Institutions and Economic Growth in Asia

This book explores the role of institutions in economic growth, looking in particular at specific Asian countries and at particular cities within those countries. It considers a wide range of factors besides institutions, including the law, cultural factors and overall government arrangements. The differences between the countries studied are highlighted, and the impact of these differences assessed: the impact of English common law on arrangements in Hong Kong, Singapore and Malaysia; sharia law in Malaysia; the differing lengths of time of colonial rule; the extent to which Chinese family businesses control an economy. Also studied are the degree to which the law is effectively applied, and a range of other social, economic and cultural factors. The book's conclusions as to which factors have the greatest impact will be of considerable interest to economists of Asia and those interested in economic growth more widely.

Flora Huang is Senior Lecturer in Law at the University of Essex, UK.

Horace Yeung is a Lecturer in Commercial Law at the University of Leicester, UK.

Routledge Economic Growth and Development Series
Series Editor
Linda Yueh
Fellow by Special Election in Economics at St Edmund Hall and Director of the China Growth Centre, University of Oxford, UK.

The aim of the series is to publish a series of books that applies rigorous economic analysis to the field of economic growth and development. The scope includes regional and country-specific studies, as well as cross-country comparisons, to examine the evidence surrounding the pressing and interesting questions on the growth prospects of developed and developing countries.

1 **Chinese Companies and the Hong Kong Stock Market**
Flora Xiao Huang and Horace Yeung

2 **China's Securities Market**
Towards Efficient Regulation
Jing Bian

3 **Institutions and Economic Growth in Asia**
The Case of Mainland China, Hong Kong, Singapore and Malaysia
Flora Huang and Horace Yeung

Institutions and Economic Growth in Asia

The Case of Mainland China, Hong Kong, Singapore and Malaysia

Flora Huang and Horace Yeung

Routledge
Taylor & Francis Group
LONDON AND NEW YORK

First published 2018
by Routledge

2 Park Square, Milton Park, Abingdon, Oxfordshire OX14 4RN
52 Vanderbilt Avenue, New York, NY 10017

Routledge is an imprint of the Taylor & Francis Group, an informa business

First issued in paperback 2020

British Library Cataloguing-in-Publication Data
A catalogue record for this book is available from the British Library

Library of Congress Cataloging-in-Publication Data
A catalog record for this book has been requested

ISBN: 978-1-138-69973-1 (hbk)
ISBN: 978-0-367-59188-5 (pbk)

Typeset in Times New Roman
by Wearset Ltd, Boldon, Tyne and Wear

This book is dedicated to Beverley, Lilyanna, and our parents.

Contents

Figures

Tables

Preface and acknowledgements

This book project is a natural outcome of two seemingly separate and yet interconnected projects, namely 'Growth without Institutions: The Qianhai Experiment' (funded by Sino-British Fellowship Trust, 1 April 2013 to 31 March 2015, Project Ref: RL10G0217) and 'A Tale of Three Cities – Unravelling the Common Law Advantage' (funded by the British Academy/Leverhulme Trust, 1 September 2013 to 31 August 2015, Project Ref: RL10G0243). By adding to and consolidating the findings of these two projects, this book presents a comprehensive, systematic and holistic analysis regarding the growth story of five Asian commercial and financial centres (Singapore, Kuala Lumpur, Hong Kong, Shanghai and Shenzhen) across four economies/jurisdictions (Singapore, Malaysia, Hong Kong and China).

With the generous financial support of the aforementioned funding bodies, we managed to travel to Asia and take advantage of the excellent research facilities at, in no particular order, the Universities of Hong Kong and Malaya, the Chinese University of Hong Kong, the National University of Singapore, East China Normal University, China University of Political Science and Law, Hong Kong Central Library and National Library Singapore. We must also acknowledge the support given by our home institutions, namely the Universities of Essex and Leicester, especially for their generous academic study leave policy, which allowed us to spend some precious time away from teaching to complete this project.

Furthermore, Flora would like to acknowledge the financial support given by the Erasmus+ Programme of the European Union to facilitate her visit to the University of Macau to conduct some follow-up research for this book.

Since 2013, we have benefited from the discussions with our colleagues and friends regarding various parts of this book, through different meetings, seminars and conferences. We would like to thank all of them collectively, to avoid the risk of missing any one of the important names. Meanwhile, we must thank certain people individually because of their substantial contributions to this book. The foremost is the editor of the book series, Linda Yueh, who participated in a conference organised by us about the Chinese financial markets. This conference was generously supported by the Newton Fund. The insights given by Linda and other speakers have helped us to enrich the perspectives and parts of the book on China. Moreover, we must thank the team at Routledge and its associates, including Peter Sowden, Lucy McClune, Leela Vathenen, Steve Turrington, and Matt Deacon, for guiding us through various stages of the book production process.

Finally, the views and opinions expressed in this book are our own and do not reflect the position of our home institutions, funders and publisher. Also, any errors in the work remain our own responsibility.

FH and HY
October 2017

Abbreviations

1MDB	1Malaysia Development Berhad
ACCA	Association of Chartered Certified Accountants
ACFTA	ASEAN-China Free Trade Agreement
AEC	ASEAN Economic Community
AFTA	ASEAN Free Trade Area
APEC	Asia-Pacific Economic Cooperation
ASEAN	Association of Southeast Asian Nations
BTA	bilateral trade agreement
CAD	Commercial Affairs Department
CAO	China Aviation Oil
CEO	chief executive officer
CEPT	Common Effective Preferential Tariff
CEPA	Closer Economic Partnership Arrangement
CLRC	Corporate Law Reform Committee
CO	Companies Ordinance
COO	certificates of origin
CPC	Communist Party of China
CSFTA	Sino-Singaporean Free Trade Agreement
CSRC	China Securities Regulatory Commission
DBS	Development Bank of Singapore
EDB	Economic Development Board
ETP	Economic Transformation Programme
EU	European Union
FDI	Foreign Direct Investment
FSA	Financial Services Authority
FTA	Free Trade Agreement
FTZ	free trade zone
GATT	General Agreement on Tariffs and Trade
GDP	Gross domestic product
GFCI	Global Financial Centres Index
GLC	government-linked company
GNI	gross national income
GNP	gross national product

HICOM	Heavy Industries Corporation of Malaysia
HK$	Hong Kong dollars
HKEx	Hong Kong Stock Exchange
HKLR	Hong Kong Listing Rules
ICAC	Independent Commission Against Corruption
ICBC	Industrial and Commercial Bank of China
IFC	International Finance Corporation
IMF	International Monetary Fund
IOSCO	International Organisation of Securities Commissions
IPO	initial public offering
MAS	Monetary Authority of Singapore
MOU	Memorandum of Understanding
MMOU	Multilateral Memorandum of Understanding
MORC	Memorandum of Regulatory Cooperation
NDP	New Development Policy
NEM	New Economic Model
NEP	New Economic Policy
NPC	National People's Congress
NVP	National Vision Policy
OBOR	One Belt One Road
OECD	Organisation for Economic Co-operation and Development
PAP	People's Action Party
PBOC	People's Bank of China
PSA	Port of Singapore Authority
PTA	Preferential Tariff Arrangement
QFII	Qualified Foreign Institutional Investors
R&D	research and development
RM	Malaysian ringgit
RMB	renminbi
RTAs	Regional Trade Agreements
SC	Securities Commission
SCSC	State Council Securities Committee
SEZ	Special Economic Zone
SFC	Securities and Futures Commission
SFO	Securities and Futures Ordinance
SG$	Singapore dollars
SOE	state-owned enterprise
SZSE	Shenzhen Stock Exchange
TEU	twenty-foot equivalent unit
TPP	Trans-Pacific Partnership
TVE	township and village enterprise
UAE	United Arab Emirates
UK	United Kingdom
UMNO	United Malays National Organisation
US	United States of America
US$	United States dollars
WTO	World Trade Organisation

List of court cases and regulatory instruments

Court cases

Australia

Marchesi v. *Barnes* [1970] VR 434 206

China

DaMing Group 78n153
Guangxia Company 58
XianFan Trust and Investment Company 56

Hong Kong

HKSAR v. *Donald Tsang* (ESCC3247/15) 135n213
HKSAR v. *Rafael Hui* (FACC No. 12 of 2016) 135n213
Waddington Ltd v. *Chan Chun Hoo Thomas and others* [2008] (FACV 15/2007) 113

Malaysia

Securities Commission Malaysia v. *Yeow Kheng Chew and others* (High Court of Malaya at Kuala Lumpur: WA-22NCC-300–07/2017) 228n133

Singapore

Chew Kong Huat v. *Ricwil (Singapore) Pte Ltd* [2000] 1 SLR 385 179n82
ECRC Land Pte Ltd v. *Wing On Ho Christopher* [2004] 1 SLR 105 179n82
Ting Sing Ning v. *Ting Chek Swee* [2008] 1 SLR 197 160–1

United Kingdom

Aberdeen Railway Co. v. *Blaikie Bros* (1854) 1 Macq 461 HI 128n67
Burland v. *Earle* [1902] AC 83 180n119

Regulatory instruments

Australia

Bilateral/regional/international

Canada

China

Hong Kong

Malaysia

New Zealand

Singapore

United Kingdom

United States

1 Introduction

It may not be easy to define the word 'institution'. According to Acemoglu and colleagues, economists and historians have long emphasised the importance of institutions.[1] The institutions hypothesis claims that societies with a social organisation that encourages investment will prosper. As put by North, 'Institutions are the rules of the game in a society or, more formally, are the humanly devised constrains that shape human interaction.'[2] Whilst saying that 'there is no unanimity in the definition of this concept [of institution]', Hodgson tries to define institutions as 'systems of established and prevalent social rules that structure social interactions' and thus 'language, money, law, systems of weights and measures, table manners, and firms (and other organisations)' are all institutions.[3]

A wide array of parameters must be taken into account to explain the growth stories of the cities. The research by North first, then La Porta and colleagues, not only generated interest from the academic research community, but also from policy makers and regulators with regards to the underlying effects of different institutions on sustainable economic growth and the promotion of efficient financial systems.[4] Using mainland China, Hong Kong, Malaysia and Singapore as case studies, this book project can enrich the understanding of how various factors (such as law, politics, culture, etc.) can contribute to economic development. By drawing on their development experience, this study seeks to confirm and advise academics, policy makers and regulators on the principles which should inform the design of relevant institutions which are important to development. Also, this study endeavours to take into account a range of parameters which can potentially be linked with economic growth such as different branches of law, questions of legal effectiveness, as well as social, political and cultural factors which are vaguely summarised as 'Asian values' by, for example, the late legendary Singaporean leader Lee Kuan Yew. The study will examine and confirm the role of each of these factors in the context of each economy or jurisdiction, and its cities.

Regulation is widely regarded as one of the foundations of economic and financial growth. For example, the 'Doing Business' project of the World Bank provides objective measures of business regulations in 185 economies. Empirically, the importance of the legal institutions is supported by the 'legal origins' hypothesis that legal systems have a long-run impact on depth of financial markets.[5] However, Roe has indicated that a political economy-based explanation seems stronger than the legal origins hypothesis.[6] He argues that continental social democracies did not provide institutions that markets need, so that the financial markets in continental Europe have flourished to a lesser degree than their Anglo-American counterparts. While the work of La Porta and others from a legal perspective and that of Roe from a political perspective have produced a great deal of discussion, the effect of culture appears to be relevant too. From a cultural perspective, laws and rules are used to prevent uncertainties in the behaviour of other people. Therefore, people will look for 'a structure in their organisations, institutions, and relationships which makes events clearly interpretable and predictable'.[7]

With a range of relevant factors, such as legal rules, politics and culture, the core objective of this book project is to put these factors into the context of the growth stories of five Asian commercial and financial centres (Singapore, Kuala Lumpur, Hong Kong, Shanghai and Shenzhen) across four economies/jurisdictions (Singapore, Malaysia, Hong Kong, China).

In essence, the following research questions will be asked:

- What are the required institutions of a commercial and financial centre?
- How are these institutions contributing to the success of the four selected Asian economies?
- How is the growth story of each of them the same or different from another?
- In the face of globalism/regionalism, what will be the prospects of growth for them?

Although La Porta and colleagues' research was so ground-breaking and sparked a great many debates, it has been subjected to many criticisms, in particular with respect to its quantitative methodology. As a result, this study seeks to focus more on qualitative contextual analyses, a gap left by the quantitative studies, and enquire into the effects of various factors on the countries/cities with respect to development. The primary aim is to look for any legal rules (and their enforcement), policies and perception of the political and socio-cultural profiles of the cities that can inform its success. Furthermore, because of the expertise of the authors, more attention will be given to the legal factors, but with a caveat and understanding that they are not necessarily the dominant factor in economic development.

The four economies are connected by certain similarities but at the same time have their own characteristics. For example, in all cases, there is a strong presence of a Chinese community. For Malaysia, the Chinese might be an ethnic minority compared to Malays, but its economy is indeed tightly controlled by Malaysian-Chinese entrepreneurs such as Lim Goh Tong and Kuok Hock Nien. Hong Kong, Malaysia and Singapore might have been former British colonies and therefore able to take advantage of an inherited English system, but they are also different in certain ways. For example, Hong Kong has always been an autonomous region, but is not a sovereign state like Malaysia, Singapore and China. On the other hand, as a part of Malaysia before, Singapore appears to have shared many similarities with Kuala Lumpur, but the influence of Islamic traditions in the Malaysian system has complicated the situation. Even within the same nation, the growth stories of Shenzhen and Shanghai are different. For example, the former is more geared towards technology, but the latter focuses on finance.

More generally the four economies can be linked up by the notion 'Asian values'. The 'Asian values' thesis was initially promulgated by the Singaporean former prime minister Lee Kuan Yew and the Malaysian former prime minister Mahathir Mohamad, to explain the root of Asia's remarkable growth over the previous decades. They claimed that the cultural inclination to respect authority and hard work allows East Asian countries to pursue liberal economic policies without democracy.[8] Since then, this thesis has gained political prominence in many Asian countries, especially as it is often articulated in government rhetoric and official statements to object to Western liberalism.[9] The traditional Asian values were explained as 'harbour deep resentment against the West for its past colonialism'.[10] Recently, Asian values have been developed and reframed to a new model for economic development characterised by high national savings, economy as top priority for government, cautious and prudent policies, and modernised laws.[11]

In Asian countries with a Confucianism-influenced culture, caution and prudence, as one of the most fundamental accounting concepts, stipulate that a conservative approach should be adopted in determining profits. Revenues and profits should never be overstated. Conversely, provisions are made for all known liabilities. The Western world has enjoyed 200 years of prosperity and Westerners perhaps forgot that the worst could come at any time. On the other hand, for Asian countries, mass civil disorders and wars have occurred continuously. Economic development in the Asian region has substantially been lagging behind their Western counterparts. This is actually a blessing in disguise. Asian people would never forget prudence is one of the virtues that are most useful to individuals. Prosperity is by no means automatic.

Considering elsewhere in the world, the following weaknesses in Latin American financial systems echoed some of the problems which hinder the deepening of domestic financial markets: (1) low savings rates; (2) an unstable macroeconomic environment; (3) a range of structural factors mostly economic and institutional in nature; (4) highly volatile capital inflows.[12] Asian countries, in contrast, have exhibited some completely different characteristics. China, Hong Kong, Singapore, Malaysia and some other East and Southeast Asian developing nations have accumulated large current account surpluses while large current account deficits have emerged in the Western world (this is also what the Westerners blame as the cause of crisis).[13] A key driver of this has been very high savings rates in countries like China and Singapore. From a cultural perspective, some Westerners can live from pay cheque to pay cheque. However, most Asian countries have experienced turbulent times. Asians save more because they know from experience the importance of preparing for rainy days. From a growth perspective, these savings can be channelled to domestic development. From a political economy perspective, holding an abundant amount of foreign debts has given Asian countries the competitive edge on various policy issues.

Amidst a consequential shift of economic and financial gravity to the East after the Global Financial Crisis 2007–08, this book seeks to provide a holistic and comprehensive account of the economic growth of four selected economies/jurisdictions and the cities within them. It is composed of eight chapters (including this introductory Chapter 1). Chapter 2 will consider the underlying institutional requirements for economic growth, and has the major goal of setting out the necessary ingredients for a successful commercial and financial centre. These will be then applied to the subsequent assessments for each of the economies and their cities in subsequent chapters. A spectrum of factors may be relevant to economic development. Some general preconditions will be examined but with an understanding that particular markets may have their own story. Some scholars, most notably La Porta and colleagues, have long stressed the importance of law and regulation. The specific role of law and its enforcement will be examined. Other factors, such as politics and culture, are also considered.

Chapter 3 will be the start of four largely parallel chapters which discuss the growth experience of the selected economies in this book. Chapter 3 will entail an assessment of China's development, in particular Shanghai and Shenzhen via the analytical framework laid down in Chapter 2. It will first compare and contrast the country's state of economy before and after its economic reform in 1978. Subsequently, the growth stories of Shanghai and Shenzhen will be studied. The role played by legal, political and cultural factors and market infrastructure will be discussed. The chapter will also consider if the tremendous growth rate in China in the past three decades is sustainable before a conclusion is made.

Chapter 4 concerns the development of Hong Kong via the analytical framework laid down in Chapter 2. It will first compare and contrast the city's state of economy before and after its handover in 1997. Subsequently, the role played by legal, political and cultural factors and market infrastructure underlying its success will be discussed. The chapter will also consider, for example, if the uncertainty in the political situation Hong Kong, such as the Umbrella Movement in 2015, will adversely affect the future of the city.

Chapter 5 will proceed to consider Singapore. It will first compare and contrast the city's state of economy before and after its independence in 1965. Subsequently, the role played by legal, political and cultural factors and market infrastructure underlying its success will be discussed. The chapter will also consider whether the city can continue its success in the post-Lee Kuan Yew era.

Chapter 6 will be the last of the four parallel chapters and concerns the development of Malaysia via the analytical framework laid down in Chapter 2. It will first compare and contrast the country's state of economy before and after its independence in 1957, in particular the status of Kuala Lumpur as an Islamic financial centre. Subsequently, like previous chapters, the role played by legal, political and cultural factors and market infrastructure underlying its success will be discussed.

Chapter 7 considers the growing interdependence of the cities in the age of globalisation, by discussing the cooperation models between economies. China, as the second largest economy in the world and the major trading partners of a number of economies, has an influential role in determining global growth. It is particularly the case for Hong Kong, which has a unique economic, socio-political relationship with China. However, there are other growth opportunities for Singapore and Malaysia, with the Association of Southeast Asian Nations (ASEAN), the once hopeful Trans-Pacific Partnership and China's One Belt One Road initiative. This chapter will examine different models of cooperation between the economies.

Chapter 8 is the conclusion; it draws on all the important theoretical and empirical findings in previous chapters, wraps up the past, present and future development of the economies and Asia as a region, and discusses the implications of the Asian case to the world.

Notes

1 Daron Acemoglu *et al.* (2002), 'Reversal of Fortune: Geography and Institutions in the Making of the Modern World Income Distribution' in *Quarterly Journal of Economics*, **117**, p. 1262.
2 Douglass North (1990), *Institutions, Institutional Change and Economic Performance*, Cambridge: CUP, p. 3.
3 Geoffrey Hodgson (2006), 'What Are Institutions?' in *Journal of Economic Issues*, **40**, p. 2.
4 North (1990), op. cit.; Rafael La Porta *et al.* (1997), 'Legal Determinants of External Finance' in *Journal of Finance*, **52**; Rafael La Porta *et al.* (1998), 'Law and Finance' in *Journal of Political Economy*, **106**; Rafael La Porta *et al.* (2000), 'Investor Protection and Corporate Governance' in *Journal of Financial Economics*, **58**.
5 Other than the research by La Porta and colleagues, see also Simeon Djankov *et al.* (2008), 'The Law and Economics of Self-dealing' in *Journal of Financial Economics*, **88**; and John Armour *et al.* (2009), 'Shareholder Protection and Stock Market Development: An Empirical Test of the Legal Origins Hypothesis' in *Journal of Empirical Legal Studies*, **6**.
6 Mark Roe (2006), 'Legal Origins, Politics and Modern Stock Markets' in *Harvard Law Review*, **120**.
7 Geert Hofsted (1994), *Cultures and Organizations*, London: HarperCollins, p. 116.
8 Molly Elgin (2010), 'Asian Values: A New Model for Development' in *Stanford Journal of East Asian Affairs*, **10**, p. 135.
9 Chang Yau Hoon (2004), 'Revisiting the Asian Values Argument used by Asian Political Leaders and its Validity' in *The Indonesian Quarterly*, **32**, p. 156.
10 Inoue Tatsuo (1999), 'Liberal Democracy and Asian Orientalism' in Joanne Bauer and Daniel Bell (eds.), *The East Asian Challenge for Human Rights*, Cambridge: CUP, p. 28.
11 Molly Elgin (2010), op. cit.; and Erik Thorbecke and Henry Wan (2004), 'Revisiting East (and South East) Asia's Development Model' Cornell Conference Papers on Seventy Five Years of Development. Online. Available at: http://citeseerx.ist.psu.edu/viewdoc/download?doi=10.1.1.573.6957&rep=rep1&type=pdf.
12 Andrew Sheng (2008), 'Building National and Regional Financial Markets' in Kohli, Harinder (ed.), *Growth and Development in Emerging Market Economies*, London: Sage, p. 181.

13 Ben Bernanke (2009), 'Asia and the Global Financial Crisis' Federal Reserve Bank of San Francisco's Conference on Asia and the Global Financial Crisis. Online. Available at: www.federalreserve.gov/newsevents/speech/bernanke20091019a.htm.

References

Acemoglu, Daron; Johnson, Simon; and Robinson, James (2002), 'Reversal of Fortune: Geography and Institutions in the Making of the Modern World Income Distribution' in *Quarterly Journal of Economics*, **117**.

Armour, John; Deakin, Simon; Sarkar, Prabirjit; Siems, Mathias; and Singh, Ajit (2009), 'Shareholder Protection and Stock Market Development: An Empirical Test of the Legal Origins Hypothesis' in *Journal of Empirical Legal Studies*, **6**.

Bernanke, Ben (2009), 'Asia and the Global Financial Crisis' Federal Reserve Bank of San Francisco's Conference on Asia and the Global Financial Crisis. Online. Available at: www.federalreserve.gov/newsevents/speech/bernanke20091019a.htm.

Djankov, Simeon; La Porta, Rafael; Lopez-de-Silanes, Florencio; and Shleifer, Andrei (2008), 'The Law and Economics of Self-dealing' in *Journal of Financial Economics*, **88**.

Elgin, Molly (2010), 'Asian Values: A New Model for Development' in *Stanford Journal of East Asian Affairs*, **10**.

Hodgson, Geoffrey (2006), 'What Are Institutions?' in *Journal of Economic Issues*, **40**.

Hofsted, Geert (1994), *Cultures and Organizations*, London: HarperCollins.

Hoon, Chang Yau (2004), 'Revisiting the Asian Values Argument used by Asian Political Leaders and its Validity' in *The Indonesian Quarterly*, **32**.

La Porta, Rafael; Lopez-de-Silane, Florencio; Shleifer, Andrei; and Vishny, Robert (1997), 'Legal Determinants of External Finance' in *Journal of Finance*, **52**.

La Porta, Rafael; Lopez-de-Silane, Florencio; Shleifer, Andrei; and Vishny, Robert (1998), 'Law and Finance' in *Journal of Political Economy*, **106**.

La Porta, Rafael; Lopez-de-Silane, Florencio; Shleifer, Andrei; and Vishny, Robert (2000), 'Investor Protection and Corporate Governance' in *Journal of Financial Economics*, **58**.

North, Douglass (1990), *Institutions, Institutional Change and Economic Performance*, Cambridge: CUP.

Roe, Mark (2006), 'Legal Origins, Politics and Modern Stock Markets' in *Harvard Law Review*, **120**.

Sheng, Andrew (2008), 'Building National and Regional Financial Markets' in Kohli, Harinder (ed.), *Growth and Development in Emerging Market Economies*, London: Sage.

Tatsuo, lnoue (1999), 'Liberal Democracy and Asian Orientalism' in Joanne Bauer and Daniel Bell (eds.), *The East Asian Challenge for Human Rights*, Cambridge: CUP.

Thorbecke, Erik and Wan, Henry (2004), 'Revisiting East (and South East) Asia's Development Model' Cornell Conference Papers on Seventy Five Years of Development. Online. Available at: http://citeseerx.ist.psu.edu/viewdoc/download?doi=10.1.1.573.6957&rep=rep1&type=pdf.

2 Institutions and growth

Setting the scene

The role of institutions has become one of the most popular research areas as a result of the rise of New Institutional Economics in the 1980s.[1] The study of institutions is important as it provides an explanation of international differences in economic development, which in turn can provide the direction of policy reform proposals both for international organisations such as the World Bank and OECD, as well as the governments of different countries. Different types of institutions have been examined by scholars in an abundant number of studies with a view to providing a plausible explanation for cross-country differences in economic growth. So far, the findings have been far from clear. By drawing on the views of these studies, this chapter seeks to set out a systematic analytical framework for subsequent chapters, such that each of the possible relevant institutions are to be put into the specific context of the four chosen economies, namely, China, Hong Kong, Singapore and Malaysia, to provide a holistic and comprehensive account of their respective growth stories.

To ensure that this chapter and subsequent analyses are not overwhelmed by the varieties of institutions which have been examined by academic studies thus far, the chapter will categorise all of them into four broad types, namely legal, political, cultural and economic. This chapter is divided into five sections. The first part will discuss the term 'institutions' as a generic concept in economics and set out the boundary discussions within this chapter, as well as the book as a whole. Particularly in this part, the dynamics and interdependence of institutions will be highlighted. The second part will move on to discuss the first of the four broad types of institutions, legal institutions. Property rights have traditionally played an overwhelmingly prominent role in the entire literature on institutions and economic growth. Yet, this part is predominantly motivated by the concern on shareholder rights underlined by La Porta and colleagues, arguably as one of the two research teams which have made path-breaking contributions in institutional economics.[2] The third part will look at political institutions. The concern lies in how political orientation and democracy can influence economic growth. The fourth part is about cultural institutions. The main issues here include cultural values, trust and religion. The fifth part is about economic institutions, a loosely defined term used in this book, which covers certain more tangible institutions not examined by the previous parts, such as financial markets and container ports. The final part will conclude. This chapter seeks to be as comprehensive as possible but with an understanding that it is virtually impossible to explore every single possible institution ever unearthed and examined by scholars.

What matters?

The study of institutions can be traced back to as early as 1899 when Veblen said:

> The evolution of social structure has been a process of natural selection of institutions. The progress which has been and is being made in human institutions and in human character may be set down, broadly, to a natural selection of the fittest habits of thought and to a process of enforced adaptation of individuals to an environment which has progressively changed with the growth of the community and with the changing institutions under which men have lived.[3]

Hamilton further claimed that 'the proper subject-matter of economic theory is institutions' and coined the term 'institutional economics', which concerns how the institutions shapes economic behaviour.[4] This has planted the seed of the more recent development in the research of the role of institutions in economic development.[5] According to Acemoglu and colleagues, economists and historians have long emphasised the importance of institutions.[6] For example, North and Thomas have explained how the institutional changes brought about by trade and commercial activities led to the Glorious Revolution in seventeenth-century England.[7] In their account of growth, they argued that 'growth will simply not occur unless the existing economic organisation is efficient'.[8] In other words, the fundamental explanation of comparative growth is differences in institutions. Similarly, Engerman and Sokoloff contend that the differentials in paths of development across countries have long been of central concern to scholars, especially economic historians and economists.[9] The explanations offered for the contrasting records in growth have most often focused on institutions and highlighted the variation across societies in conditions relevant to growth. In the view of Acemoglu and colleagues, institutions matter for economic growth because they shape the incentives of key economic actors in society.[10] As a result, differences in institutions are the major source of cross-country differences in economic growth as institutions not only determine the aggregate potential of the economy, but also an array of economic outcomes. It is unlikely that all individuals and groups will prefer the same set of institutions (and hence their economic consequences) owing to a conflict of interest among various groups and individuals over the choice of institutions. Therefore, institutions are endogenous.[11]

Varieties of growth models

Different growth models emerge as a result of the diversity of institutions and their combination. The neoclassical growth model, as proposed by Solow and

Swan, emphasises the role of capital accumulation.[12] In this model, it is assumed that labour productivity grows continually and exogenously. This change in productivity of labour is thought to arise from technological improvement. In response, the capital stock is continually increased, allowing for a continual expansion in the level of output and consumption. The basic weakness of this neoclassical model was the driving force behind the development of the class of endogenous growth models.[13] This literature has been wide and varied. Although they differ in their details, in the end, what this class of models points to as differences in development are differences in institutions across time and countries. Another model, known as the AK model, addresses the shortfall of the neoclassical model by treating technology as an endogenous variable determined within the economic system. This model predicts that a country's long-run growth rate will depend on economic factors such as thrift and the efficiency of resource allocation. The AK model, which was first proposed by Harrod and Domar, combines the virtues of the Solow-Swan model and the consideration of substitutable factors.[14] For example, productivity may depend upon the total amount of capital that has been accumulated by firms. Each of these two models discussed have their pros and cons.[15] On the one hand, it is believed that the AK approach can account for the persistently positive growth rates in most countries worldwide, whereas the neoclassical model cannot explain it. On the other hand, advocates of the neoclassical model argue that the AK model cannot explain cross-country or cross-regional convergence. Amongst other alternative models, there is the Schumpeterian model which is essentially based on the idea that growth is generated by innovations and new technologies also destroy the results of previous innovations.[16] Compared to the AK model, the Schumpeterian model has the advantage of presenting an explicit analysis of the innovation process underlying economic growth. However, a notable difficulty with this model is the absence of capital in the analysis by assuming perfect financial markets whereas in reality markets work much better in some countries than in others.[17] Amidst different theories and models, a more general critique by North and Thomas is that, while the studies provide many insights about the mechanisms of economic growth, they are incapable of providing a fundamental explanation of economic growth.[18] Some of the factors explored, such as innovation and capital accumulation, 'are not causes of growth; they are growth'.

Importance and dynamics of institutions

The institutions hypothesis alleges that societies with a social organisation that provides encouragement for investment will prosper. This new movement of institutional economics has generally identified itself as an attempt to extend the range of neoclassical theory by explaining the institutional factors traditionally taken as givens, such as property rights and governance structures.[19] Yet it is not easy to give 'institutions' a precise definition. As put by North, 'Institutions are the rules of the game in a society or, more formally, are the humanly devised constraints that shape human interaction.'[20] Greif extends the notion of institution so that it encompasses not only the rules of game as in North, but more generally all forms of economic organisations and the set of beliefs that shape the interaction between economic agents.[21] Whilst saying that 'there is no unanimity in the definition of this concept [of institution]', Hodgson tries to define institutions as 'systems of established and prevalent social rules that structure social interactions' and thus 'language, money, law, systems of weights and measures, table manners, and firms (and other organisations)' are all institutions.[22] Such a broad definition clearly adds to the complexity of what matters for economic development.

North categorises human exchange as 'political, social, or economic'.[23] Likewise, Acemoglu and colleagues distinguish three fundamental causes of growth.[24] The first set of theories emphasises the importance of economic institutions, which influence economic outcomes by shaping economic incentives. The second set emphasises geography and the third emphasises the importance of culture. However, the relevant variables can go beyond that. Over time, different types of institutions have been reviewed by scholars, including but not limited to finance,[25] law,[26] politics,[27] trade,[28] culture,[29] technology,[30] education,[31] colonial origin,[32] etc.

These institutions are not standalone but are interlinked. For example, a country's legal system is normally dependent on its colonial origin.[33] A further example is that culture can be thought to influence equilibrium outcomes for a given set of institutions.[34] As suggested by Acemoglu, there is much more work to be done in unbundling the broad cluster of institutions.[35] For this, two contrasting views exist in institutional economics.

> The top down view of institutions sees them as determined by laws written by political leaders. In contrast, the bottom up view sees institutions instead as emerging spontaneously from the social norms, customs, traditions, beliefs and values of individuals within a society, with the written law only formalising what is already mainly shaped by the attitudes of individuals.[36]

The implications of these two contrasting views are that, in the former case, drastic institutional reforms are possible to foster economic growth, whereas in the latter case, institutional change is always gradual, evolutionary rather than revolutionary as heavily constrained by pre-existing institutions.

With a view to covering as many of the institutions as possible and at the same time maintaining a digestible analytical framework for subsequent chapters, this chapter will adopt the categorisation of North, a Nobel-winning pioneer in institutional economics, by discussing the political, social or economic institutions in further detail. On top of that, taking into account the gravity of debates generated by the research of La Porta and colleagues on the importance of legal institutions, it will also form an integral part of our discussions.[37]

Legal institutions

The importance of legal institutions in economic development has long been discussed by classical economists, from Adam Smith to Karl Marx.[38] The concern has been the role of property rights in the process. The term property right refers to an owner's right to use a good or asset for consumption and/or income generation. It can also include the right to transfer it to another party, in the form of a sale, gift or bequest. A property right also typically conveys the right to contract with other parties by renting, pledging or mortgaging a good or asset, or by allowing other parties to use it, for example, in an employment relationship. Around two decades ago, La Porta and colleagues made a path-breaking contribution by giving greater prominence to the role of the state in codifying and protecting such rights, using cross-country data.[39] They examined legal rules covering the protection of corporate shareholders and creditors, the origin of these rules and the quality of their enforcement in 49 countries. According to their findings, the legal environment, including both legal rules and their enforcement, matters for the size and extent of a country's capital market. This is because a good legal environment protects potential financiers against expropriation by entrepreneurs. Investors are willing to surrender funds in exchange for securities and therefore expand the scope of capital markets. Based on their findings, they also claimed that French civil law countries with the weakest investor protection have smaller and narrower capital markets.[40] Such classification using legal families, with little regard to each particular country's 'demand for law' in the first place, later attracted criticisms from other scholars.[41] Furthermore, Spamann makes the criticism that many of the initial results from La Porta and colleagues are not robust to the correction of coding errors.[42] Legal rules differ across many relevant dimensions, in particular in international comparison. It is simply very difficult to draw the lines in each of them by variable definitions. As suggested by Siems, it is overly simplistic to examine how different legal families shape finance.[43] Furthermore, the causal link between the rise of dispersed ownership, strong shareholder protection and the development of stock markets may not be apparent.[44] They convincingly coexist, in addition to the empirical evidence by La Porta and colleagues, as observed by Black, a 'strong markets' equilibrium works in the following way:

> Strong investor protection produces high prices, which encourage honest companies to issue shares. This increases share prices and encourages more honest issuers to issue shares. Outside investors then generate political support for strong investor protection.[45]

In contrast to La Porta and others' accounts, Coffee and Cheffins have shown the opposite sequence in the UK and the US, that financial markets developed first, and then created a political demand for investor protection.[46] Further, as indicated by Dam, securities markets did blossom in the US and the UK in the nineteenth and early twentieth centuries before modern securities regulation was introduced.[47] Unfortunately, the unregulated markets were vulnerable to various forms of manipulation and abuse. As a result, in the US, Federal intervention in the 1930s by introducing the Securities Act of 1933 and the Securities Exchange Act of 1934 was justified by a contention of market failure.[48]

Based on La Porta and colleagues' original research design, other scholars have made adjustments to increase the robustness. For example, Djankov and colleagues have looked at a new measure of legal protection of minority shareholders against expropriation by corporate insiders: the anti-self-dealing index, as opposed to the index of anti-director rights adopted by La Porta and colleagues.[49] The index was calculated for 72 countries and focused on private enforcement mechanisms, such as disclosure, approval and litigation, governing a specific self-dealing transaction. According to their findings, the index was sharply higher in common law countries than in French civil law countries. Also, the index was believed to be a statistically significant and economically strong predictor of a variety of measures of stock market development across countries. These results generally supported the findings of the earlier work by La Porta and colleagues. On the other hand, in light of the causality issue on whether law is a cause of growth or a result of it, as opposed to examining legal rules at a specific point of time as in the research of La Porta and colleagues and also Djankov and colleagues, Armour and colleagues have used a time series dataset to demonstrate the potential impact of legal changes on the stock market.[50] They found no evidence of a positive correlation between both, despite agreeing that common law systems were more protective of shareholder interests than civil law ones. Despite the conclusion from whether 'law matters' being far from clear, the seminal study by La Porta and colleagues has phenomenally highlighted the importance of legal institutions in the study of economic development.

The role of legal institutions in fostering a good business environment is also underlined by the World Bank's 'Doing Business' project.[51] This project provides objective measures of business regulations and their enforcement across 190 economies and selected cities at the subnational and regional level. The first 'Doing Business' report, published in 2003, covered five indicator sets and 133 economies. The most recent report in 2017 covers 11 indicator sets and 190 economies. Amongst these, the Protecting Minority Investors indicator is perhaps the most relevant in light of La Porta and colleagues' research. The minority investor protection index measures the extent of protection from conflicts of interest and shareholders' rights in corporate governance.[52] The higher the index indicates a better protection of investors' interests. The maximum score is 10. OECD high-income countries on average get a score of 6.5 in 2017. In the context of this book, it is worth highlighting that Singapore, Hong Kong and Malaysia occupies the top three positions among 190 economies in protecting minority investors (see Table 2.1). Singapore gets a score of 8.3, whereas Hong Kong and Malaysia both get a score of 8. On the other hand, China is ranked 123rd with a rather low score of 4.5, illustrating a potential regulatory gap between it and the three economies also covered by this book. However, this does not necessarily reveal a grave concern about the legal institutions in China. If one looks at another dataset, there can be an entirely different conclusion. In light of the panel dataset covering a range of developed and developing countries from Armour and colleagues, they discovered that a significant upward

Table 2.1 Protecting minority investors index of selected economies, 2017

	OCED high income countries	*Singapore*	*Hong Kong*	*Malaysia*	*China*
Score (max: 10)	6.5	8.3	8	8	4.5
Rank (out of 190 economies)	–	1st	Joint 3rd	Joint 3rd	123rd

Source: World Bank, 'Doing Business' (2017). Online. Available at: www.doingbusiness.org.

movement in the level of shareholder protection was made by China between 1995 and 2005.[53] China experienced a jump in its shareholder protection score from 5 to 6.5. According to Armour and colleagues' shareholder protection index, although the UK and the US were the top performers in 2005 (with scores of slightly more than 7), China was more protective of shareholders' interests than some developed countries such as Germany and Switzerland. This dataset has since been updated to 2013.[54] It has been suggested that between 1990 and 2013 China experienced the 'biggest increase in shareholder protection' amongst 30 countries studied.[55] China, Russia and France were the top performers in shareholder protection in 2013, performing even better than the UK and the US.[56] This again may reveal the problem of converting laws into numbers. While statistical analysis is widely utilised in the field of social science with a view to reducing complexity, giving legal rules 'ones' and 'zeros' may reduce the 'richness of detail' in legal research.[57] As criticised by Rodrik, econometric tests of the causes of growth are inherently suspect.[58]

Role of law

La Porta and colleagues argue that optimal regulatory arrangements can be distilled down to three broad hypotheses.[59] The very liberal approach implies that the optimal government policy is to leave securities markets unregulated because the market and some general legal mechanisms are sufficient for the markets to prosper.[60] A less liberal approach suggests law is necessary owing to the consideration of enforcement costs and opportunistic behaviour of market players. One option is the standardisation of the private contracting framework to improve market discipline and private litigation through securities law. Ultimately, governmental intervention may be desirable when all existing markets, legal mechanisms and private enforcement incentives are deemed insufficient. Therefore, a public enforcer is needed to support trade. Public enforcement may work because the enforcer is independent and focused. A typical regulatory system of capital market entails three tiers of regulation.[61] Company law represents the bottom tier of regulation as it applies to all companies, both public and private companies. Securities law represents the second tier of regulation, in that it is only relevant to companies which issue securities to the public. Listing rules represent the top tier of regulation and are relevant only to a relatively small group of companies whose securities are admitted to listing. Together, there are dedicated regulators who oversee the market. They are normally the exchanges themselves and a separate specialised public agency, such as the Securities and Exchange Commission of the US.

Berle and Means in 1932 outlined a picture of separation of ownership and control in modern corporation.[62] Their thesis was that the separation of ownership from management had resulted in shareholders being unable to exercise any form of effective control over boards of directors, who were theoretically appointed by them to represent their interests. Adam Smith in his *Wealth of Nations* observed that 'being the managers rather of other people's money than of their own, it cannot be well expected that they [directors] should watch over it with the same anxious vigilance'.[63] The agency problem which Adam Smith identified was in fact inherent in the relationship between the providers of capital and their agents who put that capital to use. Corporate shareholders have certain well-defined interests in the operation of companies, in the distribution of income and in the public security markets. As outlined in Berle and Means' book, in general, the company should be made to earn the maximum profit compatible with a reasonable degree of risk.[64] Second, a proportion of these profits should be distributed as the best interests of the business permit. Finally, the shares should remain freely marketable at a fair price. Ensuring these expectations can be met is the motivation behind the call for investor protection.

Corporate law seeks to perform two general functions.[65] First, it establishes the corporate form. One major benefit of choosing the corporate form over other business forms, such as sole proprietorship and partnership, as that it provides the feature of limited liability. Limited liability shields investors from the firm's liability thereby encouraging people to invest by keeping risk under control. Second, the law attempts to control conflicts of interest among corporate constituencies. For this, three generic agency problems can arise in business firms. The first type involves the classic agency problem identified by Adam Smith. The problem lies in assuring that the managers are responsive to the shareholders' interest rather than pursuing their own personal interests. The second agency problem involves the conflict between majority and minority shareholders. The former generally have a tendency to expropriate the latter. The third problem lies in ensuring that corporate insiders do not behave opportunistically toward outsiders such as creditors, workers and consumers.[66] On the other hand, the two other levels of regulation, the securities law and the listing rules, seek to fulfil two objectives: (1) to ensure that the prices of publicly traded securities are reasonably well-informed and (2) to ensure that public shareholders are protected by effective corporate governance arrangements once they become shareholders.[67] Different legal strategies are, accordingly, employed to protect the interests of investors. For example, the entry strategy includes mandatory disclosure for new issues of shares by listed companies and then continuing disclosure.[68] The trusteeship strategy involves the empowerment of a disinterested third party to screen companies that wish to enter the stock market.[69] The rules and standards strategy concerns the acceptable characteristics and behaviour of listed companies.[70]

Enforcement

Effective law enforcement is a primary concern for any legal system. While formal legal rules are easier for economists, for instance La Porta and colleagues, to code, measure and incorporate into their regression equations, these rules may have little to do with the reality of actual practice, particularly in developing countries.[71] Enforcement can be broadly classified into two categories: (1) a public enforcement mechanism where the law gives the regulator the responsibility to gather information and pursue the offence; (2) a private enforcement mechanism which serves as the means for the private parties to sue and recoup losses in a court. The financial world is changing rapidly, but laws are usually rigid. Pistor and Xu have pointed out that the emergence of regulators is a response to both market failures and incomplete law.[72] The gap between legal theory and actual practice can be filled by public enforcement when the regulatory authority is equipped with broad powers of investigation, in order to detect financial crimes and a wide variety of remedies with which to proceed. On the other hand, private actions are considered as a necessary supplement to public enforcement activities.[73] In addition to the functions fulfilled by public enforcement, i.e. justice and deterrence, civil remedies can compensate the wronged. However, there are concerns that the efficacy of private lawsuits may be seriously compromised.[74] Existing empirical evidence is in fact not adequate enough for scholars to give any conclusive opinions regarding the relative value of public and private enforcement in relation to financial development.

For public enforcement, a quantifiable approach to measuring enforcement is to focus on inputs and outputs. Jackson and Roe have tried to measure the intensity of public enforcement based on budgetary resources and staffing levels.[75] Higher budget and greater staffing allow the regulator to conduct more activities, for instance, investigation of wrongdoing, market surveillance and writing rules. In their opinion, other attributes of the regulatory agency, such as independence and high levels of agency authority, are of little value to effective public enforcement if the agency is not given sufficient resources to function properly. According to their findings, countries allocate very different levels of resources to financial oversight, reflecting the differing roles of financial markets among jurisdictions. Financial centres like Hong Kong and Luxembourg had the highest staffing and budgets.[76] They are jurisdictions where financial activity plays a disproportionately large role in the domestic economy. Considering the securities regulation costs per billion dollars of stock market capitalisation, countries with a common law tradition dwarfed those with a civil law tradition.[77] This finding coincides with La Porta and colleagues' claim that investor protection is better in common law countries. As measured by budgets and staffing, the common law nations are more regulatory than civil law nations. Nevertheless, the casual connection between common law origin and high government spending may be obscure.[78]

At the output level, enforcement can be measured either in terms of the number of actions brought or the aggregate financial sanctions levied. The enforcement actions brought by the Financial Services Authority in the UK and the Securities Exchange Commission in the US were higher than those brought by the federal financial supervisory body in Germany.[79] This finding may not be conclusive, but is consistent with the belief that enforcement is important to the success of a securities market. Certainly, the enforcement intensity may vary even among the strongest markets. Coffee claims that the UK opts for an advisory and consulting relationship with the regulated entities, but the US adopts a 'deterrent' approach by emphasising enforcement actions and the imposition of sanctions as the principal means by which to cause regulated entities to comply.[80] In terms of monetary sanctions, those imposed in the US exceeded those imposed in the UK.[81] Among transition economies, Dam has found that the difference in size of the equity markets in Poland and the Czech Republic shows the significance of public enforcement.[82] Poland created an independent and highly motivated regulator to enforce the rules, but the Czech Republic, in contrast, left enforcement to an unmotivated office in the finance ministry. From 1995 to 2001, the Polish market increased over fivefold with the Czech market size essentially unchanged.

In contrast, La Porta and colleagues strongly advocate the role of private enforcement.[83] Both extensive disclosure requirements and standards of liability facilitating investor recovery of losses are associated with larger stock markets. However, the problem with their argument is that private enforcement of law in some leading markets, for example the UK, is not entirely efficient or widely utilised.[84] In common law countries, the difficulty for a member of a company seeking to cure maladministration of the company by legal action is that the courts have usually avoided hearing such claims, owing to the *Foss* v. *Harbottle* rule in English law.[85] The company itself is the only proper plaintiff. While shareholders have the incentives and also various rights given to them by law to protect themselves, a legal framework will not be complete without providing access to remedies when the worst happens. In Miller's view, compared to the US, the derivative action in England has not been a significant part of the corporate law landscape both because of restrictive substantive limitations on its use and because of the rule of lawyer's fees that prevent the emergence of an entrepreneurial class of lawyers specialising in class action and derivative litigation.[86] Furthermore, though evidence shows that private enforcement in the US imposes greater financial penalties than public enforcement, corporate officers and insiders rarely contribute to class action settlements, with the aggregate cost of such actions actually falling on largely diversified shareholders.[87] So, the real effect of private enforcement may be questionable.

The relative value of public and private enforcement is a key issue for understanding how financial markets deepen and broaden. During the course of financial market development in England and the US, both countries started off with a pure court regime.[88] As markets grew, courts found themselves in a position where they could not apply the law to deter future harm. Stock exchanges and subsequently an independent regulatory agency began to assume regulatory functions. Owing to the fact that the measures of both public and private enforcement, as well as their effectiveness, are highly imperfect, present empirical findings about legal enforcement and stock markets may be flawed.[89] Even though some results reveal a fairly robust relationship between the intensity of public enforcement and the size of a country's capital markets, they do not suggest that public enforcement is more important than private enforcement. Indeed, some financial indicators seem to be linked more strongly to private enforcement indices than to public enforcement measures.[90] Further improvements can perhaps be made to yield better understanding of both mechanisms of enforcement and how they interact.

Political institutions

While La Porta and colleagues have pointed out the importance of legal foundation in terms of shareholder protection to capital market development, Roe has indicated that the political economy-based theories seem stronger than the legal origins theory.[91] He argues that continental social democracies did not provide institutions that securities markets need, such that the markets in continental Europe have flourished to a lesser degree than their Anglo-American counterparts. In social democracies, employees are protected from actions that a company would often take to maximise the shareholder's value. The goals between employees and shareholders often do not intersect. Employees prefer high wages and shareholders prefer lower wages. There is even an investment horizon problem. Employees are risk-averse because, unlike a shareholder, who can have a diversified investment portfolio, their human capital is tied up in the company. Therefore, Roe's argument is that 'where labour's influence is strong, concentrated ownership should persist as a countervailing power and, hence, equity markets should develop less strongly' and he supports his argument by showing the correlation between political orientation and ownership structure.[92] Furthermore, political forces can also have direct influence. For example, in the continental system, those in power want to exercise more control through a bank-centred system because large banks are subject to more state control than securities markets.[93] This is clearly another political explanation of weak markets.

Understanding the degree of state control appears to be a more realistic approach to looking at the development of some transition economies, particularly those former or current communist regimes, such as China. In the opinion of Aoki, the whole transition path can be classified into three stages: the communist regime, the transition process and the post-transition regime.[94] At the first stage, all enterprises are owned by the state and the management of the enterprises is appointed by the state organs. Gradually, all enterprises are transformed into corporations, but the corporate ownership and control is in the process of being defined. At the final stage, the corporate governance structure is well-defined. There are due processes governed by law in dealing with issues like the appointment of management. When countries are still at their first and second stages, politics should inevitably be taken into account.

Some scholars have emphasised the politics and finance view that centralised or powerful governments tend to be incompatible with financial development.[95] The proper functioning of financial institutions and markets requires limitations on government discretion. The political story given by Roe, regarding the success of the US, is that low government involvement has always been a tradition and firms experienced less interference. As a result, norms like shareholder wealth maximisation flourished easily. Across the Atlantic, Britain's securities markets first developed when it had a laissez-faire policy, though according to Roe, British history fits 'awkwardly' with a purely political theory because many companies were still held by family blockholders before late 1970s.[96] While legal protection for minority shareholders might have prompted convergence along American lines, Cheffins has agreed that, at present, it is not possible to account in a fully satisfactory manner for the rise of the Berle and Means corporations in the UK.[97] This shows the limitation of the political arguments. However, political force can still act a supplement to the legal explanation supported by La Porta and colleagues from a path-dependence perspective. The form of legal rules is often shaped by political considerations. Social democracies will tend to have rules which favour employees, instead of investors. This is not favourable to the development of securities markets.

The relationship between political power and economic development is complex. According to Acemoglu and colleagues, political power can lead to major changes in political institutions and therefore in economic institutions and economic growth.[98] Examples of political institutions include the form of government, for example democracy, and the extent of constraints on politicians and political elites. As mentioned before, colonial origin may have an effect on the legal origin and thereby the economic performance of a country. On the other hand, there is also a political dimension in colonial origin. Acemoglu and colleagues contend that the colonisation of much of the world by Europeans provides such a large-scale natural experiment.[99] The colonisation experience transformed the institutions in many diverse lands conquered and controlled by Europeans. Most importantly, Europeans imposed very different sets of institutions in different parts of the global empire. The institutions created during the colonial era normally persist after independence. This experience can provide evidence which conclusively establishes the central role of institutions in development.

In addition to colonial origin, some scholars have examined the relationship between democracy and growth. Przeworski and Limongi have presented a summary of theoretical arguments in the direction of both positive and negative effects of democracy on growth.[100] On the one hand, it is thought that only democratic institutions can constrain the state to act in the general interest. From this view, dictatorships of any stripe are a source of inefficiency. Government's role is seen in providing law and order, enforcing contracts and defending private parties from external threats, as well as providing those inputs to private production that are not efficiently supplied by the market. On the other hand, there are also arguments against democracy. First, some have proposed that democracy generates an explosion of demands for current consumption.[101] These demands, in turn, threaten profits; hence they reduce investment and retard growth. Democracy is thus inimical to economic development. Proponents of this view therefore conclude that dictatorships are therefore better able to force savings and launch economic growth. Second, some have observed that dictators tended to behave in a 'developmentalist' fashion, especially from the experience of the Far East and Latin America.[102] In this view, it is thought that the state has a role to play to make the economy function efficiently and the state wants to perform this role well. To do this, the state must be insulated from private pressures. There is empirical evidence to support either side. Cross-country regressions by Barro have pointed to a positive correlation between income and democracy, that is richer countries tend to be more democratic.[103] Similarly, Aghion and colleagues have shown that richer counties tend to have less insulated political institutions.[104] However, it is worth noting that these relationships are between democracy and income, not democracy and growth. In contrast, Mulligan and colleagues have found no correlation between democracy and policies such as education spending, pensions and welfare, corporate taxation, openness to trade, and other policies that may affect growth.[105] Setting the far from clear impact of democracy on growth aside, the Economist Intelligence Unit's Democracy Index provides a snapshot of the state of democracy worldwide for 165 independent states and two territories.[106] According to the 2016 Democracy Index almost one-half of the world's countries can be considered to be democracies of some sort, but the number of 'full democracies' has declined from 20 in 2015 to 19 in 2016. The US has been downgraded from a 'full democracy' to a 'flawed democracy' because of a further erosion of trust in government and elected officials there. In the context of this book, out of the four economies to be explored in depth, Malaysia, Hong Kong and Singapore are considered as 'flawed democracies', whereas China is regarded as having an authoritarian regime (see Table 2.2). If one believes in the role of democracy in growth, it can easily be assumed that Malaysia, Hong Kong and Singapore should share similar economic performance while China is clearly the odd one out. The distinction is even more revealing by taking colonial origin into account. All three economies used to be British colonies, but not China. Their political and other institutional conditions will be further discussed and analysed in subsequent chapters to see whether Malaysia, Hong Kong and Singapore are really similar, and to what extent China is different from the others.

Table 2.2 Democracy index of selected economies, 2016

	Malaysia	*Hong Kong*	*Singapore*	*China*
Score	6.54	6.42	6.38	3.14
Ranking	65th	68th	70th	136th
Category	Flawed Democracy	Flawed Democracy	Flawed Democracy	Authoritarian

Source: The Economist Intelligence Unit.

Cultural institutions

According to Aghion and Howitt, the study of the effect of culture on economic growth is a relatively recent trend which has taken off after the new millennium.[107] Culture here refers to 'individual and collective beliefs, social norms, and various attributes of individuals' preferences that are somehow influenced by their environment, but typically slow moving'.[108] From a cultural perspective, laws and rules are used to prevent uncertainties in the behaviour of other people. Therefore, people will look for 'a structure in their organisations, institutions, and relationships which makes events clearly interpretable and predictable'.[109] Within a company, there are laws and rules, which can be either formal or informal, controlling the rights and duties of employers and employees. Inherently, culture is largely local and cannot be easily transplanted. The culture of a country is not a combination of properties of the 'average citizen', but is a set of likely reactions of citizens with a common mental programming.[110] Such reactions are often found in the same society.

The Inglehart-Welzel Cultural Map, based on the data from the World Values Survey, asserts that there are two major dimensions of cross cultural variation in the world: (1) traditional values versus secular-rational values; and (2) survival values versus self-expression values.[111] On the first dimension, traditional values emphasise the importance of religion, parent-child ties, deference to authority and traditional family values. People who embrace these values also reject divorce, abortion, euthanasia and suicide. These societies have high levels of national pride and a nationalistic outlook. In contrast, secular-rational values have the opposite preferences to the traditional values. These societies place less emphasis on religion, traditional family values and authority. Divorce, abortion, euthanasia and suicide are seen as relatively acceptable. On the second dimension, survival values place emphasis on economic and physical security. It is linked with a relatively ethnocentric outlook and low levels of trust and tolerance. In contrast, self-expression values give high priority to environmental protection, growing tolerance of foreigners, gays and lesbians and gender equality, and rising demands for participation in decision making in economic and political life.

Relating back to the legal institutions, studying the cultural value of a place is important because it can promote or undermine law-abidingness.[112] Such value is usually acquired during childhood and early adolescence. As a result, the influence of culture on individuals largely occurs before people have reached a stage where they recognise and respond to the rule-of-law norm. This sometimes makes the cultural factors more influential than the legal factors. Unfortunately, according to Licht and colleagues, particular cultural profiles in some regions are less compatible with good governance than with the profiles of West European and English-speaking countries.[113] This perhaps can explain why the capital markets in some countries are weaker and also indicate the challenges faced by some emerging economies. The opinion of Black is particularly insightful in that the discussion of corporate governance should be based upon a culture of honesty before taking the control and monitoring mechanisms into account.[114] This powerful opinion highlights the importance of culture and there is empirical evidence to support it.

Zak and Knack have used cross-country data over a sample of 41 countries to show that mutual trust among individuals is positively correlated with growth and investment.[115] They characterised the social, economic and institutional environments in which trust will be high, and showed that low trust environments reduce the rate of investment. Another attempt at instrumenting for trust is by Guiso and colleagues, who have shown how mutual trust among individuals or across individuals in different countries has an impact on trade and other economic outcomes, and they instrumented mutual trust using measures of genetic resemblance.[116] As recognised by them, the inherent difficulty in looking at culture is that it is so broad and the channels through which it can enter the economic discourse so ubiquitous that it is difficult to design testable, refutable hypotheses. One way to capture the component of trust is by looking at the religious and ethnic background of people.

As for religious belief, Barro and McCleary have used international survey data on religiosity for a broad panel of countries to investigate the effects of attendance at religious services and religious beliefs on economic growth.[117] It is thought that higher religious beliefs stimulate growth because they help to sustain aspects of individual behaviour that enhance productivity. On the other hand, higher such attendance can depress growth because it signifies a larger use of resources by the religion sector. According to the World Values Survey, among China, Singapore, Malaysia and Hong Kong, religion is notably important in Malaysia, less so in Singapore and arguably rather unimportant in Hong Kong and China (see Table 2.3).

Furthermore, from an organisational theory perspective, Lawton indicates that while the original Western concept of the corporate entity creates a 'juristic person' separate and distinct from its members, the culture of a place can entail correspondingly different expectations of the company.[118] On the one hand, there may be certain uniformities of culture and business practice in some English-speaking developed economies as a result of the heavy influence of the Anglo-Saxon system. On the other hand, divergencies arise from differing cultural and legal systems in other parts of the world. Contrary to the Berle and Means

Table 2.3 Response to survey question: importance of religion in life (%)

	China	*Hong Kong*	*Malaysia*	*Singapore*
Very important	2.6	12.1	84.8	43.1
Rather important	8	21.3	12	33.6
Not very important	29.6	43.8	2.9	17.8
Not at all important	49.8	22.6	0.2	5.4
No answer	0.8	0.2	0	0.1
Do not know	9.2	0	0	0

Source: World Values Survey.

theory, statistical evidence suggests that controlling shareholders, maybe the state but more often a family, are present in most large companies.[119] The Western concept of separate legal personality can play a role in safeguarding minority shareholders' interests because there is a real separation between family/state and company. There is an impersonal pattern of possession in Britain, the US, Australia, Canada and New Zealand.[120] However, Chinese companies, for example, show different characteristics. As opposed to the separation of ownership and control, professionalisation, bureaucratisation and neutralisation, Chinese companies retain characteristics of small-scale family businesses such as paternalism, personalism, opportunism and flexibility, even when conducting a very large scale of operations.[121] Private benefits of control are therefore much higher. The notable presence of Chinese businessmen and companies in the four economies studied by this book may underline the role of culture in their respective growth stories.

Economic institutions

Acemoglu defines economic institutions as those which 'comprise such things as the structure of property rights, the presence of markets, and the contractual opportunities available to individuals and companies'.[122] Apparently, property rights in the form of shareholder's interests have already been covered by the part on legal institutions above. Therefore, in this book, the term 'economic institutions' are loosely used to described the institutions that are more tangible in nature and not already covered by the three categories of institutions above.

The presence of a functional financial market can be a factor influencing economic development. The primary role of a stock market is the allocation of ownership of the economy's capital stock.[123] The market is a developed system which creates more information about investment projects and can therefore guide investors' funds to better uses.[124] Specialisation, as well as acquisition and dissemination of information, is encouraged to reduce the cost of aggregating dispersed savings, thereby facilitating investment.[125]

The market is often viewed as the most efficient allocation of capital in some cases because of the shortcomings of bank finance. In the presence of asymmetric information, banks generally finance only well-established, safe borrowers, while stock markets can encourage more risky, productive and innovative projects.[126] Furthermore, equity markets allow companies to rely more on equity and less on debt, creating a less risky financial structure in the event of an economic downturn.[127] On the other hand, investors are generally reluctant to relinquish control of their savings for long periods, despite the fact that many high-return projects require a long-term commitment of capital. A liquid stock market can enable more investment to occur because savers can buy and sell quickly and cheaply whenever they wish to alter their portfolios, especially with the development of technology.[128] Moreover, stock markets provide a vehicle for investors to diversify risk.[129] With a diversified investment portfolio, investors may shift part of their savings into higher-return projects, which can foster economic growth. Such growth can also come from the mitigation of agency cost because corporate control is enhanced through stock markets.[130]

To illustrate the importance of stock markets, some scholars have tried to examine the empirical relationship between stock markets and economic growth. A cross-sectional study of 39 countries over the period 1980–88, by Atje and Jovanovic, has suggested that the relative size of a country's stock market helps to explain subsequent growth in gross domestic product per capita.[131] Building on Atje and Jovanovic's study, Levine and Zervos have subsequently confirmed that there is a strong correlation between overall stock market development and long-term economic growth.[132] However, in contrast to the supporting opinions, Harris has found no hard evidence that the level of stock market activity helps to explain growth in per capita output.[133] Despite the debates, Carlin and Mayer are quite right to say that very little is known about the way in which financial structures bear on economic performance.[134] The studies have been restricted to assessments of whether there is a link between financial and economic performance. They have failed to address the range of other questions that lie at the heart of debates about financial systems, for example, the effect of corporate and legal structures. Policies concerning the structure of financial and corporate systems should be sensitive to different stages of economic development.[135] There is no such thing as 'one size fits all'. The absence of a highly developed system of financial markets is not necessarily an indication that a country's economy is somehow backward or underdeveloped.[136] Out of the four economies studied by this book, two of them, China and Hong Kong, have some of the largest stock markets in the world (see Figure 2.1).

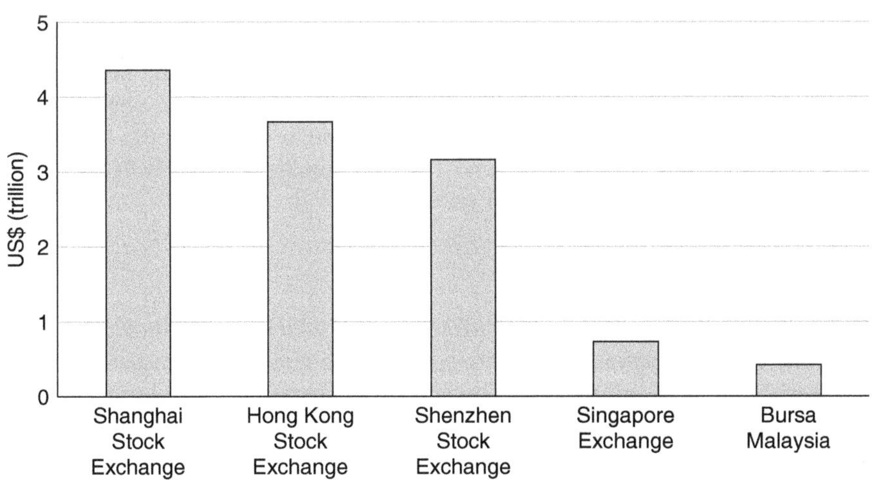

Figure 2.1 Comparative market capitalisation of the stock markets, May 2017 (US$ trillion).

Source: World Federation of Exchanges.

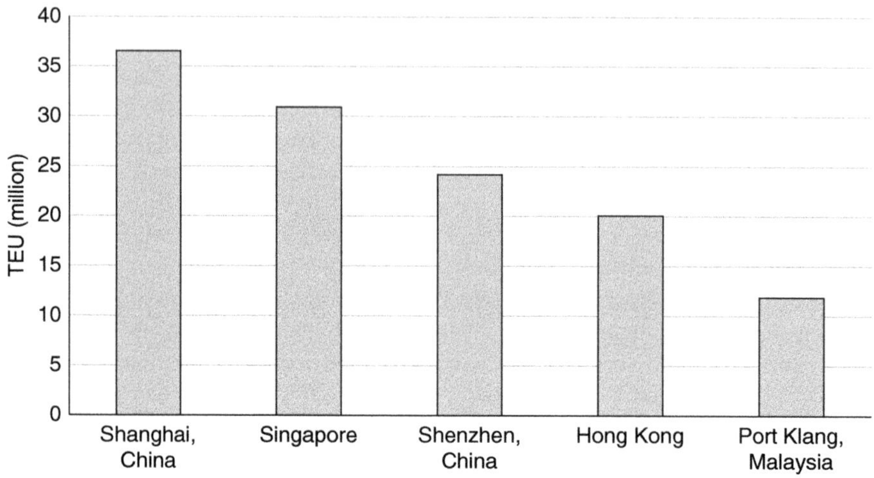

Figure 2.2 Comparative cargo volume handled by the ports, 2015 (million TEU).
Source: World Shipping Council.

In addition to the presence of markets, geography can be a cause of cross-country differences in economic performance.[137] First, climate may be an important determinant of work effort, incentives, or even productivity. This is especially true in the context of agricultural productivity.[138] Second, the burden of infectious disease may be higher in certain geographical locations but not others.[139] This may explain the underdevelopment of Africa, where diseases like malaria and AIDS are widespread. Furthermore, a superior geographical location is an obvious advantage in trade. Out of the four economies studied by this book, three of them, China, Hong Kong and Singapore have some of the busiest container ports in the world (see Figure 2.2). Shanghai, Singapore and Shenzhen are the top three ports in the world. Hong Kong and Malaysia are not too far behind in fifth and twelfth places respectively. Their economies can clearly benefit from the volume of trade handled by their ports.

Concluding remarks

This chapter has discussed a range of institutions which are confirmed by prior academic studies as influential in economic growth under the four general headings, legal, political, cultural and economic. This chapter has also brought in the four economies studied by this book at certain point to provide some preliminary comparisons before their respective experiences are discussed further in subsequent chapters.

The importance of legal institutions has been highlighted by La Porta and colleagues.[140] This part has explained how company law, together with other applicable rules and regulations, plays a role in protecting the interests of shareholders, thereby encouraging people to invest and expanding the scope of economic growth. Hong Kong, Malaysia and Singapore all have good laws in this regard as confirmed by the World Bank's 'Doing Business' reports. China has also made impressive progress in the past decades via another study conducted by the Cambridge Centre for Business Research.[141] A specific dimension of legal institutions is enforcement; this can take the form of public enforcement and private enforcement. It is not adequate to ensure that good laws are in place. At the same time, it is crucial to ensure that those laws can be enforced if needed.

Turning to the political institutions, one dimension is the political orientation of an economy. If it favours entrepreneurs and shareholders, it is believed that markets can flourish easily. Also, it is believed that a small posture of the government is beneficial to the market. Within the context of politics, scholars have been particularly interested in the role of democracy on economic growth. The findings have been rather inconclusive. Some say it is important to ensure adequate constrains are in place on politicians and political elites to foster and sustain economic growth. Some say dictators are keen on development and constraints on them in the form of democracy will indeed prove a hindrance to them in doing their job. In this case, the authoritarian regime in China apparently is an advantage. Colonial origin is also relevant, which may plant the seed of discussion for future chapters as Hong Kong, Singapore and Malaysia are former British colonies.

Turning to cultural conditions, this can echo the part on legal institutions in that legal deterrence is sometimes not the only mechanism to regulate opportunistic behaviour in the markets. Ethics, conscience, pride and reputation can also provide effective incentives in guiding the decision making of people. Scholars have studied the specific effects of trust and religion on economic development. The cross-country differences in cultural profiles may provide a plausible explanation for the differing degrees of development across the world. Confucianism can affect the cultural values in the Chinese communities present in the four countries, but Malaysia is particularly influenced by the religious beliefs of its people.

As for the economic factors, they can provide a good example of the interaction between institutions. More precisely, the legal explanation provided by La Porta and colleagues is that law helps to deepen the financial markets, thereby facilitating economic growth. The markets provide an allocation mechanism to channel capital to businessman and entrepreneurs and help to create growth. On the other hand, certain economies may possess a superior geographical location, such as having a fine seaport. Vibrant, or even world-class, financial markets and container ports are found in China, Hong Kong, Singapore and Malaysia supporting their economic growth.

In a nutshell, by building on the discussions and evidence of a large body of academic studies on the role of institutions in economic development, the chapter should have set out a sound analytical framework to enable a systematic comparison of the institutional factors behind the growth stories of the four economies studied in this book.

Notes

1 Ha-Joon Chang (2011), 'Institutions and Economic Development: Theory, Policy and History' in *Journal of Institutional Economics*, **7**, p. 473.
2 Rafael La Porta *et al.* (1997), 'Legal Determinants of External Finance' in *Journal of Finance*, **52**; Rafael La Porta *et al.* (1998), 'Law and Finance' in *Journal of Political Economy*, **106**; Rafael La Porta *et al.* (2000), 'Investor Protection and Corporate Governance' in *Journal of Financial Economics*, **58**. The other team is Acemoglu and colleagues. For example, Daron Acemoglu *et al.* (2001), 'The Colonial Origins of Comparative Development: An Empirical Investigation' in *American Economic Review*, **91**; Daron Acemoglu *et al.* (2002), 'Reversal of Fortune: Geography and Institutions in the Making of the Modern World Income Distribution' in Quarterly Journal of Economics, **117**. See Philippe Aghion and Peter Howitt (2009), *The Economics of Growth*, Cambridge: MIT Press, p. 237. Naturally, this chapter will make use of the contributions from both teams.
3 Thorstein Veblen (1899), *The Theory of the Leisure Class: An Economic Study of Institutions*, p. 87. Online. Available at: http://moglen.law.columbia.edu/LCS/theoryleisureclass.pdf.
4 Walton Hamilton (1919), 'The Institutional Approach to Economic Theory' in *American Economic Review*, **9**. See also Geoffrey Hodgson (2000), 'What is the Essence of Institutional Economics' in *Journal of Economic Issues*, **34**.
5 Malcolm Rutherford (2001), 'Institutional Economics: Then and Now' in *Journal of Economic Perspectives*, **15**, p. 187.
6 Acemoglu *et al.* (2012), op. cit., p. 1262.
7 Douglass North and Robert Thomas (1976), *The Rise of the Western World: A New Economic History*, Cambridge: CUP, pp. 146–156.
8 Ibid. p. 2.
9 Kenneth Sokoloff and Stanley Engerman (2000), 'History Lessons: Institutions, Factor Endowments, and Paths of Development in the New World' in *Journal of Economic Perspective*, **14**. In their study, they particularly examine economies of the Americas.
10 Daron Acemoglu *et al.* (2005), 'Institutions as a Fundamental Cause of Long-Run Growth' in Philippe Aghion and Steven Durlauf (eds), *Handbook of Economic Growth: Volume 1A*, Amsterdam: Elsevier, pp. 389–390.
11 Ibid. p. 390.
12 Robert Solow (1956), 'A Contribution to the Theory of Economic Growth' in *Quarterly Journal of Economics*, **70**; and T.W. Swan (1956), 'Economic Growth and Capital Accumulation' in *Economic Record*, **32**.
13 Larry Jones and Rodolfo Manuelli (2005), 'Neoclassical Models of Endogenous Growth: The Effects of Fiscal Policy, Innovation and Fluctuations' in Philippe Aghion and Steven Durlauf (eds), *Handbook of Economic Growth: Volume 1A*, Amsterdam: Elsevier, p. 15.
14 Roy Harrod (1939), 'An Essay in Dynamic Theory' in *Economic Journal*, **49**; and Evsey Domar (1946), 'Capital Expansion, Rate of Growth, and Employment' in *Econometrica*, **14**.
15 Aghion and Howitt (2009), op. cit., p. 56.
16 Ibid. p. 85. See also Joseph Schumpeter (1942), *The Theory of Economic Development*, Cambridge: Harvard University Press, for the origin of how this model is named.
17 Aghion and Howitt (2009), op. cit., pp. 99–100.
18 North and Thomas (1976), op. cit., p. 2.
19 Rutherford (2001), op. cit.
20 Douglass North (1990), *Institutions, Institutional Change and Economic Performance*, Cambridge: CUP, p. 3.

21 Avner Greif (2006), *Institutions and the Path to the Modern Economy: Lessons from Medieval Trade*, Cambridge: CUP.
22 Geoffrey Hodgson (2006), 'What Are Institutions?' in *Journal of Economic Issues*, **40**, p. 2.
23 North (1990), op. cit., p. 3.
24 Acemoglu *et al.* (2005), p. 397.
25 See, for example, Schumpeter (1942), op. cit.; Ronald McKinnon (1973), *Money and Capital in Economic Development*, Washington D.C.: Brookings Institution; Robert King and Ross Levine (1993), 'Finance and Growth: Schumpeter Might Be Right' in *Quarterly Journal of Economics*, **108**; and also see this chapter's section on 'Economic institutions' below.
26 See, for example, Franco Modigliani and Enrico Perotti (1997), 'Protection of Minority Interest and the Development of Security Markets' in *Managerial and Decision Economics*, **18**; Thorsten Beck and Ross Levine (2005), 'Legal Institutions and Financial Development' in Claude Menard and Mary Shirley (eds), *Handbook of New Institutional Economics*, Dordrecht: Springer; and also see this chapter's section on 'Legal institutions' below.
27 See for example, Adam Przeworski and Fernando Limongi (1993), 'Political Regimes and Economic Growth' in *Journal of Economic Perspectives*, **7**; and Robert Barro (1999), 'Determinants of Democracy' in *Journal of Political Economy*, **107**; and also see this chapter's section on 'Political institutions' below.
28 See for example, Daron Acemoglu and Jaume Ventura (2002), 'The World Income Distribution' in *Quarterly Journal of Economics*, **117**.
29 See for example, William Easterly and Ross Levine (1997), 'Africa's Growth Tragedy: Policies and Ethnic Divisions' in *Quarterly Journal of Economics*, **112**; and also see this chapter's section on 'Cultural institutions' below.
30 See for example, Eric Bartelsman and Mark Doms (2000), 'Understanding Productivity: Lessons from Longitudinal Microdata' in *Journal of Economic Literature*, **38**.
31 See for example, Gregory Mankiw *et al.* (1992), 'A Contribution to the Empirics of Economic Growth' in *Quarterly Journal of Economics*, **107**.
32 See for example, Acemoglu *et al.* (2001), op. cit.
33 See for example, Daniel Klerman *et al.* (2011), 'Legal Origin or Colonial History?' in *Journal of Legal Analysis*, **3**.
34 Avner Greif (1994), 'Cultural Beliefs and the Organization of Society: A Historical and Theoretical Reflection on Collectivist and Individualist Societies' in *Journal of Political Economy*, **102**.
35 Daron Acemoglu (2009), *Introduction to Modern Economic Growth*, Princeton: Princeton University Press, p. 136.
36 William Easterly (2008), 'Institutions: Top Down or Bottom Up?' in *American Economic Review: Papers and Proceedings*, **98**, p. 95.
37 La Porta *et al.* (1997, 1998, 2000), op. cit.
38 Timothy Besley and Maitreesh Ghatak (2010), 'Property Rights and Economic Development' in Dani Rodrik and Mark Rosenzweig (eds), *Handbook of Development Economics Vol. 5*, Amsterdam: Elsevier, p. 4526.
39 La Porta *et al.* (1997, 1998, 2000), op. cit.
40 Ibid.
41 See for example, Daniel Berkowitz *et al.* (2003), 'Economic Development, Legality and the Transplant Effect' in *European Economic Review*, **47**, and Mathias Siems (2007), 'Legal Origins: Reconciling Law and Finance and Comparative Law' in *McGill Law Review*, **52**. A mere categorisation of a system as common law or civil law disregards deeper legal structures. La Porta and colleagues subsequently attempted a further interpretation and addressed several objections to the empirical claim that legal origins matter in Rafael La Porta *et al.* (2008), 'The Economic Consequences of Legal Origins' in *Journal of Economic Literature*, **46**.

42 Holger Spamann (2010), 'The "Antidirector Rights Index" Revisited' in *Review of Financial Studies*, **23**.
43 Siems (2007), op. cit.
44 John Coffee (2001), 'The Rise of Dispersed Ownership: The Roles of Law and the State in the Separation of Ownership and Control' in *Yale Law Journal*, **111**; Brian Cheffins (2001), 'Does Law Matter? The Separation of Ownership and Control in the United Kingdom' in *Journal of Legal Studies*, **30**; and Mark Roe (2006), 'Legal Origins, Politics and Modern Stock Markets' in *Harvard Law Review*, **120**.
45 Bernard Black (2001), 'The Legal and Institutional Preconditions for Strong Securities Markets' in *UCLA Law Review*, **48**, p. 784.
46 See Coffee (2001), op. cit., pp. 65–66 and Cheffins (2001), op. cit., pp. 483–484.
47 Kenneth Dam (2006), *The Law-Growth Nexus*, Washington D.C.: Brookings Institution, pp. 188–189.
48 Roberta Romano (1998), 'Empowering Investors: A Market Approach to Securities Regulation' in *Yale Law Journal*, **107**, p. 2367. The framework of securities legislation in the US consists of seven related but separate statutes that are administered by the Securities and Exchange Commission.
49 Simeon Djankov *et al.* (2008), 'The Law and Economics of Self-dealing' in *Journal of Financial Economics*, **88**.
50 John Armour *et al.* (2009), 'Shareholder Protection and Stock Market Development: An Empirical Test of the Legal Origins Hypothesis' in *Journal of Empirical Legal Studies*, **6**.
51 World Bank (2017), 'Doing Business'. Online. Available at: www.doingbusiness.org.
52 Important parameters include the extent of disclosure, director liability, shareholder rights and suits, etc.
53 Armour *et al.* (2009), op. cit.
54 This is available via Mathias Siems (2016), 'CBR Extended Shareholder Protection Index'. Online. Available at: www.repository.cam.ac.uk/bitstream/handle/1810/256566/cbr-spi-30-countries-codebook-and-methodology.pdf?sequence=9&isAllowed=y. See also Dionysia Katelouzou and Mathias Siems (2015), 'Disappearing Paradigms in Shareholder Protection: Leximetric Evidence for 30 Countries, 1990–2013' in *Journal of Corporate Law Studies*, **15**.
55 Katelouzou and Siems (2015), op. cit., p. 133.
56 Ibid. p. 134.
57 Dam (2006), op. cit., p. 171.
58 Dani Rodrik (2003), 'Introduction: What Do We Learn from Country Narratives?' in Dani Rodrik (ed.), *In Search of Prosperity: Analytic Narratives on Economic Growth*, Princeton: Princeton University Press, pp. 9–10. He further said, 'econometric results can be found to support any and all … categories of arguments. However, very little of this econometric work survives close scrutiny'.
59 Rafael La Porta *et al.* (2006), 'What Works in Securities Laws?' in *Journal of Finance*, **61**, pp. 1–3.
60 This theory is advocated by Chicago school of economists such as Ronald Coase. In this situation, issuers of securities have an incentive to disclose all available information to obtain higher prices simply because failure to disclose would cause investors to assume the worst. Furthermore, auditors and underwriters can credibly certify the quality of securities to safeguard their reputation.
61 Iain MacNeil and Alex Lau (2001), 'International Corporate Regulation: Listing Rules and Overseas Companies' in *International and Comparative Law Quarterly*, **50**.
62 Adolf Berle and Gardiner Means (1991), *The Modern Corporation and Private Property*, London: Transaction Publishers.
63 Adam Smith (1776), *An Inquiry into the Nature and Causes of the Wealth of Nations*, para.V.1.107. Online. Available at: www.econlib.org/library/Smith/smWN.

html. A contemporary and landmark analysis of the agency problem was seen in Michael Jensen and William Meckling (1976), 'Theory of the Firm: Managerial Behaviour, Agency Costs and Ownership Structure' in *Journal of Financial Economics*, **3**.

64 Berle and Means (1991), op. cit., p. 114.

65 John Armour *et al.* (2017), 'Agency Problems and Legal Strategies' in John Armour *et al.* (eds), *The Anatomy of Corporate Law: A Comparative and Functional Approach*, Oxford: OUP, pp. 29–30.

66 But note, a 'shareholder value' approach traditionally has dominated the corporate world. As famously said by Milton Friedman, 'there is one and only one social responsibility of business – to use its resources and engage in activities designed to increase its profits so long as it stays within the rules of the game, which is to say, engages in open and free competition without deception or fraud.' See Milton Friedman (1970), 'The Social Responsibility of Business is to Increase Its Profits' in *New York Times* (13 September 1970). This is to be contrasted with the rising concern of corporate social responsibility. See e.g. Archie Carroll (1991), 'The Pyramid of Corporate Social Responsibility: Toward the Moral Management of Organizational Stakeholders' in *Business Horizons*, **34**.

67 Luca Enriques *et al.* (2017), 'Corporate Law and Securities Markets' in John Armour *et al.* (eds), *The Anatomy of Corporate Law: A Comparative and Functional Approach*, Oxford: OUP, pp. 243–258. See also Louise Gullifer and Jennifer Payne (2015), *Corporate Finance Law: Principles and Policy*, Oxford: Hart, p. 487.

68 Enriques *et al.* (2017), op. cit., pp. 245–252.

69 Ibid. pp. 256–257.

70 Ibid. p. 257.

71 John Coffee (2007), 'Law and the Market: The Impact of Enforcement' in *University of Pennsylvania Law Review*, **156**, p. 244.

72 Katharina Pistor and Chenggang Xu (2002), 'Law Enforcement under Incomplete Law: Theory and Evidence from Financial Market Regulation' Columbia Law and Economic Working Paper No. 222. Online. Available at: http://ssrn.com/abstract=396141.

73 Harvey Pitt and Karen Shapiro (1990), 'Securities Regulation by Enforcement: A Look Ahead at the Next Decade' in *Yale Journal on Regulation*, **7**, p. 182.

74 Howell Jackson and Mark Roe (2009), 'Public and Private Enforcement of Securities Laws: Resource-based Evidence' in *Journal of Financial Economics*, **93**.

75 Ibid.

76 Ibid. p. 216. They both have budgets of more than US$300,000 per billion of GDP.

77 See Coffee (2007), op. cit., p. 259. The adjusted regulatory cost for the US is US$83,943 per billion dollars of stock market capitalisation, around the same level as Hong Kong (US$73,317) and Singapore (US$95,406), but below that of Australia (US$279,587), Canada (US$220,515) and the UK (US$138,159). For civil law countries, Germany has a very low regulatory cost of US$8,896 per billion dollars of stock market capitalisation, below France (US$19,041) and Sweden (US$33,573).

78 Jackson and Roe (2009), op. cit., p. 233.

79 Coffee (2007), op. cit., pp. 261–262.

80 Ibid.

81 Ibid.

82 Dam (2006), op. cit., p. 189.

83 La Porta *et al.* (2006), op. cit.

84 Armour *et al.* (2009), op. cit.

85 *Foss* v. *Harbottle* (1843) 2 Hare 461.

86 Geoffrey Miller (1998), 'Political Structure and Corporate Governance: Some Points of Contrast between the United States and England' in *Columbia Business Law Review*, **1998**, p. 75.

87 Coffee (2007), op. cit.
88 Pistor and Xu (2002), op. cit., p. 35.
89 Jackson and Roe (2009), op. cit., p. 38.
90 For instance, see La Porta *et al.* (2006), op. cit.
91 Mark Roe (2003), *Political Determinant of Corporate Governance*, Oxford: OUP.
92 Roe (2006), op. cit., p. 503.
93 Coffee (2001), op. cit., p. 75. Power seeking nationalists use banks as their agents and these banks resist the rise of rivals, the securities markets, for their business.
94 Masahiko Aoki (1995), 'Controlling Insider Control: Issues of Corporate Governance in Transition Economies' in Masahiko Aoki and Hyung-Ki Kim (eds), *Corporate Governance in Transitional Economies: Insider Control and the Role of Banks*, Washington D.C.: World Bank, p. 6.
95 Thorsten Beck *et al.* (2001), 'Law, Politics, and Finance' World Bank Policy Research Working Paper No. 2585. Online. Available at: http://ssrn.com/abstract=269118.
96 Roe (2003), op. cit., pp. 98–102.
97 Cheffins (2001), op. cit.
98 Acemoglu *et al.* (2005), p. 393.
99 Ibid. p. 407.
100 Przeworski and Limongi (1993), op. cit.
101 Samuel Huntington (1968), *Political Order in Changing Societies*, New Haven: Yale University Press.
102 Przeworski and Limongi (1993), op. cit., pp. 55–56.
103 Barro (1999), op. cit.
104 Philippe Aghion *et al.* (2004), 'Endogenous Political Institutions' in *Quarterly Journal of Economics*, **116**.
105 Casey Mulligan *et al.* (2004), 'Do Democracies Have Different Public Policies than Nondemocracies?' in *Journal of Economic Perspectives*, **18**.
106 Economist Intelligence Unit (2017), 'Democracy Index 2016'. Online. Available at www.eiu.com/topic/democracy-index. The Democracy Index is based on five categories: electoral process and pluralism; civil liberties; the functioning of government; political participation; and political culture. Based on their scores on a range of indicators within these categories, each country is then itself classified as one of four types of regime: 'full democracy'; 'flawed democracy'; 'hybrid regime'; and 'authoritarian regime'.
107 Aghion and Howitt (2009), op. cit., p. 421.
108 Ibid.
109 Geert Hofsted (1994), *Cultures and Organizations*, London: HarperCollins, p. 116.
110 Ibid. pp. 110–113.
111 The Inglehart–Welzel cultural map of the world a scatter plot created by political scientists Ronald Inglehart and Christian Welzel based on the World Values Survey. See World Values Survey Association (2017), 'World Values Survey'. Online. Available at www.worldvaluessurvey.org.
112 Amir Licht *et al.* (2007), 'Culture Rules: The Foundations of the Rule of Law and Other Norms of Governance' in *Journal of Comparative Economics*, **35**.
113 Ibid. A study was conducted based on a comparison between a taxonomy of corporate governance regimes according to legal families and a classification of countries according to their shared cultural values.
114 Bernard Black (2000), 'The Core Institutions that Support Strong Securities Markets' in *Business Lawyer*, **55**.
115 Paul Zak and Stephen Knack (2001), 'Trust and Growth' in *Economic Journal*, **111**.
116 Luigi Guiso *et al.* (2006), 'Does Culture Affect Economic Outcomes?' in *Journal of Economic Perspectives*, **20**.
117 Robert Barro and Rachel McCleary (2003), 'Religion and Economic Growth' in *American Sociological Review*, 68.

118 Philip Lawton (1996), 'Berle and Means, Corporate Governance and the Chinese Family Firm' in *Australian Journal of Corporate Law*, **6**, p. 23.
119 Rafael La Porta *et al.* (1999), 'Corporate Ownership around the World' in *Journal of Finance*, **64**.
120 Lawton (1996), op. cit., pp. 27–28.
121 Ibid. In the Chinese context, personal connections or *guanxi* have remained a key element of Chinese organisation.
122 Acemoglu (2009), op. cit., p. 120.
123 Eugene Fama (1970), 'Efficient Capital Markets: A Review of Theory and Empirical Work' in *Journal of Finance*, **25**.
124 Raymond Atje and Boyan Jovanovic (1993), 'Stock Markets and Development' in *European Economic Review*, **37**.
125 Philip Arestis *et al.* (2001), 'Financial Development and Economic Growth: The Role of Stock Markets' in *Journal of Money, Credit and Banking*, **33**, p. 18.
126 Guglielmo Caporale *et al.* (2004), 'Stock Market Development and Economic Growth: the Causal Linkage' in *Journal of Economic Development*, **29**, p. 36. Venture capitalists are often the financiers for new start-ups. Stock markets provide these venture capitalists with an exit strategy. It is therefore argued that there is a link between the stock market and the venture capital market. See for example, Bernard Black and Ronald Gilson (1999), 'Does Venture Capital Require an Active Stock Market?' in *Journal of Applied Corporate Finance*, **11**.
127 Stijn Claessens *et al.* (2000), 'Stock Markets in Transition Economies' Financial Sector Discussion Paper No. 5. Online: Available at: http://ssrn.com/abstract=240703.
128 Ross Levine and Sara Zervos (1996), 'Stock Market Development and Long-Run Growth' in *World Bank Economic Review*, **10**, p. 326.
129 Ibid. p. 327.
130 Asli Demirguc-Kunt and Ross Levine (1996), 'Stock Markets, Corporate Finance and Economic Growth: An Overview' in *World Bank Economic Review*, **10**, p. 231. Although a diffuse ownership structure will reduce the incentives for investors to monitor the management carefully, the countervailing argument is that a remuneration package tied to stock performance and takeover threats are possible ways to align the interests of managers and owners. Also, the presence of institutional investors and securities analysts can potentially enhance monitoring.
131 Atje and Jovanovic (1993), op. cit.
132 Levine and Zervos (1996), op. cit., p. 327.
133 Richard Harris (1997), 'Stock Markets and Development: A Re-assessment' in *European Economic Review*, **41**.
134 Wendy Carlin and Colin Mayer (2003), 'Finance, Investment and Growth' in *Journal of Financial Economics*, **69**.
135 Ibid. p. 193.
136 Franklin Allen and Douglas Gale (2000), *Comparing Financial Systems*, Cambridge: MIT Press, p. 127.
137 Acemoglu *et al.* (2005), op. cit., pp. 399–400.
138 Jeffrey Sachs (2001), 'Tropical Underdevelopment' NBER Working Paper No. 8119. Online. Available at: www.nber.org/papers/w8119.
139 Paul Milligan and Michael Thomas (1986), 'Relationships between Development and Disease' in *Environmentalist*, **6**.
140 La Porta *et al.* (1997, 1998, 2000), op. cit.
141 Armour *et al.* (2009), op. cit.

References

Acemoglu, Daron (2009), *Introduction to Modern Economic Growth*, Princeton: Princeton University Press.

Acemoglu, Daron; Johnson, Simon; and Robinson, James (2001), 'The Colonial Origins of Comparative Development: An Empirical Investigation' in *American Economic Review*, **91**.

Acemoglu, Daron; Johnson, Simon; and Robinson, James (2002), 'Reversal of Fortune: Geography and Institutions in the Making of the Modern World Income Distribution' in *Quarterly Journal of Economics*, **117**.

Acemoglu, Daron; Johnson, Simon; and Robinson, James (2005), 'Institutions as a Fundamental Cause of Long-Run Growth' in Philippe Aghion and Steven Durlauf (eds), *Handbook of Economic Growth: Volume 1A*, Amsterdam: Elsevier.

Acemoglu, Daron and Ventura, Jaume (2002), 'The World Income Distribution' in *Quarterly Journal of Economics*, **117**.

Aghion, Philippe; Alesina, Alberto; and Trebbi, Francesco (2004), 'Endogenous Political Institutions' in *Quarterly Journal of Economics*, **116**.

Aghion, Philippe and Howitt, Peter (2009), *The Economics of Growth*, Cambridge: MIT Press.

Allen, Franklin and Gale, Douglas (2000), *Comparing Financial Systems*, Cambridge: MIT Press.

Aoki, Masahiko (1995), 'Controlling Insider Control: Issues of Corporate Governance in Transition Economies' in Masahiko Aoki and Hyung-Ki Kim (eds), *Corporate Governance in Transitional Economies: Insider Control and the Role of Banks*, Washington D.C.: World Bank.

Arestis, Philip; Demetriades, Panicos; and Luintel, Kul (2001), 'Financial Development and Economic Growth: The Role of Stock Markets' in *Journal of Money, Credit and Banking*, **33**.

Atje, Raymond and Jovanovic, Boyan (1993), 'Stock Markets and Development' in *European Economic Review*, **37**.

Armour, John; Deakin, Simon; Sarkar, Prabirjit; Siems, Mathias; and Singh, Ajit (2009), 'Shareholder Protection and Stock Market Development: An Empirical Test of the Legal Origins Hypothesis' in *Journal of Empirical Legal Studies*, **6**.

Armour, John; Hansmann, Henry; and Kraakman, Reinier (2017), 'Agency Problems and Legal Strategies' in Reinier Kraakman; John Armour; Paul Davies; Luca Enriques; Henry Hansmann; Gerard Hertig; Klaus Hopt; Hideki Kanda; Mariana Pargendler; Wolf-Georg Ringe; and Edward Rock (eds), *The Anatomy of Corporate Law: A Comparative and Functional Approach*, Oxford: OUP.

Barro, Robert (1999), 'Determinants of Democracy' in *Journal of Political Economy*, **107**.

Barro, Robert and McCleary, Rachel (2003), 'Religion and Economic Growth' in *American Sociological Review*, 68.

Bartelsman, Eric and Doms, Mark (2000), 'Understanding Productivity: Lessons from Longitudinal Microdata' in *Journal of Economic Literature*, **38**.

Beck, Thorsten; Demirgüç-Kunt, Asli; and Levine, Ross (2001), 'Law, Politics, and Finance' World Bank Policy Research Working Paper No. 2585. Online. Available at: http://ssrn.com/abstract=269118.

Beck, Thorsten and Levine, Ross (2005), 'Legal Institutions and Financial Development' in Claude Menard and Mary Shirley (eds), *Handbook of New Institutional Economics*, Dordrecht: Springer.

Berkowitz, Daniel; Pistor, Katharina; and Richard, Jean-Francois (2003), 'Economic Development, Legality and the Transplant Effect' in *European Economic Review*, **47**.

Berle, Adolf and Means, Gardiner (1991), *The Modern Corporation and Private Property*, London: Transaction Publishers.

Besley, Timothy and Ghatak, Maitreesh (2010), 'Property Rights and Economic Development' in Dani Rodrik and Mark Rosenzweig (eds), *Handbook of Development Economics Vol. 5*, Amsterdam: Elsevier.

Black, Bernard (2000), 'The Core Institutions that Support Strong Securities Markets' in *Business Lawyer*, **55**.

Black, Bernard (2001), 'The Legal and Institutional Preconditions for Strong Securities Markets' in *UCLA Law Review*, **48**.

Black, Bernard and Gilson, Ronald (1999), 'Does Venture Capital Require an Active Stock Market?' in *Journal of Applied Corporate Finance*, **11**.

Caporale, Guglielmo; Howells, Peter; and Soliman, Alaa (2004), 'Stock Market Development and Economic Growth: the Causal Linkage' in *Journal of Economic Development*, **29**.

Carlin, Wendy and Mayer, Colin (2003), 'Finance, Investment and Growth' in *Journal of Financial Economics*, **69**.

Carroll, Archie (1991), 'The Pyramid of Corporate Social Responsibility: Toward the Moral Management of Organizational Stakeholders' in *Business Horizons*, **34**.

Chang, Ha-Joon (2011), 'Institutions and Economic Development: Theory, Policy and History' in *Journal of Institutional Economics*, **7**.

Cheffins, Brian (2001), 'Does Law Matter?: The Separation of Ownership and Control in the United Kingdom' in *Journal of Legal Studies*, **30**.

Claessens, Stijn; Djankov, Simeon; and Klingebiel, Daniela (2000), 'Stock Markets in Transition Economies' Financial Sector Discussion Paper No. 5. Online: Available at: http://ssrn.com/abstract=240703.

Coffee, John (2001), 'The Rise of Dispersed Ownership: The Roles of Law and the State in the Separation of Ownership and Control' in *Yale Law Journal*, **111**.

Coffee, John (2007), 'Law and the Market: The Impact of Enforcement' in *University of Pennsylvania Law Review*, **156**.

Dam, Kenneth (2006), *The Law-Growth Nexus*, Washington D.C.: Brookings Institution.

Demirguc-Kunt, Asli and Levine, Ross (1996), 'Stock Markets, Corporate Finance and Economic Growth: An Overview' in *World Bank Economic Review*, **10**.

Djankov, Simeon; La Porta, Rafael; Lopez-de-Silanes, Florencio; and Shleifer, Andrei (2008), 'The Law and Economics of Self-dealing' in *Journal of Financial Economics*, **88**.

Domar, Evsey (1946), 'Capital Expansion, Rate of Growth, and Employment' in *Econometrica*, **14**.

Easterly, William (2008), 'Institutions: Top Down or Bottom Up?' in *American Economic Review: Papers and Proceedings*, **98**.

Easterly, William and Levine, Ross (1997), 'Africa's Growth Tragedy: Policies and Ethnic Divisions' in *Quarterly Journal of Economics*, **112**.

Economist Intelligence Unit (2017), 'Democracy Index 2016'. Online. Available at www.eiu.com/topic/democracy-index.

Enriques, Luca; Hertig, Gerard; Kraakman, Reinier; and Rock, Edward (2017), 'Corporate Law and Securities Markets' in Reinier Kraakman; John Armour; Paul Davies; Luca Enriques; Henry Hansmann; Gerard Hertig; Klaus Hopt; Hideki Kanda; Mariana Pargendler; Wolf-Georg Ringe; and Edward Rock (eds), *The Anatomy of Corporate Law: A Comparative and Functional Approach*, Oxford: OUP.

Fama, Eugene (1970), 'Efficient Capital Markets: A Review of Theory and Empirical Work' in *Journal of Finance*, **25**.

Friedman, Milton (1970), 'The Social Responsibility of Business is to Increase Its Profits' in *New York Times* (13 September 1970).

Greif, Avner (1994), 'Cultural Beliefs and the Organization of Society: A Historical and Theoretical Reflection on Collectivist and Individualist Societies' in *Journal of Political Economy*, **102**.

Greif, Avner (2006), *Institutions and the Path to the Modern Economy: Lessons from Medieval Trade*, Cambridge: CUP.

Guiso, Luigi; Sapienza, Paola; and Zingales, Luigi (2006), 'Does Culture Affect Economic Outcomes?' in *Journal of Economic Perspectives*, **20**.

Gullifer, Louise and Payne, Jennifer (2015), *Corporate Finance Law: Principles and Policy*, Oxford: Hart.

Hamilton, Walton (1919), 'The Institutional Approach to Economic Theory' in *American Economic Review*, **9**.

Harris, Richard (1997), 'Stock Markets and Development: A Re-assessment' in *European Economic Review*, **41**.

Harrod, Roy (1939), 'An Essay in Dynamic Theory' in *Economic Journal*, **49**.

Hodgson, Geoffrey (2000), 'What is the Essence of Institutional Economics' in *Journal of Economic Issues*, **34**.

Hodgson, Geoffrey (2006), 'What Are Institutions?' in *Journal of Economic Issues*, **40**.

Hofsted, Geert (1994), *Cultures and Organizations*, London: HarperCollins.

Huntington, Samuel (1968), *Political Order in Changing Societies*, New Haven: Yale University Press.

Jackson, Howell and Roe, Mark (2009), 'Public and Private Enforcement of Securities Laws: Resource-based Evidence' in *Journal of Financial Economics*, **93**.

Jensen, Michael and Meckling, William (1976), 'Theory of the Firm: Managerial Behaviour, Agency Costs and Ownership Structure' in *Journal of Financial Economics*, **3**.

Jones, Larry and Manuelli, Rodolfo (2005), 'Neoclassical Models of Endogenous Growth: The Effects of Fiscal Policy, Innovation and Fluctuations' in Philippe Aghion and Steven Durlauf (eds), *Handbook of Economic Growth: Volume 1A*, Amsterdam: Elsevier.

Katelouzou, Dionysia and Siems, Mathias (2015), 'Disappearing Paradigms in Shareholder Protection: Leximetric Evidence for 30 Countries, 1990–2013' in *Journal of Corporate Law Studies*, **15**.

King, Robert and Levine, Ross (1993), 'Finance and Growth: Schumpeter Might Be Right' in *Quarterly Journal of Economics*, **108**.

Klerman, Daniel; Mahoney, Paul; Spamann, Holger; and Weinstein, Mark (2011), 'Legal Origin or Colonial History?' in *Journal of Legal Analysis*, **3**.

La Porta, Rafael; Lopez-de-Silane, Florencio; and Shleifer, Andrei (1999), 'Corporate Ownership around the World' in *Journal of Finance*, **64**.

La Porta, Rafael; Lopez-de-Silane, Florencio; and Shleifer, Andrei (2006), 'What Works in Securities Laws?' in *Journal of Finance*, **61**.

La Porta, Rafael; Lopez-de-Silane, Florencio; and Shleifer, Andrei (2008), 'The Economic Consequences of Legal Origins' in *Journal of Economic Literature*, **46**.

La Porta, Rafael; Lopez-de-Silane, Florencio; Shleifer, Andrei; and Vishny, Robert (1997), 'Legal Determinants of External Finance' in *Journal of Finance*, **52**.

La Porta, Rafael; Lopez-de-Silane, Florencio; Shleifer, Andrei; and Vishny, Robert (1998), 'Law and Finance' in *Journal of Political Economy*, **106**.

La Porta, Rafael; Lopez-de-Silane, Florencio; Shleifer, Andrei; and Vishny, Robert (2000), 'Investor Protection and Corporate Governance' in *Journal of Financial Economics*, **58**.

Lawton, Philip (1996), 'Berle and Means, Corporate Governance and the Chinese Family Firm' in *Australian Journal of Corporate Law*, **6**.

Levine, Ross and Zervos, Sara (1996), 'Stock Market Development and Long-Run Growth' in *World Bank Economic Review*, **10**.

Licht, Amir; Goldschmidt, Chanan; and Schwartz, Shalom (2007), 'Culture Rules: The Foundations of the Rule of Law and Other Norms of Governance' in *Journal of Comparative Economics*, **35.**

MacNeil, Iain and Lau, Alex (2001), 'International Corporate Regulation: Listing Rules and Overseas Companies' in *International and Comparative Law Quarterly*, **50**.

Mankiw, Gregory; Romer, David; and Weil, David (1992), 'A Contribution to the Empirics of Economic Growth' in *Quarterly Journal of Economics*, **107**.

McKinnon, Ronald (1973), *Money and Capital in Economic Development*, Washington D.C.: Brookings Institution.

Miller, Geoffrey (1998), 'Political Structure and Corporate Governance: Some Points of Contrast between the United States and England' in *Columbia Business Law Review*, **1998**.

Milligan, Paul and Thomas, Michael (1986), 'Relationships between Development and Disease' in *Environmentalist*, **6**.

Modigliani, Franco and Perotti, Enrico (1997), 'Protection of Minority Interest and the Development of Security Markets' in *Managerial and Decision Economics*, **18**.

Mulligan, Casey; Gil, Ricard; Sala-i-Martin, Xavier (2004), 'Do Democracies Have Different Public Policies than Nondemocracies?' in *Journal of Economic Perspectives*, **18**.

North, Douglass (1990), *Institutions, Institutional Change and Economic Performance*, Cambridge: CUP.

North, Douglass and Thomas, Robert (1976), *The Rise of the Western World: A New Economic History*, Cambridge: CUP.

Pistor, Katharina and Xu, Chenggang (2002), 'Law Enforcement under Incomplete Law: Theory and Evidence from Financial Market Regulation' Columbia Law and Economic Working Paper No. 222. Online. Available at: http://ssrn.com/abstract=396141.

Pitt, Harvey and Shapiro, Karen (1990), 'Securities Regulation by Enforcement: A Look Ahead at the Next Decade' in *Yale Journal on Regulation*, **7**.

Przeworski, Adam and Limongi, Fernando (1993), 'Political Regimes and Economic Growth' in *Journal of Economic Perspectives*, **7**.

Rodrik, Dani (2003), 'Introduction: What Do We Learn from Country Narratives?' in Dani Rodrik (ed.), *In Search of Prosperity: Analytic Narratives on Economic Growth*, Princeton: Princeton University Press.

Roe, Mark (2003), *Political Determinant of Corporate Governance*, Oxford: OUP.

Roe, Mark (2006), 'Legal Origins, Politics and Modern Stock Markets' in *Harvard Law Review*, **120**.

Romano, Roberta (1998), 'Empowering Investors: A Market Approach to Securities Regulation' in *Yale Law Journal*, **107**.

Rutherford, Malcolm (2001), 'Institutional Economics: Then and Now' in *Journal of Economic Perspectives*, **15**.

Sachs, Jeffrey (2001), 'Tropical Underdevelopment' NBER Working Paper No. 8119. Online. Available at: www.nber.org/papers/w8119.

Schumpeter, Joseph (1942), *The Theory of Economic Development*, Cambridge: Harvard University Press.

Siems, Mathias (2007), 'Legal Origins: Reconciling Law and Finance and Comparative Law' in *McGill Law Review*, **52**.

Siems, Mathias (2016), 'CBR Extended Shareholder Protection Index'. Online. Available at: www.repository.cam.ac.uk/bitstream/handle/1810/256566/cbr-spi-30-countries-codebook-and-methodology.pdf?sequence=9&isAllowed=y.

Smith, Adam (1776), *An Inquiry into the Nature and Causes of the Wealth of Nations*. Online. Available at: www.econlib.org/library/Smith/smWN.html.

Sokoloff, Kenneth and Engerman, Stanley (2000), 'History Lessons: Institutions, Factor Endowments, and Paths of Development in the New World' in *Journal of Economic Perspective*, **14**.

Spamann, Holger (2010), 'The "Antidirector Rights Index" Revisited' in *Review of Financial Studies*, **23**.

Solow, Robert (1956), 'A Contribution to the Theory of Economic Growth' in *Quarterly Journal of Economics*, **70**.

Swan, T.W. (1956), 'Economic Growth and Capital Accumulation' in *Economic Record*, **32**.

Veblen, Thorstein (1899), *The Theory of the Leisure Class: An Economic Study of Institutions*. Online. Available at: http://moglen.law.columbia.edu/LCS/theoryleisureclass.pdf.

World Bank (2017), 'Doing Business'. Online. Available at: www.doingbusiness.org.

World Values Survey Association (2017), 'World Values Survey'. Online. Available at www.worldvaluessurvey.org.

Zak, Paul and Knack, Stephen (2001), 'Trust and Growth' in *Economic Journal*, **111**.

3 China

In the previous chapter, the necessary institutional foundations of economic growth were analysed. It can be seen that the legal institutions of a country are essential ingredients. Furthermore, factors such as politics, culture and other institutional conditions should be considered to form the most comprehensive picture. This book concerns the institutional foundations of economic growth in the context of Asia. This chapter has the task of discussing the situation of China by utilising the analytical framework laid down in the previous chapter. How have the institutional factors played a role in bringing about the miracle of Chinese economic growth? Hopefully, this chapter will provide an answer to this question by carefully putting the considerations set out in the previous chapter into the specific context of China. This chapter will start with the historical development of the Chinese economy both before and after the economic reform was initiated in 1978. It will then focus on the domestic legal conditions. Both laws-on-the-books and laws-in-action will be considered. Then, it will examine how politics and other factors such as culture influence the country. In summary, this chapter is the starting point of the four chapters (including this one) which explore the institutional conditions of the economies selected by this book, namely, China, Hong Kong, Singapore and Malaysia.

Economic growth of China

China is increasingly playing an important and influential role in development and in the global economy. China has been the largest contributor to world growth since the global financial crisis of 2008.[1] Different milestones have been achieved over the past decades.[2] China surpassed Japan in terms of nominal GDP in 2010, making the Chinese economy the world's second largest, just behind the US. China has grown at a rate of 9.9 per cent over the past decades. China's GDP in 2016 stood at US$11.2 trillion. For a snapshot of its GDP growth and how it is compared to other economies like the US and India, see Figure 3.1. The poverty rate fell from more than 65 per cent to less than 10 per cent, meaning that some 500 million people were lifted out of poverty. Other growth indicators include: four of the world's top five banks are now Chinese; 115 Chinese companies are on the Global Fortune 500 list in 2017.[3] China is

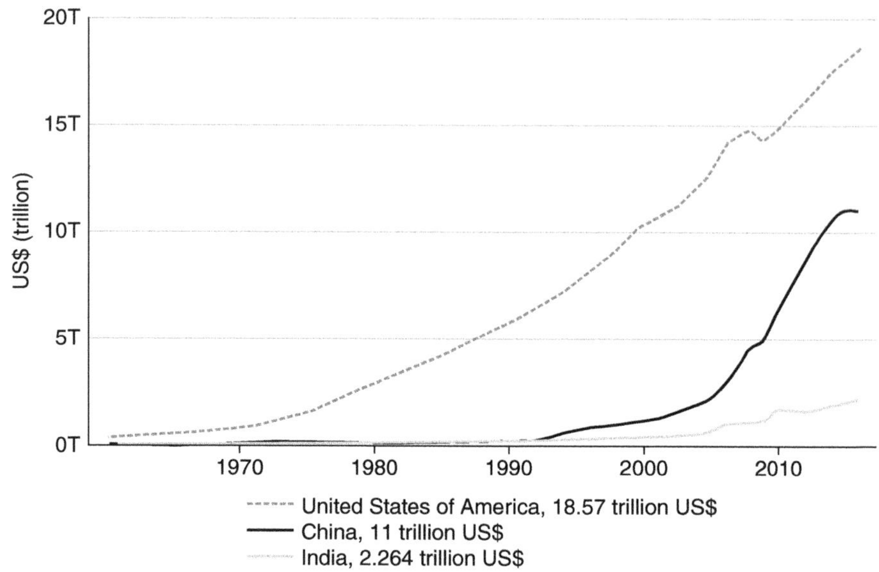

Figure 3.1 Comparative GDP of China, US and India (US$ trillion).

Source: World Bank.

home to the world's second-largest highway network, the world's three longest sea bridges, and six of the world's ten largest container ports.

Planned economy before 1978

From 1937 to 1949 China endured eight years of war with Japan and three and a half years of civil war. As a result, per capita GDP in 1952 had fallen back to the 1890 level.[4] After the founding of the People's Republic of China in 1949, according to Chinese government statistics, China's real GDP grew at an average annual rate of 6.7 per cent from 1953 to 1978, although the accuracy of these data has been questioned by many analysts.[5] It is thought that during this period, Chinese government officials (especially at the sub-national levels) often exaggerated production levels for a variety of political reasons. Some put China's actual average annual real GDP during this period at 4.4 per cent.[6]

The First Five-Year Plan (1952–57) was 'an unusually successful program of economic development'.[7] The plan was modelled on the Soviet experience of collectivisation and industrialisation in 1928–39 with significant Soviet assistance.[8] For example, close to 6,000 Soviet advisors helped establish and operate the 156 large-scale capital intensive projects. Meanwhile, China received the most advanced technology available within the Soviet Union, and in some cases this was the best in the world. By the mid-1950s, modern technology was adopted on a large scale in industry.[9] More efficient methods of agricultural production were implemented, including: (1) increase in irrigated areas; (2) increased multiple cropping; (3) afforestation; (4) improved seeds; (5) increased collection and application of organic fertilizers.[10] Afterwards, China's economy went downhill under the leadership of Chairman Mao Zedong, especially during the Great Leap Forward from 1958 to 1960 and the Cultural Revolution from 1966 to 1976.

It is believed that the Great Leap Forward led to a massive famine and reportedly the deaths of up to 45 million people.[11] During this time, all private property disappeared, including private plots, livestock, farm buildings and cash income. Rural markets were closed. Communes were created to take over responsibility for local administration, local tax collection, provision of healthcare and education, supervision of agricultural production, rural industrial construction and service activity in their area:[12] 123 million peasant households were dragooned into 26,000 giant people's communes, each with an average of 4,600 peasant households and about 6,700 workers. These people were mobilised to support the expansion of industry and construction, such as large irrigation and land reclamation projects, and to build and operate 'backyard iron furnaces'. Between 1959 and 1961 about 30 million people were diverted from farming to these other pursuits. As a result, agricultural output per capita in 1961 was 31 per cent lower than in 1957.[13] Contrary to the official story, which pinned the blame for disaster mainly on bad weather, Li and Yang contend that the main culprit was the Great Leap Forward policies.[14] Meanwhile, industrial employment rose sharply. It is estimated that national iron and steel production more than tripled between 1957 and 1960.[15] Massive diversion of agricultural resources to industry at the inception of the Great Leap Forward reduced grain output in 1959. The excessive extraction of food grain from peasants in 1958 and again in 1959 severely reduced food available for consumption in rural areas, igniting a famine in some regions in 1959. The famine soon spread to much of the countryside in 1960. Weakened by malnutrition, peasants could not exert sufficient labour input into planting or harvesting crops, leading to sharp declines in grain output. Adverse weather conditions exacerbated the output collapse. According to Bridgham, the combined effect of irrational economic policy, successive bad harvests and the Soviet withdrawal of technicians in the summer of 1960 dealt the Great Leap Forward programme of economic development a shattering blow.[16] The termination of Soviet aid to Chinese industry in 1960 was a serious blow as well, as it stopped many ambitious investment projects which were semi-finished.[17]

In 1962 there was a change in policy.[18] Farm management was switched to much smaller production teams of about 30 families, as opposed to giant communes. Private plots were restored, farm markets were reopened, communal eating was discontinued and major resources were allocated to provide modern inputs such as fertilisers, electrification and tractors. These policies continued throughout the Cultural Revolution until the beginning of economic reform in 1978. The period of 1962–66 was regarded as a period of recovery from the disaster of the Great Leap Forward.[19] The planning and ideology persisted but was softer and less brutal than in the 1950s. Agriculture grew by 35 per cent from the low of 1962 to the peak of 1966, but was still 25 per cent below the peak of 1958.[20] Manufacturing also grew quickly and recovered to the pre-crisis peak of 1957 in 1964, and increased by almost 60 per cent from the low of 1961 to the peak of 1966.[21]

Afterwards, there was a dip in industrial output during the disturbances of the Cultural Revolution. But as a whole, the actual disruption caused by the Cultural Revolution was far less certain than that resulting from the Great Leap Forward of 1958–60. Some estimate that workers' strikes, battles between workers and Red Guards and the use of the railroads to transport Red Guards around the country cost China around two years of reduced output during the peak of the Cultural Revolution.[22] As put by Perkins, 'the Cultural Revolution at its peak (1967–68) was a severe but essentially temporary interruption.'[23] Despite the exceptional importance of the events of the Cultural Revolution for the country, the economic implications were contended to be much more muted.[24] Naughton argued for a slightly more nuanced breakdown during the whole ten-year period of the Cultural Revolution.[25] The New Leap in 1970 was a period of militarisation of the economy that also instituted some principles of the Great Leap Forward. The 1972–76 period was that of consolidation and drift. It started with the economic problems of the 1970s where heavy industry development was both increasingly inefficient and outstripped the agricultural facilities to provide food, before a new more moderate course was started in 1972–74 by Zhou Enlai. According to some empirical evidence, more revolutionary regions were slower to industrialise, had lower levels of education and per-capita output.[26] Worryingly, these effects are large in magnitude, detectable more than 30 years later.

Economic reform and growth after 1978

It all started in December 1978 when the Third Plenary Session of the Eleventh Central Committee of the Communist Party of China (CPC) marked a new historical period of *gaige kaifang*, the twin strategies of economic reform and opening up. Before that, the traditional socialist system of China and the development strategy of prioritizing heavy industry, together with different political campaigns such as the Great Leap Forward and the Cultural Revolution, had not brought China prosperity. The process of economic reforms was introduced and implemented slowly and pragmatically, as famously illustrated by the old Chinese saying of 'crossing the river by feeling each stone'.[27]

The Ten Year Plan for Economic Development 1976–85 was drawn up in 1975, emphasising the priority to heavy industry. The Plan was not abandoned completely. Party policy was encapsulated in the slogan 'readjusting, restructuring, consolidating and improving the national economy'. Economic policy making between 1979 and 1982 was dominated by the theme 'Readjustment'.[28] One main problem identified was agriculture.[29] A two-pronged approach was introduced to address the agricultural problems. Rural economic policy was liberalised and the terms of trade of agriculture improved. Rural economic reform was first introduced in Xiaogang Village, Anhui Province. Production and farming work was contracted to households. Such a household responsibility system initially attracted limited support from the CPC Central Committee, but subsequently its legitimacy was affirmed and it eventually received a high appraisal.[30] The system was trialed for three years, then extended for 15 years in 1984, before a further extension of 30 years in 1993.

Meanwhile, there was considerable change in the structure of ownership. Running in parallel to the agricultural reform was a relaxation in the restrictions on farmers' non-agricultural activities, resulting in the development of township and village enterprises (TVEs). These TVEs are economic units which are either collectively owned, or mainly owned and controlled by rural residents.[31] On the other hand, the state sector has undergone significant changes since the economic reform began in 1979. The share of state-owned enterprises (SOEs) in the country's industrial output dropped from 78 per cent in 1978 to 27 per cent in 1997.[32] SOEs now only dominate a handful of industries such as oil and gas mining, transportation, telecommunications, financial services and utilities. A macro view is that the government has privatised large parts of its economy. Officials regarded the large number of state companies as a burden. Intensifying competition in many sectors involved reducing the rents that SOEs enjoyed. Private ownership was viewed as the answer to the governance problems inherited from the state sector. In terms of micro-implementation, the government adopted a retreat/retain (2-R) strategy.[33] The principle was 'grasp the big, let go of the small'. It retreated from competitive sectors, where small and medium-sized state enterprises operated. Meanwhile, in so-called strategic industries, where large SOEs were common, control was retained.

The retreat strategy was more straightforward. Since the beginning of the early 1980s, the proposal to reform in China has had three broad phases: the state's withdrawal from the operational decisions of SOEs, then from administrative oversight and ultimately from ownership. This was clearly reflected in the decline in the relative share of the exclusively state-owned companies in the economy and the emergence of hybrid structures co-owned by state entities and non-state actors.[34] SOEs were incorporated and the sale of control rights, most often to employees, closely followed. How to improve the performance of these companies became the problem of the new owners rather than the state.

By contrast, the retain strategy was more complicated. Launched in 1958, the Great Leap Forward Movement emphasised the development of heavy industries, especially iron and steel.[35] Several unrealistically high targets of industrial development were proposed. As a matter of logic, a profit-oriented company would allocate their resources to the sectors that yielded the highest returns. At the time, there was a strong demand for light industry products. The technological structure of light industries catered well to the comparative advantages of the Chinese economy. An inappropriate consumption-to-production ratio meant the heavy industry-oriented development strategy distorted the economy. Under these conditions, a perceived solution was to grant the SOEs and their managers autonomy in production and management. Certain piecemeal reforms took place in 1979–84.

Outputs from SOEs in excess of the planned targets were allowed to be sold at market prices. This was intended to stimulate production to meet market demand. Furthermore, the powers to choose what goods to buy and sell were devolved to managers. However, these reforms were inadequate to deal with all the problems that arose from flawed incentives and an increasingly competitive environment.

In the 1990s, policymakers turned to diversified shareholdings as an alternative to earlier reforms.[36] The privatisation campaign in China had clear 'Chinese characteristics'. In contrast to those in Russia and Eastern Europe, there was no transfer of control from the state to private hands.[37] The Chinese government introduced a special mechanism to prevent the loss of state control when companies went public. A distinct feature that separated China's stock market from those in other countries was the creation of state shares and legal person shares, which both carry significant constraints on tradability. These shares are generally state-owned or state-controlled. A typical public company had about one-third of its shares in state, legal person and tradable shares respectively. By holding two-thirds of most companies' shares, the state could ensure that it has the power to direct and influence their activities. Following the non-tradable shares reform, these shares are now tradable, but this does not necessarily indicate the state's immediate willingness to relinquish control and sell all its shares to the public, at least not for strategic SOEs.[38] According to the figures from the State-owned Assets Supervision and Administration Commission of China, as of the end of 2015, the state still held 80 per cent of shares in a typical SOE.[39]

Corporatisation (sometimes known as securitisation) refers to the legal and financial restructuring of SOEs through their conversion into joint stock companies. The corporatisation campaign in China was a two-step process. It first restructured SOEs into shareholding companies to be listed on a stock exchange. This caused many socio-economic and legal debates in China because such reform might change the nature of socialist public ownership. These debates involved a wide range of issues, from the fundamental principles of socialism and the efficiency of alternative economic and business forms to shareholders' rights.[40] In light of corporate governance, it was hoped that corporatisation would achieve three goals:[41] (1) change the ownership structure of the SOEs that have both state and non-state institutional shareholders in addition to small individual shareholders; (2) separate the state from business operation for enterprises to achieve full autonomy; and (3) improve managerial incentives by installing shareholders with the incentives and abilities to monitor the managers. One of the major goals was to establish a clear mechanism of company control and management. The aim was to leave the decision-making authority to boards of directors, which should supposedly be profit-oriented and free from direct intervention by state administrative organisations.[42] This can be contrasted with the time when China was still a centrally planned economy, the government directly ran SOEs, set their annual output targets, and left SOEs with little autonomy in making commercial decisions.

In the 1980s, when China began its economic reform, the state sector dominated its economy, accounting for nearly four-fifths of output.[43] In comparison, it accounts for less than one-fifth of output today.[44] The state sector stood still, with a vibrant private sector developing rapidly around it. The Fortune Global 500 list may provide some insights to this. According to their 2015 list, 98 companies were based in China, including those headquartered in Hong Kong.[45] This put China second only to the US which had 128 companies on the list. The top 12 Chinese companies were all state-owned. They included massive banks, such as the big four state-owned banks, and oil companies, such as Sinopec, China National Petroleum and China National Offshore Oil. Of the 98 Chinese companies on the list, only 22 were private. Fast forward two years to 2017, Tencent, the Chinese tech giant, passed Wells Fargo to become the world's tenth most valuable public company after nine American companies on the list including Apple, Alphabet, Microsoft and Amazon in the top four.[46] Furthermore, another Chinese tech giant, Alibaba's IPO on the New York Stock Exchange in 2014 raising US$25 billion remains the world's biggest.[47] Tencent and Alibaba were set up by entrepreneurs and now billionaires Ma Huateng and Jack Ma respectively. The two companies are not SOEs or former SOEs.

China's economic performance over the past 30 years has been remarkable. The World Bank attributed this impressive growth record to various unique factors.[48] First, China was praised for carrying out market-oriented reforms in a gradual, experimental way and by providing incentives for local governments. The pre-existing SOEs remained supported whilst the development of private enterprises was encouraged. Also, localities were often allowed to adopt their own unique institutions tailored to their specific situations. Second, economic reforms and growth were made a national objective and therefore collective efforts were mobilised for that, whilst social stability was successfully maintained amid a period of rapid economic and structural change. Third, steady integration occurred at both domestic and international levels. For the former, major infrastructure investments were made to connect regions and the interior to the coast. For the latter, with the establishment of special economic zones and accession into the WTO, China was able to bring in foreign investments, advanced technologies and managerial expertise. This is consistent with the idea of 'appropriating capitalism for the good of socialism'. Finally, local governments at various levels were allowed to compete with each other in attracting investment, developing infrastructure and improving the local business environment. The resulting fierce competition between local governments and regions became a strong driver of growth.

Growth of Shenzhen

Amidst the economic reform, another important policy initiative was the establishment of four Special Economic Zones (SEZs) in Shenzhen, Shantou, Zhuhai of Guangdong Province (all in late 1979) and in Xiamen Fujian Province (October 1980). The SEZs are formally defined as:

> A small area demarcated within a country's territory and suitably insulated for adopting special and flexible policies in external economic activities to attract and encourage foreign investments.[49]

Before 1978, Shenzhen was merely a 'sleepy border town' lying north of the then British colony, Hong Kong, in southern China.[50] It was the major source of illegal immigrants into the then booming capitalist haven of Hong Kong, where the GDP per capita was HK$25,081 in 1979 (as opposed to RMB606 in Shenzhen).[51] At that time, Shenzhen's size was merely three square kilometres with a population of over 30,000 people, while nowadays it occupies 1,991.64 square kilometres of land with a population of 10.63 million.[52] The drivers of economy have changed dramatically too. While the agricultural sector made up 37 per cent of GDP in 1979, it dropped to 0.1 per cent in 2012.[53] In contrast, secondary industries have grown dramatically over the years. In 1979, secondary industries contributed only 20.5 per cent of GDP but in 2012 the figure had increased to 44.3 per cent. The tertiary sector's contribution to GDP had increased from 42.5 per cent to 55.6 per cent over the same period.

Wu Nansheng, the ex-mayor of the Shenzhen SEZ, outlined the three functions of Shenzhen in 1981: first, to understand capitalist society; second, to experiment with different policies; and third, to study foreign advanced technology and management.[54] Wu's successor, Lang Xiang, later further elaborated the advantages of the SEZ. Through preferential policies, Shenzhen could use large amounts of foreign investment in a better way, which would eventually benefit the country as a whole. Furthermore, by dealing regularly with foreign capital, China could observe and understand the operation of the modern capitalist world. Finally, through cooperation, China could learn modern management methods and train professionals. In summary, the characteristics of SEZs are as follows:[55]

1 Various public utilities such as water supply and electricity are well prepared and it is expected that the investment climate will be very favourable for foreign investment.
2 Preferential treatment in regard to tax, use of land, etc., is given to enterprises in order to attract their investment.
3 The manufactured goods are intended to be exported.
4 The Special Zones operate in a manner similar to a free market economy.

In relation to the accompanying legal framework, China's enactment of the *Joint Venture Law*, which permitted overseas enterprises to undertake joint ventures with Chinese nationals, enabled the possibility of direct foreign investment.[56] To further enhance credibility to outside investors, officials in Guangdong wanted to write the SEZs into law.[57] The response from the National People's Congress was the approval of the *Regulations for the Special Economic Zones in Guangdong Province* ('SEZ Regulations' hereinafter) on 26 August 1980. The law consisted of six chapters and 26 articles. There were three main provisions. First, goods produced in the SEZ are primarily for export and the operation of these enterprises would be free from state intervention.[58] Second, foreign investors were entitled to preferential treatment in the form of low tax rates and exemption from duties.[59] Third, the enterprises are free to manage their labour as they would in a free market economy.[60]

According to Article 1 of the SEZ Regulations, the SEZs would encourage foreign citizens, overseas Chinese, people from Hong Kong and Macau and their companies and enterprises to open factories and set up enterprises and other establishments with their own investment or in joint ventures with Chinese nationals. In other words, the Regulations effectively sanctioned the existence of wholly-foreign-owned enterprises on Chinese soil for the first time since 1949. Although most of the investors engaged in labour-intensive industrial production, they were actually allowed to participate in 'all projects that have positive significance for international economic cooperation and technical exchanges'.[61] Despite the apparent freedom, there remained a 'theme of strongly guarded socialist political authority and national sovereignty as key prerequisites to the zones' deliberate loosening of socialist economic principles'.[62] Enterprises and individuals in the SEZs must still abide by the laws, decrees and pertinent provisions of China.[63] Also, a new, omni-competent organ, the Guangdong Provincial Administrative Committee for the SEZs was established to ensure retention by the government of the broadest possible administrative, political and judicial authority in the zones.[64] Investors wishing to open factories or set up various economic undertakings were required to apply to the Committee for approval.[65]

As regards preferential treatment, the preferential rate of income tax levied on the enterprises in the SEZs was 15 per cent, much lower than the 33 per cent rate levied on joint ventures outside the SEZs with the progressive taxation from 20 per cent up to 40 per cent for foreign enterprises.[66] Furthermore, raw and semi-processed materials, machinery and equipment, and other capital goods necessary for production that are imported by enterprises in the SEZ would be exempted from import duties.[67] The lawful profit that an investor receives could be remitted abroad through the Bank of China or other banks in the special zones, despite the existence of tight currency control in China.[68] As regards labour management, like other countries, the terms in an employment relationship would be defined by an employment contract and the employees would be protected by various measures for labour protection.[69] However, one distinctive socialist feature was contained in Article 19 of the SEZ Regulations. Whilst the investors had the autonomy to hire foreign personnel for their needs, a labour service company was set up centrally in each of the SEZs to handle the recruitment of Chinese workers. The investors themselves might be able to recruit local workers only if consent was given by the SEZ Administrative Committee.

However, despite some regulations being in place, Nishitateno believed the law remained short on specifics and also contained ambiguities.[70] Fenwick went further to allege that inadequacies in the Regulations led to several major problems in SEZ development.[71] First, the zones were meant to attract global foreign investment, but the reality was investors almost solely came from Hong Kong, largely owing to the unwillingness of international investors accepting the absence of a detailed, comprehensive legal framework for SEZ investment. Second, the sectoral concentration of foreign investment in the SEZs was unbalanced. A disproportionate amount of Shenzhen's investment was concentrated in real estate projects, as opposed to industrial development which the state hoped to focus on. Third, a substantial number of foreign firms withdrew from Shenzhen shortly after the promulgation of the Regulations. In response to these problems, the National People's Congress introduced new sets of supplementary SEZ regulations, covering the problem areas of immigration, business registration, labour and land issues.[72]

According to Yeung and colleagues, Shenzhen was the most 'special' among the four SEZs, first, with the greatest freedom to explore innovations; second, with its success.[73] Among Shenzhen's innovations were the implementation of a new contract labour and wage system, a tender system for projects and a land auction system. In 1981, the four zones accounted for 59.8 per cent of total FDI in China, with Shenzhen accounting for the lion's share at 50.6 per cent and the other SEZs roughly 3 per cent each, although the four zones just represented about 20 per cent of the national total FDI by the end of 1985.[74] This could be understandable as, by 1984, the four zones no longer enjoyed their exclusive status. In that year China further opened 14 coastal cities to overseas investment.[75]

From 1980 to 1984, Shenzhen grew at a phenomenal 58 per cent annual rate and its economy expanded sixfold during the period.[76] The secondary sector has been the primary source for the phenomenal growth.[77] Industrial production, especially labour-intensive, light industrial manufacturing, has been mainly responsible for the speedy expansion in the secondary sector. In addition to the input of capital, one advantage of fostering foreign investment is the input of technological know-how. Shenzhen used to be an important base for the production of low-end electronic products.[78] Over time, the city has been steadily upgrading in terms of technological sophistication.[79] Shenzhen is becoming a centre for high-technology industries and the base of leading domestic high-tech firms or subcontractors manufacturing world-renowned branded products, such as Huawei Technology, ZTE Corporation, Tencent and Foxconn Technology Group.[80]

Founded by Ren Zhengfei in 1987, Huawei has grown from a small company with a turnover of just US$5,680 to a global company with a turnover of over US$39 billion, and with business presence in over 170 countries and a staff of 170,000 in 2014. Huawei is a private business, wholly owned by its employees, with 82,471 employees owning shares in the company. According to the International Data Corporation, Huawei was the third largest mobile phone manufacturer in the world in the first quarter of 2017, with 10 per cent of market share, just behind Samsung (23.3 per cent) and Apple (14.7 per cent).[81] In the case of Tencent, it was founded in 1998 by Ma Huateng and others with the backing of Naspers, a South Africa-based multinational internet and media group. In 2004, Tencent went public on the Hong Kong Stock Exchange. The company is a leading provider of Internet value-added services, such as a social network called WeChat, in China. Its headquarters is in Nanshan District of Shenzhen. According to Barron's, Tencent became Asia's largest company by market capitalisation in September 2016.[82]

On 19 January 1992, Deng Xiaoping arrived at Shenzhen as part of his Southern Excursion with a view, it was believed, to find out the success of his economic experiment.[83] Deng made the following remarks:

> We should be bolder than before in conducting reform and opening to the outside and have the courage to experiment.... Once we are sure that something should be done, we should dare to experiment and break a new path. That is the important lesson to be learned from Shenzhen.[84]

This famous quote from Deng seems to summarise the development of Shenzhen well. Since 1978, amidst over three decades of economic reform in China, the city has never hesitated to innovate, so that it has successfully evolved from a tiny border town of just over 30,000 people into a modern international metropolis.

Growth of Shanghai

Unlike Shenzhen, Shanghai was not able to take advantage of the first mover advantage during the initiation of economic reform. But, differently from Shenzhen, Shanghai used to boast the most highly developed urban amenities in Asia outside of Tokyo.[85] Therefore, the city just needed to recover its pre-1949 glory, rather than building everything from scratch. For example, the first stock market was established in Shanghai in the 1890s. At that time, Shanghai was considered one of the premier international finance centres of the Far East. At its peak, the shares of 76 companies were admitted for trading, 22 of them banks.[86] In 1949, when the communist government came to power, stock exchanges were viewed as one of the most prominent symbols of an oppressive capitalist regime and were forced to close down. After 1949, the city experienced more than 30 years of neglect and disinvestment.[87]

Like Shenzhen, the drivers of economy in Shanghai have evolved over time since the start of economic reform. But as opposed to Shenzhen where agriculture used to be the focus of the economy in the past, in Shanghai there has been a shift of reliance from secondary industries to the tertiary sector. The agricultural sector made up only 4 per cent of GDP in 1979 and dropped to 0.6 per cent in 2012.[88] Meanwhile, tertiary industries have grown dramatically over the years. In 1979, the sector contributed only 18.8 per cent of GDP but in 2012 the figure increased to 60.4 per cent. In contrast, the secondary industries' contribution to GDP had decreased from 77.2 per cent to 39 per cent over the same period.

Despite being designated as a coastal open city in 1984, during the first decade of the reform era, Shanghai fell behind other major coastal cities in attracting investments.[89] One obvious reason is that Shanghai was not able to receive the same preferential policies of the four SEZs in Guangdong and Fujian provinces. Furthermore, there was a 'winner takes all' situation. The more successful cities were able to attract more inflow of foreign capital and therefore invest in infrastructure to attract more FDI. For example, in the period from 1981 to 1991, except in the years of 1988 and 1989, Shenzhen was always more capable of attracting FDI than Shanghai (see Figure 3.2).

A breakthrough finally came when Jiang Zemin and Zhu Rongji, former mayors of Shanghai, came to power. On 18 April 1990, the Chinese State

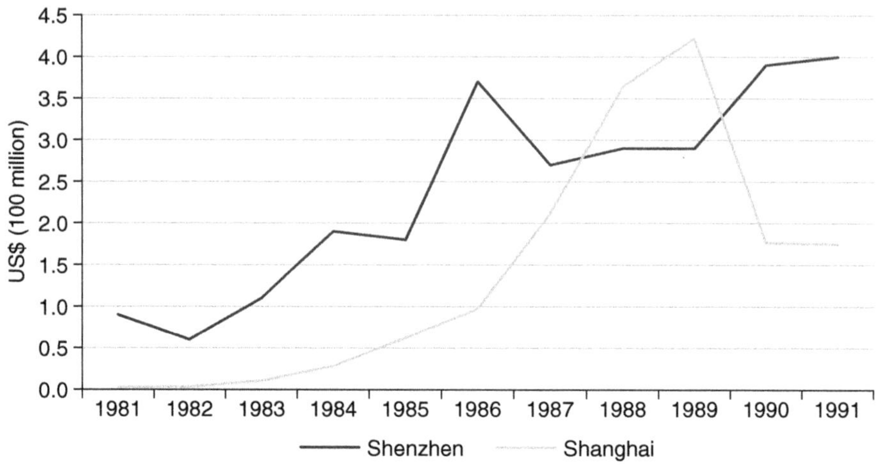

Figure 3.2 Direct foreign investments of Shenzhen and Shanghai, 1981–91 (US$ 100 million).

Source: Shenzhen and Shanghai Statistical Yearbooks (various years).

Council declared that it would open Pudong New Area to foreign investment and promised to apply many of the policies previously available only in the five SEZs.[90] This decision began the revival of Shanghai as the financial and commercial centre of China. Shanghai is divided by the Huangpu River into eastern and western parts. At that time, the western part, Puxi, was the developed centre whilst the eastern part, Pudong, was largely undeveloped. Pudong, effectively recognised as the sixth SEZ, would enjoy the same preferential policies as discussed before, such as a more market-orientated business environment than the rest of China, reduced tax rates, exemptions from customs, etc.[91] However, in some instances Pudong was able to go even beyond them to demonstrate China's commitment to reform, in line with the decision of the Fourteenth Central Committee of the CPC in 1992 to establish a 'socialist market economy'. The applicable policies were contained in the *Regulations of the Shanghai Municipality for the Encouragement of Foreign Investment in the Pudong New Area* ('Pudong Regulations' hereinafter) issued by Shanghai Municipality on 10 September 1990.

Pudong is an investment area consisting of four distinct zones: Lujiazui Finance and Trade Zone, Waigaoqiao Free Trade Zone, Jinqiao Export Processing Zone and Zhangjiang High-Tech Development Zone. These four zones were designed to take in their locational advantage, and differ in investment emphasis.[92] Lujiazui is a finance and trade zone intended for financial institutions and regional headquarters of foreign firms, forming the economic core of Shanghai together with the Bund, the traditional financial centre across the river. On the other hand, the other three zones are oriented toward manufacturing activities.

Whilst the policies on a par with those offered to the five SEZs could potentially provide a favourable business environment to the manufacturing zones, investors in Pudong have been offered particularly favourable conditions for operating financial and business services.[93]

One of the major characteristics of Pudong that distinguish it from the five SEZs is the specific mentioning of the special policies granted to foreign financial institutions, For example, according to the *Pudong Regulations*, like companies in other SEZs, they are entitled to a reduced tax rate of 15 per cent.[94] However, in addition to that, these financial institutions are entitled to tax exemption during their first profitable year, and enjoy a 50 per cent reduction subsequently in the second and third profitable years.[95] Indeed, Shanghai has a strong root in finance. As mentioned before, during the 1920s and 1930s, Shanghai was a leading financial centre in the Far East with active trading on its securities market. After the economic reform in 1986, the Jing'an District Branch of the Shanghai Trust and Investment, a subsidiary of the Industrial and Commercial Bank of China, started over-the-counter trading of shares and underwrote for Feile Audio Equipment, probably 'the first share' in new China.[96] After the establishment of a stock exchange in Shanghai, an important reform was a pilot scheme to issue RMB-denominated shares to foreign investors aimed at attracting foreign capital to the securities market.[97] These shares, known as B-shares, are domestically listed shares, denominated in RMB but subscribed to and traded in US$ or HK$ by overseas investors. In November 1991, Shanghai Vacuum Electron Devices Company issued 1 million special RMB-denominated shares at par of RMB100 each to overseas investors. The company was listed on the Shanghai Stock Exchange in February 1992, becoming the first B-share in China's securities market. Whilst the Shenzhen Stock Exchange apparently has catered for small and medium-sized enterprises by setting up a special board for them in May 2005, the Shanghai Stock Exchange's focus has always been large state-owned enterprises. For example, the big four state-owned banks are listed in Shanghai (and Hong Kong), as opposed to Shenzhen. Agricultural Bank of China's IPO was the world's largest in 2010.[98] For the trend of growth of the two exchanges, see Figure 3.3. It is also worth noting that the Shanghai Stock Exchange is now the fourth largest stock exchange in the world.[99]

At the same time, the city's ability to attract foreign investments has been growing from strength to strength, dwarfing Shenzhen's position as the first official SEZ (see Figure 3.4). In 2000, 254 of the Fortune 500 companies invested or established offices in Shanghai, including Alcatel, Volkswagen, General Motors, NEC, DuPont and IBM.[100] International financial and banking institutions include Citibank, Standard Chartered and Bank of America, and HSBC also established a base there to provide important financial services.[101]

After more than three decades of economic reform in China, it is safe to say that Shanghai has regained its pre-1949 eminence, if not better.

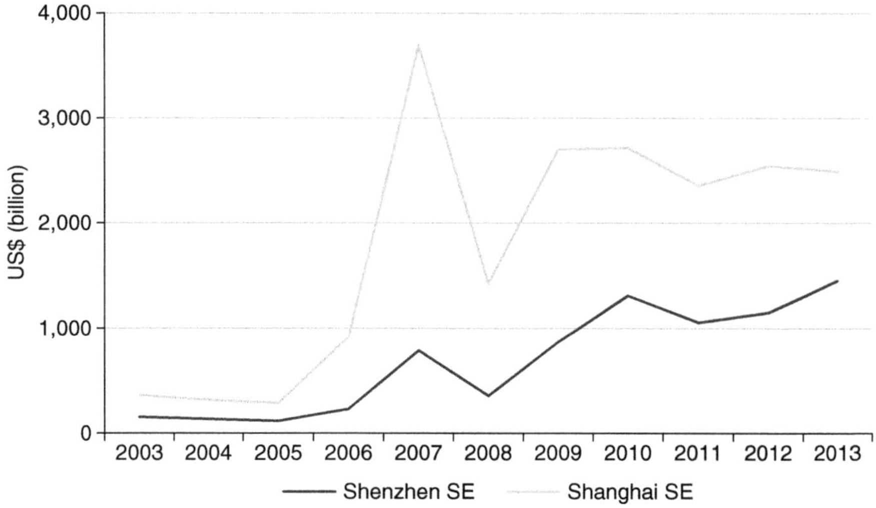

Figure 3.3 Market capitalisation of Shanghai and Shenzhen stock exchanges, 2003–13 (US$ billion).

Source: World Federation of Exchanges.

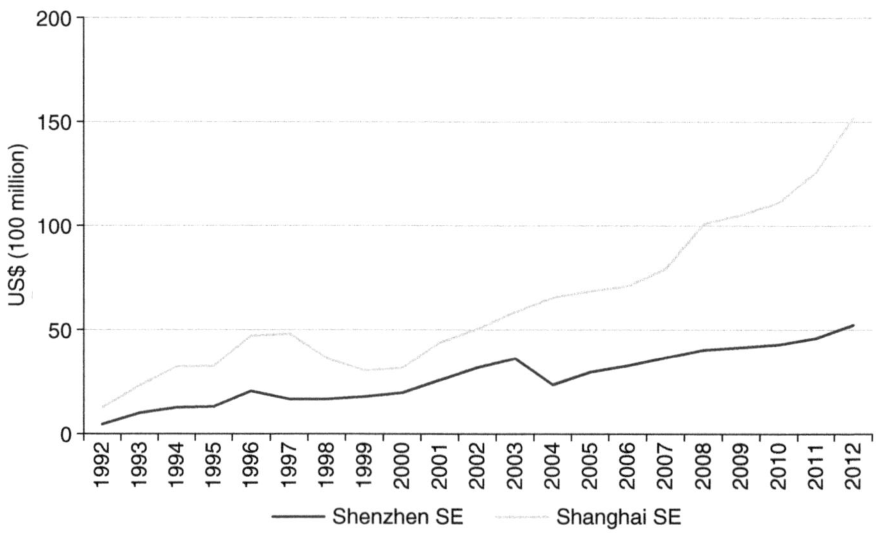

Figure 3.4 Direct foreign investments of Shenzhen and Shanghai, 1992–2012 (US$ 100 million).

Source: Shenzhen and Shanghai Statistical Yearbooks (various years).

Legal institutions

In response to the economic reforms, various laws were introduced as the supporting institutions.[102] According to Lubman, it was important as the market economy relies on private law to serve as a framework to facilitate transactions defining the rights and duties created by business arrangements.[103] Two laws related to foreign investment, the *Law on Wholly Foreign-owned Enterprises* and the *Law on Sino-foreign Cooperative Joint Venture Enterprises*, were promulgated in 1986 and 1988 respectively. For the SOE reform, the *Law on Industrial Enterprises Owned by the Whole People*, an early draft of the Company Law 1993, reaffirmed the Communist Party's explicit desire that the ownership and management of SOEs 'be appropriately separated'.[104] The regulatory response to the emergence of domestic enterprises came in 1992. The *Standard Opinion for Limited Liability Companies* and the *Standard Opinion for Companies Limited by Shares* were issued as interim measures before the promulgation of a comprehensive set of company laws. The first Company Law, based on previous draft regulations and the two *Standard Opinions*, was passed on 29 December 1993 and became effective on 1 July 1994.

The law served two main functions: (1) to establish a modern enterprise system compatible with the social market economy; and (2) to lay out the legal basis for regulating different types of companies. The Company Law has since been amended (to a limited extent) twice, in 1999 and 2004, with more radical changes introduced in 2005 and 2013.[105] The early Company Law was designed to pursue a distinctive mission in the socialist state of China, which was to build an economic system that maintains socialist principles and goals.[106] In sharp contrast, the Company Law 2005 clearly stated that its aims are to 'protect the legitimate rights and interests of companies, shareholders and creditors' and, at the same time, 'to promote the development of the socialist market economy'.[107] Until the Company Law came into effect on 1 July 1994, China was unique in having shareholding companies and a securities market operating without either company law or securities law.[108] Over time, new laws were introduced or old laws were reformed for other areas of commercial law.[109] Although the early legal framework was heavily criticised, it is believed that the current framework (laws-on-the-books) nowadays is comparable to developed countries, despite the doubt of whether other relevant supporting institutions are adequate.[110]

As discussed in Chapter 2, the goal of corporate and financial laws should start from the mitigation of the agency problem and attainment of efficient markets. For the former, the focus is placed on how shareholders can be protected from opportunistic managers or some predatory controlling shareholders, whereas the success of the latter hinges on the disclosure duties of companies and their managers. On the face of it, today's general regulatory framework of markets and companies in China seems no different from that of developed markets. For example, regarding information disclosure, under the Company Law, listed companies are required to establish a financial and accounting system that must comply with relevant laws and regulations.[111] They are also required to prepare financial statements at the end of each financial year.[112] According to the Securities Law, an annual report must include the following: (1) company profile; (2) financial accounting report and business report of the company; (3) profile of the directors, supervisors and senior management personnel and their shareholdings; (4) the actual controlling party of the company and others.[113] Furthermore, financial accounting reports must be prepared in accordance with laws and regulations, for example, the Accounting Law of China and the *Enterprise Financial and Accounting Reports Regulations* issued by the State Council. Such reports are required to be audited by an accounting firm. The information disclosed by issuers and listed companies must be authentic, accurate and complete and must contain no false or misleading statements or major omissions.[114]

In relation to corporate governance, the Code of Corporate Governance for Listed Companies, which was issued in 2002, sets forth the basic principles for the corporate governance of listed companies.[115] A listed company must introduce independent directors to its board of directors, and they should account for at least one-third of the board. Directors' duties are also covered by law.[116] For related-party transactions, timely information disclosure is required by the China Securities Regulatory Commission (CSRC). Also, the director representing a related party is required to withdraw from voting when the board or the shareholders' meeting is deliberating and voting on the related party transaction.[117] With respect to market regulations, insider dealing, market manipulation and other securities frauds are banned. Any individuals or institutions involved bears the civil and/or criminal liability depending on the severity of the crime.[118]

Quality of the laws

The most notable improvement in shareholder protection was provided by the Company Law 2005, and the current Company Law 2013 generally follows its predecessor. Under English law, the fiduciary duties of directors can be divided into two parts: a duty of loyalty and a duty of care. The duty of loyalty generally refers to the requirements: to act *bona fide* for the benefit of the company; to exercise directors' powers for their proper purpose; and not to allow any conflict between their duties as directors and personal interests. The similar concept of good faith can be found in the early Company Law, but not a duty of care. Directors of domestic companies were required to faithfully perform their duties, maintain the interests of their company and not take advantage of their positions to seek personal gains.[119] They were prohibited from engaging personally or assisting others in the business operation of a competing company, which may damage the interests of the company they are serving.[120] By contrast, the early Company Law did not provide for a duty of care. As a result, the amended law expressly commits directors, supervisors and senior officers of Chinese companies to uphold both 'duties of loyalty and care' to their companies.[121]

In the context of China, where a concentrated ownership pattern is predominant, the mitigation of majority–minority conflicts is perhaps more imminent than principal–agent conflicts. Unfortunately, shareholders' duties were not provided in detail by the early Company Law.[122] This clearly revealed a major shortfall in the early regulatory framework. Likewise, one of the most important changes in the new Company Law is to curb the abuse of controlling shareholders' powers, which is in conflict with the interests of the company. The new law renders them liable to pay compensation for any loss the company suffers as a result of taking advantage of their positions.[123] It has been suggested that the intention of the regulatory authorities was to stall opportunistic affiliated transactions by imposing severe civil compensation liability on the parties of the transactions.[124] This is important in at least two ways. First, controlling shareholders, who are often the state or governmental organisations, are typically able to appoint and remove board members. Minority shareholders have little or no power over management. Second, minority shareholders are especially powerless against the self-interested actions of controlling shareholders. In China, various self-interested arrangements can be seen, from the direct misappropriation of funds to providing a guarantee or loan for relatives and friends. The current law provides additional causes of action that might be used by minority shareholders against controlling shareholders, one important area not covered by the first Company Law.

Other than limiting the opportunistic behaviour of managers and controlling shareholders, another safeguard for minority shareholders is to provide them with an exit strategy. In a typical situation, controlling shareholders might try to prevent minority shareholders from realising the value of their investments by withholding dividends or forcing them out of the business on unfavourable terms. Without an exit strategy in the early law, in a few special cases now, shareholders can request the company buy back their shareholdings at a reasonable price.[125] Yet, this might not be a useful protection mechanism to shareholders given that there is no definition of what 'a reasonable price' really means and because shareholders need to file a petition to a people's court to enforce their exit rights. In a listed company, shareholders might avoid the hassles and be better off selling their shares on the open market.

Information is important in both investor and shareholder protection. Listing prospectuses allow prospective shareholders to make informed investment decisions. On the other hand, existing shareholders' participation in the decision-making process requires their access to information, mainly disseminated via regular financial reports and ad hoc announcements. As the content of a prospectus in China is regulated by a separate prospectus rule issued by the CSRC, the early Company Law gave shareholders the right to review and examine company documents.[126] At the basic level, this meant shareholders could, usually upon payment of a fee, obtain documents and information including a copy of the company articles, personal information of company officers, financial reports, minutes of shareholders' meetings and so on. To allow shareholders to effectively exercise their decision rights, since the Company Law 2005, they can request any director, supervisor or senior managers to attend the shareholders' meeting and respond to the enquiries of shareholders.[127] More importantly, their right to know can also be exercised outside this meeting. Other than the usual disclosures, the new law grants shareholders the power to examine the company's accounts. This access is particularly crucial because some accounting anomalies may be reflected in the accounting records rather than the financial statements.

Further, shareholders' meetings are a forum where shareholders, as the owners, can formally exercise their control rights. In comparison with the early Company Law, the current law elaborates greatly on the procedures to be followed in shareholders' meetings. First, shareholders' meetings can pass resolutions on hiring, dismissing and terminating accounting firms as well as matters proposed by shareholders representing 3 per cent or more of the shareholders entitled to vote.[128] Second, shareholders have the right to propose new matters in writing, which must be included in the agenda of the meetings. Third, shareholders are entitled to receive prior individual notice, with information prescribed by the provisions, regarding a meeting.[129] Moreover, cumulative voting is now permitted (but not mandatory) under the Company Law, giving a minority shareholder a better chance to elect a director to represent their interests.[130] According to empirical evidence, a majority of Chinese listed firms have formally embraced cumulative voting.[131]

Lastly, the Chinese state has always been sceptical about losing control in various industries and companies. Under the early Company Law, specific private placements of shares were banned.[132] The early position was that a joint-stock company could be established either by promotion or by issuing shares to 'non-specific' targets. For example, the government in the late 1990s banned share issues to employees.[133] Its concern was the opaqueness involved in the private placement process. This somewhat contradicted the goal of economic form, which was to foster a more diversified ownership structure. In contrast, offering shares to 'specific' targets, which mainly refer to institutional investors, is now expressly allowed.[134] The presence of institutional investors is widely regarded as a mechanism to enhance corporate governance.

Although China seems to have vastly improved its laws, it is worth noting that the legal ideology between the East and West might not necessarily be the same. 'Rule by law' refers to the instrumental use of law by the state to govern, whereas the 'rule of law' refers to a normative and political theory of the relationship of legal institutions and the political state focusing on a theory of limited government through the separation of powers among executive, legislative and judicial organisations.[135] The current situation in China seems to be the former. Indeed, Tomasic has alleged that the privileges of incorporation and limited liability under the Company Law in China were 'jealously guarded by the state' and the state would closely monitor the actions of incorporated companies.[136] Milhaupt and Pistor have further alleged that China's commitment to the rule of law has been weakened by other governance mechanisms.[137] For instance, while the Company Law 1993 stipulated the conditions under which a company could issue shares to the public, they were complemented shortly afterwards by a set of regulations promulgated by the State Council and the CSRC. MacNeil has confirmed this by indicating that there has been an extensive state regulation of company formation in the sense that approval must be obtained from the relevant government departments in addition to satisfying the requirements of the Company Law.[138] The laws in China are rapidly changing. For example, the Company Law, which came into effect in 1994, was revised in 1999, 2004, 2005 and 2013. Although undeniably the laws have been revised and improved, whether those enforcing the laws can keep up with the changes is questionable. To investigate the legal and institutional conditions of China, one must look into the laws-in-action as well as the laws-on-the-books.[139]

According to Tomasic and Fu, both the early Company Law and Securities Law were in many aspects almost immediately out of date after their passage, and it was left to the Supreme People's Court to issue interpretations of these statutes and to regulatory bodies such as the CSRC to promulgate regulations, guidelines and interpretation to fill in the holes and gaps.[140] The traditional emphasis of Chinese legal culture has been on administrative and criminal sanctions, but not on civil liability and procedural law.[141] In terms of public enforcement, it is possible for the CSRC to bring criminal or administrative actions against companies and their officers who have been engaged in market misconduct.[142] In terms of private enforcement, investors have had much less success in seeking compensation through the courts by way of civil actions, despite the existence of legal provisions that seem to allow for such actions.[143] In practice, Pistor and Xu have stated that the private enforcement of investor rights has been virtually absent in China, not because of a lack of demand for them, but because courts have restricted investor lawsuits.[144] The sections below will examine the public and private enforcement of corporate and securities law in China.

Public enforcement

The CSRC is the competent authority supervising the securities markets in China.[145] It formulates the relevant rules and regulations on the supervision and administration of the securities market.[146] It also carries out supervision on the issuance, listing and trading of securities.[147] Issuers, listed companies, stock exchanges, organisations in the securities industry such as securities companies, clearing houses and stockbrokers as well as professionals such as auditors and lawyers, are all under the supervision of the CSRC.[148] It is empowered by law to investigate and deal with violations of the laws and regulations.[149] The CSRC's supervision over listed companies covers information disclosure, corporate governance, related parties transactions and mergers and acquisitions.

The Chinese regulator has been inclined to seek mainly administrative penalties rather than criminal penalties via the court system.[150] The CSRC uses three primary tools to sanction listed companies: correction orders; formal warnings or fines; and a bar from participation in the securities markets, although in theory directors, managers and even controlling shareholders can be subjected to criminal liability.[151] The first administrative case of insider trading was announced in 1994, in which the violator, the Shanghai securities brokerage division of the

XianFan Trust and Investment Company, was fined by the CSRC.[152] This was the first attempt to enforce securities market rules. Later, in 1996, the first administrative case against false disclosure and misleading statements in connection with securities trading was decided.[153] However, there were concerns that the administrative penalties imposed were not effective. Managers and intermediaries responsible for misleading or cheating investors were not actually fined personally. It was usually the listed companies that were fined, so that ultimately the shareholders (state entities especially) bore the cost. In the case of state-owned companies, punitive fines might not provide the desired deterrent effect. This is because a company can easily absorb the fines as a cost of business, which in turn falls on the state entities and finally on the public.

A quantifiable approach to measuring enforcement is to focus on inputs and outputs. Generally, for inputs, the funding available to the regulator will be the point of focus.[154] Unfortunately, this information is not publicly available in China. For human resources inputs, the CSRC has a number of seasoned and highly experienced staff from other jurisdictions, for example, Laura Cha and Anthony Neoh from Hong Kong, and it has actively sought cooperation from regulators in the US and other parts of the world.[155] However, the middle and lower executive levels often lack both expertise and experience. In general, it is argued that the CSRC is not very effective at identifying and prosecuting frauds.[156] Other criticisms include its susceptibility to political pressure. The CSRC is a ministry-level commission. It is financed by and answerable to the State Council. Therefore, it is common that a company chairman has a higher rank than a CSRC official and, as a result, it can be difficult for the CSRC to deal with the company effectively.[157] However it is worth noting, if one considers the number of staff, the ratio of staff to market capitalisation was four times more than that in the US in 2008.[158] Xu and colleagues indicate that there is a salient pattern of selective enforcement. Privately owned listed firms face a harsher regulatory environment in terms of both the number and severity of sanctions from regulators, whereas state-owned and, particularly, central-government-controlled firms enjoy the most favourable treatment, although the gap has been reduced in recent years.[159]

For outputs, the CSRC initiates investigations based on a number of leads. These leads include complaints from investors and information from insiders or former employees of companies. The CSRC also conducts the on-going surveillance of listed companies and has a practice of regular reviews and random investigations. The results of these investigations are made public if wrongdoing is found. Between 1997 and 2001, the CSRC published 205 formal rulings in total, including 15 for market manipulation, two for the dissemination of wrongful information, nine for insider trading and 39 for violation of disclosure rules.[160] This number was far lower than that of the US and UK, which often had more than 500 and 100 enforcement cases brought by the national regulator per year respectively.[161] This can be partly explained by the size of markets. The size of China's market and the number of listed companies were then small. Yet, considering that the private enforcement of securities law in China remained uncommon, such a number of public enforcement alone might not be a strong deterrent to market misconduct. The number of enforcement actions in 2002 and 2003 were about double those of 1999 and 2000.[162] The main violations were major failures to disclose information, false statements, a delay in disclosing information and inflated profits. According to a report compiled by the Shenzhen Stock Exchange (SZSE), in 2007 around 80 per cent of the enforcement actions were also related to information disclosure offences, whereas there were only nine cases related to insider trading and market manipulation.[163] There were two major reasons for this. The investigation of insider trading and market manipulation cases is often complicated. Therefore, more time is required and a lot of cases are still to be published. Second, some cases were reclassified as information disclosure offenses for ease of prosecution. Although these explanations make perfect sense, it is doubtful whether the CSRC has the determination and resources to prosecute complicated but serious offences. According to the same SZSE report, the CSRC's administrative commands often hindered market mechanisms, and the poor implementation of regulations, including some laws flawed from the start, left the market open to exploitation.[164] But a recent investigation presented a more optimistic picture. Based on public enforcement outcomes from documents disclosed by listed firms, Xu and colleagues reveal that law enforcement outputs have increased significantly since 2011, thanks to the efforts of the CSRC's 38 regional offices.[165] This confirms both enforcement input and output.

An effective legal regime should combine both private and public enforcement. It is still hard to say if the CSRC, which is empowered by the Securities Law to produce a single strong regulator, is experienced enough or whether its enforcement intensity (both *ex ante* and *ex post*) is sufficiently strong.[166] However, as Pistor and Xu have rightly pointed out, it is difficult to interpret enforcement activities in the absence of comparative data.[167] For instance, in 2003, when total enforcement procedures reached 51, there were 1,278 listed companies in China, implying that at most one in 25 companies was the subject of any kind of enforcement activities.[168] To compare, in the same year, there were 175 enforcement cases brought by the Financial Services Authority (FSA) when there were 2,692 listed companies on the London Stock Exchange, implying a ratio of around 1:15. In the US, the ratio was around 1:10.[169] Unfortunately, the data are simply not comparable because the FSA's numbers for enforcement actions cover all aspects of the financial services industry, including banking, pensions and insurance. Also, enforcement actions done in an informal manner were not included. The raw data might not have told the whole story. A comparison between that of the US and China is not conclusive either, because low public enforcement intensity can be complemented by other mechanisms. There might be other functional substitutes such as private enforcement or the existence of professional institutional investors. In the UK, where both private and public enforcement is weaker than in the US, the role of institutional investors is large.[170] Unfortunately, in China, institutional investors did not actually emerge until the new millennium. Xu and colleagues contend that despite increased public enforcement, due to the lack of a reliable private enforcement regime and the limitations of monetary penalties, the general enforcement of securities law is still apparently weak.[171] Therefore, there is a need to investigate the private enforcement situation.

Private enforcement

As discussed in Chapter 2, in addition to the functions fulfilled by public enforcement (i.e. justice and deterrence), civil remedies have the advantage of compensating the wronged. Unfortunately, the private enforcement of investor rights was once non-existent.[172] The World Bank's 'Doing Business' studies once awarded China two out of ten for a shareholder's ability to sue officers and directors for misconduct.[173] In the past, the rights of shareholders were very weak in China. Under the early Company Law, where shareholders were conferred certain rights, those rights were provided mainly without any mention of civil remedies.[174] Only since the Company Law 2005 has private enforcement been facilitated. The most notable feature is the introduction of a derivative-like action. For the first time, the concept of derivative action was introduced in the new Company Law to strengthen the protection of minority shareholders. Since the company is an independent legal entity, individual shareholders have not been able to bring actions against company directors under previous laws. However, Article 151 of the current Company Law gives rise to certain shareholders' rights to bring a derivative lawsuit.[175] Shareholders can sue, on behalf of the company, the directors, senior officers or supervisors who violated any laws or administrative regulations or the company's articles of association, in the performance of their official duties, causing losses to the company. This is a derivative action-like mechanism because the right to sue still vests in the company, rather than its shareholders. Accordingly, the compensation recovered belongs to the company, instead of individual shareholders.

The first civil compensation attempt on account of false statements occurred in 1998.[176] The case was dismissed by the court because of a lack of direct causal link between the false disclosure and the loss. However, it was suggested that the actual reason for this decision was because the court believed that the case should be referred to the CSRC to determine.[177] This indicates the reliance on administrative measures, rather than formal legal mechanisms, in China. Private litigation began to take off only in 2001 in response to fraud at Guangxia Company. The Guangxia case is a benchmark case for private securities litigation in China, and is often referred to as 'China's Enron'.[178] In total, 1,000 cases were filed in Wuxi, Jiangsu province, against Guangxia alone.[179] This shocked the key government officials because they had always thought in terms of administrative sanctions instead of judicial remedies. These events evidenced the need for a drastic legal overhaul. Disappointed investors started to demonstrate in front of the CSRC building. Key officials from the CSRC initiated meetings with the Supreme People's Court, urging the court to assume a more significant role in regulating the securities market through adjudicating cases.[180] In September

2001, the Supreme People's Court issued a notice directing all lower courts not to accept private securities lawsuits temporarily until the further clarification of the appropriate judiciary procedures.[181] In January 2003, a circular was issued setting out more detailed procedural rules for dealing with securities cases.[182] From 1 February 2003, Chinese courts have been able to adjudicate private securities litigation on the basis of rules issued by the Supreme People's Court in the circular. In the opinion of Zhu, these procedural rules, in conjunction with other relevant provisions of law, such as the Company Law, the Securities Law and the Civil Procedure Rule, have finally provided courts with the guidelines necessary to address claims from investors.[183]

China's court system was undoubtedly slow to react to the demand for the private enforcement of securities cases, considering that both domestic stock exchanges commenced their operation in the early 1990s. There were two reasons for this, according to an insider of the CSRC.[184] First, despite the general provisions set out in the Securities Law 1998, there were no specific rules and guidelines as to the implementation of private securities litigation. Second, given the huge disparity in the quality of judges among courts nationwide and the lack of precedents, there would have been many inconsistent judgments, which might have made the situation more chaotic.

The effect of the circular was immediate; more than 900 private securities suits were brought by investors.[185] This illustrated the demand for private securities litigation. In practice, the courts appeared to be uncertain about how to apply the rules.[186] Even though actions could be initiated, courts tended to refuse to make a judgment, and none was settled by a court judgment in favour of the investors.[187] The ban on all private securities cases in 2001 to 2003 showed that both the *ex ante* and *ex post* threat of private enforcement was weak. Furthermore, according to the 2003 circular, claimants can only sue in the court where the headquarters of the listed company is located. Previously, according to the Civil Procedure Rule of China, investors had enjoyed the right to sue either in their own domicile or at the location of the company's operation. The new restriction raised the concern of local protectionism. Judges and courts in China, especially at the lower level, often lack independence because governments at the same level control them through appointment and budgetary powers.[188] The integrity of the legal structure can easily be undermined by political influence. In fact, this influence is very strong in China. According to a study of the nature and extent of private securities litigation in China, examining whether private securities litigation has been effectively carried out during the first decade since it was formally permitted by China's highest court in 2002, there has been a much lower number than expected of securities civil suits in China during the ten-year study period, but the percentage of recovery in China is significantly higher than that in the US.[189] In particular, the local courts are found to be dysfunctional in handling securities civil cases. There remains a need to improve the Chinese legal regime for private enforcement.

Political institutions

Despite the changes of leadership since 1978, the orientation of Chinese political ideology has followed Deng Xiaoping's model of 'socialism with Chinese characteristics' closely. Traditionally, institutional innovations in China were supposedly consistent with a Marxist-Leninist-Maoist ideology that could not be challenged.[190] However, Jiang Zemin's 'Three Represents' legitimised the inclusion of capitalists and private entrepreneurs within the Chinese Communist Party. More recently, Hu Jintao's 'Harmonious Society' slightly adjusted China's focus from economic growth to overall societal balance and harmony. His 'Scientific Outlook on Development' aims to achieve 'coordinated development, all-round development, and sustainable development'.[191] The current leader, Xi Jinping, reaffirmed in 2013 the position of Deng Xiaoping Theory, Three Represents and Scientific Outlook on Development in pursuing 'socialism with Chinese characteristics'.[192] Xi himself also presents a new a set of personal and national ideals called the 'China Dream'.[193]

According to Coase and Wang, the resistance to market reform throughout the 1980s did not come from the people or government officials, but originated from China's remaining commitment to socialism.[194] The idea of establishing a socialist market economy was confirmed by the Fourteenth Central Committee of the CPC in 1992. The whole process of reform proceeded into the 1990s and beyond. The establishment of two formal securities exchanges took place at around the same time. The Shanghai Stock Exchange was founded on 26 November 1990 and opened for its first trading day on 19 December 1990. The Shenzhen Stock Exchange was founded in the same year, on 1 December, and formally opened for trading on 3 July 1991. There have been numerous concerns over reinterpreting Marxism and leaping into a 'socialist market economy with Chinese characteristics'. Would the introduction of a capital market be consistent with socialist economic division and production? Deng Xiaoping once made the following remarks:

> Securities, stock markets, are they good or evil? Are they dangerous or safe? Are they unique to capitalism or also applicable to socialism? Let's try and see. Let's try for one or two years; if it goes well, we can relax controls; if it goes badly, we can correct or close it. Even if we have to close it, we may do it quickly, or slowly, or partly. What are we afraid of? If we maintain this attitude, then we will not make big mistakes.[195]

For the Chinese leaders, the use of non-socialist development and the taste of capitalism are only the tools to get China into the 'socialist utopia'.[196] In this sense, capitalist means can be borrowed and utilised for the building of socialism. But socialism remains the basic system. The Chinese Constitution essentially recognised only socialist ownership.[197] Deng was widely credited as the great architect of the Chinese economic reform. China's post-Cultural Revolution economic reforms have been based on Deng Xiaoping's 'Socialism with

Chinese characteristics', a theory of incorporating capitalism into central planning to increase productivity, advance Chinese culture and enhance the interests of the people.[198] The only difference between socialism and capitalism, Deng argued, was that socialism relied on central planning whereas capitalist planning was determined by market forces of supply and demand. Since central and market planning were designed to influence economic outcomes, both are consistent with socialism. To achieve socialism, Deng hinted that China must go through capitalism, but its usage must be controlled by the state. Thus he insisted that incorporating capitalist ideas into reforms was not violating the Four Cardinal Principles, consisting of upholding the following: (1) the socialist path; (2) the people's democratic dictatorship; (3) the leadership of the CPC; and (4) Maoist thought and Marxism-Leninism.[199] Such a belief has arguably been influenced by Chen Yun, a participant in Deng Xiaoping's coalition for economic reform.[200] In 1978, Chen Yun was elected as a member to the Chinese Communist Party's Politburo and its standing committee, the apex of power. He postulated the 'bird cage' thesis that the proper relationship between the planned and market economy is that of a 'bird in a cage', meaning the planned economy was the cage that confined the bird in the market. With Deng at the helm and Chen Yun as principal economic strategist, China's new leaders, sensing the great magnitude and urgency of the crisis confronting the country after the Cultural Revolution, began to jettison key components of Mao Zedong's legacy.[201] They repudiated Mao's Cultural Revolution, renounced most of his economic theories and reinstated virtually all of his purged opponents. In place of Mao's insistence on austerity, egalitarianism, self-sacrifice, self-reliance and perpetual class struggle, they advocated incentive-driven production responsibility systems, decentralised state administration, expanded use of market, and sharply increased international economic and technological involvement.

Deng stepped down from top positions in 1989, and completely retired from the political scene in 1992. This left his successor, Jiang Zemin, to continue the reform. Jiang Zemin's Three Represents refer to what the CPC stands for:

> It represents the development trends of advanced productive forces. It represents the orientations of an advanced culture. It represents the fundamental interests of the overwhelming majority of the people of China.[202]

According to Jia, the efforts of Jiang to promote the traditional Party lines through the Three Represents Campaign are a result of the rising need to maintain the legitimacy of the Communist Party's rule.[203] Since the mid-1990s, various social problems, especially rising layoffs from SOEs as a result of the SOE reform, have become increasingly poignant. The rising unemployment and rapidly widening income gap shadowed the Party's economic legitimacy and previous justifications of the reform policies because the fruit of economic growth was not enjoyed by a large portion of population, while socialism by definition means equality and common wealth. The rising dissatisfaction with reform and strong support of socialism drove the post-Deng leadership to debate the socialist nature of China's economic growth. The large-scale political campaigns that the leadership under Jiang Zemin resumed, including the Three Represents Campaign, were aimed at emphasising the socialist characteristics of the reform. Taking place earlier than the Three Represents Campaign was *sanjiang* (Three Emphases). It is noticeable that Jiang Zemin first urged Party leaders to stress politics, the most important aspect of *sanjiang*, in 1995.[204] On the one hand, it is believed that the major target of *sanjiang* was to strengthen the centre's control over local leaders. On the other hand, *sanjiang*, together with its measures to strictly punish corrupt officials and highly praise outstanding and selfless Party members, sent a strong message that the Party was energetic and able to cleanse itself whenever possible. Compared with *sanjiang*, which emphasised the disciplinary side of the Party orthodoxy, the Three Represents theory stressed the CPC's reform or development side.[205] In other words, the Party can adjust itself to changing times because it represents the development trend of China's advanced productive forces and the orientation of China's advanced culture. Therefore, it seems that the move to allow private entrepreneurs, who are playing an increasingly important role in the Chinese economy, to join the Party can be explained as the CPC's reform measure to advance economic development.

Although it is observed that Hu Jintao regularly invoked the Three Represents since he had come to power in 2002, he might have different approaches to understanding the Three Represents, which reflect different personalities, different leadership agendas and different political interests.[206] Jiang Zemin raised to prominence the idea of 'governing the country through law' and discussed the need for greater institutionalisation if the CPC is to act more as a ruling party and less as a revolutionary party. In contrast, Hu Jintao presented himself in a much more populist guise than did the more formal and remote Jiang. In fact, Hu put forward the idea of *sange tiejin* (Three Closenesses) in 2003 to illustrate this image.[207] Furthermore, his vision of a 'Harmonious Society' thus follows in the footsteps of previous policy discourses to map out the direction of China's socioeconomic development as well setting the tone for national policies.[208] Hu inherited an increasingly disparate society: widening regional disparities, a tattered social and welfare system, massive unemployment, structural poverty and rising environmental concerns.[209] Mounting social and political problems called into question the CPC's governing capacity, while uncontrolled and widespread corruption and misconduct by cadres and government officials further tarnished the party's image. Hu therefore sought to ditch its erstwhile infatuation with economic growth to pursue a more sustainable mode of development. In line with this vision, Hu Jintao and his government were promoting a new approach to development called the 'Scientific Development Concept'. This approach aims to correct the presumed overemphasis in recent years on the pursuit of increases in GDP, which encourages the generation of false figures and dubious construction projects along with neglect for the social welfare of those left behind in China.[210]

However, despite all these new ideologies, one recurrent concern has been the legitimacy of the CPC rule. There has not been a legitimate mandate to govern via a democratic election. As discussed in the previous chapter, there is a varied position regarding the role of democracy in development. One view is that dictatorship is the best path to development. The story of China appears to fit in this view well. Under the Chinese Constitution, the most powerful organ of state is the National People's Congress (NPC), effectively China's parliament.[211] Only the NPC has the power to amend the Constitution. Amendments to the Constitution must be proposed by the NPC Standing Committee or by one-fifth or more of the NPC deputies, and they must be passed by a two-thirds majority vote of all deputies. It has the power to enact and amend all major laws. Also, it will determine major state issues, such as examining and approving the report on the plan for national economic and social development and on its implementation, as well as examining and approving the report on the central and local budgets and their implementation. Most importantly, the NPC has the role to elect and appoint members to central state organs. The NPC elects the Chairman, Vice Chairmen, Secretary-General and other members of its Standing Committee and the President and the Vice President of the People's Republic of China. The congress is made up of nearly 3,000 delegates elected by China's provinces, autonomous regions, municipalities and the armed forces. To many, it is little more than a rubber stamp for party decisions.[212] About 70 per cent of its delegates, and almost all its senior figures, are also party members.[213] Their loyalty is to the party first, the NPC second. In other words, despite what is said in the constitution, the party's political bureau (Politburo) is the real nexus of all power in China.[214] The 24-member Politburo is elected by the party's central committee. But real power lies with its smaller standing committee. This essentially means that every significant decision affecting China's 1.3 billion people is first discussed and approved by a handful of people. This perhaps explains why the vision of an individual, such as Deng, can be easily translated into some nationwide policies, such as the creation of SEZs, initiating and sustaining China's miraculous economic growth.

Cultural institutions

The corporate culture of China may not be compatible with the best corporate governance practices. Standard legal protections are essential in a scenario where investors are too naïve to protect themselves.[215] There can be both governance and regulatory strategies. However, both are problematic in the context of China, largely because of the dominance of state-owned companies. First, absolute control in these companies is still retained by the state. Second, enforcement, both public and private, against these companies has been problematic as discussed. In addition, Chinese companies retain characteristics of small family businesses such as paternalism, personalism, opportunism and flexibility, even when conducting large operations. There is not a culture of honesty. Corruption is widespread in China with excessive entertainment, embezzlement, bribery and moonlighting.[216] Personal connections (*guanxi*) have remained a key element of Chinese organisations. China's traditional business culture is characterised by discretionary power, secrecy, a substantial government role in large-scale production and personal connections. Conversely, it is commonly asserted that securities markets depend on the rule of law, transparency and the interactions of private parties who are often strangers.

However, before making a serious accusation that China is ‘corrupt’, one needs to distinguish between *guanxi* and corruption. *Guanxi* can be legitimate and can provide a ‘positive cultural framework for building and maintaining warm and lasting relationships in China’.[217] On the other hand, corruption can be generally defined as ‘the abuse of entrusted power for private gain’ and is prohibited by law.[218] *Guanxi* is omnipresent within Chinese society; it is a moral code proscribing proper social behaviour within Chinese culture, and prescribes rules for the development, maintenance and use of connections.[219] *Guanxi* has had this role for thousands of years and can be traced back to Confucian concepts.

Max Weber used to refer to Confucianism as the religion of China.[220] Confucianism is the way of life propagated by Confucius in ancient China and has been followed by the Chinese people for more than two millennia.[221] It is still the substance of learning, the source of values and the social code of the Chinese. Its influence has also extended to other countries, particularly Korea, Japan and Vietnam. As a teacher of humanity, Confucius stated his ambition in terms of concern for human beings: ‘To bring comfort to the old, to have trust in friends, and to cherish the young’ (from *Lunyu*, the Analects of Confucius). Confucius’s vision of the way to develop a moral community began with a holistic reflection on the human condition. On the question of Confucianism remaining relevant to the contemporary Chinese society, Hu provides two factors of consideration.[222] First, Confucianism has gained influence in a rising China. The reforms initiated by Deng Xiaoping have undermined the communist ideology, changed China’s socioeconomic system and increased China’s international status. One consequence has been Confucianism’s re-emergence out of the ashes of communist rule. Second, in the 1980s, many had heaped praise on Confucianism for its contribution to the success of the East Asian model. As it had taken credit for the economic miracle, ‘Asian values’, especially those of Confucianism, took some of the blame for the financial crisis.

The word *guanxi* is not found in the Confucian classics. Instead, the word *lun* is used.[223] The literal term *lun* seeks to capture some of the most essential aspects of the ancient Chinese social system and its political and moral philosophy. The first meaning of *lun* pertains to the paramount importance of human relationships. The fundamental Confucian assumption about humankind is that individuals exist in relation to others. The Five Cardinal Relationships (*wulun*) are: ruler–subject, father–son, husband–wife, elder brother–younger brother and friend–friend. The second meaning of *lun* is social order. In hierarchical differentiation, members of each relationship enjoyed unequal rights and obligations so that sovereign, father, husband, elder brother, the senior friend had more prerogatives and authority than the subject, son, wife, younger brother and the junior friend. Horizontally, the self is at the centre of a series of concentric circles, while socially related others were differentiated in terms of their closeness to the self. Finally, *lun* refers to moral principles regarding interactive behaviours of related parties.

Guanxi practice begins with developing a relationship.[224] It consists of relationships based on family ties, familiar connections and with strangers. A good *guanxi* relationship develops over time through multiple interactions and exchanges, creating a web of reciprocal obligations and indebtedness. Yang made the key distinction between *guanxi* and *guanxi* practice to understand manner of social and economic relations in China.[225] *Guanxi* alone refers to the personal relations and other social ties that people develop through their lives through normal interactions. In contrast, *guanxi* practice refers to the deliberate and strategic cultivation and use of social relations. The structure of the lending and trade relations that emerged in China's business groups reflected the various strategies managers used to reduce uncertainty and opportunism and to avoid dependence as the groups emerged. A particularly common strategy was to develop new lending and trade relations where prior social ties existed.[226] In the Chinese environment, however, trust is a normative and an essential part of a relationship.[227] This is to be contrasted with a Western business environment in which trust is separate from the contractual basis of the alliance, and trust is generated over time through long-term interaction. For these reasons, trust among Western businesspeople is more difficult to generate and maintain, but less problematic than among Chinese businesspeople.

The ubiquity of *guanxi* makes trustworthiness a primary quality of people.[228] From an individual's point of view, trust is necessarily generated, maintained and sanctioned within the small group of people with whom one has relationships. In contrast, for Western societies, laws are universally applicable. Laws provide generalised institutional foundations for groups that may vary tremendously in size and function. As a result, as revealed by Liebman and Milhaupt, the role of reputational sanctions imposed by the stock exchanges has been a major mechanism of punishment and deterrent in the Chinese capital market.[229] This casts doubt on the meaning of looking at the substantive legal rules in the context of China because an informal unorthodox form of governance is practiced there instead of a strictly legal mechanism. Potter has examined the role of *guanxi* in the Chinese legal system in the context of legal culture and by reference to the attitudes and behaviour of Chinese legal actors.[230] According to him, the role of *guanxi* in China is often seen as operating in juxtaposition to the role of law and legal institutions, and its importance in China is attributed to the weakness of institutions for managing social, economic and political relations, and allocating resources.

The impact of *guanxi* on economic performance is not known with precision. It may be viewed as an informal network allowing the bypassing of the inefficiencies inherent in a Communist bureaucracy.[231] In this sense, *guanxi* may be seen as a substitute for the rule of law. Meanwhile, several theories have been used to explain the *guanxi*–performance link.[232] One example is the social capital theory. According to social capital theory, social ties provide access to valuable resources which can be used to achieve a variety of positive outcomes. In fact, social capital itself is considered one type of resource that is embedded within, available through and derived from the network of ties. As such, social capital theory recognises the importance of social ties among individuals and organisations and posits that tangible advantageous outcomes, such as privileged access to knowledge and information, preferential opportunities, enhanced reputation and so on, can be obtained through the network of ties. There are three benefits of social capital.[233] First, social capital provides access to information through broader sources and with better quality, enhanced relevance and greater timeliness. Second, influence, control and power resulting from possessing social capital allow organisations to get things done and achieve their goals. Third, strong social norms and belief provide solidarity that encourages compliance and reduces the need for formal controls. In the context of China, social ties and networks formed by managers with other managers and government officials bring social capital to the organisations to which they belong.[234] Managers' social capital can be transferred to their organisations because managerial ties involve managers using their ties and networks to exchange favours and reciprocal obligations for organisational purposes. Through the maintained and accumulated social capital derived from their social ties, managers and organisations are able to reap the information, control and solidarity benefits that allow organisations to operate more efficiently and to compete more effectively, which is conducive to overall organisational performance.

Nonetheless, the difference between corruption and legitimate *guanxi* is often a matter of degree.[235] Despite the general perception that corruption is bad and the presence of empirical evidence showing the economic cost of corruption, the OECD highlighted a major puzzle, known as the 'Asian Paradox', in the discussion of the corruption–growth nexus which is the combination of rapid growth and high levels of perceived corruption in many Asian economies, including China.[236] But this can be contrasted with the historical experience of Singapore and Hong Kong. Both of them introduced stringent anticorruption policies at low levels of development, while their subsequent economic growth and development has been quite spectacular.

Role of market infrastructure

During the development of Shenzhen, it has been envisaged that the city would become a regional centre of commerce, trade, finance and transportation.[237] Supporting high-tech and other advanced industry will be modern service sectors such as logistics and finance. The primary container ports are Yantian in the east, and Shekou and Chiwan in the west. For a long period of time, Hong Kong has been viewed as the Chinese mainland's main gateway to the rest of the world, thanks to its strategic location and modern facilities, such as financial system and transportation network, thereby enabling it to take advantage of a large volume of entrepot trade.[238] However, from 1979 to 2004, the Shenzhen Port invested over RMB30 billion into port infrastructure and related areas boosting its profile and usability.[239] According to the Eleventh Five-Year Plan (2006–10), Shenzhen was committed to improving the infrastructure of the logistics industry, to build the city into a key supply chain service base in South China, as well as an influential logistics hinge city in the Asian Pacific Region. Meanwhile, Shanghai also invested an accumulative amount of RMB1,384 billion in fixed assets in the 1990s, building the infrastructures required to attract investors.[240] For example, Shanghai port only began to handle container shipping in 1983, but now it is the largest port in the world.[241] According to the statistics of 2015 from the World Shipping Council, out of the top ten ports in the world, seven of them are located in China (including Hong Kong).[242] Apart from Shanghai, Shenzhen and Hong Kong which were in the first, third and fifth positions respectively, other important ports in mainland China include, Ningbo, Qingdao, Guangzhou and Tianjin. Incidentally, all these cities were designated as coastal open cities, together with Shanghai, in 1984, while Shenzhen has been able to enjoy a more enviable status as a SEZ since 1979, as discussed before.

As for a robust financial market, it is undeniable that like most countries in the world including many developed countries (except the US and UK), China has been relying much more heavily on financial intermediaries such as banks than markets to channel capital to business.[243] For example, bank credit still accounts for close to 90 per cent of funds raised by the corporate sector.[244] However, the non-performing loans problem in the Chinese banking system meant that the state had to find a way out. The problem of the Chinese bank-centred system can be explained by several factors.[245] First, state-controlled banks have remained dominant in the banking sector. The state ownership of banks has reduced competition and lessened the pressure on banks to operate on a commercial, profit-oriented basis. Second, there is a lack of good internal credit assessment capabilities in many banks. The reason behind most of the non-performing loans in the past was the directed lending policies of the government to fund SOEs regardless of their profitability. Third, these state-owned banks have a decentralised structure. Lending decisions are made at the local branch level, which is susceptible to influence from local government and favouritism towards local SOEs. This diffuse structure of banks and many SOEs makes it difficult for banks to collect and share useful information to make an informed lending decision.

The over-reliance on a single mode of finance has apparently driven China to consider a diversification of domestic fund-raising channels. Long before the establishment of a formal establishment, there was an attempt from a company in Shenzhen to raise funds from the public. In July 1983, United Investment Corporation of Bao'an County in Guangdong Province placed a public offering advertisement in the Shenzhen Special Economic Zone Daily, announcing the issuance of shares guaranteed by the county government to raise US$6.6 million.[246] This was the first company to place a public offering advertisement in a newspaper after 1949. Furthermore, in September 1987, Shenzhen Special Zone Securities Firm, the first professional securities firm in China, was established.[247] Finally, as mentioned before, the SZSE was established in December

1990. As a formal set of securities law was not in place, Shenzhen Municipal Government introduced a series of administrative measures.[248]

The operation of the exchange was not without problems. For example, on 10 August 1992, a serious shortage of IPO subscription application forms, combined with poor organisation and other irregular practices, resulted in violent protests by potential retail investors in Shenzhen.[249] The incident triggered the Chinese government's decision to set up a national regulatory body to supervise activities on the equity market. The response was the establishment of the State Council Securities Committee (SCSC) and the CSRC in October of the same year.[250] The exchange has been steadily developing since then. Towards the new millennium, there was an idea from the State Developing Planning Commission to establish a market for growth enterprises, the Chinese equivalent to the NASDAQ.[251] This certainly coincided with Shenzhen's position as a centre for high-technology industries. The Growth Enterprise Board of China was eventually launched in 2009. Apparently, comparing to its counterpart in Shanghai, the SZSE has been relatively lacklustre. For example, according to the statistics as of June 2017, Shenzhen was just the eighth largest stock exchange in the world (in terms of market capitalisation), compared to Shanghai at fourth and Hong Kong at seventh.[252] However, according to the recent Global Financial Centre Index which measures the competitiveness of a financial centre, Shenzhen was placed at eighteenth position, two above Shanghai at twentieth.[253] More importantly, Shenzhen has the Growth Enterprise Board (now known as ChiNext), like other junior bourses around the world, which has less stringent admission standards and is capable of providing emerging businesses with a valuable fund-raising channel.[254]

Determinants of future growth

Despite repeated attempts for the government to update its laws, the rule of law in China is still perceived as weak, as exemplified by the World Bank Governance Indicators 2015 putting the country at the 44th percentile in this regard. This is especially true for the country's intellectual property rights protection. As indicated by the Embassy of the United States in Beijing, despite stronger statutory protection following China's WTO accession, China 'continues to be a haven for counterfeiters and pirates'.[255] Lax legal protection is not necessarily a disadvantage. For example, several tech giants in China have allegedly imitated their Western counterparts. Tencent's QQ messenger is believed to be 'an imitation of an Israeli service called ICQ' and Xiaomi is hailed as 'Apple of the East'.[256] Another example will be the effects of enhanced labour protection. After the introduction of the Labour Contract Law in 2007, the resulting rising cost of China's famously cheap labour has immediately dented the labour intensive manufacturing sector in Guangdong Province.

There is a tension between the economic benefits of law and compliance costs. The manufacturing sector officially makes up about 50 per cent of gross domestic product in China and China's coastal manufacturing belt has been better known as the workshop of the world. The additional costs involved may not be a problem to large state-owned enterprise because of their capability to absorb the costs. However, smaller-scale manufacturing is clearly struggling, especially amid a global recession.[257] Millions of factories are being squeezed from all sides by rising costs, labour shortages, shrinking margins and a collapse in new orders from overseas. Many small manufacturers face the prospect of going out of business owing to government policies and immutable demographic and economic forces that make low-end production in China increasingly untenable. Pressures from the labour law may encourage factories to close rather than pay what they owe to workers under the law. Companies avoid paying claims by liquidating or by just disappearing without properly settling their business. In 2008, more than 15,000 enterprises in Guangdong, the manufacturing-heavy southern province, shut their doors.[258] For example, after their factory closed, workers from the Shatangbu Yifa Rubber and Hardware Factory in Shenzhen filed for the back-pay and severance promised under a contract required by the law. The Hong Kong-based owner disappeared. That left many migrant workers stranded without enough money to return to their hometowns hundreds of miles away. Enforcement of the laws remains an imminent issue. With reports emerging of layoffs preceding its implementation, and company closures or relocations to cheaper jurisdictions afterwards, it has been widely believed that the new law would add considerable burden to employers. There are undoubtedly comprehensive improvements to worker rights. However, all these represent costs to a company. The impact can be particularly devastating considering that labour intensive productions have been the major economic driver in China. After the new law came into effect and the financial crisis, there have been epidemic closures of factories across the Pearl River and Yangtze River Deltas.

Other than labour costs, the simultaneous increase in living and operational costs can be a concern. For example, homes in Shenzhen were sold at an average of RMB49,259 per square metre (or US$690 a square foot) in April 2016, as much as the Rockridge neighborhood in Oakland in the US, a pricey part of the San Francisco Bay Area, where home prices averaged US$704 a square foot.[259] The fact that China has been migrating to high value-added industries may mitigate the impact.

Another strategy is to continue to adhere to its commitment to opening up. In April 2009, the State Council made an official announcement on its goal of turning Shanghai into an international finance and shipping centre by 2020.[260] In line with this national strategy, a report concerning the construction of China's first free trade zone (FTZ) in Shanghai was submitted to the regulatory authorities and attracted great attention in 2011.[261] The State Council official approved the establishment of the China (Shanghai) Pilot Free Trade Zone in August 2013; this would first span 28.78 square kilometres in the city's Pudong New Area, including Waigaoqiao Free Trade Zone, Waigaoqiao Bonded Logistics Park, Pudong International Free Trade Zone and Yangshan Free Trade Port Area. The zone was officially launched on 29 September 2013.

Indeed, after his appointment as General Secretary of the Chinese Communist Party in March 2012, Xi Jinping chose Shenzhen as the destination for his first inspection tour. Shenzhen is symbolic in a sense that it is one of the first SEZs and one of the significant stops on Deng Xiaoping's 'Southern Tour' in 1992. Xi's visit signalled his approval of historical reform models and his decision to use the Shanghai FTZ as a testing ground for economic reform echoes Deng's use of similarly purposed SEZs.[262]

Right before its official launch, the *Framework Plan for the China (Shanghai) Pilot Free Trade Zone* ('Framework Plan' hereinafter) was issued to outline the first batch of initiatives that set the tone and scale of the FTZ.[263] The Framework Plan first affirmed 'socialism with Chinese characteristics' to promote reform and development by opening up the economy. Other than Deng Xiaoping Theory, Jiang Zemin's 'Three Represents' and Hu Jintao's 'Scientific Outlook on Development', Xi Jinping's 'China Dream' was formally recognised in the plan.[264] The vision is that the FTZ will be developed into a zone with convenient investment and trading procedure, full convertibility of currencies, effective and efficient goods supervision, and investor-friendly regulatory environment. To achieve the aim, a list of tasks and measures was set out. For example, to transform government functions, administration transparency and information disclosure mechanisms would be enhanced.[265]

As for trade in services and goods, various measures are also in place. Financial services, transportation services, commerce and trade services, professional services, cultural services and public services sectors are selected to be enlarged and opened, and market access restrictions, such as requirements concerning the qualification of investors, limitations on foreign participation, restrictions concerning business scope, etc., will be suspended or cancelled.[266] The innovation is a 'negative list', a key reform in the zone, which shows sectors where foreign investment is banned or restricted within the zone. There are no restrictions for anything not on the list. In relation to trade in goods, initiatives such as upgrading the international shipping services and developing the joint effect of the Waigaoqiao port, the Yangshan port and Pudong airport were laid out.[267] For financial innovation, the aim is to promote RMB capital account convertibility, financial market liberalisation, cross-border use of RMB and a market approach to financial asset pricing.[268] Favourable legal and tax measures would also be introduced to promote investment and trade, for example, adjustments to the laws of business associations involving foreign parties and tax deferral payment on income derived from asset valuation appreciation.[269]

Concluding remarks

China's tremendous economic growth has been the direct result of a comprehensive set of carefully planned and executed reforms formulated towards the end of 1970s under the leadership of the legendary Chinese leader Deng Xiaoping. For a few decades before that, the Chinese economy had been severely hampered by a series of misplaced economic policies and political turbulences. The Chinese economy has taken off since the commencement of the economic reform in 1978.

The actual changes can be neatly summarised by the twin strategies of reform and opening-up (*gaige* and *kaifang* in Chinese). First, there was the SOE reform. Control over industries and production has not been completely shifted from the state sector to private hands. China's economic reform has not been the privatisation experienced by many former communist countries in the Soviet Union. Instead, it has been a process of corporatisation, which entailed the adoption of corporate form, restructuring and instituting stock ownership without necessarily relinquishing the state's controlling interest in the means of production. Second, China has been opening up its markets to the outside world. One key policy was the introduction of SEZs, an area with special and flexible policies in external economic activities to attract and encourage foreign investments. Shenzhen, as one of the first SEZs, has clearly taken advantage of a first mover advantage to become one of the economic centres in China.

At the same time, institutional conditions have been improved over time to accompany the economic reform. Company and securities laws have been introduced and amended over time to provide entrepreneurs with a functional business form to commence their venture and also protect the rights of outside investors. There is also a fundamental shift in political ideology to accommodate the economic reform. The ideological dilemma faced by the Chinese Communist Party was a choice between a strictly socialist model, a partially privatised model and a *laissez-faire* capitalist model. China has not been shy in reiterating its commitment to socialism. The first pronouncement of the Company Law 1993 stated the purpose of 'maintaining the social economic order and promoting the development of a socialist market economy'. It appeared that a *laissez-faire* economy was not an option. By contrast, the initiation of economic reform was meant to move society away from socialism. It seemed that somewhere in between was the way to go. In Chinese terms, the path to reform by recasting Western corporate law was an attempt 'to make a foreign construction readily adaptable to serving China, in the course of building socialism'.[270] On the other hand, culture remains a key element in influencing the organisational and economic structures in China. *Guanxi* can be a mechanism to overcome inefficiencies in bureaucracies, but at the same time can create social problems like corruption. Finally, China has been making a lot of capital investments in improving its infrastructure to ensure that modern economic demands can be met. The country has the largest ports to provide excellent transportation links. Also, two stock exchanges were established to provide an additional channel of national capital, apart from the pre-existing state-owned banking sector which has been plagued by various problems. All these institutional changes may point to the conclusion that the Chinese economic miracle is far from an unintentional coincidence, but rather is a set of calculated moves to form an integrated strategy of economic development. Future sustainable economic growth will hinge on whether continual innovations of reform and opening-up can be seen.

Notes

1 World Bank (2017), 'China Overview'. Online. Available at: www.worldbank.org/en/country/china/overview.
2 World Bank (2013), *China 30*, Washington D.C.: World Bank, p. 4.
3 Business Insider (2017), 'These are the 23 Biggest Global Banks – all with more than $1 trillion of assets' Online. Available at: http://uk.businessinsider.com/the-biggest-banks-in-the-world-2017-4/#22-postal-savings-bank-of-china-china-119-trillion-2. China Daily (2017), '115 Chinese Firms on Fortune Global 500 List 2017'. Online. Available at: www.chinadaily.com.cn/business/2017-07/21/content_30202343.htm.
4 Angus Maddison (2007), *Chinese Economic Performance in the Long Run*, Paris: OECD, p. 53.
5 Wayne Morrison (2015), 'China's Economic Rise: History, Trends, Challenges, and Implications for the United States' Congressional Research Service Report. Online. Available at: https://fas.org/sgp/crs/row/RL33534.pdf.
6 Maddison (2007), op. cit., p. 60.
7 Nicholas Lardy (1987), 'Economic Recovery and the 1st Five-Year Plan' in Roderick MacFarquhar and John Fairbank (eds.), *The Cambridge History of China*, Cambridge: CUP, p. 157.
8 Anton Cheremukhin *et al.* (2015), 'The Economy of People's Republic of China from 1953' CEPR Discussion Paper No. 10764. Online. Available at: http://cepr.org/active/publications/discussion_papers/dp.php?dpno=10764.
9 Lardy (1987), op. cit., p. 144.
10 Cheremukhin *et al.* (2015), op. cit., p. 21.
11 Morrison (2015), op. cit. p. 3.
12 Maddison (2007), op. cit., p. 73.
13 Ibid.
14 Wei Li and Dennis Yang (2005), 'The Great Leap Forward: Anatomy of a Central Planning Disaster' in *Journal of Political Economy*, **113**.
15 Ibid.
16 Philip Bridgham (1967), 'Mao's "Cultural Revolution": Origin and Development' in *China Quarterly*, **29**, p. 4.
17 Maddison (2007), op. cit., p. 83.
18 Ibid. p. 74.
19 Cheremukhin *et al.* (2015), op. cit., p. 22.
20 Ibid.
21 Ibid.
22 Dwight Perkins (1991), 'China's Economic Policy and Performance' in Roderick MacFarquhar and John Fairbank (eds.), *The Cambridge History of China*, Cambridge: CUP, pp. 482–483.
23 Ibid. p. 486.
24 Cheremukhin *et al.* (2015), op. cit., p. 23.
25 Barry Naughton (1995), *Growing Out of the Plan*, Cambridge: CUP, p. 76.
26 Liang Bai (2014), 'Economic Legacies of the Cultural Revolution' LSE Economic History Working Paper. Online. Available at: www.lse.ac.uk/economichistory/seminars/economichistory/papers14-15/cultural-revolution.pdf.
27 Although such a Chinese mentality of prudence was adopted by Deng Xiaoping, it was indeed proposed and said repeatedly by Chen Yun as early as 1950, who was the Chairman of the CPC Central Advisory Commission between 1988 and 1992, one of the most influential leaders of China known as 'the Eight Elders' during the 1980s and 1990s. See People's Daily Online (2014), 'Mozhe Shitou Guohe Gaige Fangfa de Lailongqumai' [The Origin of "Crossing the River by Feeling each Stone"]. Online. Available at: http://dangshi.people.com.cn/n/2014/0409/c85037-24858259.html.

28 Chris Bramall (2009), *Chinese Economic Development*, Abingdon: Routledge, p. 331.
29 Naughton (1995), op. cit., p. 76.
30 Gong Gang (2012), *Contemporary Chinese Economy*, Abingdon: Routledge, p. 30.
31 Linda Yueh (2010), *The Economy of China*, Cheltenham: Edward Elgar, p. 49.
32 Yiping Huang, (2001), *China's Last Steps across the River: Enterprise and Banking Reforms*, Canberra: Asia Pacific Press, p. 57.
33 Stephen Green and Guy Liu (2005), 'China's Industrial Reform Strategy: Retreat and Retain' in Stephen Green and Guy Liu (eds), *Exit the Dragon? Privatisation and State Control in China*, Oxford: Blackwell, p. 15.
34 Statistically, the dominance of SOEs in the Chinese economy has been diminishing from accounting for 76 per cent of annual gross industrial output in 1980 to only around 15 per cent in 2006. However, in some public utility industries including water, electricity, thermal energy and fuel, the market share of SOEs still exceeds 50 per cent in order to protect public interests. See Sanlin Jin and Yuanyuan Wei (2006), 'Extent of Government Ownership or Control of the Means of Production and Enterprises' in Xiaoxi Li (ed.), *Assessing the Extent of China's Marketisation*, Aldershot: Ashgate, pp. 239–242.
35 Justin Lin *et al.* (2003), *The China Miracle: Development Strategy and Economic Reform*, Hong Kong: Chinese University Press, p. 57.
36 Green and Liu (2005), op. cit., p. 17.
37 See for example, Bernard Black *et al.* (2000), 'Russian Privatisation and Corporate Governance: What Went Wrong?' in *Stanford Law Review*, **52** and Lan Cao (1995), 'The Cat that Catches Mice: China's Challenge to the Dominant Privatisation Model' in *Brooklyn Journal of International Law*, **21**.
38 For more about the non-tradable shares reform, see Horace Yeung (2009), 'Non-tradable Share Reform in China: A Review of Progress' in *Company Lawyer*, **30**.
39 People's Daily Online (2017), 'Guoqi Hungai Dayou Kandian' [Highlight of Mixed SOE Reform]. Online. Available at http://paper.people.com.cn/rmrbhwb/html/2017-03/09/content_1755936.htm. Of these SOEs, 338 were listed companies. This can be contrasted with a 2005 survey, when it was revealed that out of 835 companies listed on the Shanghai Stock Exchange at the end of 2005, 662 had state shares, accounting for 50.8 per cent of the total shares. Shanghai Stock Exchange (2006), *Corporate Governance Report* 2006, Shanghai: Fudan University Press, p. 28.
40 Jianfu Chen (1993), 'Securitisation of State-owned Enterprises and the Ownership Controversy in the PRC' in *Sydney Law Review*, **15**, p. 60.
41 Jean Chen (2005), 'Corporatisation of China's State-owned Enterprises and Corporate Governance' in David Brown and Alasdair MacBean (eds.), *Challenges for China's Development – An Enterprise Perspective*, Abingdon: Routledge, p. 60. In November 1993, the Chinese Communist Party put forward the concept of 'modern corporate framework', emphasising the separation of ownership and management and encouraging the development of diverse ownership structures.
42 Chen (1993), op. cit., p. 65.
43 Economist (2017), 'Reform of China's Ailing State-owned Firms is Emboldening Them'. Online. Available: www.economist.com/news/finance-and-economics/21725293-outperformed-private-firms-they-are-no-longer-shrinking-share-overall.
44 Ibid.
45 Scott Cendrowski (2015), 'China's Global 500 Companies are Bigger than Ever – and Mostly State-owned' in *Fortune* (22 July 2015).
46 Scott Cendrowski (2017), 'Tencent Just Passed Wells Fargo as the World's 10th Biggest Company' in *Fortune* (6 April 2017).
47 Nicole Bullock (2014), 'Alibaba IPO Hits Record $25bn' in *Financial Times* (22 September 2014).
48 World Bank (2013), op. cit., pp. 4–6.

49 Chi Keung Leung (1986) 'Spatial Redeployment and the Special Economic Zones in China: An Overview' in Y.C. Jao and Chi Keung Leung (eds), *China's Special Economic Zones*, Hong Kong: OUP, p. 10.
50 Mee Kam Ng (2003), 'City Profile: Shenzhen' in *Cities*, **20**.
51 See Ng (2003), op. cit., p. 430 for the GDP data of Hong Kong. The data for Shenzhen came from Marco Di Tommaso *et al.* (2012), *Southern China: Industry, Development and Industrial Policy*, Abingdon: Routledge, p. 67. In 2013, the GDP per capita for two cities were HK$295,701 (up 1,179 per cent) and RMB136,947 (up 22,599 per cent) respectively. The 2013 data came from the Census and Statistics Department of Hong Kong and the Statistics Bureau of Shenzhen.
52 Data from Di Tommaso *et al.* (2012), op. cit., p. 66 and the Statistics Bureau of Shenzhen.
53 Data from the Statistics Bureau of Shenzhen Municipality.
54 Yin-Wang Kwok (1986), 'Structure and Policies in Industrial Planning in the Shenzhen Special Economic Zone' in Y.C. Jao and Chi Keung Leung (eds), *China's Special Economic Zones*, Hong Kong: OUP, p. 40.
55 Sonoko Nishitateno (1983), 'China's Special Economic Zones: Experimental Units for Economic Reform' in *International and Comparative Law Quarterly*, **32**, p. 177.
56 The law was adopted by the Second Session of the Fifth National People's Congress on 1 July 1979 and became effective on 6 July.
57 Ronald Coase and Ning Wang (2012), *How China Became Capitalist*, Basingstoke: Palgrave Macmillan, p. 62.
58 SEZ Regulations, arts. 9–10.
59 SEZ Regulations, Chapter III.
60 SEZ Regulations, Chapter IV.
61 SEZ Regulations, art. 4.
62 Ann Fenwick (1984), 'Evaluating China's Special Economic Zones' in *International Tax and Business Lawyer*, **2**, p. 381.
63 SEZ Regulations, art. 2.
64 SEZ Regulations, art. 3. The functions and powers of the Committee were stipulated in Article 23.
65 SEZ Regulations, art. 7.
66 SEZ Regulations, art. 14 and Nishitateno (1983), op. cit., pp. 178–179.
67 SEZ Regulations. art. 13.
68 SEZ Regulations. art. 15.
69 SEZ Regulations. arts. 21–22.
70 Nishitateno (1983), op. cit., p. 178.
71 Fenwick (1984), op. cit., p. 384.
72 Ibid. p. 386. These regulations were *Provisional Entry/Exit Regulations (Guangdong Special Economic Zones)*; *Provisional Regulations for Business Registration (Guangdong Special Economic Zones)*; *Provisional Labour and Wage Regulations (Guangdong Special Economic Zones)*; and *Provisional Land Regulations for Shenzhen Special Economic Zone*.
73 Yue-man Yeung *et al.* (2009), 'China's Special Economic Zones at 30' in *Eurasian Geography and Economics*, **50**, p. 224.
74 Ibid.
75 These cities were: Dalian, Qinhuangdao, Tianjin, Yantai, Qingdao, Lianyungang, Nantong, Shanghai, Ningbo, Wenzhou, Fuzhou, Guangzhou, Zhanjiang and Beihai.
76 Yeung *et al.* (2009), op. cit., p. 225. The comparable annual growth rates during the same period were 32 per cent, 9 per cent and 13 per cent for Zhuhai, Shantou and Xiamen respectively. Over the same period, China as a whole expanded 1.5 times, 3 times for Zhuhai, 1.4 for Shantou, and 1.6 for Xiamen.
77 Wei Ge (1999), 'Special Economic Zones and the Opening of the Chinese Economy: Some Lessons for Economic Liberalization' in *World Development*, **27**, p. 1272.

78 For example, as early as 1985, Shenzhen's output of television sets and radio-cassette recorders accounted for one-sixth and one-third, respectively, of the national total. See Yeung *et al.* (2009), op. cit., pp. 229–230.
79 Xie Wei (2000), 'Acquisition of Technological Capability through Special Economic Zones (SEZS): The Case of Shenzhen SEZ' in *Industry and Innovation*, **7**, p. 203.
80 According to Gartner, a leading technology research and consulting company, among the top ten best-selling mobile phone companies in 2013, ZTE and Huawei were ranked the fifth and sixth respectively, behind Samsung, Nokia, Apple and LG Electronics. Indeed, there were three more Chinese companies on the top ten list, including TCL Communication, Lenovo and Yulong. See Gartner (2014), 'Market Share Analysis: Mobile Phones, Worldwide, 4Q13 and 2013'. Online. Available at: www.gartner.com/doc/2665319. Tencent is now the fourth largest internet company behind Google, Amazon and Ebay in terms of market capitalisation. Internet companies refer to those that conduct the majority of its business on the internet. See BBC (2014), 'Tencent and Alibaba Battle for Internet Dominance in China'. Online. Available at: www.bbc.co.uk/news/business-26540666. Foxconn is the world's largest contract manufacturer, known for assembling famous electronic goods like Apple's iPhone and iPad. Its Shenzhen Longhua campus, covering 2.5 square kilometres, employed 240,000 people. See Economist (2012), 'When Workers Dream of a Life beyond the Factory Gates'. Online. Available at: www.economist.com/news/business/21568384-can-foxconn-worlds-largest-contract-manufacturer-keep-growing-and-improve-its-margins-now.
81 International Data Corporation (2017), 'Smartphone Vendor Market Share, 2017 Q1'. Online. Available at www.idc.com/promo/smartphone-market-share/vendor.
82 Barron's (2016), 'Tencent Surges To Become Asia's Largest Company By Market Cap'. Online. Available at: www.barrons.com/articles/tencent-surges-to-become-asias-largest-company-in-market-cap-1473059889.
83 Coase and Wang (2012), op. cit., p. 116.
84 People's Daily Online (1992) 'Excerpts from Talks Given in Wuchang, Shenzhen, Zhuhai and Shanghai'. Online. Available at http://english.peopledaily.com.cn/dengxp/vol. 3/text/d1200.html.
85 Weiping Wu (1999), 'City Profile: Shanghai' in *Cities*, **16**, p. 207.
86 Robin Brayshaw and Z. Teng (1995), 'Re-emergence of the Chinese Stock Market' in John Blake and Simon Gao (eds), *Perspectives on Accounting and Finance in China*, Abingdon: Routledge, p. 93.
87 Wu (1999), op. cit., p. 208.
88 Data from the Statistics Bureau of Shanghai.
89 Yehua Wei and Chi Kin Leung (2005), 'Development Zones, Foreign Investment, and Global City Formation in Shanghai' in *Growth and Change*, **36**, p. 20.
90 Bin Xue Sang (1993), 'Pudong: Another Special Economic Zone in China? An Analysis of the Special Regulations and Policy for Shanghai's Pudong New Area' in *Northwestern Journal of International Law and Business*, **14**, p. 136. The official approval came two years later in 1992.
91 Refer to the discussions of the SEZ Regulations above.
92 Wei and Leung (2005), op. cit., p. 26.
93 Le-Yin Zhang (2003), 'Economic Development in Shanghai and the Role of the State' in *Urban Studies*, **40**, p. 1557.
94 Pudong Regulations, art. 7.
95 Ibid.
96 China Securities Regulatory Commission (2008), *China Capital Markets Development Report*, Beijing: China Financial Publishing, p. 158. On 14 November 1986, Deng Xiaoping met a New York Stock Exchange delegation and especially gave them a share of Shanghai Feile Audio Equipment Company as a gift.

97 Ibid. p. 170. From a legal perspective, A-shares issued by Chinese companies that are listed and traded in the Shanghai or Shenzhen Stock Exchanges can only be sold to and held by Chinese investors. See the *Standard Opinion for Companies Limited by Shares*, an early version of China's company law, which outlined the nature of different types of shares. An exception to this will be those under the Qualified Foreign Institutional Investors scheme. The scheme, launched in 2003, allows licensed foreign investors to buy and sell RMB-denominated A-shares in Chinese stock exchanges (in Shanghai and Shenzhen). The Chinese stock market remains largely closed off to foreign investors owing to China's exercise of tight capital controls which restrict the movement of assets in-and-out of the country.

98 Jamil Anderlini (2010), 'AgBank IPO Officially the World's Biggest' in *Financial Times* (13 August 2010).

99 The top 5 are: New York Stock Exchange, NASDAQ, Tokyo Stock Exchange, Shanghai Stock Exchange and London Stock Exchange, according to market capitalisation. Data from the World Federation of Exchanges, as of June 2017.

100 Shahid Yusuf and Weiping Wu (2002), 'Pathways to a World City: Shanghai Rising in an Era of Globalisation' in *Urban Studies*, **39**, pp. 1226–1227.

101 Wei and Leung (2005), op. cit., p. 23.

102 Previous attempts to put the law-growth nexus into the context of China include: Franklin Allen *et al.* (2005), 'Law, Finance, and Economic Growth in China' in *Journal of Financial Economics*, **77**; Kenneth Dam (2006), *The Law-Growth Nexus*, Washington D.C.: Brookings Institution, pp. 232–278; Horace Yeung and Flora Huang (2013), 'Growth without Institutions? The Case of China' in *Durham Law Review*, **3**; and Ding Chen and Simon Deakin, (2015), 'On Heaven's Lathe: State, Rule of Law, and Economic Development' in *Law and Development Review*, **8**.

103 Stanley Lubman (1999) *Bird in a Cage: Legal Reform in China after Mao*, Stanford: Stanford University, p. 174.

104 The law was enacted by the National People's Congress in 1988.

105 The 2005 amendments enhanced shareholder rights in a number of aspects. See Flora Huang (2010), 'Modernising the Chinese Capital Market: Old Problems and New Legal Responses' in *International Company and Commercial Law Review*, **21**. The recent company law amendments in 2013 removed the requirement for companies to have a minimum level of capitalisation. It is expected to encourage more entrepreneurs to start their own businesses fostering the growth of the individual economic sector. See PwC China (2014), 'China's Amended Company Law Facilitating More Business'. Online. Available at www.pwccn.com/home/eng/chinatax_news_jan2014_1.html.

106 See Robert Art and Minkang Gu, (1995) 'China Incorporated: the First Corporation Law of the People's Republic of China' in *Yale Journal of International Law*, **20**, pp. 273–274.

107 See art. 1 of the Company Law 2005.

108 Until the first set of securities laws came into effect in 1999, the Company Law had been supplemented by the *Interim Regulations on Share Issuing and Trading*, issued in May 1993 by the State Council Securities Committee, to help regulate the stock market. The Chinese Securities Law was adopted by the Standing Committee of the National People's Congress on 29 December 1998, effective as of 1 July 1999, amended on 28 August 2004 and revised 27 October 2005, effective as of 1 January 2006. The law was amended for the second time in 2013 and third time in 2014. The current version is the Securities Law 2014.

109 The Labour Law of China was adopted on 5 July 1994 and came into effect on 1 January 1995. In a decade since then, not much has been done to protect labour rights. A breakthrough came when the Labour Contract Law was adopted on 29 June 2007 and came into force on 1 January 2008. This was amended in 2013. The

Property Law was adopted by the National People's Congress in 2007 and came into effect on 1 October.

110 For example, Lubman criticised that Chinese legal reform tended to use numerous general terms to express vague legal standards. See Lubman (1999), op. cit., p. 186. As briefly mentioned in the previous chapter, China is now amongst the top performers of shareholder protection, see Dionysia Katelouzou and Mathias Siems (2015), 'Disappearing Paradigms in Shareholder Protection: Leximetric Evidence for 30 Countries, 1990–2013' in *Journal of Corporate Law Studies*, **15**. But laws-in-action can remain an issue. For example, Yeung expressed his concerns over the quality of Chinese judges and legal profession. See Horace Yeung (2014), 'Transferability of English Legal Concepts and Skills in China with respect to Corporate Regulation' in Georges Depeyrot (ed.), *When Orient and Occident Meet*, Wetteren: Moneta, pp. 347–348.

111 Company Law 2013, art. 163.

112 Ibid. art. 164.

113 Securities Law 2014, art. 66.

114 Ibid. art. 63.

115 The Code is applicable to all listed companies within the boundary of China. The requirements of the Code must be followed when listed companies formulate or amend their articles of association or rules of governance.

116 Company Law 2013, art. 147.

117 Company Law 2013, art. 124.

118 Prohibited trading behaviour is stipulated in Chapter III Section IV of the Securities Law.

119 Company Law 1993, art. 59.

120 Ibid. art. 61.

121 Company Law 2005, art. 148; Company Law 2013, art. 147.

122 Minkang Gu (2006), *Understanding Chinese Company Law*, Hong Kong: Hong Kong University Press, p. 120. Nevertheless, it was still possible to identify a few of them in the law. For example, shareholders were required to respect and comply with the articles of association, see Company Law 1993, art. 11. Also, they had the duty to pay capital contributions and not to withdraw their investment after a company is established, see Company Law 1993, arts. 25 and 34.

123 Company Law 2005, art. 21; Company Law 2013, art. 21. Controlling shareholders are those holding half or more of shares or the equivalent voting powers.

124 Jian Fu and Jie Yuan (2006), *PRC Company and Securities Laws: A Practical Guide*, Singapore: CCH, p. 548.

125 Company Law 2005, art. 75; Company Law 2013, art. 74. The circumstances include: (1) the company's resolution not to distribute profits to its shareholders for five consecutive years despite the company being profitable for those five years; (2) a merger or split of the company or transfer of the major assets of the company, or (3) renewal of the company's operation term after its expiration or events triggering dissolution.

126 Company Law 1993, arts. 32 and 110. The law only specifies three types of documents: (1) the articles of association; (2) the minutes of shareholders' meetings; and (3) the financial statements.

127 Company Law 2005, art. 151; Company Law 2013, art. 150.

128 Company Law 2005, art. 103; Company Law 2013, art. 102.

129 Ibid.

130 Company Law 2005, art. 106; Company Law 2013, art. 105.

131 Chao Xi and Yugang Chen (2014), 'Does Cumulative Voting Matter? The Case of China: An Empirical Assessment' in *European Business Organization Law Review*, **15**.

132 Company Law 1993, art. 74.

133 Jian Fu and Jie Yuan (2006), *PRC Company and Securities Laws: A Practical Guide*, Singapore: CCH, p. 70.
134 Company Law 2005, art. 78; Company Law 2013, art. 77.
135 Eric Orts (2001), 'The Rule of Law in China' in *Vanderbilt Journal of Transnational Law*, **34**, p. 94.
136 Roman Tomasic (1995), 'Company Law and the Limits of the Rule of Law in China' in *Australian Journal of Corporate Law*, **4**, p. 473. According to Article 19 of the Company Law 1993, a company must provide the necessary conditions for the establishment of the organisation of the Communist Party of China and the carrying out of party activities within a company.
137 Curtis Milhaupt and Katharina Pistor (2008), *Law and Capitalism*, Chicago: University of Chicago Press, p. 142.
138 Iain MacNeil (2002), 'Adaptation and Convergence in Corporate Governance: The Case of Chinese Listed Companies' in *Journal of Corporate Law Studies*, **2**, p. 302.
139 For the importance of legal enforcement, see John Coffee (2007), 'Law and the Market: The Impact of Enforcement' in *University of Pennsylvania Law Review*, **156**.
140 Roman Tomasic and Jane Fu (2005), 'Regulation and Corporate Governance of China's Top 100 Listed Companies: Whither the Rule of Law' Research Committee on the Sociology of Law Conference Paper. Online. Available at: https://papers.ssrn.com/sol3/papers.cfm?abstract_id=2712610.
141 Zhiwu Chen (2003), 'Capital Markets and Legal Development: The China Case' in *China Economic Review*, **14**, p. 454.
142 See Chapter XI of the Securities Law 2014.
143 See for example, arts. 20 (for abuse of shareholder's rights) and 152 (derivative suit) of the Company Law 2005 and art. 69 of the Securities Law 2005 (for civil liability of false recording, misleading statement and material omission made by issuers and securities companies).
144 Katharina Pistor and Chenggang Xu (2005), 'Governing Stock Markets in Transition Economies: Lessons from China' in *American Law and Economics Review*, **7**, p. 191.
145 Securities Law 2014, art. 178.
146 Ibid. art. 179(1).
147 Ibid. art. 179(2).
148 Ibid. arts. 179(3) and 179(4).
149 Ibid. art. 179(7).
150 Benjamin Liebman and Curtis Milhaupt (2008), 'Reputational Sanctions in China's Securities Market' in *Columbia Law and Review*, **108**.
151 For a list of possible legal liabilities arising from securities market crimes and the resulting penalties, see Chapter XI of the Securities Law 2014.
152 Chen (2003), op. cit., p. 461.
153 In this case, the DaMing Group (a listed company of ShengLi YouTian), and the underwriter firm, accounting and auditing firm, and law firm that each provided service to facilitate the IPO of the DaMing Group were prosecuted by the CSRC for misrepresentation of the listed company's outstanding share structure, omitting material facts, and false statements in its IPO Prospectus.
154 See, for example, Howell Jackson and Mark Roe (2009), 'Public and Private Enforcement of Securities Laws: Resource-based Evidence' in *Journal of Financial Economics*, **93**.
155 As of 2016, CSRC has signed 63 MOUs with securities and/or futures regulators from 58 countries or regions. The MOUs facilitate information exchange, cross-border assistance and dialogue on policies and regulation.
156 Gongmeng Chen *et al.* (2005), 'Is China's Securities Regulatory Agency a Toothless Tiger? Evidence from Enforcement Actions' in *Journal of Accounting and Public Policy*, **24**.
157 Tomasic and Fu (2005), op. cit., p. 24.

158 Flora Huang (2010), 'In Defence of China's Public Enforcement in Equity Market' in *International Company and Commercial Law Review*, **21**, pp. 333.
159 Wenming Xu *et al.* (2017), 'An Empirical Analysis of the Public Enforcement of Securities Law in China: Finding the Missing Piece of the Puzzle' in *European Business Organization Law Review*, **18**.
160 Katharina Pistor and Chenggang Xu (2005a), 'Governing Emerging Stock Markets: Legal vs Administrative Governance' in *Corporate Governance*, **13**, p. 8.
161 Coffee (2007), op. cit., p. 269.
162 Chen *et al.* (2005), p. 466.
163 This report appeared briefly on 16 July on the official website of the SZSE before being removed. An anonymous source at the SZSE told Caijing that exchange officials had asked the web manager to remove the report that night because 'further review is needed about the content, and it will be published in the future when the timing is right'. See Zhou Huan and Cao Zhen (2008), 'Shenzhen Bourse Report Blasts Regulators' in *Caijing Magazine* (18 July 2008).
164 Ibid. The report said the CSRC had expanded its jurisdiction with little oversight, and oversaw a wide range of issues including professional standards, business approvals, IPO regulation, and investor education. Meanwhile, CSRC gave itself the right to make rules and supervise the nation's bourses, and assumed a bailout role during market troubles.
165 Wenming Xu *et al.* (2017), op. cit.
166 There has been a debate on the relationship between enforcement intensity and market competitiveness. The Securities and Exchange Commission of the US and the Financial Services Authority of the UK have different regulatory philosophy, but both markets are successful. The former has taken a more proactive approach while the latter has had a more laid-back approach. Ferran has tried to explain the difference by suggesting that a successful principle-based regulatory strategy that relies heavily on *ex ante* compliance may be capable of producing the desired deterrent effect. See Eilis Ferran (2008), 'Capital Market Competitiveness and Enforcement' Working Paper. Online. Available at: http://ssrn.com/abstract=1127245.
167 Pistor and Xu (2005), op. cit., p. 195.
168 Ibid.
169 Ibid. There were 6,159 listed companies and the number of enforcement actions was 679.
170 Myners recognised the highly-developed equity culture and the professionalisation of investment in the UK as 'key national assets', see Paul Myners (2001), 'Institutional Investment in the United Kingdom: A Review' Report to HM Treasury. Online. Available at: http://archive.treasury.gov.uk/pdf/2001/myners_report.pdf. See also John Armour (2009), 'Enforcement Strategies in UK Corporate Governance: A Roadmap and Empirical Assessment' in John Armour and Jennifer Payne (eds.), *Rationality in Company Law*, Oxford: Hart, p. 71, for a comprehensive assessment of the UK's enforcement strategies.
171 Wenming Xu *et al.* (2017), op. cit.
172 Zhong Zhang (2007), 'Legal Deterrence: the Foundation of Corporate Governance – Evidence from China' in *Corporate Governance: An International Review*, **15**, p. 756. Zhang believed that the old Company Law had not clearly conferred on shareholders the standing to bring derivative actions. Also, shareholders' right to take on private securities action was substantially restricted by the court system. Pistor and Xu shared similar opinion that private enforcement of securities cases have virtually been absent in China. See Pistor and Xu (2005), op. cit., p. 191.
173 Dam (2006), op. cit., p. 236.
174 Craig Andersen and Bingna Guo (2006), 'Corporate Governance under the New Company Law (Part 2): Shareholder Lawsuits and Enforcement' in *China Law and Practice* (May 2006).

175 Under the provision, a shareholder or a group of shareholders holding one per cent or more of shares in the company for 180 consecutive days may submit a request in writing to the board of directors or board of supervisors to file a lawsuit with a people's court. The law further provides that if the request is refused or the circumstances are urgent, the shareholders shall have the right to file a lawsuit directly in their own name to protect the interests of the company.

176 Naomi Li (2004), 'Civil Litigation against China's Listed Firms: Much Ado about Nothing?' Royal Institute of International Affairs: Asia Programme Working Paper No. 13. Online. Available at: www.chathamhouse.org/sites/files/chathamhouse/public/General/wpfeb04.pdf. According to Article 77 of the *Provisional Regulations on the Administration of Issuing and Trading of Stocks*, the responsible directors, supervisors and/or managers of the issuer or distributing securities company would be jointly and severally liable for any damages arising from false representation in the course of securities trading (art. 63 of the Securities Law 1998 and art. 69 of the Securities Law 2005 and 2014).

177 Ibid.

178 Located in Ningxia province, Guangxia was listed on the SZSE in 1994 as a manufacturer of floppy disks and related products. After experiencing poor and deteriorating performance for the first five years, the company reported unprecedented high earnings per share. Consequently, the company' share price shot up from RMB14 to RMB76 in one year. Later, Caijing Magazine played the role as a whistle blower and the CSRC launched an investigation. It turned out that the reported earnings as well as many sales records and contracts were fabricated. See Franklin Allen *et al.* (2008), 'China's Financial System: Past, Present, and Future' in Loren Brandt and Tom Rawski (eds.), *China's Great Economic Transformation*, Cambridge: CUP.

179 Pistor and Xu (2005), op. cit., p. 192.

180 Chen (2003), op. cit.,p. 464.

181 *Notice Concerning Temporarily Not Accepting Civil Compensation Cases Related to Securities* (issued by the Supreme People's Court on 21 September 2001).

182 *Several Regulations Concerning the Adjudication of Civil Compensation Securities Cases Based upon Misrepresentation* (issued by the Supreme's People's Court on 9 January 2003).

183 Sanzhu Zhu (2005), 'Civil Litigation Arising from False Statements on China's Securities Market' in *North Carolina Journal of International Law and Commercial Regulation*, **31**, pp. 381–382. For example, art. 63 of the Securities Law 1998 expressly mentioned civil liability and compensation of losses caused by false statement and art. 17 of the 2003 circular specifies that a false statement on the securities market is defined as a false recording, misleading statement, material omission or improper disclosure.

184 Li (2004), op. cit., p. 4.

185 Walter Hutchens (2003), 'Private Securities Litigation in China: Material Disclosure about China's Legal System?' in *University of Pennsylvania Journal of International Economic Law*, **24**, p. 600.

186 Li (2004), op. cit., p. 10.

187 Ibid.

188 Hutchens (2003), op. cit., p. 621.

189 Hui Huang (2013), 'Private Enforcement of Securities Law in China: A Ten-Year Retrospective and Empirical Assessment' in *American Journal of Comparative Law*, **61**.

190 Stanley Lubman (1991), 'Studying Contemporary Chinese Law: Limits, Possibilities and Strategy' in *American Journal of Comparative Law*, **39**, p. 318.

191 Hu's own explanation of his idea during a trip to Jiangxi, as quoted in Joseph Fewsmith (2004), 'Promoting the Scientific Development Concept' in *China Leadership Monitor*, **11**.

192 Jinping Xi (2013), 'Haobu Dongyao Jianchi he Fazhan Zhongguotese Shehuizhuyi' [Unswervingly Adhere to and Develop Socialism with Chinese Characteristics] in *People's Daily* (19 February 2013). Online. Available at: http://theory.people.com.cn/n/2013/0219/c352499-20529681.html.
193 BBC (2013), 'What does Xi Jinping's China Dream Mean?'. Online. Available at: www.bbc.co.uk/news/world-asia-china-22726375.
194 Coase and Wang (2012), op. cit., p. 96.
195 Speech made by Deng Xiaoping on his Southern Excursion in 1992. See China Securities Regulatory Commission (2008), op. cit., p. 161.
196 Based on this theory, the socialist system will evolve into four phases: from capitalism to the primary stage of socialism, then to the advanced stage of socialism and finally to communism. See Yebi Hu (1993), *China's Capital Market*, Hong Kong: Chinese University Press, p. 67.
197 Constitution of China, art. 6. In 1988, an amendment of the constitution expressly authorised the development of a private economy. See art. 11 of the Constitution, which provides the following: 'The state permits the private sector of the economy to exist and developing within the limits prescribed by law. The private sector of the economy is a complement to the socialist public economy.'.
198 Ken Moak and Miles Lee (2015), 'Deng Xiaoping Theory' in Ken Moak *et al.* (eds), *China's Economic Rise and Its Global Impact*, New York: Palgrave Macmillan, p. 91.
199 Ibid.
200 James Wang (2002), 'Chen Yun' in Edwin Leung (ed.), *Political Leaders of Modern China: A Biographical Dictionary*, Santa Barbara: Greenwood, p. 22.
201 Richard Baum (1994), *Burying Mao: Chinese Politics in the Age of Deng Xiaoping*, Princeton: Princeton University Press, p. 4.
202 People's Daily Online (2006), 'Three Represents'. Online. Available at http://english.cpc.people.com.cn/66739/4521344.html.
203 Hepeng Jia (2004), 'The Three Represents Campaign: Reform the Party or Indoctrinate the Capitalists?' in Cato *Journal*, **24**, pp. 264–266.
204 Ibid. pp. 266–267.
205 Ibid. pp. 267–268.
206 Joseph Fewsmith (2003), 'Studying the Three Represents' in *China Leadership Monitor*, **8**.
207 The ideas are getting closer to reality, the masses, and life.
208 Yongnian Zheng and Sow Keat Tok (2007), '"Harmonious Society" and "Harmonious World": China's Policy Discourse under Hu Jintao' University of Nottingham China Policy Institute Briefing Series Issue 26. Online. Available at: https://nottingham.ac.uk/cpi/documents/briefings/briefing-26-harmonious-society-and-harmonious-world.pdf.
209 Ibid. para. 3.2.
210 Fewsmith (2004), op. cit.
211 Constitution of China, art. 57.
212 BBC (2012), 'How China is Ruled: National People's Congress'. Online. Available at: www.bbc.co.uk/news/world-asia-pacific-13908155.
213 Ibid.
214 BBC (2012), 'How China is Ruled: Politburo'. Online. Available at: www.bbc.co.uk/news/world-asia-pacific-13904441.
215 John Armour *et al.* (2017), 'Transactions with Creditors' in Reinier Kraakman *et al.* (eds*), The Anatomy of Corporate Law: A Comparative and Functional Approach*, Oxford: Oxford University Press.
216 According to the 2016 Corruption Index released by the Transparency International, China was ranked seventy-ninth out of 176 countries. The perceived level of corruption in China remained high.

217 Jacob Harding (2014), 'Corruption or Guanxi? Differentiating Between the Legitimate, Unethical, and Corrupt Activities of Chinese Government Officials' in *Pacific Basin Law Journal*, **31**, pp. 128–129.
218 Transparency International (2017), 'What is Corruption?'. Online. Available at: www.transparency.org/what-is-corruption/#define. See also, Criminal Law, art. 386.
219 Harding (2014), op. cit., p. 130.
220 Max Weber (1964), *The Religion of China: Confucianism and Taoism*, New York: Macmillan.
221 Weiming Tu (2017), 'Confucianism' in *Encyclopedia Britannica*. Online. Available at: www.britannica.com/topic/Confucianism.
222 Shaohua Hu (2007), 'Confucianism and Contemporary Chinese Politics' in *Politics and Policy*, **35**, p. 136.
223 Xiao-Ping Chen and Chao Chen (2004), 'On the Intricacies of the Chinese Guanxi: A Process Model of Guanxi Development' in *Asia Pacific Journal of Management*, **21**, pp. 307–308.
224 Harding (2014), op. cit., p. 131.
225 Mayfair Yang (1994), *Gifts, Favors and Banquets: The Art of Social Relationships in China*, Ithaca: Cornell University Press.
226 Lisa Keister (2004), 'Guanxi in Business Groups: Social Ties and the Formation of Economic Relations' in Thomas Gold *et al.* (eds), *Social Connections in China Institutions, Culture, and the Changing Nature of Guanxi*, Cambridge: CUP, p. 82.
227 Wai Keung Chung and Gary Hamilton (2001), 'Social Logic as Business Logic: Guanxi, Trustworthiness and the Embeddedness of Chinese Business Practices' in Richard Appelbaum *et al.* (eds), *Rules and Networks: The Legal Culture of Global Business Transactions*, Oxford: Hart, pp. 337–339.
228 Ibid. pp. 339–340.
229 Liebman and Milhaupt (2008), op. cit.
230 Pitman Potter (2004), 'Guanxi and the PRC Legal System: From Contradiction to Complementarity' in Thomas Gold *et al.* (eds), *Social Connections in China Institutions, Culture, and the Changing Nature of Guanxi*, Cambridge: CUP, p. 180.
231 Thomas Dunfee and Danielle Warren (2001), 'Is Guanxi Ethical? A Normative Analysis of Doing Business in China' in *Journal of Business Ethics*, **32**, p. 197.
232 Yadong Luo *et al.* (2012), 'Guanxi and Organizational Performance: A Meta-Analysis' in *Management and Organization Review*, **8**.
233 Ibid. p. 146.
234 Ibid.
235 Harding (2014), op. cit., p. 129.
236 OECD (2013), 'Issues Paper on Corruption and Economic Growth'. Online. Available at: www.oecd.org/g20/topics/anti-corruption/Issue-Paper-Corruption-and-Economic-Growth.pdf.
237 Mee Kam Ng and Wing-Shing Tang (2004), 'The Role of Planning in the Development of Shenzhen, China: Rhetoric and Realities' in *Eurasian Geography and Economics*, **45**, p. 206.
238 In essence, Hong Kong would import the goods manufactured in China and re-export them to the rest of the world. See Dong-Wook Song (2002), 'Regional Container Port Competition and Co-operation: The Case of Hong Kong and South China' in *Journal of Transport Geography*, **10**, p. 100.
239 Alexander McKinnon (2011), 'Hong Kong and Shenzhen Ports: Challenges, Opportunities and Global Competitiveness' Hong Kong Centre for Maritime and Transportation Law Working Paper. Online. Available at: www.cityu.edu.hk/slw/HKCMT/Doc/Working_Paper_3_-_Shenzhen_-_Final_(v6).pdf.
240 Zhang (2003), op. cit., p. 1554.
241 Before 1983, Shanghai was essentially a domestic economy and had little direct trade with the outside world except for the former Soviet Union. Occasional trade

was handled through Hong Kong. See James Wang and Brian Slack (2004), 'Regional Governance of Port Development in China: A Case Study of Shanghai International Shipping Center' in *Maritime Policy and Management*, **31**, p. 362.

242 World Shipping Council (2017), 'Top 50 World Container Ports 2015'. Online. Available at: www.worldshipping.org/about-the-industry/global-trade/top-50-world-container-ports.

243 See for example, the charts of bank credit and stock market capitalisation to GDP of selected economies in Alan Winters and Shahid Yusuf (2007), *Dancing with Giants: China, India, and the Global Economy*, Washington D.C.: World Bank, p. 114.

244 World Bank (2013), op. cit., p. 116.

245 McKinsey Global Institute (2006), 'Putting China's Capital to Work: The Value of Financial System Reform'. Online. Available at: www.mckinsey.com/mgi/publications.

246 China Securities Regulatory Commission (2008), op. cit., p. 156.

247 Ibid. p. 160.

248 These were introduced in May 1990 and included: banning illegal off-floor trading; imposing a 0.5 per cent stamp duty on both sellers and buyers; setting a daily price change ceiling and floor limits of 10 per cent; increasing the number of branches; and enhancing the disclosure of market information and the provision of proper guidance to the public. Later, in May 1991, the Government introduced the *Provisional Measures of Shenzhen Municipality for Administration of the Issuance and Trading of Shares* and subsequently in January 1992, the *Provisional Regulations of Shenzhen Municipality Concerning Joint Stock Limited Companies*. See ibid. p. 161.

249 See ibid. p. 160.

250 The two bodies were set up to oversee the securities market on behalf of the State Council. The SCSC was composed of the heads of ministries and commissions such as the State Commission for Restructuring and Economic Reform, the State Planning Commission, the Ministry of Finance, and the People's Bank of China. It was responsible for higher level oversight for securities market to develop long-term strategies, draft relevant laws, rules and regulations, and coordinate different levels of government. On the other hand, the CSRC was responsible for frontline regulation by supervising the trading activities, securities firms, and listed companies. In April 1998, the two were consolidated into one regulator, the CSRC.

251 For the full story, see Horace Yeung (2010), 'Just Another Casino? The Case of Launching the Growth Enterprise Board in China' in *International Company and Commercial Law Review*, **21**.

252 Data from the World Federation of Exchanges.

253 Z/Yen Group (2014), 'The Global Financial Centres Index 15'. Online. Available at: www.zyen.com/research/gfci.html.

254 According to the World Bank, smaller businesses which contributed some 60 per cent of China's GDP, accounted for only 15 per cent of outstanding credit, most of which from banks. This showed that the financial market could have allocated resources more fairly. See World Bank (2008), *Doing Business in China* Washington D.C.: World Bank, p. 18.

255 Embassy of the United States in Beijing (2016), 'Intellectual Property Rights'. Online. Available at: http://beijing.usembassy-china.org.cn/protecting_ipr.html.

256 Scott Cendrowski (2015), 'Tencent Turns Venture Capitalist to Conquer China's Digital Wallet' in *Fortune* (22 July 2015), and BBC (2016), 'Xiaomi: Has the "Apple of the East" lost its shine?'. Online. Available at: www.bbc.co.uk/news/business-37175056.

257 Jamil Anderlini and Rahul Jacob (2011), 'Global Decline Drags Down Chinese Factories' in *Financial Times* (1 December 2011).

258 Sky Canaves (2009), 'Factory Closures Strain China's Labour Law' in *Wall Street Journal* (17 January 2009).

259 Yuan Li (2016), 'How Shenzhen Mimics Silicon Valley' in *Wall Street Journal* (1 June 2016).

260 The *Opinions of the State Council on Promoting the Development of Shanghai's Modern Service Industry and Advanced Manufacturing Industry, and Promoting the Construction of Shanghai International Financial Centre and International Shipping Centre* were issued on 14 April 2009.

261 Ying Wang (2011), 'Shanghai to Develop Bonded Areas into FTZ' in *China Daily* (12 November 2011).

262 American Chamber of Commerce in Shanghai (2013) 'Navigating the FTZ' in *Insight Magazine* (November 2013), p. 26.

263 The English version of this Framework Plan is available from the official website of the FTZ, available at: http://en.shftz.gov.cn/laws/general.

264 Framework Plan, section 1.1. The term 'China Dream' was first used by Xi in November 2012. He used the term numerous times in his first address to the nation as head of state on 17 March 2013. See BBC (2013), op. cit.

265 Framework Plan, section 2.1.

266 Framework Plan, section 2.2. A detailed list of services sectors to open up is contained in the appendix of the Plan. Market access restrictions will be relaxed in most sectors, except in respect of banks, information and communication services.

267 Framework Plan, section 2.3.

268 Framework Plan, section 2.4.

269 Framework Plan, sections 2.5 and 3.2. Certain administrative examination and approval requirements under *Law of the People's Republic of China on Wholly Foreign Owned Enterprises*, and *Law of the People's Republic of China on Sino-Foreign Cooperative Joint Venture Companies* will be temporarily adjusted.

270 Art and Gu (1995), op. cit., p. 280.

References

Allen, Franklin; Qian, Jun; Qian, Meijun (2005), 'Law, Finance, and Economic Growth in China' in *Journal of Financial Economics*, **77**.

Allen, Franklin; Qian, Jun; Qian, Meijun (2008), 'China's Financial System: Past, Present, and Future' in Loren Brandt and Tom Rawski (eds.), *China's Great Economic Transformation*, Cambridge: CUP.

American Chamber of Commerce in Shanghai (2013) 'Navigating the FTZ' in *Insight Magazine* (November 2013).

Anderlini, Jamil (2010), 'AgBank IPO Officially the World's Biggest' in *Financial Times* (13 August 2010).

Anderlini, Jamil and Jacob, Rahul (2011) 'Global Decline Drags Down Chinese Factories' in *Financial Times* (1 December 2011).

Andersen, Craig and Guo, Bingna (2006), 'Corporate Governance under the New Company Law (Part 2): Shareholder Lawsuits and Enforcement' in *China Law and Practice* (May 2006).

Armour, John (2009), 'Enforcement Strategies in UK Corporate Governance: A Roadmap and Empirical Assessment' in John Armour and Jennifer Payne (eds.), *Rationality in Company Law*, Oxford: Hart.

Armour, John; Hertig, Gerard; and Kanda, Hideki (2017), 'Transactions with Creditors' in Reinier Kraakman; John Armour; Paul Davies; Luca Enriques; Henry Hansmann; Gerard Hertig; Klaus Hopt; Hideki Kanda; Mariana Pargendler; Wolf-Georg Ringe; and Edward Rock (eds), *The Anatomy of Corporate Law: A Comparative and Functional Approach*, Oxford: OUP.

Art, Robert and Gu, Minkang (1995) 'China Incorporated: the First Corporation Law of the People's Republic of China' in *Yale Journal of International Law*, **20**.

Bai, Liang (2014), 'Economic Legacies of the Cultural Revolution' LSE Economic History Working Paper. Online. Available at: www.lse.ac.uk/economichistory/seminars/economichistory/papers14-15/cultural-revolution.pdf.

Barron's (2016), 'Tencent Surges To Become Asia's Largest Company By Market Cap'. Online. Available at: www.barrons.com/articles/tencent-surges-to-become-asias-largest-company-in-market-cap-1473059889.

Baum, Richard (1994), *Burying Mao: Chinese Politics in the Age of Deng Xiaoping*, Princeton: Princeton University Press.

BBC (2012), 'How China is Ruled: National People's Congress'. Online. Available at: www.bbc.co.uk/news/world-asia-pacific-13908155.

BBC (2012), 'How China is Ruled: Politburo'. Online. Available at: www.bbc.co.uk/news/world-asia-pacific-13904441.

BBC (2013), 'What does Xi Jinping's China Dream Mean?'. Online. Available at: www.bbc.co.uk/news/world-asia-china-22726375.

BBC (2014), 'Tencent and Alibaba Battle for Internet Dominance in China'. Online. Available at: www.bbc.co.uk/news/business-26540666.

BBC (2016), 'Xiaomi: Has the "Apple of the East" lost its shine?'. Online. Available at: www.bbc.co.uk/news/business-37175056.

Black, Bernard; Kraakman, Reinier; and Tarassova, Anna (2000), 'Russian Privatisation and Corporate Governance: What Went Wrong?' in *Stanford Law Review*, **52**.

Bramall, Chris (2009), *Chinese Economic Development*, Abingdon: Routledge.

Brayshaw, Robin and Teng, Z. (1995), 'Re-emergence of the Chinese Stock Market' in John Blake and Simon Gao (eds), *Perspectives on Accounting and Finance in China*, Abingdon: Routledge.

Bridgham, Philip (1967), 'Mao's "Cultural Revolution": Origin and Development' in *China Quarterly*, **29**.

Bullock, Nicole (2014), 'Alibaba IPO Hits Record $25bn' in *Financial Times* (22 September 2014).

Business Insider (2017), 'These are the 23 Biggest Global Banks – all with more than $1 trillion of assets'. Online. Available at: http://uk.businessinsider.com/the-biggest-banks-in-the-world-2017-4/#22-postal-savings-bank-of-china-china-119-trillion-2.

Canaves, Sky (2009), 'Factory Closures Strain China's Labour Law' in *Wall Street Journal* (17 January 2009).

Cao, Lan (1995), 'The Cat that Catches Mice: China's Challenge to the Dominant Privatisation Model' in *Brooklyn Journal of International Law*, **21**.

Cendrowski, Scott (2015), 'China's Global 500 Companies are Bigger than Ever – and Mostly State-owned' in *Fortune* (22 July 2015).

Cendrowski, Scott (2015), 'Tencent Turns Venture Capitalist to Conquer China's Digital Wallet' in *Fortune* (22 July 2015).

Cendrowski, Scott (2017), 'Tencent Just Passed Wells Fargo as the World's 10th Biggest Company' in *Fortune* (6 April 2017).

Chen, Ding and Deakin, Simon (2015), 'On Heaven's Lathe: State, Rule of Law, and Economic Development' in *Law and Development Review*, **8**.

Chen, Gongmeng; Firth, Michael; Gao, Daniel; and Rui, Oliver (2005), 'Is China's Securities Regulatory Agency a Toothless Tiger? Evidence from Enforcement Actions' in *Journal of Accounting and Public Policy*, **24**.

Chen, Jean (2005), 'Corporatisation of China's State-owned Enterprises and Corporate Governance' in David Brown and Alasdair MacBean (eds.), *Challenges for China's Development – An Enterprise Perspective*, Abingdon: Routledge.

Chen, Jianfu (1993), 'Securitisation of State-owned Enterprises and the Ownership Controversy in the PRC' in *Sydney Law Review*, **15**.

Chen, Xiao-Ping and Chen, Chao (2004), 'On the Intricacies of the Chinese Guanxi: A Process Model of Guanxi Development' in *Asia Pacific Journal of Management*, **21**.

Chen, Zhiwu (2003), 'Capital Markets and Legal Development: The China Case' in *China Economic Review*, **14**.

Cheremukhin, Anton; Golosov, Mikhail; Guriev, Sergei Guriev; and Tsyvinski, Aleh (2015), 'The Economy of People's Republic of China from 1953' CEPR Discussion Paper No. 10764. Online. Available at: http://cepr.org/active/publications/discussion_papers/dp.php?dpno=10764.

China Daily (2017), '115 Chinese Firms on Fortune Global 500 List 2017'. Online. Available at: www.chinadaily.com.cn/business/2017-07/21/content_30202343.htm.

China Securities Regulatory Commission (2008), *China Capital Markets Development Report*, Beijing: China Financial Publishing.

Chung, Wai Keung and Hamilton, Gary (2001), 'Social Logic as Business Logic: Guanxi, Trustworthiness and the Embeddedness of Chinese Business Practices' in Richard Appelbaum; William Felstiner; and Volkmar Gessner (eds), *Rules and Networks: The Legal Culture of Global Business Transactions*, Oxford: Hart.

Coase, Ronald and Wang, Ning (2012), *How China Became Capitalist*, Basingstoke: Palgrave Macmillan.

Coffee, John (2007), 'Law and the Market: The Impact of Enforcement' in *University of Pennsylvania Law Review*, **156**.

Dam, Kenneth (2006), *The Law-Growth Nexus*, Washington D.C.: Brookings Institution.

Di Tommaso, Marco; Rubini, Lauretta; Barbieri, Elisa (2012), *Southern China: Industry, Development and Industrial Policy*, Abingdon: Routledge.

Dunfee, Thomas and Warren, Danielle (2001), 'Is Guanxi Ethical? A Normative Analysis of Doing Business in China' in *Journal of Business Ethics*, **32**.

Economist (2012), 'When Workers Dream of a Life beyond the Factory Gates'. Online. Available at: www.economist.com/news/business/21568384-can-foxconn-worlds-largest-contract-manufacturer-keep-growing-and-improve-its-margins-now.

Economist (2017), 'Reform of China's Ailing State-owned Firms is Emboldening Them'. Online. Available: www.economist.com/news/finance-and-economics/21725293-outperformed-private-firms-they-are-no-longer-shrinking-share-overall.

Embassy of the United States in Beijing (2016), 'Intellectual Property Rights'. Online. Available at: http://beijing.usembassy-china.org.cn/protecting_ipr.html.

Fenwick, Ann (1984), 'Evaluating China's Special Economic Zones' *in International Tax and Business Lawyer*, **2**.

Ferran, Eilis (2008), 'Capital Market Competitiveness and Enforcement' Working Paper. Online. Available at: http://ssrn.com/abstract=1127245.

Fewsmith, Joseph (2003), 'Studying the Three Represents' in *China Leadership Monitor*, **8**.

Fewsmith, Joseph (2004), 'Promoting the Scientific Development Concept' in *China Leadership Monitor*, **11**.

Fu, Jian and Yuan, Jie (2006), *PRC Company and Securities Laws: A Practical Guide*, Singapore: CCH.

Gang, Gong (2012), *Contemporary Chinese Economy*, Abingdon: Routledge.

Gartner (2014), 'Market Share Analysis: Mobile Phones, Worldwide, 4Q13 and 2013'. Online. Available at: www.gartner.com/doc/2665319.

Ge, Wei (1999), 'Special Economic Zones and the Opening of the Chinese Economy: Some Lessons for Economic Liberalization' in *World Development*, **27**.

Green, Stephen and Liu, Guy (2005), 'China's Industrial Reform Strategy: Retreat and Retain' in Stephen Green and Guy Liu (eds), *Exit the Dragon? Privatisation and State Control in China*, Oxford: Blackwell.

Gu, Minkang (2006), *Understanding Chinese Company Law*, Hong Kong: Hong Kong University Press.

Harding, Jacob (2014), 'Corruption or Guanxi? Differentiating Between the Legitimate, Unethical, and Corrupt Activities of Chinese Government Officials' in *Pacific Basin Law Journal*, **31**.

Hu, Yebi (1993), *China's Capital Market*, Hong Kong: Chinese University Press.

Huan, Zhou and Zhen, Cao (2008), 'Shenzhen Bourse Report Blasts Regulators' in *Caijing Magazine* (18 July 2008).

Huang, Flora (2010), 'In Defence of China's Public Enforcement in Equity Market' in *International Company and Commercial Law Review*, **21**.

Huang, Flora (2010), 'Modernising the Chinese Capital Market: Old Problems and New Legal Responses' in *International Company and Commercial Law Review*, **21**.

Huang, Hui (2013), 'Private Enforcement of Securities Law in China: A Ten-Year Retrospective and Empirical Assessment' in *American Journal of Comparative Law*, **61**.

Huang, Yiping (2001), *China's Last Steps across the River: Enterprise and Banking Reforms*, Canberra: Asia Pacific Press.

Hutchens, Walter (2003), 'Private Securities Litigation in China: Material Disclosure about China's Legal System?' in *University of Pennsylvania Journal of International Economic Law*, **24**.

Hu, Shaohua (2007), 'Confucianism and Contemporary Chinese Politics' in *Politics and Policy*, **35**.

International Data Corporation (2017), 'Smartphone Vendor Market Share, 2017 Q1'. Online. Available at www.idc.com/promo/smartphone-market-share/vendor.

Jackson, Howell and Roe, Mark (2009), 'Public and Private Enforcement of Securities Laws: Resource-based Evidence' in *Journal of Financial Economics*, **93**.

Jia, Hepeng (2004), 'The Three Represents Campaign: Reform the Party or Indoctrinate the Capitalists?' in *Cato Journal*, **24**.

Jin, Sanlin and Wei, Yuanyuan (2006), 'Extent of Government Ownership or Control of the Means of Production and Enterprises' in Xiaoxi Li (ed.), *Assessing the Extent of China's Marketisation*, Aldershot: Ashgate.

Katelouzou, Dionysia and Siems, Mathias (2015), 'Disappearing Paradigms in Shareholder Protection: Leximetric Evidence for 30 Countries, 1990–2013' in *Journal of Corporate Law Studies*, **15**.

Keister, Lisa (2004), 'Guanxi in Business Groups: Social Ties and the Formation of Economic Relations' in Thomas Gold; Doug Guthrie; and David Wank (eds), *Social Connections in China Institutions, Culture, and the Changing Nature of Guanxi*, Cambridge: CUP.

Kwok, Yin-Wang (1986), 'Structure and Policies in Industrial Planning in the Shenzhen Special Economic Zone' in Y.C. Jao and Chi Keung Leung (eds), *China's Special Economic Zones*, Hong Kong: OUP.

Lardy, Nicholas (1987), 'Economic Recovery and the 1st Five-Year Plan' in Roderick MacFarquhar and John Fairbank (eds.), *The Cambridge History of China*, Cambridge: CUP.

Leung, Chi Keung (1986) 'Spatial Redeployment and the Special Economic Zones in China: An Overview' in Y.C. Jao and Chi Keung Leung (eds), *China's Special Economic Zones*, Hong Kong: OUP.

Li, Naomi (2004), 'Civil Litigation against China's Listed Firms: Much Ado about Nothing?' Royal Institute of International Affairs: Asia Programme Working Paper No. 13. Online. Available at: www.chathamhouse.org/sites/files/chathamhouse/public/General/wpfeb04.pdf.

Li, Wei and Yang, Dennis (2005), 'The Great Leap Forward: Anatomy of a Central Planning Disaster' in *Journal of Political Economy*, **113**.

Li, Yuan (2016), 'How Shenzhen Mimics Silicon Valley' in *Wall Street Journal* (1 June 2016).

Liebman, Benjamin and Milhaupt, Curtis (2008), 'Reputational Sanctions in China's Securities Market' in *Columbia Law and Review*, **108**.

Lin, Justin; Cai, Fang; and Li, Zhou (2003), *The China Miracle: Development Strategy and Economic Reform*, Hong Kong: Chinese University Press.

Lubman, Stanley (1991), 'Studying Contemporary Chinese Law: Limits, Possibilities and Strategy' in *American Journal of Comparative Law*, **39**.

Lubman, Stanley (1999) *Bird in a Cage: Legal Reform in China after Mao*, Stanford: Stanford University.

Luo, Yadong; Huang, Ying; and Wang, Stephanie (2012), 'Guanxi and Organizational Performance: A Meta-Analysis' in *Management and Organization Review*, **8**.

Maddison, Angus (2007), *Chinese Economic Performance in the Long Run*, Paris: OECD.

MacNeil, Iain (2002), 'Adaptation and Convergence in Corporate Governance: The Case of Chinese Listed Companies' in *Journal of Corporate Law Studies*, **2**.

McKinnon, Alexander (2011), 'Hong Kong and Shenzhen Ports: Challenges, Opportunities and Global Competitiveness' Hong Kong Centre for Maritime and Transportation Law Working Paper. Online. Available at: www.cityu.edu.hk/slw/HKCMT/Doc/Working_Paper_3_-_Shenzhen_-_Final_(v6).pdf.

McKinsey Global Institute (2006), 'Putting China's Capital to Work: The Value of Financial System Reform'. Online. Available at: www.mckinsey.com/mgi/publications.

Milhaupt, Curtis and Pistor, Katharina (2008), *Law and Capitalism*, Chicago: University of Chicago Press.

Moak, Ken and Lee, Miles (2015), 'Deng Xiaoping Theory' in Ken Moak and Miles Lee (eds), *China's Economic Rise and Its Global Impact*, New York: Palgrave Macmillan.

Morrison, Wayne (2015), 'China's Economic Rise: History, Trends, Challenges, and Implications for the United States' Congressional Research Service Report. Online. Available at: https://fas.org/sgp/crs/row/RL33534.pdf.

Myners, Paul (2001), 'Institutional Investment in the United Kingdom: A Review' Report to HM Treasury. Online. Available at: http://archive.treasury.gov.uk/pdf/2001/myners_report.pdf.

Naughton, Barry (1995), *Growing Out of the Plan*, Cambridge: CUP.

Ng, Mee Kam (2003), 'City Profile: Shenzhen' in *Cities*, **20**.

Ng, Mee Kam and Tang, Wing-Shing (2004), 'The Role of Planning in the Development of Shenzhen, China: Rhetoric and Realities' in *Eurasian Geography and Economics*, **45**.

Nishitateno, Sonoko (1983), 'China's Special Economic Zones: Experimental Units for Economic Reform' in *International and Comparative Law Quarterly*, **32**.

OECD (2013), 'Issues Paper on Corruption and Economic Growth'. Online. Available at: www.oecd.org/g20/topics/anti-corruption/Issue-Paper-Corruption-and-Economic-Growth.pdf.

Orts, Eric (2001), 'The Rule of Law in China' in *Vanderbilt Journal of Transnational Law*, **34**.

People's Daily Online (1992) 'Excerpts from Talks Given in Wuchang, Shenzhen, Zhuhai and Shanghai'. Online. Available at http://english.peopledaily.com.cn/dengxp/vol. 3/text/d1200.html.

People's Daily Online (2006), 'Three Represents'. Online. Available at http://english.cpc.people.com.cn/66739/4521344.html.

People's Daily Online (2014), 'Mozhe Shitou Guohe Gaige Fangfa de Lailongqumai' [The Origin of 'Crossing the River by Feeling each Stone']. Online. Available at: http://dangshi.people.com.cn/n/2014/0409/c85037-24858259.html.

People's Daily Online (2017), 'Guoqi Hungai Dayou Kandian' [Highlight of Mixed SOE Reform]. Online. Available at http://paper.people.com.cn/rmrbhwb/html/2017-03/09/content_1755936.htm.

Perkins, Dwight (1991), 'China's Economic Policy and Performance' in Roderick MacFarquhar and John Fairbank (eds.), *The Cambridge History of China*, Cambridge: CUP.

Pistor, Katharina and Xu, Chenggang (2005), 'Governing Stock Markets in Transition Economies: Lessons from China' in *American Law and Economics Review*, **7**.

Pistor, Katharina and Xu, Chenggang (2005a), 'Governing Emerging Stock Markets: Legal vs Administrative Governance' in *Corporate Governance*, **13**.

Potter, Pitman (2004), 'Guanxi and the PRC Legal System: From Contradiction to Complementarity' in Thomas Gold; Doug Guthrie; and David Wank (eds), *Social Connections in China Institutions, Culture, and the Changing Nature of Guanxi*, Cambridge: CUP.

PwC China (2014), 'China's Amended Company Law Facilitating More Business'. Online. Available at www.pwccn.com/home/eng/chinatax_news_jan2014_1.html.

Sang, Bin Xue (1993), 'Pudong: Another Special Economic Zone in China? An Analysis of the Special Regulations and Policy for Shanghai's Pudong New Area' in *Northwestern Journal of International Law and Business*, **14**.

Shanghai Stock Exchange (2006), *Corporate Governance Report* 2006, Shanghai: Fudan University Press.

Song, Dong-Wook (2002), 'Regional Container Port Competition and Co-operation: The Case of Hong Kong and South China' in *Journal of Transport Geography*, **10**.

Tomasic, Roman (1995), 'Company Law and the Limits of the Rule of Law in China' in *Australian Journal of Corporate Law*, **4**.

Tomasic, Roman and Fu, Jane (2005), 'Regulation and Corporate Governance of China's Top 100 Listed Companies: Whither the Rule of Law' Research Committee on the Sociology of Law Conference Paper. Online. Available at: https://papers.ssrn.com/sol3/papers.cfm?abstract_id=2712610.

Transparency International (2017), 'What is Corruption?'. Online. Available at: www.transparency.org/what-is-corruption/#define.

Tu, Weiming (2017), 'Confucianism' in *Encyclopedia Britannica*. Online. Available at: www.britannica.com/topic/Confucianism.

Wang, James (2002), 'Chen Yun' in Edwin Leung (ed.), *Political Leaders of Modern China: A Biographical Dictionary*, Santa Barbara: Greenwood.

Wang, James and Slack, Brian (2004), 'Regional Governance of Port Development in China: A Case Study of Shanghai International Shipping Center' in *Maritime Policy and Management*, **31**.

Wang, Ying (2011), 'Shanghai to Develop Bonded Areas into FTZ' in *China Daily* (12 November 2011).

Weber, Max (1964), *The Religion of China: Confucianism and Taoism*, New York: Macmillan.

Wei, Xie (2000), 'Acquisition of Technological Capability through Special Economic Zones (SEZS): The Case of Shenzhen SEZ' in *Industry and Innovation*, **7**.

Wei, Yehua and Leung, Chi Kin (2005), 'Development Zones, Foreign Investment, and Global City Formation in Shanghai' in *Growth and Change*, **36**.

Winters, Alan and Yusuf, Shahid (2007), *Dancing with Giants: China, India, and the Global Economy*, Washington D.C.: World Bank.

World Bank (2008), *Doing Business in China* Washington D.C.: World Bank.

World Bank (2013), *China 30*, Washington D.C.: World Bank.

World Bank (2017), 'China Overview'. Online. Available at: www.worldbank.org/en/country/china/overview.

World Shipping Council (2017), 'Top 50 World Container Ports 2015'. Online. Available at: www.worldshipping.org/about-the-industry/global-trade/top-50-world-container-ports.

Wu, Weiping (1999), 'City Profile: Shanghai' in *Cities*, **16**.

Xi, Chao and Chen, Yugang (2014), 'Does Cumulative Voting Matter? The Case of China: An Empirical Assessment' in *European Business Organization Law Review*, **15**.

Xi, Jinping (2013), 'Haobu Dongyao Jianchi he Fazhan Zhongguotese Shehuizhuyi' [Unswervingly Adhere to and Develop Socialism with Chinese Characteristics] in *People's Daily* (19 February 2013). Online. Available at: http://theory.people.com.cn/n/2013/0219/c352499-20529681.html.

Xu, Wenming; Chen, Jianwei; and Xu, Guangdong (2017), 'An Empirical Analysis of the Public Enforcement of Securities Law in China: Finding the Missing Piece of the Puzzle' in *European Business Organization Law Review*, **18**.

Yang, Mayfair (1994), *Gifts, Favors and Banquets: The Art of Social Relationships in China*, Ithaca: Cornell University Press.

Yeung, Horace (2009), 'Non-tradable Share Reform in China: A Review of Progress' in *Company Lawyer*, **30**.

Yeung, Horace (2010), 'Just Another Casino? The Case of Launching the Growth Enterprise Board in China' in *International Company and Commercial Law Review*, **21**.

Yeung, Horace (2014), 'Transferability of English Legal Concepts and Skills in China with respect to Corporate Regulation' in Georges Depeyrot (ed.), *When Orient and Occident Meet*, Wetteren: Moneta.

Yeung, Horace and Huang, Flora (2013), 'Growth without Institutions? The Case of China' in *Durham Law Review*, **3**.

Yeung, Yue-man; Lee, Joanna; Kee, Gordon (2009), 'China's Special Economic Zones at 30' in *Eurasian Geography and Economics*, **50**.

Yueh, Linda (2010), *The Economy of China*, Cheltenham: Edward Elgar.

Yusuf, Shahid and Wu, Weiping (2002), 'Pathways to a World City: Shanghai Rising in an Era of Globalisation' in *Urban Studies*, **39**.

Z/Yen Group (2014), 'The Global Financial Centres Index 15'. Online. Available at: www.zyen.com/research/gfci.html.

Zhang, Le-Yin (2003), 'Economic Development in Shanghai and the Role of the State' in *Urban Studies*, **40**.

Zhang, Zhong (2007), 'Legal Deterrence: the Foundation of Corporate Governance – Evidence from China' in *Corporate Governance: An International Review*, **15**.

Zheng, Yongnian and Keat Tok, Sow (2007), '"Harmonious Society" and "Harmonious World": China's Policy Discourse under Hu Jintao' University of Nottingham China Policy Institute Briefing Series Issue 26. Online. Available at: https://nottingham.ac.uk/cpi/documents/briefings/briefing-26-harmonious-society-and-harmonious-world.pdf.

Zhu, Sanzhu (2005), 'Civil Litigation Arising from False Statements on China's Securities Market' in *North Carolina Journal of International Law and Commercial Regulation*, **31**.

4 Hong Kong

In the previous chapter, the development of China's economy, especially with respect to its legal, political, cultural and other institutional foundations, was considered. China indeed has a close connection with the rise of Hong Kong. As this chapter will proceed to discuss, for a long period of time, as is still true today, Hong Kong has been playing an important role in China's development and the city has been taking advantage of this role economically. In this chapter, again using the analytical framework set out in Chapter 2, a comprehensive account of Hong Kong's economic growth will be conducted. First, the chapter will start from the economic development of Hong Kong, both during and after the colonial era. Then, the legal, political, cultural and other institutional conditions of Hong Kong will be examined in turn. Before a conclusion is made, this chapter will highlight the concern over the city's ability to preserve its institutional strengths largely inherited from its colonial era. This chapter is the second of the four chapters which explore the institutional conditions of the economies selected by this book, namely, China, Hong Kong, Singapore and Malaysia.

Economic growth of Hong Kong

Hong Kong is certainly one of the most advanced economies and a very competitive one. According to the IMD's World Competitiveness Yearbook 2017, Hong Kong was crowned as the world's most competitive economy for the second consecutive year.[1] Hong Kong stood out and was again ranked first among the 63 economies assessed, followed by Switzerland, Singapore and the US. In light of the news, Paul Chan, Hong Kong's Financial Secretary, highlighted the competitive edge of the city, including 'the open and free market principle, the fine tradition of the rule of law, an efficient public sector and a robust institutional framework'.[2] The report assessed each economy on four competitiveness factors: economic performance, government efficiency, business efficiency and infrastructure, each consisting of five sub-factors. Among the four competitiveness factors, Hong Kong's rankings in 'government efficiency' and 'business efficiency' both stayed at the top position globally. The ranking in 'infrastructure' also showed an improvement, climbing slightly up from twenty-first to twentieth. On the other

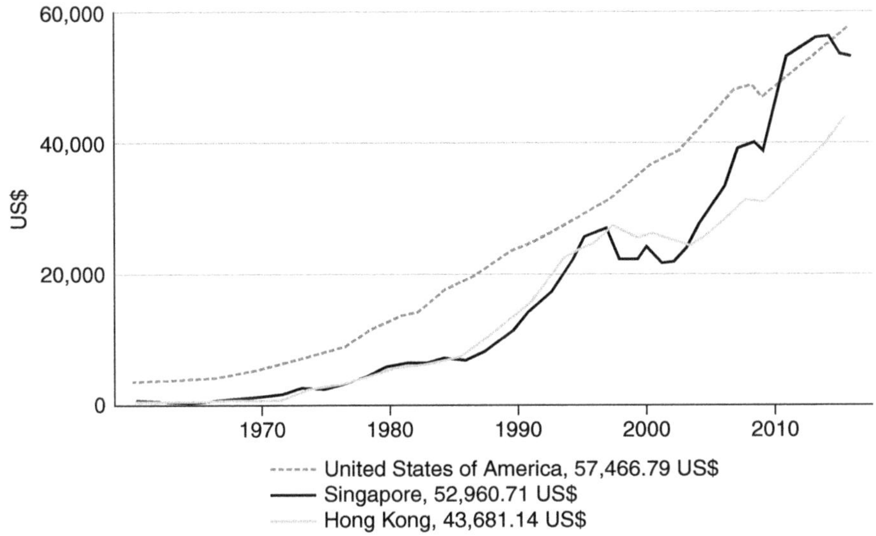

Figure 4.1 Comparative GDP per capita growth of Hong Kong, Singapore and US (US$).

Source: World Bank.

hand, the ranking in 'economic performance' fell from fifth to eleventh, generally reflecting Hong Kong's moderated overall economic growth in 2016 relative to that of 2015 amid internal and external unsteadiness. Hong Kong's raw GDP is certainly not comparable to economies like the US and China, as a city with a population of some seven million people. To trace Hong Kong's economic development from the 1960s, it can be seen from Figure 4.1 that, for a long period of time, the city has grown strongly alongside its close competitor in the Asian region, Singapore, in terms of GDP per capita. Both cities were looking on course to get close to, if not surpass, the level of the US just before the Asian Financial Crisis in 1998. However, Hong Kong apparently has not recovered as well as its competitor: the GDP per capita of Singapore did surpass the US after 2010 while Hong Kong has been trailing behind by a significant gap. This seems to capture the story of Hong Kong well, strong growth under the British colonial rule and lacklustre performance after the handover of its sovereignty back to China.

Economic development as a British colony

Hong Kong is situated at the southeastern tip of the mainland of China, with a total area of about 1,104 square kilometres covering Hong Kong Island, Kowloon and the New Territories and Islands. Out of the economies studied by this book, it is only larger than Singapore which has an area of 692.7 square kilometres. Economic activities in the city can be traced back to the Ming

(1368–1644) and Qing (1644–1911) dynasties, when considerable quantities of Ming blue-and-white porcelain were collected and excavated from Lantau Island of Hong Kong.[3] The local porcelain industry continued well into the early twentieth century, spanning a period of 500 years. At that time, there was a population of about 3,650 scattering over 20 villages and hamlets, and 2,000 fishermen lived on board their boats in the sheltered harbour, one of Hong Kong's natural assets. Victoria Harbour was strategically located on the trade routes of the Far East, and was soon to become the hub of a burgeoning entrepot trade with China.

Hong Kong's development into a commercial centre began with British settlement in 1841.[4] During this time, the First Opium War broke out. Under the Treaty of Nanking signed in 1842, Hong Kong Island was ceded to Britain. As a result of the Treaty, five Chinese ports, including Canton, were also opened for trade. The commercial treaty was embodied in a supplementary Treaty of Humen (Treaty of the Bogue) in October 1843, by which the Chinese were allowed free access to Hong Kong Island for trading purposes. The Second Anglo-Chinese War (1856–58) arose out of disputes over the interpretation of the earlier treaties and over the boarding of the Arrow, a British vessel, by Chinese in search of suspected pirates. The War led to the cession of Kowloon under the Convention of Peking in 1860. Under the Second Convention of Peking in 1898 which arose as a result of another war involving other European countries and Japan, the New Territories, comprising the area north of Kowloon up to the Shenzhen River, were leased for 99 years. This largely set out the boundary of Hong Kong as it currently is and planted the seed of the handover of sovereignty in 1997.

The population rose from 32,983 in 1851 to 878,947 in 1931.[5] Hong Kong became a centre of Chinese emigration and trade with Chinese communities abroad. Ocean-going shipping using the port increased from 2,889 ships in 1860 to 23,881 in 1939. Meanwhile, public and utility services developed, including the Hong Kong and China Gas Company in 1861, the Peak Tram in 1885, the Hongkong Electric Company in 1889, China Light and Power in 1903, the electric tramways in 1904 and the Kowloon-Canton Railway, completed in 1910. Trading in Hong Kong in company shares could also be traced back to about 1860. In 1891 the Association of Stockbrokers in Hong Kong was formed, changing its name to the Hong Kong Stock Exchange in 1914.[6] Until the 1930s, Shanghai dominated international finance in East Asia. The political and economic chaos that plagued China through the 1930s and 1940s, however, dislodged Shanghai from its dominant position and Hong Kong soon replaced it as the regional financial centre.[7] In the immediate post-war years, a rush of banks sprang up to service the swelling population of Hong Kong and to manage the deluge of flight capital from China. This prompted the enactment of the Banking Ordinance of January 1948, which remained in force until 1965. The Sino-Japanese conflict fought over the Chinese homeland in the 1930s led to a doubling of Hong Kong's population. It was estimated that nearly 100,000 entered in 1937, 500,000 in 1938 and 150,000 in 1939, bringing the total population to the peak of about 1.8 million in 1940.[8] Some describe pre-war Hong Kong as a 'pre-industrial society'.[9] It is believed the number of factories and workshops rose from 3,000 to 7,500 between 1927 and 1940. Based on the number of workers employed, the top five industries were: shipyards (10,426 workers); knitting factories (6,745 workers); spinning and weaving factories (6,151 workers); metal wares (3,926 workers); and rubber factories (2,019 workers).[10] Some useful trade data during that period are also available.[11] From 1931 to 1938, 37 per cent of Hong Kong's imports came from China, of which 30 per cent were consumed locally, 10 per cent were re-exported to China and 70 per cent were re-exported to non-Chinese countries. Meanwhile, the Chinese market accounted for 40 per cent of Hong Kong's exports. Of the exports to China, 10 per cent were produced locally, 11 per cent originated in other parts of China and 79 per cent consisted of re-exports of non-Chinese origin. Hence, 80 per cent of the imports from China and 90 per cent of the exports to China represented entrepot trade. Hong Kong's entrepot trade accounted for 25 per cent of China's exports and 19 per cent of China's imports.

During the Second World War, the Japanese military conquered and occupied Hong Kong for three years and eight months. Trade virtually disappeared, currency lost its value, food supplies were disrupted, and government services and public utilities were seriously impaired.[12] After the end of the Second World War, as a result of the civil war in China, Hong Kong received an influx of immigrants unparalleled in its history. Hundreds of thousands of people mainly from Guangdong Province, Shanghai and other commercial centres entered Hong Kong during 1949 and the spring of 1950. The population has continued to grow, reaching four million by 1971, five million by 1980, six million by 1994 and now over seven million.[13]

After the Second World War, China conducted most of its trade through Hong Kong and the Hong Kong–China trade recovered to pre-war levels.[14] Hong Kong's exports to China trebled during the period 1948–50, representing 38 per cent of total Chinese imports. Hong Kong's imports from China also rose to 25 per cent of total Chinese exports in 1950. The city's role as an entrepot for the China trade was then abruptly terminated when China entered the Korean War and the United Nations subsequently imposed a trade embargo on China. The city's post-war recovery was dealt a mortal blow. Exports to China dropped from HK$1,604 million in 1951 to HK$520 million in 1952.[15] With the loss of the China trade, Hong Kong was forced to develop its manufacturing industries. The prime movers of the industrialisation process were emigrant entrepreneurs from Shanghai, who brought not only capital but also technical and managerial know-how.[16]

Rapid economic growth in Hong Kong began with its economic transformation from an entrepot to an industrial city in the 1950s. In the 1960s and early 1970s, Hong Kong experienced a process of rapid industrialisation accompanied by a high rate of income growth. The city adopted an outward-looking policy of export-oriented industrialism from the very beginning. During the period 1961–82, the average annual growth rate of real GDP was 9.5 per cent.[17] There were two structural changes in the period. The first phase occurred in the 1950s and 1960s, when there was a shift of resources to the manufacturing sector. The second phase began in the early 1970s, and the direction has been toward the development of financial services. In 1980, for the first time, the contribution of financial services (26 per cent) surpassed that of manufacturing (25 per cent).[18] In the same period, the economy of Hong Kong was highly industrialised and export-oriented. Manufactured exports accounted for over 90 per cent of total exports.[19] Clothing was the single most important industry, accounting for more than one-third of Hong Kong's total exports. Traditional established industries included textiles, footwear and plastic articles. Other industries like toys and dolls, electronics, and watches and clocks were emerging with rapid growth.

These industries were undergoing changes over that period to keep up with the global competitive market.[20] In the early 1950s the bulk of Hong Kong's clothing (largely to the US) were of low quality knitwear. However, the imposition of quotas in the early 1960s provided an incentive for local manufacturers to upgrade quality and increase value added in order to maximise their return under the quota. The effect of this has been a steady shift to higher quality garments. Textiles were the foundation of Hong Kong's industrialisation. Cotton weaving, which was the first sector of the industry to develop, was started in the 1920s by local Cantonese weavers on a traditional handicraft basis. Early weaving factories produced primarily low quality, heavy grey cotton yardage for domestic consumption and export to Southeast Asian markets. The foundation of the whole textile industry was laid by Shanghai industrialists who, in 1947–50, brought their machinery and skills from China. As a result of growing world demand and increasing trade restrictions on cotton textile trade, the industry has moved increasingly into the production of cotton/synthetic and synthetic yarns and fabrics. Some of these industries were world leaders in their respective markets.[21] For some years Hong Kong has been the world's number-one exporter of toys and dolls, followed at some distance by Taiwan, Japan and the US, in that order. Also, the city was the world's number-one exporter of plastic flowers, followed by Taiwan, West Germany and South Korea. Hong Kong billionaire, Li Ka Shing, had a humble beginning making plastic flowers. Hong Kong was the world's number-one exporter of watches in terms of quantity. However, the output was basically confined to the assembly of imported parts. The watches produced in Hong Kong therefore either had relatively low value-added content or were largely for the lower price range of the market.

While the economy was growing well, another transformation was soon necessary. The percentage share of nominal GDP contributed by services increased from 67.5 per cent in 1980 to an estimated 85.2 per cent in 1997, while the corresponding figure for manufacturing decreased substantially, from 23.7 per cent in 1980 to an estimated 6.5 per cent in 1997.[22] What happened was that in the late 1970s, when mainland China launched its economic reform and adopted an open-door policy, many Hong Kong manufacturing companies relocated their labour-intensive production processes and lower value-added activities to the mainland to take advantage of the low production costs available there.

The Hong Kong economy has demonstrated a remarkable capacity to adapt to external change during the past century. The economy evolved from being an entrepot trading centre for China during the immediate post-war period into an export-oriented light manufacturing industrial city during the 1950s and 1960s. In the 1970s, the Hong Kong financial sector started as a local commercial banking community only to emerge as one of the largest financial centres in the world.[23] Towards the end of 1969, 32 new banks and branches were opened in Hong Kong. The original Hong Kong Stock Exchange, established in 1891, and the Far East Exchange opened their doors at the end of 1969. The next to start trading, the Kam Ngan Stock Exchange, opened its doors on 15 March 1971. The Kowloon Stock Exchange, the fourth exchange, opened on 5 January 1972. Altogether, these exchanges generated a turnover of HK$49,000 million in 1973, almost 25 times the level in 1969 before the advent of the Far East Exchange.

Furthermore, with the advent of China's open-door policy, Hong Kong has re-emerged as the premier entrepot trading centre serving not only China but the entire Asia Pacific region. The relationship between China and Hong Kong is unique. Indeed, Hong Kong has played a pivotal role throughout China's various stages of development, although the position of this role has constantly changed over time, from a supplier of vital supplies, then a trade middleman and finally to a financial centre. When the Communist Party of China came to power in 1949, it inherited a poor agrarian society consisting mainly of millions of small-scale self-sufficient farming households. It is believed that China imported most of its strategic supplies from Hong Kong during the Korean War, amid a trade embargo by the United Nations.[24] Following the calamity of the Great Leap Forward strategy and the Cultural Revolution, the state advocated a fundamental reorientation of China's development strategy and marked a new era of economic reform and open-door policy. The open-door policy is a vital part of China's new development strategy of intensive growth, and the motivational force for reform. The commitment to the open-door policy forced China to modify a rigid economic system to facilitate economic interactions with world markets. The role of Hong Kong in the process has been pivotal and can be summarised into four main functions: financier; trading partner; middleman; and facilitator.[25] Hong Kong is a trading partner as well as a middleman both in the commodity and services trades, including financial services, business consultancy and tourism. For example, in the 1980s, 74 per cent of Hong Kong imports from China were re-exported, accounting for 30 per cent of China's exports.[26] Half of the foreign law firms in Hong Kong provided legal advice for China's trade with Hong Kong, or for other overseas countries such as Japan or the US. China has valued Hong Kong as a contact point with the world, as a conduit of information and technology transfer, and as a market and production training ground.

With particular respect to finance, Hong Kong is the predominant source of foreign finance in China. Hong Kong has contributed to foreign loans borrowed by China in terms of: (1) direct lending; (2) loan syndication; and (3) lending from Hong Kong banks to non-bank customers in China. Beginning in 1984,

Hong Kong contributed to a substantial share of foreign loans. The combined shares of direct loans and syndicated loans from Hong Kong ranged from one-third to two-thirds of China's commercial loans in the period 1984 to 1987.[27] Furthermore, from 1979 to 1989, contracted and utilised investment in China totalled US$38 billion; US$22 billion or 59 per cent of which came from Hong Kong.[28] After 1990, a new dimension of Hong Kong's role as a financier has been to provide a fund-raising platform for Chinese companies.

Post-handover economic development

There are various indicators which point to the fact that Hong Kong is Asia's premier international financial centre.[29] Hong Kong was the world's sixth and Asia's second largest banking centre in terms of external positions in the *Bank for International Settlements Quarterly Review* for the end of 2016. International financial institutions maintain a strong presence in Hong Kong. Of the world's top 100 banks, 75 operate in the city. Of the 156 licensed banks in Hong Kong 149 were beneficially owned by parties outside Hong Kong. The combined fund management business was valued at HK$17 trillion at the end of 2015. The Hong Kong Stock Exchange ranked first worldwide in 2016 for the second consecutive year in terms of equity funds raised via IPOs. It is the seventh largest exchange in the world in terms of market capitalisation, behind the New York Stock Exchange, Tokyo Stock Exchange, NASDAQ, Euronext, London Stock Exchange and Shanghai Stock Exchange.[30] All these have driven demand for professional services along the whole service chain, including fund management, investment advice, legal and accounting services, and sales and marketing. This allows the city to develop into an all-round financial hub. It is worth noting that as of 2015, the services sector as a whole contributed 92.7 per cent of the GDP of Hong Kong.[31]

Although it is not the biggest in size, Hong Kong is arguably one of the leading international finance centres. According to the recent Global Financial Centres Index (GFCI), London and New York still lead the field and continue to be the only two truly 'global' financial centres.[32] However, Hong Kong, consistently ranked the third (but recently dropping to fourth) in the overall ranking of the GFCI, has been predicted to pose the greatest threat, among Asian cities, to the dominance of London and New York in this context.[33] Hong Kong is the strongest contender because of its historical root in finance and ability to tap into the Chinese market. *Time* magazine even came up with the term 'Nylonkong' to describe the extent to which New York, London and Hong Kong are linked by a shared economic culture, and how they have created a financial network that has come to be both an example and an explanation of globalisation.[34] Recently, the *Financial Times* even replaced New York and London with Shanghai, using a new term 'Shangkong', following a shift in financial gravity to the east.[35] The rise of Hong Kong to its present status is a miracle because when it was colonised by the British Empire in 1842, Hong Kong was merely a small fishing village.

Hong Kong's role following the handover has notably been the fund-raising hub of China. The increasing economic prominence of China is clearly reshaping the international financial system. It has grown strongly over the past decade with an average GDP growth of 9.1 per cent.[36] China has managed to maintain such a rapid pace of growth amid the financial crisis, and projections suggest this trend will continue.[37] The Hong Kong stock market used to be dependent on the property sector, but now has a more diversified structure because of the increasing importance of Chinese companies from a variety of sectors. The property sector accounted for 31 per cent of total market capitalisation at the end of 1996, but declined to 11 per cent in 2004.[38] However, the finance sector rose from 23.2 to 37 per cent in the same period as a result of the growth of HSBC, the Standard Chartered Bank and the admission of Chinese banks to the listing.[39] Furthermore, Chinese companies now have an overwhelmingly important presence on the stock exchange.

At the same time as the creation of domestic markets at the beginning of the 1990s, China began to experiment with the direct overseas listing of large and medium-sized state-owned enterprises (SOEs). To facilitate and regulate these cross-border financing activities, the State Council promulgated the *Special Regulations of the State Council Concerning Floating and Listing of Shares Overseas by Companies Limited by Shares* and the *Mandatory Provisions for Companies Listing Overseas*, with input from the Hong Kong authorities. In September 1992, the State Council published a list of the nine SOEs selected to be the first ever to issue equity overseas. In July 1993, Tsingtao Brewery, which produces the famous Chinese Tsingtao beer, became the first Chinese company to be listed on the Hong Kong Stock Exchange (HKEx).[40] Their importance reached a peak in 2008 when 465 Chinese companies (in a very broad sense) were listed on the Hong Kong market and their capitalisation accounted for 60 per cent of the HKEx's total market capitalisation.[41] Equity funds raised by these Chinese companies in the same year amounted to HK$287 billion, which was 71 per cent of the total equity funds raised through the exchange during the year.[42] One landmark listing in over two decades was the floating of China's largest state-owned bank, Industrial Commercial Bank of China (ICBC) in Hong Kong that raised US$22 billion in 2006.[43] In that year, Hong Kong attracted more IPOs than New York and London with the position of Hong Kong extraordinarily boosted by the mega Chinese bank IPOs.[44] The IPO of ICBC had remained the largest in the world until 2010 when it was surpassed by that of Agricultural Bank of China in Hong Kong and Shanghai.[45]

The overwhelming presence of Chinese companies can ring alarm bells as to whether the regulatory authorities in Hong Kong will be committed to enforcing rules and regulations against these Chinese companies, because they are not only the main source of revenue to the stock exchange, but also to the overall economy, since Hong Kong is now heavily financial service-oriented. However, since the peak in 2008, the percentage of China-related stocks has been dropping to around 40 per cent as of 2017. For the amount raised by China-related stocks and their percentage on the exchange since 1993, see Figures 4.2 and 4.3. Such a

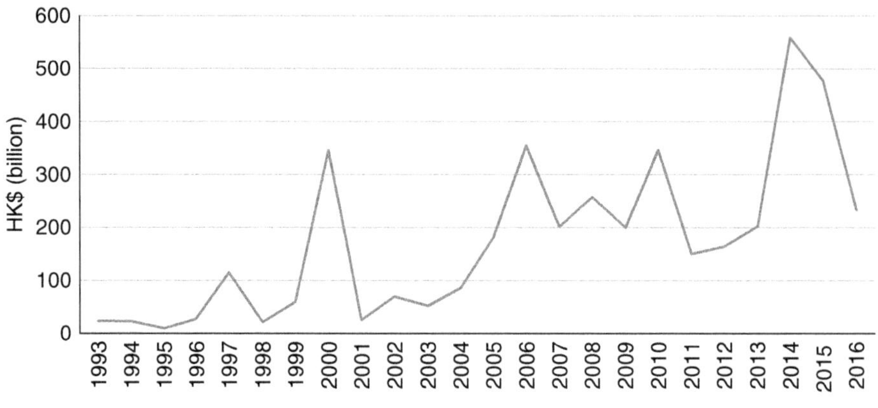

Figure 4.2 Equity funds raised by China-related companies (HKEx Main Board, HK$ billion).

Source: HKEx.

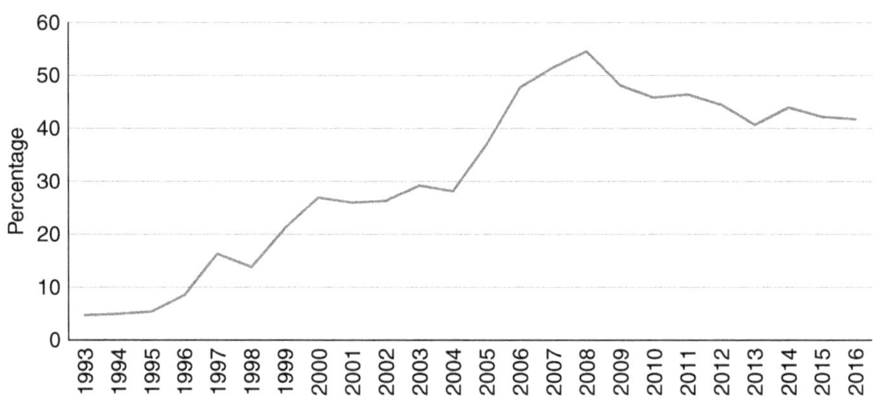

Figure 4.3 Market capitalisation percentage of China-related companies on the HKEx.

Source: HKEx.

decline has been largely a result of HKEx's move to look for alternative sources of new issuers. Until late 2006, the HKEx would accept listing applications from companies incorporated in a few jurisdictions only, such as Hong Kong, China, the Cayman Islands and Bermuda.[46] Since October 2006, it has approved over 20 other jurisdictions as acceptable overseas jurisdictions of an issuer's place of incorporation under the Hong Kong Listing Rules.[47] For example, the Russian company UC Rusal, the world's largest aluminium producer, was listed in Hong Kong in 2010. It was the first Russian IPO there.[48] Another example in the same year includes the listing of American International Group's Asian life insurance unit, AIA Group. European companies such as L'Occitane en Provence, Samsonite and Prada have also raised funds in Hong Kong.

Nonetheless, it is undeniable that the influx of Chinese companies has been the catalyst for Hong Kong to evolve into an international finance centre. Fuelled by the interests of global investors in having a share of China's impressive economic growth, the presence of overseas institutional investors in Hong Kong has increased dramatically. Local retail investors were the major contributors to the Hong Kong market in the 1990s. They contributed the largest proportion of market turnover value among all types of investors until 2000.[49] Since 2000, their dominant position has been taken by overseas institutional investors. The major overseas participants are UK investors by turnover value, followed by US investors.[50] Investors from the rest of Europe have also expanded their participation. Although China introduced the Qualified Foreign Institutional Investors (QFII) program in 2002 as a provision to enable foreign capital to access China's domestic financial markets, only large foreign financial institutions can actually benefit from the scheme.[51] However, small to medium-sized foreign investors are still able to invest in Chinese companies, through the Hong Kong market.

The Chinese stock market has so far enjoyed impressive growth as discussed in the previous chapter. This leads to the question of whether Shanghai and Shenzhen are in direct competition with Hong Kong. There are three reasons to doubt that this ever will be the case. First, it is doubtful whether China has all the tools to develop a stock market. China apparently still has something to learn from Hong Kong. This is implied by the fact that three of the big four banks in China chose to list in Hong Kong between 2005 and 2007, even though the domestic stock markets had been considerably developed and should have been capable of providing a significant amount of liquidity. Second, and following from this, it might be asked whether these cross-listed Chinese companies have something other than liquidity in mind. Finally, are these cross-listings perhaps the reason why the Chinese market could develop so quickly by learning from one of the best in the world? Apparently, the dual-listing of these companies (first in Hong Kong, then domestically) has strengthened the domestic market by bringing back their experience in a high quality market. This dual-listing model has also fostered a closer tie between the regulators in China and Hong Kong, which gives the China Securities Regulatory Commission (CSRC) an opportunity to learn from its seasoned counterpart.[52]

As more and more Chinese companies have listed overseas, the Chinese government has started to emphasise the strategic role played by cross-listings in establishing a modern corporate system. In fact, the Chinese government has stated all along that one purpose of listing companies overseas is to bring their management and performance up to international norms.[53] Furthermore, there are national political and economic objectives involved, such as showcasing China's economic power and grooming a selected group of companies for global competition.[54] From the company side, it is commonly believed that companies list abroad to broaden their investor base, raise capital for foreign acquisition or gain strategic international recognition. According to a report investigating the

Chinese companies' perception on overseas listing, over 55 per cent of the respondents reported that the capital raising capabilities are higher in overseas markets compared with mainland stock markets.[55] In terms of their preferred place of listing, Hong Kong and the US markets are the top two destinations.[56] The overall results suggest that the appeal of foreign institutional investors and international recognition are the main factors that Chinese companies consider when listing abroad. These factors are consistent with the conclusion in the previous chapter that the domestic Chinese market still needs further improvements to compete with the high quality overseas markets. However, whether Hong Kong possesses the necessary conditions of a strong market for these companies to bond themselves with is doubtful. As in the previous chapter, this will be discussed below in accordance with the factors laid down in Chapter 2.

Legal institutions

The development of Hong Kong's corporate and financial law regime has a close connection with its historical status as a colony of the British Empire. The genesis of the current framework is the Companies Ordinance (CO) of 1865 that mirrored the English Companies Act of 1862, which in turn incorporated both the Joint Stock Companies Registration and Regulation Act of 1844 and the Limited Liability Act of 1855.[57] Likewise, the Companies Act of 1908 in the UK was followed by the CO of 1911 in Hong Kong. The CO was designated as Chapter (Cap) 32 in 1933 and no further significant legislative initiative in company law was introduced until 1984, which reflected the Companies Act of 1948.[58] Since then, the law has constantly been revised.[59] The first major rewrite of the Hong Kong company law in more than a century came into effect in 2014 when the CO was re-designated as Chapter (Cap) 622. Other related rules and regulations include the Listing Rules of the HKEx, as well as the Code on Corporate Governance Practices and the Code on Takeovers and Mergers.[60]

Regarding securities law, formal regulation started in 1974 when the market crash attracted government attention and led to the introduction of legislation. In the same year, the Securities Ordinance and the Protection of Investors Ordinance became effective. They required the registration of all stockbrokers, dealers, and investment advisers. However, in the view of Gunningham, the government regulation of the stock market at this point was more apparent than real.[61] First, the government was still committed to *laissez-faire* and non-intervention. Second, the regulator was in fact starved of resources by the colonial government, which had little understanding of the complexities of financial market regulation. As a result, the Securities Commission took a passive and reactive role instead of actively monitoring markets and brokers. In 1987, when the world's securities markets braced themselves for another crash, the Hong Kong government started to realise the need to strengthen its systems and regulatory arrangements to maintain its position as the primary capital market in the Asian region. The crash of 1987 led to the appointment of the Securities Review Committee. The Securities and Futures Commission Ordinance, which passed its final reading in 1989, marked the beginning of a strong single regulator. In 1991, the Securities (Disclosure of Interests) Ordinance and Securities (Insider Dealing) Ordinance came into force. In 2003, the Securities and Futures Ordinance (SFO) consolidated and modernised all these previous ordinances regulating the securities and futures markets in Hong Kong.[62]

The Securities and Futures Commission (SFC) was established as an autonomous statutory body and is responsible for regulating the securities and futures markets in Hong Kong.[63] Its regulatory objectives, duties, functions and powers are stipulated in the SFO.[64] To keep in line with the objectives and principles of the International Organisation of Securities Commissions (IOSCO), the role of the SFC is to maintain and promote the fairness, efficiency, competitiveness, transparency and orderliness of the securities and futures industry in Hong Kong. Broadly speaking, the SFC's work involves the licensing, supervision and monitoring of intermediaries; regulation of the public marketing of unit trusts, mutual funds and other collective investment products; regulation of takeovers, mergers and other corporate activities; listing regulation for IPO applicants and issuers; supervision of markets including the exchanges and clearing houses; enforcement of securities laws and rules; and investor education. Owing to the large number of Chinese companies listed in Hong Kong, the SFC has built up a cooperation framework with the CSRC. The SFC can request investigatory assistance from the CSRC to obtain information in China and the CSRC can compel persons to provide the requested information to the SFC.[65] The SFC is also able to exercise its investigatory powers to help the CSRC in its investigations that have a Hong Kong element.

Quality of the laws

The substantive legal framework in Hong Kong to protect investors and promote market efficiency is roughly similar to that of the UK because of the influence from the English model during the colonial era before 1997. For example, both common law and statute impose on company directors certain duties to the company. Directors owe fiduciary duties to the company, which are based upon showing the utmost good faith.[66] They should not put themselves in a position where their personal interest conflicts with those of the company.[67] The new CO is revolutionary in codifying part of the directors' duties to statutorily require a director to exercise reasonable care, skill and diligence.[68] To reduce the likelihood of self-dealing by directors, the CO provides that any director of a company who is in any way, directly or indirectly, interested in a contract with the company must declare the nature of that interest.[69] The Listing Rules also prescribe the timely disclosure requirements for notifiable and connected transactions.[70] Other general disclosure duties include the requirement for a company to keep proper books of account and a report by directors dealing with the state of affairs of the company.[71] The reporting obligations of majority shareholders and company officers are also specified under the SFO.[72] Furthermore, to combat financial market crimes, there are six types of market misconduct specified:

insider dealing; false trading; price rigging; the disclosure of information about prohibited transactions; the disclosure of false and misleading information inducing transactions; and stock market manipulation.[73] These six forms of market misconduct are all subject to civil remedies and wrongdoing can be punishable as a criminal offence.[74]

The stock exchange in Hong Kong has pursued a predominantly outward looking strategy. For example, funds raised by international and Mainland companies represented 94 per cent of IPO equity funds raised in 2015.[75] A notable strength in the Hong Kong framework is the existence of a dedicated set of listing rules for foreign issuers to standardise and streamline their listing process. To ensure a level of shareholder protection for overseas companies, four major requirements can be seen in both Chapters 19 (for all non-Chinese overseas issuers) and 19A (for Chinese issuers only) in their listing rules.

First, the HKEx must be satisfied that the overseas issuer is incorporated or otherwise established in a jurisdiction where the standards of shareholder protection are at least equivalent to those provided in Hong Kong. Various rules should in principle apply to all issuers regardless of their country of incorporation unless otherwise stated. The company laws of Bermuda, the Cook Islands, the Cayman Islands and China have already been pre-vetted by the HKEx and special provisions are made for those jurisdictions as seen in Appendix 13 of the Listing Rules. A major doubt to this general principle is that Chapter 19A has apparently relaxed some requirements for Chinese cross-listings, though at the same time, some additional requirements have been added. It is difficult to assess whether the resulting shareholder protection is actually higher or lower.

Second, in relation to a localisation requirement, under Rule 8.12, a prospective issuer applying for a primary listing on the Exchange must have a sufficient management presence in Hong Kong. This will normally mean that at least two of its executive directors must be ordinarily resident in Hong Kong. This applies to all overseas issuers including those from China. Also, overseas issuers must appoint a person authorised to accept a service of process and notices on its behalf in Hong Kong.[76] In the case of registered securities, provision must be made for a register of holders to be maintained in Hong Kong or another agreed location. In addition, all documents furnished by an overseas issuer, including accounts, which are in a language other than English, must be accompanied by a certified English translation.[77] The localisation requirement ensures that investors, the HKEx and the SFC are communicating in a language they understand and the overseas company has maintained a point of contact for them.

Third, there are also specific requirements in relation to their listing documents. Overseas issuers are required under Rule 19.08 to include a summary of the provisions of the constitutive documents of the overseas issuer and the relevant regulatory provisions of the jurisdiction in which the overseas issuer is incorporated. In this regard, the listing document of a Chinese issuer must contain a summary of the relevant Chinese laws.[78] In general, the relevant Chinese law to be summarised would normally be expected to cover matters such as taxation on the issuer's income and capital, foreign exchange controls or restrictions, company law, securities regulations, any law that regulates or limits the Chinese issuer's major business and other relevant laws or regulations. For example, the following appeared in the listing document of China Construction Bank, which was listed on 27 October 2005 (before the new Company Law in China came into effect):[79]

> Hong Kong law permits minority shareholders to start a derivative action on behalf of all shareholders against directors who have committed a breach of their fiduciary duties to the company … the PRC [People's Republic of China] law does not have a form of proceedings which is the same as a derivative action.

This seems to be the entry strategy in action. The regulatory authorities must have recognised that certain shortfalls in the host country system are irremediable. It is entirely up to the investors if they want to take the risk of investing in the company.

Fourth, a further requirement related to corporate transparency is that the accounts and reports of different companies, no matter whether they are locally or overseas incorporated, should be comparable. The general rule is that accounts and reports will not normally be regarded as acceptable unless they have been audited to a standard comparable to that required in Hong Kong. The standard can be one specified by the Hong Kong Institute of Certified Public Accountants or by the International Auditing and Assurance Standards Board of the International Federation of Accountants.

On the other hand, Chinese issuers are subject to further modifications to the requirements of the Listing Rules. Rule 19A.23 requires Chinese issuers to present a certified copy of the document issued by the competent authority in China, which is the CSRC, expressly approving the issuer's listing on the HKEx and issuance of equity securities in the manner contemplated by the issuer's listing application. Furthermore, Rule 19A.03 requires that the HKEx is satisfied there are adequate communication and cooperation arrangements in place between the HKEx and CSRC. This was echoed by the signing of a Memorandum of Understanding between the CSRC and the SFC on 19 June 1993. No similar requirements are seen in Chapter 19. First, this means that Chinese companies need to pass through an additional selection and assessment process, which is undertaken by the CSRC. Second, cross-border enforcement activities are enabled and facilitated. By contrast, the same does apply to other overseas companies and is not necessary for local companies. Furthermore, in light of the foreign exchange control in China, Chinese issuers must include in their listing documents a statement of whether or not they have sufficient foreign exchange to pay forecasted or planned dividends and meet their foreign exchange liabilities.[80]

To protection investors, Chapter 19A stresses the importance of having a compliance adviser. Listing Rule 19A.05 requires that the compliance adviser retained by the Chinese issuer must have access at all times to the management and that the management must provide any information and assistance the compliance adviser might need. Although Rules 3A.26 and 3A.37 allow a Hong Kong or overseas issuer to terminate a compliance adviser's role if its work is of an unacceptable standard and appoint a replacement within three months, a more stringent requirement is provided in Rule 19A.05. A Chinese issuer should have a compliance adviser at all times in the sense that it must not terminate the role of a compliance adviser unless a replacement is in place. Furthermore, owing to the differences between Hong Kong and China's legal systems, the sponsor of a Chinese issuer is required to offer timely advice on the amendment or supplement to the Listing Rules and any new or amended law, regulation or code in Hong Kong applicable to Chinese issuers. Clearly, a compliance adviser is entrusted to safeguard the quality of Chinese issuers. A further mechanism to protect the investors is the provision of pre-emption rights. A general principle is that a shareholder should be able to protect their proportion of the total equity by having the opportunity to subscribe to any new issue of equity securities. Under Rule 13.36, the directors of an issuer must obtain the consent of shareholders in a general meeting prior to allotting, issuing or granting shares, securities convertible into shares or options, warrants or similar rights to subscribe for any shares. In the context of Chinese issuers, a special resolution of shareholders in a general meeting, and the approval by special resolutions of holders of domestic shares and overseas-listed foreign shares at separate class meetings must be sought.[81] This ensures that the interests of foreign shareholders, who are usually the minority, will not be diluted unless prior consent is sought.

Recognising that the extra-territorial enforcement of law is difficult, perhaps the most important additional requirement is the inclusion of an arbitration clause to the articles of association. Whenever any disputes or claims arise between holders of shares and the company including the directors, supervisors, manager, other senior officers or holders of domestic shares, they must be referred to arbitration.[82] A claimant can elect for arbitration to be carried out at either the China International Economic and Trade Arbitration Commission in accordance with its rules or the Hong Kong International Arbitration Centre in accordance with its rules. Once a claimant refers a dispute or claim to arbitration, the other party must submit to the arbitral body elected by the claimant. Under the Arbitration Law and the Civil Procedure Law of China, an arbitral award is final and binding on the parties.[83] If a party fails to comply with an award, the other party to the award can apply to the People's Court for enforcement. It should be noted that China acceded to the *Convention on the Recognition and Enforcement of Foreign Arbitral Awards* (also known as the 'New York Convention') pursuant to a resolution passed on 2 December 1986. The New York Convention provides that all arbitral awards made in a state that is a party to the New York Convention must be recognised and enforced by other parties to the New York Convention. Furthermore, on 18 June 1999, an arrangement was made between Hong Kong and the Supreme People's Court of China for the mutual enforcement of arbitral awards. Under this arrangement, awards made by China's arbitral authorities recognised under the Arbitration Ordinance of Hong

Kong can be enforced in Hong Kong. Hong Kong arbitration awards are also enforceable in China. By a sharp contrast, Listing Rule 19 and Appendix 13 provide no such arbitration mechanism to other overseas issuers and their investors.

Amidst mechanisms to give investors increased protection, a major concession is given to Chinese issuers. They are exempt from disclosing any related party transactions associated with the 'Chinese governmental body', which is usually their controlling shareholder. Under Rule 8.10, the HKEx requires an issuer to disclose where it has a controlling shareholder or a director with an interest in a business that competes or is likely to compete with the issuer's business. In this connection, according to Chapter 1 of the Listing Rules, 'controlling shareholder' means any shareholder or other person or group of persons, entitled to exercise or control the exercise of 30 per cent or more of the voting power at general meetings of the issuer, or who is in a position to control the composition of a majority of the board of directors. However, for the purposes of this rule, the HKEx will normally not consider the Chinese governmental body as a 'controlling shareholder'.[84] The term 'Chinese governmental body' can be interpreted very broadly according to Rule 19A.04.[85] Similarly, for purpose of the connected transaction provisions of Chapter 14A, the HKEx will normally not treat a Chinese governmental body as the connected person of a Chinese issuer.[86] This exemption can have severe implications on shareholder protection because it means that the expropriation of minority shareholders' interests via manipulated transfer pricing between state entities is unregulated.

To conclude, the standard of shareholder protection is in general high, which is supported by various evidence. As seen in the previous chapter, Armour and colleagues have created a shareholder protection index covering a range of developed and developing countries.[87] Unfortunately, unlike China, Hong Kong is not one of the jurisdictions under investigation. Still, one of their conclusions could be relevant in the context of Hong Kong. They have discovered that common law systems were generally more protective of shareholder interests than civil law ones. By contrast, it might be useful to refer back to the seminal work of La Porta and colleagues, although their work has been criticised as flawed by some scholars.[88] According to their shareholder right index, the score of Hong Kong was 5, the highest achieved in the study. This placed it in the same league as the UK and US.[89] In relation to securities regulation, Hong Kong also performed very well, even when compared with other common law jurisdictions.[90] Furthermore, Hong Kong's strength in this area is confirmed by the World Bank's 'Doing Business' report.[91] According to its Minority Investor Protection Index 2017, Hong Kong was given a score of 8, putting it in third place, amongst 190 economies. It is worth pointing out that Singapore (joint first in the index with New Zealand) and Malaysia (joint third with Hong Kong), to be covered by the next two chapters, were also doing very well. However, these are all rights on paper. The enforcement in practice, both public and private, will be examined below.

Public enforcement

Different jurisdictions have adopted different regulatory models to regulate the market. For example, comparing both sides of the Atlantic, the Securities and Exchange Commission in the US has taken a more active role in policing the market than the Financial Services Authority (FSA) in the UK. Gadinis and Jackson have tried to categorise different jurisdictions into three distinct models.[92] The continental model (France, Germany and Japan), which is described as a government-led model, preserves significant authority for central government control over securities market regulation, albeit with a relatively limited enforcement apparatus. The American model (cooperation model) assigns a broad range of power to market participants in almost all aspects of securities regulation. The English model (flexibility model), which is applicable in Hong Kong, grants significant leeway to market participants in performing their regulatory obligations, but relies on government agencies to set general policies and maintain some enforcement capacity.[93]

To identify potential breaches of relevant laws or regulations, the SFC carries out market surveillance. The first step is to identify and assess risks. For instance, the Licensing Department will identify potential licensees who could pose an unacceptable risk to investors. Then, it monitors and tracks identified risks. The Enforcement Division carries out market surveillance to gather evidence in relation to market crimes. Under the SFO, the SFC is empowered to direct any corporation, authorised financial institution, auditor and any other persons to produce information, records and documents concerning suspected cases of fraud, misfeasance or other misconduct.[94] In addition, the SFC will consider complaints from the public. For example, in 2007–08, the SFC received 1,204 public complaints of which 248 cases were referred to operational divisions for further assessment and 89 cases were investigated by the Enforcement Division.[95] Among these investigations, 73 per cent were completed within seven months.[96] There can also be referrals of cases from other law enforcers or organisations, for example, the Hong Kong Police and other overseas regulators.

Similar to other seasoned regulators in the world, the SFC has employed a spectrum of remedies including administrative, civil and criminal sanctions to deter wrongdoing and protect the market and investors. Under Sections 194 and 196 of the SFO, the SFC can impose a fine either on its own or together with other disciplinary sanctions. The SFC regards a fine as a more severe sanction than a reprimand, and a public reprimand as more severe than a private reprimand.[97] For more serious offences, the SFC will either refer civil cases to the Market Misconduct Tribunal or criminal cases to the court. The Tribunal has the jurisdiction to enquire into and punish all forms of market misconduct stipulated in Parts XIII and XIV of the SFO.[98] The types of orders made by the Tribunal include disgorgement orders, disqualification orders, government costs orders and disciplinary referral actions against wrongdoers by the relevant professional body. Between 1994 and 2007, 26 cases were heard by the Tribunal.[99] Furthermore, criminal sanctions are frequently seen. For example, in 2008–09, there were 128 criminal charges against 40 people, with 70 charges laid against 15 people for market manipulation and insider dealing.[100] The first convictions and jail sentences for insider dealing were witnessed in that year.[101]

As Coffee has suggested, the more satisfactory approach to measuring enforcement is to focus on inputs and outputs.[102] In the investigation by Jackson and Roe, the Hong Kong market had the highest staffing and budgets in 2006.[103] The direct staff per million of population ratio in Hong Kong was 59.59.[104] The US figure was 23.75, a country where the enforcement intensity is high. Concerning budgets, Hong Kong had a budget of around US$320,000 per billion GDP, whereas in markets such as the US and UK, the figures were around US$80,000.[105] All these, to a large extent, illustrate the disproportionately large role of the financial market in Hong Kong. The government is committed to preserving the integrity and efficiency of the market. The SFC has clearly possessed and spent adequate financial resources to enable its enforcement actions.[106] Between 2005 and 2015, the SFC reported annual expenditures more than trebling from HK$497 million in 2005 to about HK$1.7 billion in 2015. Despite tripling its spending over the ten-year period, the SFC still showed a surplus of more than HK$6.3 billion. Although this might reflect an *ex ante* threat of sanction, as an *ex post* basis the threat is equally high. Although the US and UK often have more than 500 and 100 enforcement cases brought by the national regulator per year respectively, Hong Kong's annual average of over 100 actions is high considering that its market is smaller than the US and the scope of regulation by the SFC is narrower than the FSA.[107] It can be seen that the public enforcement of securities regulation in Hong Kong has been comparable to the world's renowned markets. However, private enforcement is relatively weak. As indicated by Donald and Cheuk, the data on judicial actions taken pursuant to corporate and securities laws clearly show that such enforcement in Hong Kong is primarily public.[108] This sharply contrasts to jurisdictions like the US where private actions play a leading role. Such a disinclination of ligations can partly be attributed to the reluctance of ordinary Chinese to seek justice through the court to preserve harmony. After all, even though Hong Kong was under British rule for over 100 years, local people still retain a traditional Chinese mentality. However, it is notable that the private enforcement of shareholder rights in the UK has equally been rare.[109]

With specific regard to the importance of overseas issuers in Hong Kong, although Listing Rule 2.03 requires that 'all holders of listed securities are treated fairly and equally', the level of protection given to shareholders can vary. As discussed above, Chinese companies, which intend to go public via a conventional route, have to pass a fairly rigorous process and comply with a number of requirements. By contrast, those that become listed via overseas shelf companies seem to be more problematic. As indicated by Cai, the sources of bonding premiums for Chinese companies are derived from stricter accounting rules, independent directors, ownership diversification and reputational intermediaries.[110] Certain improvements in these corporate governance arrangements are readily observable. For instance, Tsingtao was the first company in China to introduce independent directors to its board.[111] Another example of observable changes is the introduction of strategic investors. A number of prominent business tycoons and companies in Hong Kong, as well as some foreign wealth funds are consistently among the list of these strategic investors.[112] This strategy has been especially common in the financial sector when the Chinese government faces intense pressure to open their financial industry to foreign investment under China's WTO entry commitments.[113] These institutional investors and independent directors are often described as the guardians of corporate governance.

By contrast, some less readily observable elements can lead to the difference in both the perceived and actual level of protection and thereby the bonding premiums. Brockman and Chung have predicted that Hong Kong-based shares are associated with lower adverse selection costs to the capital providers than are China-based shares.[114] This phenomenon can be attributed to the suboptimal management quality of Chinese companies and enforcement. The collapse of China Aviation Oil (CAO), which was listed on the Singapore Stock Exchange, revealed the problematic governance structure of Chinese state-owned companies. In 2004, CAO disclosed massive trading losses in derivative transactions and subsequently filed for court protection from creditors. In the view of Milhaupt and Pistor, this incident suggested some major oversight and compliance problems within the company.[115] Although cross-listed Chinese companies are generally the best performers of the state sector, their success is not because of entrepreneurial spirit or managerial skill, but rather their exclusive monopolistic status in their respective business.[116] One sceptical view is that the transformation of China's partially privatised (or 'corporatised' as used by many scholars) giants is plagued by structural problems associated with the transition from a planned economy to a market economy. The majority of their shares are essentially state-owned. Almost all senior appointments and their dismissals, as in the case of CAO, are initiated by state bureaucrats, instead of strict market disciplines.[117]

In theory, appropriate enforcement actions can be triggered by several institutions. First in line is clearly the stock exchange, which has admitted the company to its market and is responsible for monitoring its compliance and disclosure requirements. Sponsors, lawyers and accountants also involved in the listing process are usually entrusted by the exchange and the listing rules to duly perform their roles as gatekeepers. Finally and ultimately, a public regulatory agency is the fearsome law enforcer. In the CAO debacle, the prompt actions taken by Singapore's regulators and criminal enforcement agents were highly praised despite growing concerns about possible conflicts of interest posed by the exchange's assertive recruitment of Chinese companies while fulfilling its role of investor protection.[118] Hong Kong, as one of the most intense regulators in the world, seems to be capable of performing even better than the Singaporean side. Still, the conflicts of interest situation in Hong Kong is more severe. At the time of the CAO debacle, Chinese companies represented just 7 per cent of the combined market capitalisation of the Singapore Stock Exchange. However, by the end of May 2009, China-related shares accounted for over half of the HKEx's market capitalisation.[119]

In practice, Hong Kong cannot extend its jurisdiction across its border with China or vice versa under the virtue of 'One Country Two Systems'. Although the Hong Kong authorities have the final say over the requirements for Chinese companies and whether they are still fit to stay listed, the exchange and the SFC have always shared their supervisory roles with the CSRC and other appropriate Chinese authorities. Listing Rule 19A.03 states that the HKEx must be 'satisfied that there are adequate communication and cooperation arrangements in place between the Exchange and the relevant securities regulatory authorities in China'. This assistance from the Chinese authorities is particularly valuable to the investigations into, for example, the business operations and onsite accounts of Chinese companies. The legal basis for Chinese authorities to act also comes from Listing Rule 19A.52, which states that Chinese issuers must declare that they will observe and comply with the laws of China. Hence, in essence, the authorities just need to ensure that Chinese companies comply with the laws and regulations of their respective jurisdictions, without the need to actually enforce foreign laws.

To facilitate better cooperation, in June 1993, the SFC and HKEx entered into a Memorandum of Regulatory Cooperation (MORC) with the CSRC, the Shanghai Stock Exchange and the Shenzhen Stock Exchange. The purpose of the MORC is to enable parties, through mutual assistance and the exchange of information, to (1) accomplish the basic principles of protecting investors, (2) maintain fair, orderly and efficient markets and (3) ensure compliance with each other's laws and rules.[120] Information is exchanged in relation to several key areas, namely, insider trading, market manipulation and breaches of company legislation. The request for information by any signatories of the MORC should be made in writing, specifying the purpose for which the information is sought, a description of the conduct or suspected conduct that gives rise to the request and the link between the specified laws or regulatory requirements.[121] The signatories can also provide this information on a voluntary basis even though no request has been made.

Joint surveillance and investigation is possible under the law of each authority's jurisdictions. The substantive procedures of how this can be conducted are decided on a case-by-case basis and should be agreed in advance. The agreement will cover specific matters including details of the target entities or companies, and the documents that the signatories wish to jointly inspect.[122] The costs incurred in a joint surveillance and review will be shared. Similarly, for joint investigation, an agreed initial action plan must be prepared setting out the objectives, expected duration, funding, publicity and accountability arrangements and management of the joint investigation. Apart from the bilateral agreement, the basis for China–Hong Kong cooperation also comes from the Multilateral Memorandum of Understanding (MMOU) of the IOSCO, to which both the SFC and CSRC are signatories.[123] The basis of their cooperation has been well covered.

The SFC has not published the statistics for regulatory cooperation in its annual report since 2005. Therefore, the recent situation is unclear. Despite the existence of a formal cooperation framework among regulatory authorities, the SFC did not actively seeking assistance from foreign regulators. Conversely, a number of assistance requests were received and responded to. In 2005, the SFC received 47 requests for enforcement-related assistance.[124] Of these, 13 were requests for investigatory assistance involving the SFC in the exercise of its statutory powers and 34 were requests for information. In three cases, interviews were arranged for overseas regulators with suspects or witnesses. Criminal charges were laid in one of the cases in a foreign country. In the same year, by contrast, the SFC made just seven requests to overseas regulators and, of these, four were requests for investigatory assistance and three were for non-public information. The situation in 2004 was around the same, with 46 requests in but just six requests out.[125] This largely illustrates that the SFC might not be so committed to enforcing the law against foreign companies.

Private enforcement

In their survey of securities laws in 49 countries, La Porta and colleagues gave Hong Kong full marks in ten aspects out of 12 regarding public enforcement.[126] Private enforcement was equally strong according to the same study. It received high scores compared with the US, the UK and Australia. From these findings, they came to the interesting conclusion that laws facilitating private enforcement through disclosure and liability rules are more correlated to the growth of stock markets than public enforcement. In fact, shareholders in Hong Kong have various ways to bring an action in the event of misfeasance, and this legal framework has a large resemblance to the UK model.[127]

For example, similar to the statutory protection of minority shareholders in England, any member of a company can apply to the court for an order under Section 724 of the Companies Ordinance on the grounds that the affairs of the company are being or have been conducted in a manner unfairly prejudicial to the interests of the members.[128] Of course, this might not be useful in a public company where shareholders can choose to sell their shares via the market. Under the CO, they can also take advantage of statutory derivative actions.[129] Even earlier than the UK, Hong Kong placed derivative actions on a statutory footing in 2004 with a view to strengthening the position of minority shareholders.[130] As an exception to the rule in *Foss* v. *Harbottle*,[131] a shareholder can bring legal proceedings on behalf of the company against any director in respect of misfeasance committed against the company. Furthermore, under the SFO, shareholders have a right of action in civil proceedings for their pecuniary loss as a result of another person's contravention of market misconduct provisions.[132]

Nonetheless, in practice, these proceedings have rarely been seen. In his investigation of minority shareholder protection in Hong Kong, Lawton identified over 200 relevant shareholder actions between 1980 and 1995.[133] Among these, most of the cases were actions for just and equitable winding up under Section 177(1)(f) of the Companies Ordinance, which is essentially an equivalent of Section 122(1)(g) of the Insolvency Act 1986 in the UK. There were a considerable number of statutory minority shareholder actions under Section 724 (formerly 168A) of the Companies Ordinance in this period, but the number of derivative actions was negligible.[134] Nevertheless, it is incorrect to state that the law has never been enforced. Since the introduction of the statutory derivative actions, the number of derivative actions started (54 in 2005 to 2014) were almost twice as many as those initiated before that (29 in 1995 to 2004).[135] Hong Kong has also contributed to the development of the scope of derivative action. For example, in the case of *Waddington Limited* v. *Chan Chun Hoo Thomas*, 'multiple derivative action' was permitted to allow an action brought on behalf of a company against its directors not by a shareholder of the company itself, but by a shareholder of a company further up the corporate chain.[136] Apart from this, most cases have largely been related to small and private companies and, therefore, should have little impact on the securities market. Tyler and Ho have attributed the lack of some representative cases of minority shareholder action in Hong Kong to the Chinese disinclination for litigation and the family structure of Hong Kong companies.[137] Although the former was somewhat considered in the previous chapter both in the context of why China did not have a detailed procedural framework of private securities litigation in the past and China's Confucian society, the latter will be addressed further below in the section about the corporate culture in Hong Kong.[138]

Political institutions

The political explanation for the growth of Western securities markets given by Roe has been that if a society's institutions do not promote shareholder value, then ownership separation, which can influence the depth of a market, ought to be narrower than elsewhere.[139] Friedman referred to Hong Kong as an example of capitalism in action.[140] Indeed, he further suggested that the success of the *laissez-faire* capitalist policy in Hong Kong was a major factor in encouraging China and other countries to move away from centralised control towards a greater reliance on private enterprise and the free market.[141] In contrast to the continental system with strong labour institutions, Hong Kong has always tried to foster a flexible and competitive private sector and retain its small government posture.[142] Economists have stressed the idea that good economic institutions, especially those in the public sector, are instrumental to economic growth.[143] Non-interventionism is often regarded as one aspect of good government by economists.[144] According to the recent Index of Economic Freedom, Hong Kong ranks first (Singapore closely behind in the second place) among 180 countries in light of the degree of economic freedom.[145] This illustrates the success of the 'positive non-interventionism' policy implemented by the government since British rule, despite concern that Hong Kong has become more interventionist and more susceptible to political influence from China following the handover in 1997. Self-regulation is an important feature of the English model. In relation to a wide variety of types of activities, market participants have established, of their own accord, industrial, professional and social organisations to oversee and regulate matters of common interest.[146] The financial market regulation in Hong Kong has largely been based on self-regulation by the exchange.

The colonial government of Hong Kong was a fiscally limited and conservative state. Throughout the period of British colonial rule, public spending had taken up less than 20 per cent of GDP, in contrast with the high level of expenditure of Western countries (over 40 per cent of GDP).[147] By the 1980s the colonial government, in the words of then Financial Secretary, Sir Philip Haddon-Cave, referred to its attitude to the economy as 'positive non-interventionism'.[148] The idea is to maintain no attempt to plan the allocation of resources available to the private sector or to frustrate the operation of market forces, but recognise a responsibility on the part of the government to respond when industries with social obligations run into trouble and when an institution needs regulation to prevent inequitable practice. In the opinion of Wong, as economic policy, 'positive non-interventionism' upholds free market capitalism as official government policy.[149] But this is not to say that the government limits itself only to upholding the rule of law, protecting private property rights, maintaining open competitive markets, low taxes and free trade. The articulated position of positive non-interventionism is not to rule out all state interventions, but to accept only those for which an overwhelming deep market failure case could convincingly be made. Housing, healthcare, education and modest amounts of social welfare are examples of areas that could be justified according to the logic of 'positive non-interventionism'.

Such a principle of 'positive non-interventionism' has arguably been fading away since the transfer of sovereignty in 1997, despite that in theory it can be shielded by the principle of 'One Country Two Systems'. 'One Country, Two Systems' is a fundamental state policy formulated by Deng Xiaoping to accomplish the reunification of China by resolving the sovereignty questions of Hong Kong, Macau and Taiwan arising from a complicated historical background.[150] More specifically, this means that within the China, the mainland with its more than one billion people, will maintain the socialist system, while Hong Kong, Macau and Taiwan continue under the capitalist system. In sum, Hong Kong's current social and economic systems will remain unchanged; its legal system will remain basically unchanged; its way of life and its status as a free port and an international trade and financial centre will remain unchanged and it can continue to maintain or establish economic relations with other countries and regions. This promise will last for 50 years after 1997, as written in its constitutional document of Hong Kong, the Basic Law.[151] Furthermore, Beijing will not assign officials to the government of the Hong Kong Special Administrative Region.

Under the Basic Law, Hong Kong is an autonomous Special Administrative Region of the People's Republic of China, except in defence and foreign affairs.[152] The Basic Law guarantees that autonomy for 50 years, and designates a system of governance led by a Chief Executive and an Executive Council, with a two-tiered system of representative government and an independent judiciary.[153] The Chief Executive is the head of the Hong Kong Special Administrative Region.

He is elected by an Election Committee in accordance with the Basic Law, and is then appointed by the Central People's Government of China. Apparently, this is more democratic than the colonial government. By contrast, the government of the colonial Hong Kong was established through two constitutional documents, the Letters Patent and Royal Instructions.[154] The Letters Patent allowed for the selection of a Governor by the Crown as its representative in Hong Kong. Despite this a democratic process is in place after the handover, Summers points out the process is still largely within Beijing's control and it is virtually certain that only the favoured candidate of the central government will be elected.[155] The Chief Executive is assisted by the Executive Council in policy making and the Council advises the Chief Executive on matters relating to the introduction of bills and subsidiary legislation. The Council comprises 16 principal officials and 16 non-official members. All members are directly appointed by the Chief Executive. Besides, there is the Legislative Council which is the law making body of Hong Kong. It comprises 70 members, with 35 elected by geographical constituencies and 35 elected by functional constituencies. Again, the Legislative Council is more democratic than the one in the colonial era. Before 1985, all members of the Council were directly appointed. The first-ever elections to the Council were held in 1985. After the elections, there were 11 Official Members (including four ex officio), and 46 Unofficial Members, of which 22 were appointed by the Governor, 12 were elected from functional constituencies, one elected from among members of the Urban Council, one elected from among members of the Regional Council and ten elected by an electoral college constituency made up of members of all district boards.[156] Only in 1995 did the last Legislative Council under British rule become a fully elected legislature. Among its 60 elected Members, 30 came from functional constituencies, 20 were returned by direct elections in geographical constituencies and ten were elected by the Election Committee constituency.

However, despite a welcome move towards democracy, a worrying trend is that Hong Kong (and Beijing) is becoming more interventionist. In 1998, the Hang Seng Index reached a low point of 6,660 after the Asian Financial Crisis. As part of its actions to counter speculative attacks and manipulation, the government introduced a series of follow-through measures to further improve both the currency market and securities and futures markets.[157] The most controversial move was the purchase of shares of 33 stocks that constitute the Hang Seng Index. Goodhart and Dai have suggested that views towards this governmental intervention were divided.[158] Supporters thought that the government had the right to fight back against the speculators and protect the economy and financial markets. The opposing view was the government had a confused dual role as both the regulator and player. Furthermore, there was a serious deviation from the usual non-interventionist practice. In fact, this deviation was not only implied by its conduct but also stated explicitly by the Financial Secretary of Hong Kong in 2002.[159] More recently in 2015, Chief Executive Leung Chun Ying made his strong call for Hong Kong to ditch its laissez-faire economic policy, calling it outdated and arguing that it was time for the government to take a leading role in the city's big business decisions.[160] In addition, an even more worrying trend has been that the integrity of the legal, political and economic system in Hong Kong has been slowly compromised since 1997. For example, on the one hand, Article 2 of the Basic Law of Hong Kong states that Hong Kong has a high degree of autonomy and enjoys independent executive, legislative and judicial power, including that of final adjudication. On the other hand, after the Right of Abode cases had been decided by the Court of Final Appeal (the highest court in Hong Kong), the Hong Kong government sought the Standing Committee of the National People's Congress of China in 1999 to interpret the law in an attempt to reverse the potential adverse effect of the decision.[161] Furthermore, a series of other rulings have stirred fears that the rule of law has slowly been eroded since Hong Kong was absorbed into China.[162]

Cultural institutions

Hong Kong is a largely homogenous society, with about 94 per cent of its people being Chinese (ethnically speaking, Han Chinese). The 2011 Population Census found that there were about 451,000 non-Chinese people in Hong Kong, or about 6 per cent of the population. Out of the ethnic minorities, the major groups were Indonesians and Filipinos, who generally work as domestic helpers in Hong Kong. Hong Kong opened its doors to these maids and caretakers in the mid-1970s and now has one of the highest densities of domestic workers in the world.[163] As discussed, Hong Kong has served as the main link between China and the West for centuries. Thus, Hong Kong is a base for overseas companies engaged in Chinese ventures and functions as a conduit for goods to flow from China to the West. As such, Hong Kong is constantly in touch with both worlds. The result is that Hong Kong is an interesting blend of East and West.[164] As a capitalistic economy that developed out of a Western influence, Hong Kong is environmentally compatible with the US. On the other hand, adherence to Confucian values and traditional Chinese customs makes Hong Kong culturally comparable to China. *Guanxi* and Confucian values are still practised in Hong Kong, which has led to the dominance of family business in the city. On the other hand, unlike China and other Asian economies, it is one of the most corruption-free countries.

The rise of dispersed ownership, which has resulted from strong shareholder protection or other functional substitutes, is arguably associated with the development of stock markets.[165] Most Anglo-American corporations have a separation of management and ownership, which facilitates the growth of domestic stock markets. Despite the perception that Hong Kong is an international business centre heavily influenced by the Anglo-American model, most listed companies in Hong Kong have been controlled by families. Chen and colleagues analysed a sample of 412 publicly listed Hong Kong firms during 1995 to 1998 and found that the majority of Hong Kong firms were closely held: 61.1 per cent had a family controlling at least 30 per cent of the voting rights.[166] Data from La Porta and colleagues' survey on corporate ownership around the world were even more revealing.[167] Using 20 per cent as the criterion for control, 70 per cent of the large publicly traded companies in Hong Kong were family controlled, the highest percentage among the other 27 wealthy economies in the sample.[168] A more general and comparative picture can be seen in the study by Claessens and colleagues, who surveyed the separation of ownership and control in 2,980 publicly traded companies in nine East Asian countries, including Hong Kong, Indonesia, Japan, South Korea, Malaysia, the Philippines, Singapore, Taiwan and Thailand.[169] In some of these countries, a significant share of corporate assets rests in the hands of a small number of families. The largest ten families in Indonesia, the Philippines and Thailand controlled half of the corporate assets in the sample, while the largest ten families in Hong Kong and Korea controlled about a third of the corporate sector. The exception is Japan, where family control was insignificant. They discovered that around three-quarters of the largest 20 companies were under family control. All these studies pointed to a high concentration of family businesses in Hong Kong. But a noteworthy point is that all these studies were conducted during the very early stages of the influx of Chinese state-owned companies into the HKEx, a new survey of ownership structure nowadays may present another picture.

According to the International Finance Corporation (IFC), a family business is defined as 'a company where the voting majority is in the hands of the controlling family, including the founder(s) who intend to pass the business on to their descendants.'[170] Wong's seminal article on family business is concerned with the aspect of family ownership and the prevalence of family owned firms among privately owned Chinese commercial and industrial enterprises.[171] His argument is that because they tend to behave differently at various stages of their development cycle, these firms are not necessarily small, impermanent and conservative. Wong identifies four phases of development, namely the emergent, centralised, segmented and disintegrative stages. In the beginning, the primary source of capital of a Chinese family business is either the individual himself or his relatives. On the other hand, another format for a new business is a partnership in which financial resources are pooled by persons largely unrelated by ties by descent or marriage. This is consistent with the discussion in the previous chapter on Confucianism about different layers of family ties. Then, once a family firm is established, the firm is characterised by a highly personalised style of leadership. Centralisation in decision making entails a low degree of delegation of responsibility to subordinates. After the father-entrepreneur has relinquished control, the centralised family firm enters the third phase of its evolution and gradually becomes segmented. Finally, according to Wong, family enterprises in their Chinese guise are apparently short-lived.[172] As common wisdom has it, they seldom last beyond three generations.

Running a company in a family business form has its strengths and weaknesses.[173] In relation to strengths, the family, as the business owners, normally shows the highest dedication in seeing its business grow, prosper and get passed on to the next generations. Many family members identify with the company, and usually work harder and reinvest part of their profits into the business to allow it to grow in the long term. Furthermore, accumulation of knowledge, experience and skills within families through generations is normally seen as a priority. Also, because family businesses have their name and reputation associated with their output, they strive to increase the quality of their products or services and to maintain a good relationship. On the other hand, family businesses are usually complex in terms of governance and more problematically, there is not a set of clearly articulated business practices and procedures. As the family and its business grow larger, many inefficiencies and internal conflicts that could threaten the continuity of the business will start to surface.

Although both Ho and Lawton have agreed that family-controlled companies can make efficient decisions owing to a more personalised method of control, with less paperwork and fewer formalities, there are inherent conflicts between the controlling and minority shareholders of companies.[174] The former have high incentives to extract private benefits through their control in connected party transactions. Ho has observed that common forms of misbehaviour among controlling shareholders in Hong Kong include: unfair terms for intra-group sales of goods and services; the transfer of assets and controlling stakes at the expense of minority shareholders; and directing corporate resources to themselves.[175] The predominance of family ownership and control of companies in Hong Kong is incompatible with its rise as an international finance centre if one believes in the nexus between shareholder protection and market growth. The explanation in this case seems to be that the gain in efficiency outweighs the increase in agency costs. As claimed by Farrar, Hong Kong represents a successful story built on the twin foundations of Anglo-American law and finance and successful Chinese family business.[176] It is a spectrum of factors, rather than one single factor, that contributes to Hong Kong's achievements.

One of the factors can perhaps be that Hong Kong has long had the reputation of one of the most corruption-free countries in the world. It ranks fifteenth among 176 countries according to the recent Corruption Perceptions Index.[177] It is widely believed that this success is largely owed to the Independent Commission Against Corruption (ICAC). The ICAC was set up in 1974 to tackle corruption, marking a milestone in Hong Kong's anti-corruption history.[178] Before its establishment, corruption was rampant in the public sector. For example, controlling assets of over HK$4.3 million, Peter Godber, a Chief Police Superintendent, was under investigation in 1973.[179] It was suspected that his unearned wealth had been obtained from corrupt means. At that point, a prima facie case was established, but the police were still unable to prove that Godber's wealth was amassed through illegal means. After relentless efforts by the ICAC and with the assistance of the UK police, as he had escaped from Hong Kong earlier, Godber was arrested on 29 April 1974. The Commission is independent of the civil service and the Commissioner is answerable directly to the Chief Executive of the Hong Kong government. The ICAC is committed to fighting corruption through a three-pronged strategy of law enforcement, education and prevention to maintain Hong Kong as a fair and just society. Law enforcement is the responsibility of the Operations Department which receives, considers and investigates reports of alleged offences under the Prevention of Bribery Ordinance, the Independent Commission Against Corruption Ordinance and the Elections (Corrupt and Illegal Conduct) Ordinance. It is worth noting that the legal efforts to combat corruption had started far earlier than 1974.[180] As early as 1898, bribery was made an offence with the enactment of the Misdemeanours Punishment Ordinance. Replaced by the Prevention of Corruption Ordinance in 1948, the legislation was enforced by the Anti-Corruption Office of the Police Force. In May 1971, the Ordinance was further strengthened with new offences, heavier penalties and stronger investigative powers to become the Prevention of Bribery Ordinance of today. Apart from law enforcement, the Commission has a statutory duty to examine the practices and procedures of government departments and public bodies and to secure the revision of methods of work or procedures which may be conducive to corrupt practices. The Commissioner is also required by law to provide corruption prevention assistance on request to any member of the public. These duties are discharged by the Corruption Prevention Department. Finally, the Community Relations Department is responsible for educating the public against the evils of corruption and enlisting community support in the fight against graft. In addition to its role of fighting corruption, the ICAC has closely cooperated with the SFC to combat market misconduct by regularly reviewing the work of the SFC as well as exchanging cases and information with the SFC.[181]

Heilbrunn differentiates among four types of anti-corruption commissions in the world.[182] First is the universal model with its investigative, preventative and communicative functions. The universal model is typified by Hong Kong's ICAC. Second, the investigative model is characterised by a small and centralised investigative commission as operates in Singapore's Corrupt Practices Investigation Bureau. Both the universal and investigative models are organisationally accountable to the executive. Third, the parliamentary model includes commissions that report to parliamentary committees and are independent from the executive and judicial branches of state. The parliamentary model is epitomised by the New South Wales Independent Commission Against Corruption, Finally, the multi-agency model includes a number of offices that are individually distinct, but together weave a web of agencies to fight corruption. The US has adopted this approach. Amongst the models, the universal model entails high costs that for many governments are simply prohibitive for already limited budgets. The ICAC is another piece of convincing evidence showcasing Hong Kong's strength in public enforcement, as discussed above. From the experience of China and other Asian countries (except Singapore), the cultural values there can easily lead to corruption. But the risk is nonetheless effectively controlled by the government, as seen in Hong Kong and Singapore.

Role of market infrastructure

As discussed before, Hong Kong has strong historical roots in finance and trade. For the former, a rich investment culture could be expected among local people.

However, following the market turmoils in 1974 and 1987, ordinary investors have taken a cautious attitude towards investing in stocks. In the 1990s, six in ten Hong Kong adults put their money only into their saving accounts and not into any other financial products.[183] In the 2000s, stock market participation increased. In 2005, the SFC estimated that 28.3 per cent of Hong Kong adults traded Hong Kong stocks and 4.1 per cent traded Chinese or overseas stocks.[184] Among these investors, 42.6 per cent had received tertiary education or above.[185] This reflects the fact that many investors in Hong Kong are well educated, which can potentially reduce market volatility.[186] In addition, institutional investors accounted for 40 per cent of the local market transactions.[187] The maturity of the Hong Kong market can be further confirmed by the presence of a large body of professionals.

The changing economic conditions of Hong Kong seems largely dependent and comes as a result of the rise of China as a new economic superpower. As the old saying goes, 'chance favours the prepared mind'. The pre-existing legal, political, cultural and economic conditions of Hong Kong, plus the rapid growth of China, is the formula for success. As discussed before, since the late 1970s, Hong Kong has successfully transformed into a service-oriented economy. By 2007, around 15.7 per cent of the total labour force, which stood at 3.64 million, was employed in the financial services sector, which was higher than that of New York.[188] In fact, Hong Kong has developed a critical mass of expertise in financial services and related professional sectors. For example, Hong Kong has the fourth largest number of Chartered Financial Analysts in the world after the US, Canada and the UK.[189] The number of Certified Public Accountants grew from about 11,500 in 1995 to more than 25,000 in 2006.[190] The heavy presence of these intermediaries has provided a strong foundation to the Hong Kong market. The market is also highly internationalised. Stockbroking and fund management companies have come from all over the world to set up businesses. In Hong Kong, the first fund managers were subsidiaries of merchant banks from the UK in the late 1960s and early 1970s.[191] Many of the more recent arrivals have come from the US, as well as South Africa, Taiwan, Sweden and New Zealand.[192] All these workers in the financial services industries have contributed to the success of Hong Kong.

The presence and growth of all these market professionals and participants is by no means a coincidence. Take the accounting profession in the city as an example. To serve the multinational corporations and institutions that came to set up in Hong Kong, an accounting sector started to develop in the city from the turn of the twentieth century.[193] Lowe's firm, which became Lowe Bingham and Matthews, and leading international accounting firms such as Peat, Marwick, Mitchell and Company, offered auditing and accounting services that generally followed British standards and practices. Meanwhile, many local companies that kept books in Chinese followed their own bookkeeping methods, usually handwritten in ledger books, and were audited to varying standards by local accounting firms. In 1913, a formal system for examining auditors was established. The 17 or so successful candidates in the first examination formed the Hong Kong

Chinese Auditor Research Society. After the war, the government was keen to increase oversight of the accounting sector. Auditor qualifications were reorganised under the Companies Ordinance, which became the principal legislation governing accounting in the colony. At that time, becoming a qualified accountant usually involved the expense and time of studying overseas and working as an articled clerk to an accounting firm in the UK, which imposed a high bar for those who would like to become an accountant. This led to a call for a local professional and regulatory body with the power to standardise, oversee and uplift the profession. By 1966, there were about 200 British- and Australian-qualified chartered accountants. They gathered as the Association of Chartered Accountants in Hong Kong. Soon in the 1970s, the Professional Accountants Ordinance became part of the law of the colony. The Hong Kong Society of Accountants was established on 1 January 1973. It is estimated that there were about 1,500 accountants in Hong Kong at the dawn of the 1980s.[194] However, only two universities trained accountants at the time. To increase the number of accountants, in 1984, the Society signed an agreement with the Association of Chartered Certified Accountants (ACCA) in London to offer their exam in Hong Kong as a joint programme. People who qualified would be able to become a Hong Kong accountant as well as an ACCA qualified accountant. However, amidst the handover in 1997, the Society decided to give ACCA notice that it was going to end the joint examination and qualification scheme and develop its own programme. Under the new system, introduced in 1999, candidates must have a degree, undertake a professional training programme and pass examinations and workshops to qualify as a Hong Kong certified accountant. In 2004, the Society was renamed the Hong Kong Institute of Certified Public Accountants. In the past decades, from 566 in 1973, the number of members of the Society (now called Institute) rose to 35,533 in 2013, providing the much needed accounting support to various commercial activities which have served as an engine of Hong Kong's economic growth.[195]

Whilst human capital is undoubtedly a precious asset for Hong Kong's economic growth, the city has excellent transportation links to enable the success of its trading activities. The civil airport in Hong Kong during the colonial era was Kai Tak airport. The first commercial passenger flight 'Dorado' landed on 24 March 1936 from Penang operated by the Imperial Airways. In 1954, the Government approved a master plan for airport development. In 1958, a new northwest/southeast heading 2,529 metre runway was constructed on a promontory into Kowloon Bay. The name Hong Kong International Airport was officially adopted for Kai Tak Airport. In 1976, the Hong Kong Air Cargo Terminal was opened. Terminal 2 of the Hong Kong Air Cargo Terminal was commissioned providing an annual air cargo handling capacity of 1.5 million tonnes per annum in 1991. In 1996, Kai Tak Airport reached an important milestone when it handled 29.5 million international passengers and 1.56 million tonnes of international cargo, making it the third busiest Airport in the world for international passengers and first in the world for international cargo throughput in the world.[196] Kai Tak was closed down in 1998 and a new airport was opened.

The new international airport at Chek Lap Kok is on a 1,248 hectare site on the northern side of Lantau Island and 28 kilometres west of Kai Tak. The estimated cost for the first phase of the new airport was HK$70.3 billion, which was one of the largest construction projects commissioned by the colonial government. Indeed during the planning stage, this new airport was a source of disputes between the British and Chinese government.[197] China had concerns about the cost, financing, timing and location of the project. Above all, China was worried that Britain might be trying to bleed the territory of its financial resources before the handover. As of 2016, the airport handled 70.5 million passengers and 4.52 million tonnes of cargo.[198] It remains the busiest airport in the world by cargo traffic. Also, it has consistently been rated as one of the best airports in the world by Skytrax, an international air transport rating organisation and based in London.

Furthermore, the port of Hong Kong used to be the world's busiest container port. Since 1992, Hong Kong has been the world's busiest port in 12 years.[199] However, its development has been overshadowed by the competition from other nearby ports in the new millennium. This has come from Singapore's major efforts to become a hub port in the region, and the southern Chinese ports' successful efforts to compete directly with Hong Kong. According to Song, Hong Kong's port has expanded along with the fast economic development in Southeast Asian countries and China, and greater international trade connections between these areas and the rest of the world.[200] However, Hong Kong has been gradually losing its edge in the past two decades. The main reason is that almost every major international container shipping company is now engaged in trade with China and operates direct line services to an increasing number of Chinese ports. This clearly points to the phasing out of Hong Kong's middleman role in China's economic development. Also, internally, Hong Kong faces a capacity problem at its ports.[201] In February 1967, the Container Committee urged government and business to embrace the emerging trend for container shipping and support a purpose-built port at Kwai Tsing. It was a huge financial gamble requiring a proposed initial investment of HK$281 million, but Hong Kong grasped the nettle. The facility grew and by the 1990s was the largest container port in the world. Fast-forward to 2014 with other ports overtaking, port administrators identified 70 hectares of land adjacent to container berths for expansion, but three years later only 15 hectares has been promised, and only eight hectares are in the process of being transferred. With the airport, Hong Kong did not wait for capacity to be 100 per cent full before planning a new runway, but that has not been the case with shipping. It could be a severe lack of vision and planning on the part of the government considering that: (1) Chek Lap Kok handles between 1 and 2 per cent of Hong Kong's cargo, while the container port handles more than 90 per cent; and (2) Hong Kong's wealth has grown with the container shipping trade for five decades.[202]

Determinants of future growth

Although it is widely believed that Hong Kong's economic success has been built on the institutions left behind by its colonial ruler, ranging from a legal system based on common law to the current airport built by the colonial government, some of these institutions may be fading away following the handover, despite the Basic Law confirming that Hong Kong would largely remain unchanged under the Chinese rule. The foremost uncertainty is that the Basic Law only provides for the existing system in Hong Kong to stay until 2047, that is, 50 years after the handover.[203] After 2047, Hong Kong may be absorbed into China entirely and practice a system of 'One Country One System', rather than continue to exist as 'Special Administrative Region' which enjoys 'a high degree of autonomy and enjoy executive, legislative and independent judicial power'. There are uncertainties and worries about what will happen to Hong Kong after 2047. Albert Chen, a professor of Faculty of Law at the University of Hong Kong and a member of the Basic Law Committee which drafted the law, said that the Basic Law will continue to be effective from a legal standpoint until some amendments are made or it is abolished.[204] However, some legal issues which affect the economy directly still arise. One example is the use of land. Nowadays, most land leases are issued or renewed for a period of 50 years in Hong Kong, which means that large numbers of leases extend beyond 30 June 2047. Some have expressed doubts about the legality of this practice.[205]

Political stability is obviously a concern to all investors. Recently the tension between pro-Beijing and pro-democracy groups over how the promise of universal suffrage would be delivered to the special administrative region has unsettled the city. As John Tsang, former financial secretary of Hong Kong, remarked in August 2014, 'The uncertain political situation might lead to "a perfect financial storm".'[206] Occupy Central was a plan initiated by the pro-democracy group to mobilise more than 10,000 people to block streets in Central, the financial district of Hong Kong, if the government failed to deliver a satisfactory political reform proposal for the election of the Chief Executive in 2017. John Tsang's remark could be supported by a study from investment bank UBS earlier in April which suggested a prolonged political incident could cause stock market volatility and warned that it might take a long time for the city to regain the confidence of foreign investors and travellers.[207] The Occupy Central movement soon evolved into the Umbrella Revolution; tens of thousands of Hong Kong residents peacefully occupied major thoroughfares across the city, shuttering businesses and bringing traffic to a halt.[208]

Despite Articles 45 and 68 of the Basic Law expressly stating that the ultimate aim is the selection of the Chief Executive and election of all the members of the Legislative Council by universal suffrage upon nomination, discussions on the models, roadmap and timetable for implementing universal suffrage in Hong Kong have been attracting a great deal of discussions. On the one hand, the pro-democracy camp, represented by Occupy Central with Love and Peace, believed the government should adopt an open-minded attitude towards civil nomination. On the other hand, the pro-Beijing camp, represented by Silent Majority for Hong Kong, opposed the Occupy Central Movement and fought for 'democracy without chaos'. To clear the confusion surrounding the constitutional development in Hong Kong, both the Hong Kong government and Central

Government of China took action. In December 2013, the former issued the *Consultation Document on the Methods for Selecting the Chief Executive in 2017 and for Forming the Legislative Council in 2016* to formally commence a five-month public consultation to collect views from various sectors of the community on major issues and related questions on the two electoral methods. Subsequently, in June 2014, the State Council in China issued the White Paper on the Practice of 'One Country Two Systems' Policy in Hong Kong.

The Hong Kong Bar Association was particularly anxious about two points in the white paper. First, in relation to the theme of resolutely safeguarding the authority of the Constitution of China and the Basic Law, the Association believed that respect for the rule of law means more than 'doing things according to law'.[209] Proper self-restraint in the exercise of power and judicial independence are also important. Furthermore, the Association criticised the State Council for categorising judges and judicial officers as part of 'Hong Kong's administrators' and therefore sending a wrong message to people that 'Courts are part of the machinery of the Government and sing in unison with it'. Similarly, the Law Society of Hong Kong responded to the white paper by reiterating 'unambiguously that the rule of law and judicial independence are essential for maintaining the principle of "One Country Two Systems", as well as the stability and prosperity of Hong Kong'.[210]

Despite the divided society, several prominent authorities are optimistic about the principles of 'One Country Two Systems' and a high degree of autonomy. As put by Andrew Li, a former Chief Justice of the Court of Final Appeal, whilst recognising the inherent tensions and grey areas in the concept, he remains 'confident that, with constant vigilance, the rule of law with an independent judiciary will continue to thrive in the coming years'.[211] William Hague, former Foreign Secretary of the UK, also commented that 'Hong Kong's unique constitutional framework has worked well … [and it is] vital for the future prosperity and security of Hong Kong'.[212] Meanwhile, there were other more recent events which may suggest otherwise. First, there have been several former senior government officials jailed for corruption, including former Chief Executive, Donald Tsang, and former Chief Secretary, Rafael Hui.[213] This may have signalled the end of a corruption free era in Hong Kong and the city is becoming more like mainland China where corruption is perceived to be widespread. Second, Hong Kong has been ranked as the world's freest economy in the Index of Economic Freedom of the Heritage Foundation for 20 consecutive years, since its inception in 1995.[214] Hong Kong is particularly praised for its well protected business freedom within an efficient regulatory framework. However, by the end of 2015, five Hong Kong-based book publishers linked to the company Mighty Current went missing.[215] They eventually turned up in the custody of mainland Chinese authorities for running an independent bookstore selling politically sensitive books. Finally, six pro-democracy lawmakers in Hong Kong have been disqualified from their posts recently, sparking fears about the brutal attempts by Beijing to exert more control over internal affairs in Hong Kong.[216] This essentially means that hundreds of thousands voters have had their voices silenced in the legislative body. All of these episodes cast doubt on the credibility of the principle of 'One Country Two Systems' which forms the bedrock of Hong Kong's post-handover economy. This is not only a political problem, but it also affects other institutional advantages like the rule of law in Hong Kong.

Concluding remarks

Hong Kong's growth can be explained by its ability to capitalise on the China factor and its versatile economy which has reacted effectively to the changes in the global environment. As a British colony, Hong Kong was used mainly as an entrepot in the trade between China and the West. The 1951 UN trade embargo on China slashed trade in Hong Kong's port, forcing the colony to shift its economic focus towards export-oriented manufacturing. After the economic reform in China, the migration of labour-intensive industries to the north forced Hong Kong to transform from light manufacturing to a services industry. Hong Kong is now one of the major financial centres in the world, and is arguably the only international financial centre in China at a time when China has yet to fully open its financial markets. Hong Kong has been serving as an important fund-raising platform for Chinese companies.

Hong Kong's robust English legal system, especially in relation to corporate and financial law, has provided the essential protection for investors. One notable feature is that Hong Kong has a dedicated set of listing rules in place for Chinese companies, which provides a convincing explanation as to why Chinese companies have been especially keen to get listed in Hong Kong, amidst other possible factors such as geographical and cultural proximity. Moreover, Hong Kong has invested a lot in public enforcement to make sure that it has one of the best regulators in the world to oversee the market. Other factors have also contributed to its success. Since the colonial era, the government has maintained a positive non-interventionist approach. This laissez-faire capitalist system, together with the English legal system mentioned before, are allowed to stay in the post-handover era, thanks to the principle of 'One Country Two Systems' recognised by the Basic Law of Hong Kong, which is regarded as a mini constitution of the city. Furthermore, the dominance of family businesses in the city means that companies there have been more flexible in accommodating changes, which may provide the reason behind the city's several successful transformations. Finally, as discussed before, Hong Kong has ensured both soft and hard infrastructures are in place to support its strong economic growth.

Looking to the future, Hong Kong's success will hinge on how credible the principle of 'One Country Two Systems' is, so as to allow it to preserve a unique mix of institutional advantages. On the face of it, such a promise may expire in 2047, 50 years after the handover, as expressly stated in the Basic Law. On the other hand, there are plausible concerns that, even long before 2047, these institutional advantages may have already corroded under Chinese rule. There is a chance that Hong Kong will soon be just another city in China. If this is true, pragmatic integration with China in the form of bilateral trade relations may inevitably dictate the source of future growth. This is to be further discussed in Chapter 7.

Notes

1 IMD (2017), 'World Competitiveness Yearbook 2017 Results'. Online. Available at: www.imd.org/wcc/world-competitiveness-center-rankings/competitiveness-2017-rankings-results.
2 Hong Kong Government (2017), 'Hong Kong again Ranked the World's Most Competitive Economy'. Online. Available at: www.info.gov.hk/gia/general/201706/01/P2017060100156.htm.
3 Hong Kong Government (2017a), *Yearbook 2016*, Hong Kong: Information Services Department, p. 335.
4 Ibid. p. 336.
5 Ibid. p. 338.
6 Securities and Futures Commission (2002), *Securities Regulation in Hong Kong*, Hong Kong: Securities and Futures Commission, p. 3.
7 Catherine Schenk (2002), 'Banks and the Emergence of Hong Kong as an International Financial Center' in *Journal of International Financial Markets, Institutions and Money*, **12**, p. 323.
8 Swee-Hock Saw and Wing Kin Chiu (1975), 'Population Growth and Redistribution in Hong Kong, 1841–1975' in *Southeast Asian Journal of Social Science*, **4**, p. 126.
9 Tak-Wing Ngo (1999), 'Industrial History and the Artifice of Laissez-faire Colonialism' in Tak-Wing Ngo (ed.), *Hong Kong's History: State and Society under Colonial Rule*, Abingdon: Routledge, p. 122.
10 Ka-Che Yip *et al.* (2016), *Health Policy and Disease in Colonial and Post-Colonial Hong Kong, 1841–2003*, Abingdon: Routledge, p. 38.
11 Yun Wing Sung (1991), *The China-Hong Kong Connection: The Key to China's Open-Door Policy*, Cambridge: CUP, p. 21.
12 Hong Kong Government (2017a), op. cit., p. 340.
13 Ibid.
14 Sung (1991), op. cit., p. 21.
15 Zhigang Tao and Richard Wong (2002), 'Hong Kong: From Entrepot to Manufacturing and Then to Producer Services' in Gordon Liu (ed.), *Urban Transformation in China: Theory, Evidence and Policy*, Farnham: Ashgate.
16 Ibid.
17 Edward Chen (1987), 'Foreign Trade and Economic Growth in Hong Kong: Experience and Prospects' in Colin Bradford and William Branson (eds), *Trade and Structural Change in Pacific Asia*, Chicago: University of Chicago Press, p. 334.
18 Ibid.
19 Ibid. p. 337.
20 See James Riedel (1973), 'The Hong Kong Model of Industrialization' Kiel Discussion Papers 29. Online. Available at: www.econstor.eu/bitstream/10419/48056/1/055872107.pdf.
21 Chen (1987), op. cit, pp. 341–344.
22 Tao and Wong (2002), op. cit.
23 Securities and Futures Commission (2002), op. cit., p. 7.
24 Sung (1991), op. cit., p. 5.
25 Ibid. p. 17.
26 Ibid. pp. 16–28.
27 Ibid. pp. 95–97.
28 Ibid. p. 99.
29 Hong Kong Government (2017a), op. cit., pp. 56–84.

30 Statistics from the World Federation of Exchanges.
31 Census and Statistics Department of Hong Kong (2017), 'Gross Domestic Product (GDP) by Economic Activity'. Online. Available at: www.censtatd.gov.hk/hkstat/sub/sp250.jsp?tableID=036&ID=0&productType=8.
32 Long Finance (2017), 'The Global Financial Centres Index'. Online. Available at: www.longfinance.net/publications.html.
33 Brooke Masters (2008), 'Hong Kong Poses Threat to City' in *Financial Times* (6 October 2008).
34 Michael Elliott (2008), 'A Tale of Three Cities' in *Time Magazine* (17 January 2008).
35 Jeffrey Garten (2009), 'Amid the Economic Rubble, Shangkong will Rise' in *Financial Times* (10 May 2009).
36 See Alan Winters and Shahid Yusuf (2007), *Dancing with Giants: China, India and the Global Economy*, Washington D.C.: World Bank. China accounted for only five per cent of world GDP, but it has one-fourth of world population.
37 China Daily (2010), 'ADB Hikes China GDP Forecast'. Online. Available at: www.chinadailyasia.com/business/2010-04/14/content_42590.html.
38 Securities and Futures Commission (2004), 'The Listing of Mainland Companies on HKEx and the Implications for Hong Kong'. Online. Available at: www.sfc.hk/web/doc/EN/research/research/rs%20paper%2017.pdf.
39 Ibid.
40 In this paragraph, 'Chinese company' means a company incorporated in China. In a more general sense, the foreign listing of Chinese companies took place much earlier, with the most prominent example being the China International Trust and Investment Corporation, which was listed in Hong Kong under the name Tylfull Company (a Hong Kong incorporated company) in 1990. This chapter endeavours to consider 'Chinese companies' in both the strict and the broader sense.
41 Hong Kong Government (2009), *Yearbook 2008*, Hong Kong: Information Services Department, p. 67. Here, Chinese companies refer to those incorporated in China under the Chinese Company Law as well as those incorporated outside China but with actual business based in China and controlled by Chinese shareholders.
42 Ibid.
43 Tom Mitchell (2006), 'ICBC on Track to be World's Largest IPO' in *Financial Times* (13 October 2006).
44 A total of US$41.2 billion was raised on the HKEx alone in 2006, compared with US$37.3 billion in London and US$29.3 billion in New York. Another giant Chinese bank IPO in Hong Kong was that of Bank of China, with US$11 billion being raised in June 2006, see Tom Mitchell and Sundeep Tucker (2006), 'Hong Kong Braced for China Bank IPO' in *Financial Times* (5 October 2006).
45 Jamil Anderlini (2010), 'AgBank IPO Officially the World's Biggest' in *Financial Times* (13 August 2010). This was subsequently surpassed by the listing of Alibaba on the New York Stock Exchange in 2014.
46 Flora Huang and Horace Yeung (2013), 'Regulatory Co-operation between Securities Commissions: A Reflection from Hong Kong' in *Chinese Journal of Comparative Law*, **1**, p. 153.
47 Examples include Australia, Brazil, B.V.I., Canada (British Columbia and Ontario), Cyprus, France, India, Italy, Germany, the Isle of Man, Japan, Jersey, Luxembourg, Russia, Singapore, the UK and the US (Delaware, Nevada, and California).
48 Horace Yeung (2011), 'From Further North: The Case of Rusal's (Russian Aluminium) Listing in Hong Kong' in *International Company and Commercial Law Review*, **22**.
49 Hong Kong Stock Exchange (2004), 'Understanding Investors in the Hong Kong Listed Securities and Derivatives Markets'. Online. Available at: www.hkex.com.hk/eng/stat/research/rpaper/Documents/UIHKM.pdf.

50 Ibid.

51 China Daily (2010), 'What is QFII?'. Online. Available at: www.chinadaily.com.cn/business/2010h1results/2010-08/02/content_11079257.htm. QFII regulations relax some capital controls and allow foreign institutions to invest in RMB denominated equity and bond markets. These institutional investors are all big names such as Goldman Sachs, Morgan Stanley and some non-banks such as Yale University and Government of Singapore Investment Corporation.

52 Flora Huang and Horace Yeung (2014), *Chinese Companies and the Hong Kong Stock Market*, Abingdon: Routledge, pp. 189–202.

53 Qian Sun *et al.* (2006), 'The Choice of Foreign Primary Listing: China's Share-issue Privatization Experience' Working Paper. Online. Available at: http://cei.ier.hit-u.ac.jp/Japanese/pdf/Qian-Sun.pdf.

54 Mingyi Hung *et al.* (2012), 'Political Relations and Overseas Stock Exchange Listing: Evidence from Chinese State-Owned Enterprises' in *Journal of Accounting and Economics*, **53**.

55 Wei Liu and Xing-Hua Kang (2007), 'Study on Chinese Companies' Perception on Overseas Public Listing' in *Chinese Business Review*, **6**, p. 43.

56 Ibid.

57 Minkang Gu (2006), *Understanding Chinese Company Law*, Hong Kong: Hong Kong University Press, p. 9.

58 John Farrar (2002), 'Developing Corporate Governance in Greater China' in *UNSW Law Journal*, **25**, p. 474. The Companies Law Revision Committee was established in the early 1960s to review the company law in Hong Kong. It was subsequently replaced by the Standing Committee on Company Reform, which started the drafting work of the Companies (Amendment) Ordinance 1984.

59 Recent important amendments include the Companies (Amendment) Ordinance in 1991, 1994, 2003, 2004, 2010 and 2015.

60 The Code is essentially based on the Combined Code of the UK. Hong Kong similarly has adopted a 'comply or explain' principle. Issuers are expected to comply with, but may choose to deviate from, the code provisions. The recommended best practices are for guidance only. However, they must state whether they have complied with the code provisions set out in this Code in their interim reports and annual reports. See Appendix 14 of the Listing Rules of HKEx. Likewise, Hong Kong's system addressing issues arising from takeovers and mergers is largely based on the UK system. The Code on Takeovers and Mergers is a non-statutory set of rules regulating all aspects of these sorts of activities. At the heart of the whole system, similar to the UK is the mandatory offer requirement and a 'no frustration' rule. See Rules 4 and 26 of the Code.

61 Neil Gunningham (1990), 'Moving the Goalposts: Financial Market Regulation in Hong Kong and the Crash of October 1987' in *Law and Social Inquiry*, **15**, p. 20.

62 SFO (Cap 571, Ordinance No. 5 of 2002).

63 Ibid. s. 3. The SFC was indeed established on 1 May 1989 under the Securities and Futures Commission Ordinance (repealed in 2002).

64 Ibid. ss. 4, 5, 6 and 7.

65 Securities and Futures Commission (2007), 'Annual Report 2006–07'. Online. Available at: www.sfc.hk/sfc/doc/EN/speeches/public/annual/rep06-07/Regulation.pdf.

66 See for example, *Re Smith and Fawcett Ltd* [1942] Ch 304 CA.

67 See for example, *Aberdeen Railway Co.* v. *Blaikie Bros* (1854) 1 Macq 461 HI.

68 CO (Cap 622) s. 465. Contrast this with the UK's Companies Act 2006, s. 174. Similar to the UK, a dual subjective/objective test is adopted.

69 CO (Cap 32) s. 162(3); CO (Cap 622) s. 536. Under the old regime, directors must disclose the nature of their interests in 'contracts or proposed contracts' with the company which is of significance to the company's business. The new CO extends

the ambit of disclosure to cover any 'contracts', 'transactions' and 'arrangements' of the company in which the director has material interests.

70 Chapter 14 and 14A of the Listing Rules of Hong Kong.
71 For example, CO (Cap 32) ss. 121 and 129. The directors' report includes the following information with respect to the relevant financial year: (a) the principal activities of the company; (b) the names of the persons who were directors; (c) significant changes in assets; (d) directors' material interest in a company contract; and many others.
72 Part XV of the SFO (Cap 571).
73 Parts XIII and XIV of the SFO (Cap 571).
74 See Part XIII of the SFO (Cap 571) for civil liability and Part XIV for criminal liability. In the civil route, the standard of proof is 'on the balance of probabilities'. The criminal route is likely to be used when the government considers it has sufficient evidence to prove that a person is guilty of market misconduct 'beyond all reasonable doubt'.
75 Hong Kong Government (2016), *Yearbook 2015*, Hong Kong: Information Services Department, p. 58.
76 Hong Kong Listing Rule (HKLR) 19.05 and 19A.13.
77 Ibid. 19.55 and 19A.57.
78 Ibid. 19A.27.
79 See the Listing Document of China Construction Bank, Appendix VII-16. Shortly after that, a derivative action-like mechanism was added to the new Company Law, see art. 152 of the Company Law 2005 of China.
80 HKLR 19A.42.
81 HKLR 19A.38.
82 HKLR 19A.54.
83 The Arbitration Law was enacted by the Standing Committee of the National People's Congress on 31 August 1994 and became effective on 1 September 1995.
84 HKLR 19A.14.
85 'Chinese governmental body' includes, but not limited to: (1) China's central government, including the State Council, State Ministries and Commissions, Bureaus and Administrations directly under the State Council, State Council Offices and Institutions, Bureaus supervised by State Ministries and Commissions; (2) China's provincial-level governments, including provincial governments, municipalities directly under the central government, and autonomous regions, together with their respective administrative arms, agencies and institutions; and (3) local governments immediately under the provincial-level governments, including prefectures, municipalities and counties, together with their respective administrative arms, agencies and institutions.
86 HKLR 19A.19.
87 John Armour *et al.* (2009), 'Shareholder Protection and Stock Market Development: An Empirical Test of the Legal Origins Hypothesis' in *Journal of Empirical Legal Studies*, **6**.
88 See the relevant discussions in Chapter 2 of this book.
89 Rafael La Porta et al. (1998), 'Law and Finance' in *Journal of Political Economy*, **106**.
90 Rafael La Porta et al. (2006), 'What Works in Securities Laws?' *in Journal of Finance*, **61**.
91 World Bank (2017), 'Doing Business'. Online. Available at: www.doingbusiness.org.
92 Stavros Gadinis and Howell Jackson (2007), 'Markets as Regulators: A Survey' in *Southern California Law Review*, **80**.
93 The UK has taken a new, intrusive and direct approach after the Credit Crunch in 2007–08. For example, Hector Sants, former FSA chief executive, made the following comments in 2009, 'There is a view that people are not frightened of the FSA. I

can assure you that this is a view I am determined to correct. People should be very frightened of the FSA.' See Reuters (2009), 'Highlights – FSA Chief Promises Intrusive, Direct Regulation' Online. Available at: http://uk.reuters.com/article/uk-britain-banks-regulation-sb-idUKTRE52B27020090312.

94 SFO (Cap 571) s. 5.

95 Securities and Futures Commission (2008), 'Annual Report 2007–08'. Online. Available at: www.sfc.hk/web/doc/EN/speeches/public/annual/rep07-08/full.pdf.

96 Ibid. p. 38.

97 Securities and Futures Commission (2003), 'SFC Disciplinary Fining Guidelines'. Online. Available at: www.sfc.hk/web/EN/assets/components/codes/files-current/web/guidelines/disciplinary-fining-guidelines/SFC%20Disciplinary%20Fining%20Guidelines.pdf.

98 SFO (Cap 571) ss. 252–254.

99 Hong Kong Government (2008), *Yearbook 2007*, Hong Kong: Information Services Department, p. 77. This number included cases handled by the Insider Dealing Tribunal, the predecessor of the Market Misconduct Tribunal.

100 Securities and Futures Commission (2009), 'Annual Report 2008–09'. Online. Available at: www.sfc.hk/web/EN/published-resources/corporate-publications/annual-reports.html.

101 Ibid. The court sentenced two persons to imprisonment for 26 months and 12 months respectively. The first jailing for market manipulation was seen in the previous year. In the case, the market manipulator was sentenced to six months' imprisonment. See Securities and Futures Commission (2008), op. cit., p. 38.

102 John Coffee (2007), 'Law and the Market: The Impact of Enforcement' in *University of Pennsylvania Law Review*, **156**.

103 Howell Jackson and Mark Roe (2009), 'Public and Private Enforcement of Securities Laws: Resource-based Evidence' in *Journal of Financial Economics*, **93**, pp. 214–215.

104 Ibid.

105 Ibid.

106 David Donald and Paul Cheuk (2017), 'Hong Kong's Public Enforcement Model of Investor Protection' in *Asian Journal of Law and Society*, **4**.

107 The US and UK figures are quoted from Coffee (2007), op. cit. The figures of Hong Kong are compiled from the annual reports of the SFC. In 2006–07, there were 51 criminal prosecutions, 80 administrative actions and four cases referred to the Market Misconduct Tribunal. In 2007–08, there were 72 administrative actions. Also, 74 entities were charged in criminal proceedings and nine civil cases commenced.

108 Donald and Cheuk (2017), op. cit.

109 John Armour *et al.* (2009), 'Private Enforcement of Corporate Law: An Empirical Comparison of the US and UK' in *Journal of Empirical Legal Studies*, **6**.

110 Hua Cai (2007), 'Bonding, Law Enforcement and Corporate Governance in China' in *Stanford Journal of Law, Business and Finance*, **13**, pp. 91–102.

111 Jinsong Tan *et al.* (2007), 'An Analysis of the Characteristics of Chinese Listed Companies' Independent Director System' in *Frontiers of Business Research in China*, **1**, p. 457. In the context of the Chinese market, only until 2001, the CSRC issued the *Guiding Opinion on the Establishment of an Independent Director System in Listed Companies.*

112 Examples are Li Ka Shing and his Cheung Kong Holdings, the Kwok Brothers and their Sung Hung Kai Properties, the Government of Singapore Investment Corporation and the Qatar Investment Authority. See Chee Keong Low (2009), 'Investors and Initial Public Offerings on the Stock Exchange of Hong Kong' in *Fordham Journal of Corporate and Financial Law*, **14**, pp. 652–653.

113 This can be reflected from the three Chinese big four banks, which are listed in Hong Kong. Bank of America bought 9 per cent of China Construction Bank's ownership

in 2005. In the same year, the Royal Bank of Scotland and other parties led an investment of 10 per cent in Bank of China. In 2006, Goldman Sachs, Allianz Group and American Express purchased 10 per cent of the ICBC.

114 Dennis Chung and Paul Brockman (2003), 'Investor Protection and Firm Liquidity' in *Journal of Finance*, **58**.

115 Curtis Milhaupt and Katharina Pistor (2008), *Law and Capitalism*, Chicago: University of Chicago Press, p. 129.

116 Jing Leng (2005), 'Interaction between Domestic and Overseas Capital Markets and Corporate Governance of Chinese Listed Companies' in *Studies in International, Financial, Economic and Technology Law*, **7**, p. 311. CAO had a monopoly in market distribution of jet oil for China's domestic civil carriers. Other examples are the cellular duopoly of China Mobile and China Unicom, which are both listed in Hong Kong, as well as the oligopoly the big four banks, all of which are listed in Hong Kong.

117 Milhaupt and Pistor (2008), op. cit., p. 130.

118 Ibid. p. 134.

119 Data from the HKEx.

120 Securities and Futures Commission (2002), op. cit., pp. 218–219.

121 MORC, art. 6.

122 MORC, appendix 4.

123 In May 2002, IOSCO adopted the MMOU, the first multilateral international arrangement of its type among financial market regulators. The SFC was among the first signatories to have signed the MMOU in February 2003. The CSRC also became a party in April 2007.

124 Securities and Futures Commission (2005), 'Annual Report 2004–2005'. Online. Available at: www.sfc.hk/web/EN/published-resources/corporate-publications/annual-reports.html.

125 Securities and Futures Commission (2004), 'Annual Report 2003–2004'. Online. Available at: www.sfc.hk/web/EN/published-resources/corporate-publications/annual-reports.html.

126 La Porta *et al.* (2006), op. cit. Certainly, the idea of investigating enforcement by looking at substantive laws is logically flawed. In the survey, La Porta and colleagues analysed the specific provisions in securities laws governing IPOs in each country.

127 Misfeasance is defined under CO (Cap 32) s. 168BB(2) as fraud, negligence, default in compliance with any enactment or rule of law or breach of duty.

128 CO (Cap 622) s. 724; previously CO (Cap 32) s. 168A. See also the Companies Act 2006 of the UK s. 994 (formerly Companies Act 1985, s. 459).

129 CO (Cap 32) s. 168BC; CO (Cap 622) s. 732.

130 It was added to the ordinance by the Companies (Amendment) Ordinance 2004 (Ordinance No. 30 of 2004).

131 See *Foss* v. *Harbottle* (1843) 2 Hare 461.

132 SFO (Cap 571) s. 281. It appears that there is no equivalent in the UK.

133 Philip Lawton (2007), 'Modeling the Chinese Family Firm and Minority Shareholder Protection: The Hong Kong Experience 1980–1995' in *Managerial Law*, **49**. A total of 275 cases were identified.

134 Ibid. The numbers of CO (Cap 32) s. 177 actions, s. 168A actions and a mixture of both were 135, 24 and 116 respectively. There were only a very small number of cases pleaded as exceptions to *Foss* v. *Harbottle* and these were excluded from the analysis.

135 Félix Mezzanotte (2017), 'The Unconvincing Rise of the Statutory Derivative Action in Hong Kong: Evidence from its First 10 Years of Enforcement' in *Journal of Corporate Law Studies*, **17**.

136 *Waddington Ltd* v *Chan Chun Hoo Thomas and others* [2008] (FACV 15/2007). See also Say Goo (2010), 'Multiple Derivative Action and Common Law Derivative

Action Revisited: A Tale of Two Jurisdictions' in *Journal of Corporate Law Studies*, **10**.

137 Edward Tyler and John Ho (2004), *HKLRD Review Series 2004: Company Law*, Hong Kong: Sweet and Maxwell, p. 32.

138 See especially the part about private enforcement in China in Chapter 3 of this book.

139 Mark Roe (2005), *Corporate Governance: Political and Legal Perspectives*, Cheltenham: Edward Elgar, p. 199.

140 Milton Friedman (1997), 'The Real Lesson of Hong Kong'. Online. Available at: http://miltonfriedman.hoover.org/friedman_images/Collections/2016c21/MFlecture_05_14_1997.pdf. He said the post-war economic fortunes of Hong Kong, Great Britain and Israel formed a nice controlled experiment that demonstrated the superiority of market economies. Britain went for socialism and Hong Kong went for *laissez-faire* free markets.

141 Milton Friedman (2006), 'Hong Kong Wrong' in *Wall Street Journal* (6 October 2006). Friedman highly praised the 'positive-non-interventionism' policy implemented by former Financial Secretary, John Cowperthwaite in the 1960s.

142 Charles Goodhart and Lu Dai (2003), *Intervention to Save Hong Kong*, Oxford: OUP, p. 15.

143 See for example, Rafael La Porta *et al.* (1999), 'The Quality of Government' in *Journal of Law, Economics and Organisation*, **15**.

144 Ibid. p. 225.

145 The Heritage Foundation (2017), 'Index of Economic Freedom'. Online. Available at: www.heritage.org/Index/countries.cfm.

146 See Brian Cheffins (1997), *Company Law: Theory, Structure and Operation*, Oxford: OUP, for an evaluation of self-regulation in the UK.

147 Anthony Cheung (2000), 'New Interventionism in the Making: Interpreting State Interventions in Hong Kong after the Change of Sovereignty' in *Journal of Contemporary China*, **20**, pp. 295–296.

148 Ibid. p. 297.

149 Richard Wong (2015), 'Positive Non-interventionism as Governance Strategy' in *Hong Kong Economic Journal* (4 November 2015).

150 Xiaoping Deng (1984) 'One Country Two Systems'. Online. Available at: http://en.people.cn/dengxp/vol. 3/text/c1210.html.

151 Basic Law, art. 5.

152 Ibid. arts. 13–14.

153 Hong Kong Government (2017b), 'Government Structure'. Online. Available at: www.gov.hk/en/about/govdirectory/govstructure.htm.

154 Gavin Ure (2012), *Governors, Politics and the Colonial Office: Public Policy in Hong Kong, 1918–58*, Hong Kong: Hong Kong University Press, pp. 1–2.

155 Tim Summers (2017), 'What to Know about Hong Kong's Chief Executive Election'. Online. Available at: www.chathamhouse.org/expert/comment/what-know-about-hong-kong-s-chief-executive-election.

156 Legislative Council of Hong Kong (2017), 'History of the Legislative Council'. Online. Available at: www.legco.gov.hk/yr98-99/english/intro/hist_lc.htm.

157 Hong Kong Government (1999), *Yearbook 1998*, Hong Kong: Information Services Department. There is a dedicated part on 'Asian Financial Turmoil'.

158 Goodhart and Dai (2003), op. cit., p. 163.

159 Former Financial Secretary, Anthony Leung declared himself a believer in the free market while saying that 'proactive market enabling' should probably be a more appropriate way and a more accurate way to describe what a government should do. See Hong Kong Government (2002), 'Press Release'. Online. Available at: www.info.gov.hk/gia/general/200203/14/0314236.htm.

160 Jeffie Lam (2015), 'Hong Kong's Laissez-faire Economic Policy is "Outdated", Says CY Leung' in *South China Morning Post* (10 August 2015).

161 For more information about this case, see Hong Kong Government (1999), 'Key Issues 1998/99'. Online. Available at: www.info.gov.hk/info/sar2/rule.htm. Such a mechanism to seek interpretation is provided in Article 158 of the Basic Law.
162 One of the highest profile cases immediately after the handover was former Secretary of Justice, Elsie Leung decided not to prosecute a politically well-connected newspaper publisher on fraud accusations, see Mark Landler (1998), 'Hong Kong Rulings Stir Fears Over Law System' in *New York Times* (31 March 1998).
163 It is estimated that there are more than 336,000 among the 7.2 million in the city, comprising 10 per cent of the total working population. See John Kang (2016), 'Study Reveals 95% Of Filipino, Indonesian Helpers In Hong Kong Exploited Or Forced Labor' in *Forbes* (18 March 2016).
164 David Ralston et *al.* (1993), 'Differences in Managerial Values: A Study of U.S., Hong Kong and PRC Managers' in *Journal of International Business Studies*, **24**.
165 For a discussion for the interaction of these three spheres: law, ownership and market, see for example, John Coffee (2001), 'The Rise of Dispersed Ownership: The Roles of Law and the State in the Separation of Ownership and Control' in *Yale Law Journal*, **111**; Brian Cheffins (2001), 'Does Law Matter? The Separation of Ownership and Control in the United Kingdom' in *Journal of Legal Studies*, **30**; and Mark Roe (2006), 'Legal Origins, Politics and Modern Stock Markets' in *Harvard Law Review*, **120**.
166 Zhilan Chen *at el.* (2005), 'Ownership Concentration, Firm Performance and Dividend Policy in Hong Kong' in *Pacific-Basin Finance Journal*, **13**.
167 Rafael La Porta *et al.* (1999), 'Corporate Ownership around the World' in *Journal of Finance*, **64**.
168 Ibid.
169 Stijn Claessens *et al.* (2000), 'The Separation of Ownership and Control in East Asian Corporation' in *Journal of Financial Economics*, **58**.
170 International Finance Corporation (2011), 'IFC Family Business Governance Handbook'. Online. Available at: www.ifc.org/wps/wcm/connect/6a9001004f9f5979933c ff0098cb14b9/FamilyBusinessGovernance_Handbook_English. pdf?MOD=AJPERES.
171 Siu-lun Wong (1985), 'The Chinese Family Firm: A Model' in *British Journal of Sociology*, **36**.
172 Ibid. p. 61.
173 International Finance Corporation (2011), op. cit., pp. 12–14.
174 Philip Lawton (1996), 'Berle and Means, Corporate Governance and the Chinese Family Firm' in *Australian Journal of Corporate Law*, **6**; and Simon Ho *et al.* (2004), *The Hong Kong Financial System*, Hong Kong: OUP, pp. 383–388.
175 Ho *et al.* (2004), op. cit., pp. 386–387.
176 Farrar (2002), op. cit., p. 464.
177 Transparency International (2017), 'Corruption Perceptions Index 2016'. Online. Available at: www.transparency.org/news/feature/corruption_perceptions_index_2016.
178 Hong Kong Government (2016a), 'ICAC'. Online. Available at: www.gov.hk/en/about/abouthk/factsheets/docs/icac.pdf.
179 Independent Commission Against Corruption (2017), 'Landmark Cases'. Online. Available at: www.icac.org.hk/en/law/case/index.html.
180 Hong Kong Government (2016a), op. cit.
181 The ICAC is empowered by Independent Commission Against Corruption Ordinance (Cap 204) to investigate the offences of bribery involving civil servants, public bodies and private sector employees.
182 John Heilbrunn (2004), 'Anti-corruption Commissions: Panacea or Real Medicine to Fight Corruption?' World Bank Institute Working Paper Series 37234. Online. Available at: http://siteresources.worldbank.org/WBI/Resources/wbi37234Heilbrunn.pdf.
183 Securities and Futures Commission (2002), op. cit., p. 194.

184 Securities and Futures Commission (2006), 'Stock Investor Survey'. Online. Available at: www.sfc.hk/sfc/doc/EN/speeches/public/surveys/06/stock_investor_survey_060602.pdf.
185 Hong Kong Stock Exchange (2004), op. cit.
186 Xing has discovered that the education level of investors plays a significant role in explaining cross-country market volatility differences. See Xuejing Xing (2004), 'Why Does Stock Market Volatility Differ across Countries? Evidence from Thirty Seven International Markets' in *International Journal of Business*, **9**. Of course, the basic assumption might be that these investors have the ability to understand the risks and potential rewards of different types of investments as well as their rights as shareholders.
187 Ho *et al.* (2004), op. cit., p. 419.
188 Statistics from Hong Kong Government and New York State Department of Labour. Around 10 per cent of labour in New York City was in the financial services industry in 2007.
189 Statistics from the Chartered Financial Analysts Institute.
190 Securities and Futures Commission (2006), 'Hong Kong as a Leading Financial Centre in Asia'. Online. Available at: www.sfc.hk/web/doc/EN/research/research/rs%20paper%2033.pdf.
191 Stewart Aldcroft (2000), 'The Role and Functions of Fund Managers' in Chee Keong Low (ed.), *Financial Markets in Hong Kong*, Singapore: Springer, p. 221.
192 Ibid.
193 Hong Kong Institute of Certified Public Accountants (2013), 'The Institute at 40'. Online. Available at: http://app. 1.hkicpa.org.hk/APLUS/2013/04/pdf/22-31-Anniversary.pdf.
194 Hong Kong Institute of Certified Public Accountants (2013), 'The First Golden Age'. Online. Available at: http://app. 1.hkicpa.org.hk/APLUS/2013/06/pdf/30-anniversary.pdf.
195 Hong Kong Institute of Certified Public Accountants (2013), '40 Years of Serving Hong Kong Society'. Online. Available at: http://app. 1.hkicpa.org.hk/APLUS/2013/12/pdf/24-Infographic.pdf.
196 Civil Aviation Department of Hong Kong (2013), 'Kai Tak Airport 1925–1998'. Online. Available at: www.cad.gov.hk/english/kaitak.html.
197 John Flowerdew (1998), *The Final Years of British Hong Kong: The Discourse of Colonial Withdrawal*, Basingstoke: Palgrave Macmillan, p. 73.
198 Hong Kong Government (2017a), op. cit., p. 224.
199 Census and Statistics Department of Hong Kong (2006), 'Hong Kong Is One of the World's Busiest Container Ports'. Online. Available at: www.censtatd.gov.hk/FileManager/EN/Content_1064/B2_E.pdf.
200 Dong-Wook Song (2002), 'Regional Container Port Competition and Co-operation: The Case of Hong Kong and South China' in *Journal of Transport Geography*, **10**, pp. 101–102.
201 Stuart Heaver (2017), 'Why Hong Kong's Container Port may be in Terminal Decline, and What that would Mean for a City that Appears not to Care' in *South China Morning Post* (6 March 2017).
202 Ibid.
203 Basic Law, art. 5.
204 EJInsight (2016), 'Basic Law Remains Valid after 2047, as of Now: Law Expert'. Online. Available at: www.ejinsight.com/20160511-basic-law-remains-valid-after-2047-as-of-now-say-law-expert.
205 Danny Gittings (2013), *Introduction to the Hong Kong Basic Law*, Hong Kong: Hong Kong University Press, p. 305.
206 Julie Zhu and Mark Wembridge (2014), 'Hong Kong Pro-China Rally Draws Fake Crowd Allegations' in *Financial Times* (18 August 2014).

207 Jeffie Lam and Peggy Sito (2014), 'Occupy Central to Hit Hongkong Land, Wharf Holdings Hardest, UBS Says' in *South China Morning Post* (1 April 2014).
208 Jonathan Kaiman (2014), 'Hong Kong's Umbrella Revolution – the Guardian Briefing' in *Guardian* (30 September 2014).
209 Hong Kong Bar Association (2014), 'Response: White Paper on the Practice of "One Country, Two Systems" Policy in the Hong Kong Special Administrative Region'. Online. Available at: www.hkba.org/sites/default/files/White_Paper_Response_eng.pdf.
210 Law Society of Hong Kong (2014), 'Submission on the White Paper on the Practice of "One Country, Two Systems" Policy in the Hong Kong Special Administrative Region'. Online. Available at: www.hklawsoc.org.hk/pub_e/news/submissions/20140625.pdf.
211 Andrew Li (2014), 'Under Rule of Law, An Independent Judiciary Answers to No Political Masters' in *South China Morning Post* (15 August 2014).
212 Foreign and Commonwealth Office (2014), 'Six Monthly Reports on Hong Kong: January to June 2014'. Online. Available at: www.gov.uk/government/publications/six-monthly-reports-on-hong-kong-january-to-june-2014.
213 *HKSAR* v. *Donald Tsang* (ESCC3247/15); *HKSAR* v. *Rafael Hui* (FACC No. 12 of 2016).
214 Heritage Foundation (2017), 'Hong Kong'. Online. Available at: www.heritage.org/index/country/hongkong.
215 Nicola Smith (2017), 'Hong Kong Bookseller Abducted by China Vows to Reopen Shop in Taiwan' in *Guardian* (8 May 2017).
216 Benjamin Haas (2017), 'Hong Kong Pro-democracy Legislators Disqualified from Parliament' in *Guardian* (14 July 2017).

References

Aldcroft, Stewart (2000), 'The Role and Functions of Fund Managers' in Chee Keong Low (ed.), *Financial Markets in Hong Kong*, Singapore: Springer.

Anderlini, Jamil (2010), 'AgBank IPO Officially the World's Biggest' in *Financial Times* (13 August 2010).

Armour, John; Deakin, Simon; Sarkar, Prabirjit; Siems, Mathias; and Singh, Ajit (2009), 'Shareholder Protection and Stock Market Development: An Empirical Test of the Legal Origins Hypothesis' in *Journal of Empirical Legal Studies*, **6**.

Armour, John; Black, Bernard; Cheffins, Brian; and Nolan, Richard (2009) 'Private Enforcement of Corporate Law: An Empirical Comparison of the US and UK' in *Journal of Empirical Legal Studies*, **6**.

Cai, Hua (2007), 'Bonding, Law Enforcement and Corporate Governance in China' in *Stanford Journal of Law, Business and Finance*, **13**.

Census and Statistics Department of Hong Kong (2006), 'Hong Kong Is One of the World's Busiest Container Ports'. Online. Available at: www.censtatd.gov.hk/FileManager/EN/Content_1064/B2_E.pdf.

Census and Statistics Department of Hong Kong (2017), 'Gross Domestic Product (GDP) by Economic Activity'. Online. Available at: www.censtatd.gov.hk/hkstat/sub/sp250.jsp?tableID=036&ID=0&productType=8.

Cheffins, Brian (1997), *Company Law: Theory, Structure and Operation*, Oxford: OUP.

Cheffins, Brian (2001), 'Does Law Matter? The Separation of Ownership and Control in the United Kingdom' in *Journal of Legal Studies*, **30**.

Chen, Edward (1987), 'Foreign Trade and Economic Growth in Hong Kong: Experience and Prospects' in Colin Bradford and William Branson (eds), *Trade and Structural Change in Pacific Asia*, Chicago: University of Chicago Press.

Chen, Zhilan; Cheung, Yan-Leung; Stouraitis, Aris; and Wong, Anita (2005), 'Ownership Concentration, Firm Performance and Dividend Policy in Hong Kong' in *Pacific-Basin Finance Journal*, **13**.

Cheung, Anthony (2000), 'New Interventionism in the Making: Interpreting state interventions in Hong Kong after the change of sovereignty' in *Journal of Contemporary China*, **20**.

China Daily (2010), 'ADB Hikes China GDP Forecast'. Online. Available at: www.chinadailyasia.com/business/2010-04/14/content_42590.html.

China Daily (2010), 'What is QFII?'. Online. Available at: www.chinadaily.com.cn/business/2010h1results/2010-08/02/content_11079257.htm.

Chung, Dennis and Brockman, Paul (2003), 'Investor Protection and Firm Liquidity' in *Journal of Finance*, **58**.

Civil Aviation Department of Hong Kong (2013), 'Kai Tak Airport 1925–1998'. Online. Available at: www.cad.gov.hk/english/kaitak.html.

Claessens, Stijn; Djankov Simeon; and Lang, Larry (2000), 'The Separation of Ownership and Control in East Asian Corporation' in *Journal of Financial Economics*, **58**.

Coffee, John (2001), 'The Rise of Dispersed Ownership: The Roles of Law and the State in the Separation of Ownership and Control' in *Yale Law Journal*, **111**.

Coffee, John (2007), 'Law and the Market: The Impact of Enforcement' in *University of Pennsylvania Law Review*, **156**.

Deng, Xiaoping (1984), 'One Country Two Systems'. Online. Available at: http://en.people.cn/dengxp/vol. 3/text/c1210.html.

Donald, David and Cheuk, Paul (2017), 'Hong Kong's Public Enforcement Model of Investor Protection' in *Asian Journal of Law and Society*, **4**.

EJInsight (2016), 'Basic Law Remains Valid after 2047, as of Now: Law Expert'. Online. Available at: www.ejinsight.com/20160511-basic-law-remains-valid-after-2047-as-of-now-say-law-expert.

Elliott, Michael (2008), 'A Tale of Three Cities' in *Time Magazine* (17 January 2008).

Farrar, John (2002), 'Developing Corporate Governance in Greater China' in *UNSW Law Journal*, **25**.

Flowerdew, John (1998), *The Final Years of British Hong Kong: The Discourse of Colonial Withdrawal*, Basingstoke: Palgrave Macmillan.

Foreign and Commonwealth Office (2014), 'Six Monthly Reports on Hong Kong: January to June 2014'. Online. Available at: www.gov.uk/government/publications/six-monthly-reports-on-hong-kong-january-to-june-2014.

Friedman, Milton (1997), 'The Real Lesson of Hong Kong'. Online. Available at: http://miltonfriedman.hoover.org/friedman_images/Collections/2016c21/MFlecture_05_14_1997.pdf.

Friedman, Milton (2006), 'Hong Kong Wrong' in *Wall Street Journal* (6 October 2006).

Gadinis, Stavros and Jackson, Howell (2007), 'Markets as Regulators: A Survey' in *Southern California Law Review*, **80**.

Garten, Jeffrey (2009), 'Amid the Economic Rubble, Shangkong will Rise' in *Financial Times* (10 May 2009).

Gittings, Danny (2013), *Introduction to the Hong Kong Basic Law*, Hong Kong: Hong Kong University Press.

Goo, Say (2010), 'Multiple Derivative Action and Common Law Derivative Action Revisited: A Tale of Two Jurisdictions' in *Journal of Corporate Law Studies*, **10**.

Goodhart, Charles and Dai, Lu (2003), *Intervention to Save Hong Kong*, Oxford: OUP.

Gu, Minkang (2006), *Understanding Chinese Company Law*, Hong Kong: Hong Kong University Press.

Gunningham, Neil (1990), 'Moving the Goalposts: Financial Market Regulation in Hong Kong and the Crash of October 1987' in *Law and Social Inquiry*, **15**.

Haas, Benjamin (2017), 'Hong Kong Pro-democracy Legislators Disqualified from Parliament' in *Guardian* (14 July 2017).

Heaver, Stuart (2017), 'Why Hong Kong's Container Port may be in Terminal Decline, and What that would Mean for a City that Appears not to Care' in *South China Morning Post* (6 March 2017).

Heilbrunn, John (2004), 'Anti-corruption Commissions: Panacea or Real Medicine to Fight Corruption?' World Bank Institute Working Paper Series 37234. Online. Available at: http://siteresources.worldbank.org/WBI/Resources/wbi37234Heilbrunn.pdf.

Heritage Foundation (2017), 'Index of Economic Freedom'. Online. Available at: www.heritage.org/Index/countries.cfm.

Heritage Foundation (2017), 'Hong Kong'. Online. Available at: www.heritage.org/index/country/hongkong.

Ho, Simon; Scott, Robert; and Wong, Kie Ann (2004), *The Hong Kong Financial System*, Hong Kong: OUP.

Hong Kong Bar Association (2014), 'Response: White Paper on the Practice of "One Country, Two Systems" Policy in the Hong Kong Special Administrative Region'. Online. Available at: www.hkba.org/sites/default/files/White_Paper_Response_eng.pdf.

Hong Kong Government (1999), *Yearbook 1998*, Hong Kong: Information Services Department.

Hong Kong Government (1999), 'Key Issues 1998/99'. Online. Available at: www.info.gov.hk/info/sar2/rule.htm.

Hong Kong Government (2002), 'Press Release'. Online. Available at: www.info.gov.hk/gia/general/200203/14/0314236.htm.

Hong Kong Government (2008), *Yearbook 2007*, Hong Kong: Information Services Department.

Hong Kong Government (2009), *Yearbook 2008*, Hong Kong: Information Services Department.

Hong Kong Government (2016), *Yearbook 2015*, Hong Kong: Information Services Department.

Hong Kong Government (2016a), 'ICAC'. Online. Available at: www.gov.hk/en/about/abouthk/factsheets/docs/icac.pdf.

Hong Kong, Government (2017), 'Hong Kong again Ranked the World's Most Competitive Economy'. Online. Available at: www.info.gov.hk/gia/general/201706/01/P2017060100156.htm.

Hong Kong Government (2017a), *Yearbook 2016*, Hong Kong: Information Services Department.

Hong Kong Government (2017b), 'Government Structure'. Online. Available at: www.gov.hk/en/about/govdirectory/govstructure.htm.

Hong Kong Institute of Certified Public Accountants (2013), 'The Institute at 40'. Online. Available at: http://app.1.hkicpa.org.hk/APLUS/2013/04/pdf/22-31-Anniversary.pdf.

Hong Kong Institute of Certified Public Accountants (2013), 'The First Golden Age'. Online. Available at: http://app.1.hkicpa.org.hk/APLUS/2013/06/pdf/30-anniversary.pdf.

Hong Kong Institute of Certified Public Accountants (2013), '40 Years of Serving Hong Kong Society'. Online. Available at: http://app.1.hkicpa.org.hk/APLUS/2013/12/pdf/24-Infographic.pdf.

Hong Kong Stock Exchange (2004), 'Understanding Investors in the Hong Kong Listed Securities and Derivatives Markets'. Online. Available at: www.hkex.com.hk/eng/stat/research/rpaper/Documents/UIHKM.pdf.

Huang, Flora and Yeung, Horace (2013), 'Regulatory Co-operation between Securities Commissions: A Reflection from Hong Kong' in *Chinese Journal of Comparative Law*, **1**.

Huang, Flora and Yeung, Horace (2014), *Chinese Companies and the Hong Kong Stock Market*, Abingdon: Routledge.

Hung, Mingyi; Wong, T.J.; and Zhang, Tianyu (2012), 'Political Relations and Overseas Stock Exchange Listing: Evidence from Chinese State-Owned Enterprises' in *Journal of Accounting and Economics*, **53**.

IMD (2017), 'World Competitiveness Yearbook 2017 Results'. Online. Available at: www.imd.org/wcc/world-competitiveness-center-rankings/competitiveness-2017-rankings-results.

Independent Commission Against Corruption (2017), 'Landmark Cases'. Online. Available at: www.icac.org.hk/en/law/case/index.html.

International Finance Corporation (2011), 'IFC Family Business Governance Handbook'. Online. Available at: www.ifc.org/wps/wcm/connect/6a9001004f9f5979933cff0098cb14b9/FamilyBusinessGovernance_Handbook_English.pdf?MOD=AJPERES.

Jackson, Howell and Roe, Mark (2009), 'Public and Private Enforcement of Securities Laws: Resource-based Evidence' in *Journal of Financial Economics*, **93**.

Kaiman, Jonathan (2014), 'Hong Kong's Umbrella Revolution – the Guardian Briefing' in *Guardian* (30 September 2014).

Kang, John (2016), 'Study Reveals 95% Of Filipino, Indonesian Helpers In Hong Kong Exploited Or Forced Labor' in *Forbes* (18 March 2016).

La Porta, Rafael; Lopez-de-Silane, Florencio; and Shleifer, Andrei (1999), 'Corporate Ownership around the World' in *Journal of Finance*, **64**.

La Porta, Rafael; Lopez-de-Silane, Florencio; and Shleifer, Andrei (2006), 'What Works in Securities Laws?' in *Journal of Finance*, **61**.

La Porta, Rafael; Lopez-de-Silane, Florencio; Shleifer, Andrei; and Vishny, Robert (1998), 'Law and Finance' in *Journal of Political Economy*, **106**.

La Porta, Rafael; Lopez-de-Silane, Florencio; Shleifer, Andrei; and Vishny, Robert (1999), 'The Quality of Government' in *Journal of Law, Economics and Organisation*, **15**.

Lam, Jeffie (2015), 'Hong Kong's Laissez-faire Economic Policy is "Outdated", Says CY Leung' in *South China Morning Post* (10 August 2015).

Lam, Jeffie and Sito, Peggy (2014), 'Occupy Central to Hit Hongkong Land, Wharf Holdings Hardest, UBS Says' in *South China Morning Post* (1 April 2014).

Landler, Mark (1998), 'Hong Kong Rulings Stir Fears Over Law System' in *New York Times* (31 March 1998).

Law Society of Hong Kong (2014), 'Submission on the White Paper on the Practice of "One Country, Two Systems" Policy in the Hong Kong Special Administrative Region'. Online. Available at: www.hklawsoc.org.hk/pub_e/news/submissions/20140625.pdf.

Lawton, Philip (1996), 'Berle and Means, Corporate Governance and the Chinese Family Firm' in *Australian Journal of Corporate Law*, **6**.

Lawton, Philip (2007), 'Modeling the Chinese Family Firm and Minority Shareholder Protection: The Hong Kong Experience 1980–1995' in *Managerial Law*, **49**.

Legislative Council of Hong Kong (2017), 'History of the Legislative Council'. Online. Available at: www.legco.gov.hk/yr98-99/english/intro/hist_lc.htm.

Leng, Jing (2005), 'Interaction between Domestic and Overseas Capital Markets and Corporate Governance of Chinese Listed Companies' in *Studies in International, Financial, Economic and Technology Law*, **7**.

Li, Andrew (2014), 'Under Rule of Law, An Independent Judiciary Answers to No Political Masters' in *South China Morning Post* (15 August 2014).

Liu, Wei and Kang, Xing-Hua (2007), 'Study on Chinese Companies' Perception on Overseas Public Listing' in *Chinese Business Review*, **6**.

Long Finance (2017), 'The Global Financial Centres Index'. Online. Available at: www.longfinance.net/publications.html.

Low, Chee Keong (2009), 'Investors and Initial Public Offerings on the Stock Exchange of Hong Kong' in *Fordham Journal of Corporate and Financial Law*, **14**.

Masters, Brooke (2008), 'Hong Kong Poses Threat to City' in *Financial Times* (6 October 2008).

Mezzanotte, Félix (2017), 'The Unconvincing Rise of the Statutory Derivative Action in Hong Kong: Evidence from its First 10 Years of Enforcement' in *Journal of Corporate Law Studies*, **17**.

Milhaupt, Curtis and Pistor, Katharina (2008), *Law and Capitalism*, Chicago: University of Chicago Press.

Mitchell, Tom (2006), 'ICBC on Track to be World's Largest IPO' in *Financial Times* (13 October 2006).

Mitchell, Tom and Tucker, Sundeep (2006), 'Hong Kong Braced for China Bank IPO' in *Financial Times* (5 October 2006).

Ngo, Tak-Wing (1999), 'Industrial History and the Artifice of Laissez-faire Colonialism' in Tak-Wing Ngo (ed.), *Hong Kong's History: State and Society under Colonial Rule*, Abingdon: Routledge.

Ralston, David; Gustafson, David; Cheung, Fanny; and Terpstra, Robert (1993), 'Differences in Managerial Values: A Study of U.S., Hong Kong and PRC Managers' in *Journal of International Business Studies*, **24**.

Reuters (2009), 'Highlights – FSA Chief Promises Intrusive, Direct Regulation' Online. Available at: http://uk.reuters.com/article/uk-britain-banks-regulation-sb-idUKTRE52B27020090312.

Riedel, James (1973), 'The Hong Kong Model of Industrialization' Kiel Discussion Papers 29. Online. Available at: www.econstor.eu/bitstream/10419/48056/1/055872107.pdf.

Roe, Mark (2005), *Corporate Governance: Political and Legal Perspectives*, Cheltenham: Edward Elgar.

Roe, Mark (2006), 'Legal Origins, Politics and Modern Stock Markets' in *Harvard Law Review*, **120**.

Saw, Swee-Hock and Chiu, Wing Kin (1975), 'Population Growth and Redistribution in Hong Kong, 1841–1975' in *Southeast Asian Journal of Social Science*, **4**.

Schenk, Catherine (2002), 'Banks and the Emergence of Hong Kong as an International Financial Center' in *Journal of International Financial Markets, Institutions and Money*, **12**.

Securities and Futures Commission (2002), *Securities Regulation in Hong Kong*, Hong Kong: Securities and Futures Commission.

Securities and Futures Commission (2003), 'SFC Disciplinary Fining Guidelines'. Online. Available at: www.sfc.hk/web/EN/assets/components/codes/files-current/web/guidelines/disciplinary-fining-guidelines/SFC%20Disciplinary%20Fining%20Guidelines.pdf.

Securities and Futures Commission (2004), 'Annual Report 2003–2004'. Online. Available at: www.sfc.hk/web/EN/published-resources/corporate-publications/annual-reports.html.

Securities and Futures Commission (2004), 'The Listing of Mainland Companies on HKEx and the Implications for Hong Kong'. Online. Available at: www.sfc.hk/web/doc/EN/research/research/rs%20paper%2017.pdf.

Securities and Futures Commission (2005), 'Annual Report 2004–2005'. Online. Available at: www.sfc.hk/web/EN/published-resources/corporate-publications/annual-reports.html.

Securities and Futures Commission (2006), 'Stock Investor Survey'. Online. Available at: www.sfc.hk/sfc/doc/EN/speeches/public/surveys/06/stock_investor_survey_060602.pdf.

Securities and Futures Commission (2006), 'Hong Kong as a Leading Financial Centre in Asia'. Online. Available at: www.sfc.hk/web/doc/EN/research/research/rs%20paper%2033.pdf.

Securities and Futures Commission (2007), 'Annual Report 2006–07'. Online. Available at: www.sfc.hk/sfc/doc/EN/speeches/public/annual/rep06-07/Regulation.pdf.

Securities and Futures Commission (2008), 'Annual Report 2007–08'. Online. Available at: www.sfc.hk/web/doc/EN/speeches/public/annual/rep07-08/full.pdf.

Securities and Futures Commission (2009), 'Annual Report 2008–09'. Online. Available at: www.sfc.hk/web/EN/published-resources/corporate-publications/annual-reports.html.

Smith, Nicola (2017), 'Hong Kong Bookseller Abducted by China Vows to Reopen Shop in Taiwan' in *Guardian* (8 May 2017).

Song, Dong-Wook (2002), 'Regional Container Port Competition and Co-operation: the case of Hong Kong and South China' in *Journal of Transport Geography*, **10**.

Summers, Tim (2017), 'What to Know about Hong Kong's Chief Executive Election'. Online. Available at: www.chathamhouse.org/expert/comment/what-know-about-hong-kong-s-chief-executive-election.

Sun, Qian; Tong, Wilson; and Wu, Yujun (2006), 'The Choice of Foreign Primary Listing: China's Share-issue Privatization Experience' Working Paper. Online. Available at: http://cei.ier.hit-u.ac.jp/Japanese/pdf/Qian-Sun.pdf.

Sung, Yun Wing (1991), *The China-Hong Kong Connection: The Key to China's Open-Door Policy*, Cambridge: CUP.

Tan, Jinsong *et al.* (2007), 'An Analysis of the Characteristics of Chinese Listed Companies' Independent Director System' in *Frontiers of Business Research in China*, **1**.

Tao, Zhigang and Wong, Richard (2002), 'Hong Kong: From Entrepot to Manufacturing and Then to Producer Services' in Gordon Liu (ed.), *Urban Transformation in China: Theory, Evidence and Policy*, Farnham: Ashgate.

Transparency International (2017), 'Corruption Perceptions Index 2016'. Online. Available at: www.transparency.org/news/feature/corruption_perceptions_index_2016.

Tyler, Edward and Ho, John (2004), *HKLRD Review Series 2004: Company Law*, Hong Kong: Sweet and Maxwell.

Ure, Gavin (2012), *Governors, Politics and the Colonial Office: Public Policy in Hong Kong, 1918–58*, Hong Kong: Hong Kong University Press.

Winters, Alan and Yusuf, Shahid (2007), *Dancing with Giants: China, India and the Global Economy*, Washington D.C.: World Bank.

Wong, Richard (2015), 'Positive Non-interventionism as Governance Strategy' in *Hong Kong Economic Journal* (4 November 2015).

Wong, Siu-lun (1985), 'The Chinese Family Firm: A Model' in *British Journal of Sociology*, **36**.

World Bank (2017), 'Doing Business'. Online. Available at: www.doingbusiness.org.

Xing, Xuejing (2004), 'Why Does Stock Market Volatility Differ across Countries? Evidence from Thirty Seven International Markets' in *International Journal of Business*, **9**.

Yeung, Horace (2011), 'From Further North: The Case of Rusal's (Russian Aluminium) Listing in Hong Kong' in International *Company and Commercial Law Review*, **22**.

Yip, Ka-Che; Wong, Man Kong; and Leung, Yuen-Sang (2016), *Health Policy and Disease in Colonial and Post-Colonial Hong Kong, 1841–2003*, Abingdon: Routledge.

Zhu, Julie and Wembridge, Mark (2014), 'Hong Kong Pro-China Rally Draws Fake Crowd Allegations' in *Financial Times* (18 August 2014).

5 Singapore

Singapore has frequently been compared to Hong Kong.[1] They are both small cities with a population of around 5.6 and 7.3 million respectively in Singapore and Hong Kong.[2] They both used to be British colonies and therefore inherited the institutions left behind by the colonial ruler, most notably their legal and political systems. They both represent successful examples of economic development in Asia and are now amongst the most affluent economies in the world. Meanwhile, they are different in certain ways. Singapore has been an independent sovereign state since 1965, whilst Hong Kong has been ruled successively by Britain and then China. Further, as discussed before, the Hong Kong government has been prominent in maintaining a low profile in its economy, whilst the situation in Singapore has been quite different. Also, Singapore has a multicultural society, compared to Hong Kong's essentially Chinese society. Following on the previous two chapters which looked at the stories of China and Hong Kong, this chapter will move the discussion on to Singapore. Like the previous two chapters, with the help of the analytical framework laid down in Chapter 2, this chapter will first provide an overview of Singapore's economic development both before and after its independence. Afterwards, it will examine the legal, political, cultural and other institutional conditions of the city-state one by one, before coming to a final conclusion. This chapter is the third of the four largely parallel chapters which explore the institutional conditions of the economies selected by this book, namely, China, Hong Kong, Singapore and Malaysia.

Economic growth of Singapore

Singapore's closest competitor in the region is obviously Hong Kong. According to the IMD's World Competitiveness Yearbook 2017, Hong Kong took top spot for the second year, with Switzerland in the second place and Singapore in third.[3] Meanwhile, Singapore has taken top spot in the increasingly crucial area of digital competitiveness in a new global ranking of economies, also compiled by the IMD.[4] The new ranking measures the ability of economies to explore and adopt digital technologies that transform government practices and business models. Singapore was praised for its developed regulation which facilitates the inflow of overseas talent which complements the local pool. The rivalry of the two cities has also been seen in the Global Financial Centres Index.[5] According to the Index, London, New York and Hong Kong were consistently ranked as the top three global financial centres in the past. However, since 2016, Singapore has overtaken Hong Kong and become a contender to challenge second place New York. Hong Kong appears to have lost out to Singapore in recent years, as observed in the real GDP growth and per-capita GDP of both cities (see Figures 5.1 and 5.2). Both Hong Kong and Singapore enjoyed phenomenal growth in the

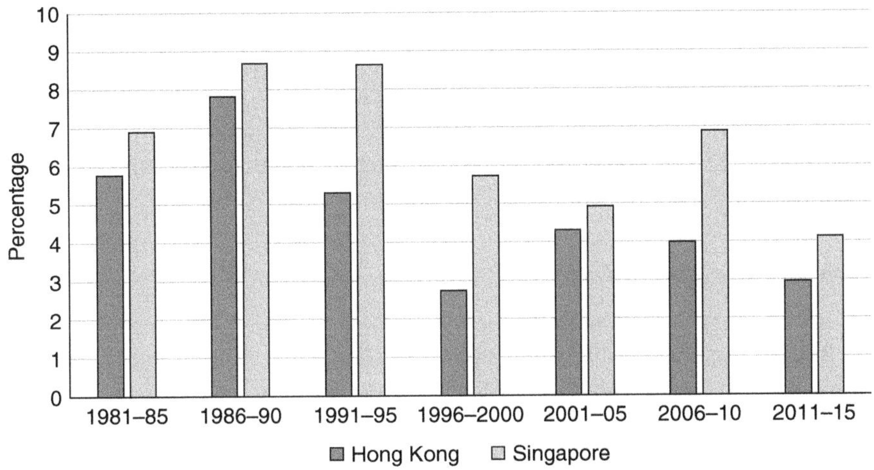

Figure 5.1 Real GDP growth (five year periods) of Hong Kong and Singapore.

Source: The Hong Kong Trade Development Council.

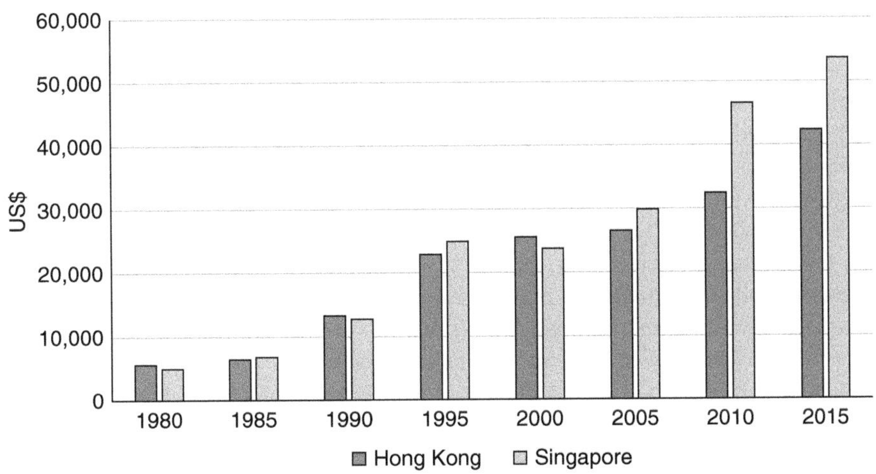

Figure 5.2 Per-capita GDP of Hong Kong and Singapore.

Source: The Hong Kong Trade Development Council.

1980s and 1990s amid their economic restructuring into services-based economies. But since 2004, Singapore's per-capita GDP has surpassed Hong Kong's. As shown in the previous chapter (see Figure 4.1), Singapore's per-capita GDP even surpassed the US after 2010 for several years in a row. In contrast, Hong Kong has not been in a position to challenge both economies. In 2016, Singapore's per-capita GDP was US$52,960, compared with US$43,681 for Hong Kong.[6] Hong Kong and Singapore are often compared in light of economic growth and various global rankings. In most rankings concerning the business environment, such as the examples above, both economies usually rank near the top. In fact, Hong Kong and Singapore share a lot in common. Both are small, open economies with no natural resources, but have developed into international trade and services centres in Asia. From a regional development perspective, the two economies are nodes connecting the hinterlands of Mainland China and ASEAN countries, which are set to strengthen economic ties and integration.

Growth before independence

History of trade in Singapore can be traced to as early as 1300.[7] Exploration in the Riau Archipelago south of Singapore has shown that many Chinese artefacts dating back to the fourteenth to sixteenth centuries were interred with the dead as burial offerings. This indicates that the people of Riau travelled to Singapore to barter sea products such as tortoise shell in exchange for Chinese products. The first Chinese trader to write about Southeast Asia was Wang Dayuan, who was born around 1311 in Nanchang which was a prosperous port in Jiangxi Province of China during the Song Dynasty. Wang used the term 'Temasek' to refer to the general area of Singapore and the nearby islands. The port-settlement of Temasek was a major regional emporium in the maritime trade between the Indian Ocean and the South China Sea. In the next several hundreds of years, internal rivalry among regional and European powers led to the rise of other port settlements and a new role for Singapore in the maritime trade of Southeast Asia. Singapore took advantage of a rapid expansion of the country trade between India and China, which was fostered by the Dutch East India Company and the British East India Company.

Sir Stamford Raffles is widely regarded as the founder of modern Singapore.[8] On 6 February 1819, Raffles, Temenggong Abdur Rahman and Sultan Hussein Shah of Johor signed a treaty that gave the British East India Company the right to set up a trading post in Singapore. It was also on this day that the British flag was formally hoisted on Singapore, marking the birth of Singapore as a British settlement. Raffles had different visions and plans that helped turn Singapore into a thriving settlement.[9] Singapore was chosen, by virtue of its strategic geographical location, to compete with other ports under the control of the Dutch. Raffles devised a set of policies and regulations that outlined the objectives of Singapore's harbour, helping to establish the settlement as a free port. He instituted the administration of justice to ensure peace and order in the thriving settlement. He founded the Resident Court, appointed magistrates, and implemented trial by jury. He also formed an institution of higher learning to educate the sons of the Malay chiefs; to teach the native languages to officers of the East India Company; and to collect the literature on the traditions, and laws and customs of the country. The first bridge in Singapore was also built by Raffles over the Singapore River.

With the arrival of the British, Singapore from 1819 to 1945 was revived as a hub for entrepot trade that attracted immigrants from China, India, the Malay Archipelago, and beyond.[10] In the beginning when Singapore was opened for trade, British merchants who had established themselves in the Straits and Bengal formed mercantile (agency) houses in Singapore for the exchange of Straits produce, opium, tea and English manufactured wares. In 1820, Alexander Johnston and Company, one of the first European agency houses, was established in Singapore. It became a firm that was closely associated with the first 70 years of Singapore's history. At this point indeed, apart from the East India Company officials, few European settlers came to Singapore during the earliest years.[11] Westerners were deterred by uncertainty as to whether Singapore would be retained as a permanent British settlement and the consequent difficulties about buying land. The first census in Singapore, which was taken in January 1824, recorded 10,683 residents comprising 74 Europeans, 16 Armenians, 15 Arabs, 4,580 Malays, 3,317 Chinese, 756 natives of India and 1,925 Bugis.[12] Subsequent censuses showed rapid population growth rates on the island and a disproportionately high ratio of men to women. From 1826 to 1867, Singapore, along with two other trading ports on the Malay Peninsula, Penang and Malacca, and several smaller dependencies, were ruled together as the Straits Settlements from the British East India Company headquarters in India.[13] In 1867, the British needed a better location than fever-ridden Hong Kong to station their troops in Asia, so the Straits Settlements were made a crown colony on 1 April and its capital Penang, ruled directly from London. By this time, Singapore had surpassed the other Straits Settlements in importance, as it had grown to become a bustling seaport with 86,000 inhabitants. Singapore also dominated the Straits Settlements Legislative Council. After the Suez Canal opened in 1869 and steamships became the major form of ocean transport, British influence increased in the region, bringing more maritime activities to Singapore. At that time, there were 60 European companies in Singapore.[14] Some were general import and export businesses, others had special interests in rubber, tin or shipping. Total trade volume reached 71 million Straits dollars in 1870, a year after the Suez Canal was opened, up from only 39 million the year before.[15] The trade boom would continue throughout the 1870s, and by 1879, the colony's total trade volume was valued at 105 million Straits dollars.[16] Before the First World War, tin was the single most important item of Singapore's export trade with the West.[17] But rubber was fast becoming important.

During the eighteenth century, the Chinese arrived to work at the newly discovered rich tin fields at places like the Indonesian island of Banka.[18] The Chinese merchants in Penang and Singapore then financed them to work at the tin-mining states along the west coast of the Malay Peninsula. The influx of Chinese miners gained momentum from 1848, when a new tin field in the Larut Valley of Perak was discovered; by 1870, more than 40,000 Chinese miners had been employed. The tin-mining industry became largely monopolised by the Chinese before the founding of the Straits Trading Company Limited on 8 November 1887. The company was formed by Herman Muhlinghaus, a German entrepreneur, and James Sword, a Scottish businessman. By 1912, the company had become the largest tin-smelting company in the world, contributing to one-third of the world's tin supply.[19] On the other hand, rubber trees were first planted in Singapore in 1877.[20] From the mid-1870s to the 1890s, experiments were carried out to make rubber planting commercially viable, yielding several breakthroughs due to the efforts of Henry Nicholas Ridley, a botanist who was the director of the Singapore Botanic Gardens. At that time, there was an explosive growth in world demand for rubber due to the burgeoning automobile industry, which was in turn fuelled by the invention of the pneumatic tyre by Dunlop in 1888. The Singapore Chamber of Commerce Rubber Association was formed in 1911 with the primary aim of regulating and controlling rubber auctions, which had increased in tandem with rubber transactions. The formation of the rubber association resulted in a wider pool of buyers and sellers, and a larger volume of rubber traded. Previously, rubber had to be sent from Singapore to London for sale, but with the establishment of the rubber association rubber could now be sold locally. Quantities of rubber sold at auctions enjoyed a five-fold increase in just two years, from 522 tons in 1912 to 2,666 tons in 1914.[21] The rubber association helped steer Singapore towards becoming the rubber capital of the world by 1920.

Singapore prospered as financial institutions, transportation, communications and government infrastructure expanded rapidly to support the booming trade and industry of the British Empire. For example, the Post Office Savings Bank was established by the British colonial government on 1 January 1877 to provide banking facilities for people in Singapore. Set up as part of the Post Office Service Department, it was the first of several savings banks established in the Straits Settlements. Between 1877 and 1940, the Post Office Savings Bank enjoyed steady growth. The number of accounts grew from 211 in 1877 to 57,000 in 1940, while total deposits increased from 19,862 to 14.3 million Straits dollars.[22] Also, steam trams started operating in Singapore on 3 May 1886 by the Singapore Tramways Company.[23]

The period between the First and Second World Wars was characterised by economic change. The emergence of economic nationalism, changes in world production and values, and the rise of new markets and suppliers, all had repercussions on the entrepot trade of Singapore.[24] The effects of the world depression led to quotas on imports and restrictions on exports. From 1929 onwards, flooding of the rubber markets caused the sharply decreasing prices and countries agreed to restrict exports and each producing country was given a basic quota. The history of tin was similar to that of rubber. In 1929 world production outstripped consumption and subsequently restrictions on production were imposed. Moreover, Singapore's position was not helped by the emergence of competitors, such as Japan and Netherlands India. At that time, whilst trade with the Malay Peninsula still constituted a major proportion, Singapore's prosperity indeed increasingly relied on its entrepot trade with wider geographical areas.[25] Sandwiched between the Indian and Pacific Oceans, Singapore's trade reflected the regional growth of around the Pacific Ocean economies. In 1935, the aggregate trade with North America, East Asia and Australasia was 36 per cent of total trade, compared with 23 per cent in 1915, and 17 per cent in 1870.[26] As put by Wong, Singapore had remained more a regional entrepot than a Malayan port.[27] This entrepot trade was made possible largely because of Sino-Western enterprise, the product of British free trade policy and admission of foreign investment, enterprise and settlers. Indeed, the population and GDP of Singapore continued to rise until its Japanese occupation during the Second World War (see Figure 5.3). In 1909, the population was around 290,000 and the GDP at that time was estimated to be 54.1 million Straits dollars. In 1939, 30 years later, the population had risen to around 730,000 and the estimated GDP was 266.3 million Straits dollars. But note that the GDP level in 1939 was actually lower than 1929 owing to development in world trade during the 1920s as outlined before.

During the Second World War, Singapore experienced three and a half years of Japanese occupation. The post-war economy was affected by the political changes. First, the Straits Settlements were dissolved on 1 April 1946. On this day, the nine Malay states and the Straits Settlements of Penang and Malacca officially formed the Malayan Union, while Singapore became a separate crown

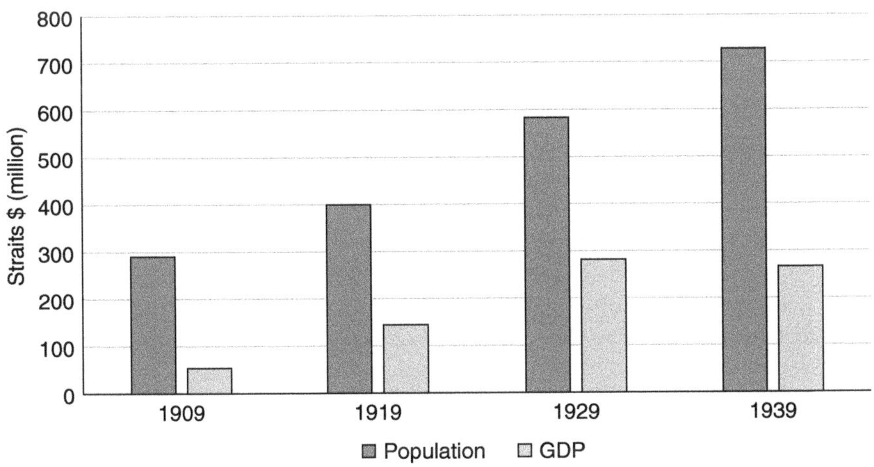

Figure 5.3 Population (in thousands) and GDP estimate (million Straits dollars), 1909–39.

Source: Ichiro Sugimoto (2011), *Economic Growth of Singapore in the Twentieth Century*, Singapore: World Scientific Publishing.

colony. Such a development could be attributed to various reasons.[28] The formation of the Malayan Union was the outcome of British planning for the post-war reorganisation of Malaya in order to improve its administrative efficiency and security, as well as in preparation for its eventual self-government. Singapore was left out of the Malayan Union due to its economic and strategic importance as a free port and naval base. Moreover, given that all persons born or domiciled in Malaya were automatically eligible for Malayan Union citizenship, the British felt that the inclusion of Singapore, with its Chinese majority, would further complicate the task of securing Malay acceptance of the scheme.

During this time, Singapore revived as a staple port serving the Malay Peninsula. Between 1939 and 1959, the export volume of primary commodities increased almost two and a half times.[29] Meanwhile, petroleum exports expanded substantially during the 1950s, and by mid-decade, were four times greater in volume than in 1939. Royal Dutch Shell maintained the Far Eastern headquarters of its tanker fleet at Singapore, and Caltex began operations there in 1959. When oil refining operations were inaugurated at the port in 1960, Singapore was already the largest storage and distribution base for petroleum in Southeast Asia.[30] On the other hand, Singapore's trade still depended on rubber. Throughout the 1950s, rubber normally accounted for two-fifths to over a half of Singapore's exports.[31]

Recognising that the city was highly dependent on entrepot trade and the provision of services to British military bases, on 21 March 1957, the Singapore Industrial Promotion Board was instituted. The main task of the board was to promote and develop the various industries in the Colony of Singapore. Measures were introduced to attract new enterprises to Singapore and encourage expansion of existing companies.[32] In the next year, the Constitutional Agreement was signed in London on 28 May 1958 and self-government achieved after Singapore held general elections in 1959. The first government of the State of Singapore was sworn in on 5 June with Lee Kuan Yew as Prime Minister. The new government quickly set up the Economic Development Board (EDB) in 1961 as a replacement for the Singapore Industrial Promotion Board, and made it both a financial institution for industry and an industrial corporation to establish new industries and open industrial estates. The Singapore Industrial Promotion Board, which had received a revolving fund of SG$1 million and a staff consisting only of a manager and a confidential secretary, was found to be too small to be effective on the scale required to promote industrialisation and growth. In sharp contrast, the EDB was given a capital of SG$100 million over a four-year period from 1961 to 1964 for its industrial development plan.[33] According to the World Bank, since 1960, the EDB has been Singapore's one-stop and lead government agency for planning and executing economic strategies to enhance Singapore's position as a global hub for business and investment.[34]

Post-independence economy

The self-governing State of Singapore joined the Federation of Malaysia in 1963 and became totally independent in 1965, nearly 20 years after it was made a

British crown colony. Lee Kuan Yew's People's Action Party (PAP) has been the dominant political force since independence. Lee once said the idea of an independent Singapore was a 'political, economic, and geographical absurdity'.[35] Singapore was an island of around 580 squares kilometres with no natural resources, no hinterland and no industry at the time of independence. In 1965, Singapore's nominal GDP per capita was around US$500, around the same level as Mexico and South Africa.[36] Industrial strife was common. The unemployment rate was close to 9 per cent. To create job opportunities following the massive unemployment and labour unrest, an environment conducive to industrial development had to be formed, thus leading to the birth of the Jurong Industrial Estate, the first of many such estates on the island.

The EDB has been responsible for investment promotion and the continued economic success of Singapore. During the early years, to attract foreign investment, 'pioneer status' was given by the EDB to many industries with attendant tax holidays, tariff protection and other benefits.[37] Encouraging investments through tax incentives can be exemplified by the Economic Expansion Incentives (Relief from Income Tax) Act 1967. Under the Act, tax exemption given to companies with pioneer status was generous. In comparison to those paying the standard Singapore corporation tax, pioneer status lowered the actual cost of each dollar of new investment in Singapore to around 80 cents.[38] Pioneer status has remained Singapore's basic investment incentive and is still granted to most foreign investors. Other than granting financial incentives, the EDB targeted industries regarded as desirable, by using criteria such as employment potential and growth potential, as well as value added. As a result of EDB decisions, foreign investment concentrated in petrochemicals, pharmaceuticals and, above all, the electronics industry.[39] One notable example is the emergence of the disk drive industry. The industry started in 1982 when the EDB, offering generous investment incentives, attracted Seagate. Soon, most other multinational disk drive manufacturers were drawn to Singapore because of the attractive subsidies. Since the late 1980s, Singapore has emerged as a major regional hub for magnetic hard disk drive assembly operations, accounting for about half of the world's total output.[40] This demonstrated two strategic decisions by Singapore: first, to focus on export-led industrialisation and, second, to attract global multinational corporations as vehicles to achieve industrial growth.[41] At this point, Singapore's manufacturing industry evolved to become more sophisticated and included computer parts, peripherals, software packages and silicon wafers.

Various economic indicators can confirm Singapore's early success.[42] By the close of the 1960s, manufacturing had become the lead sector of Singapore's economic growth, contributing 18 per cent of GDP. By the early 1970s, Singapore reached full employment. During the period 1965–86, Singapore achieved high rates of GDP growth: between 8 and 10 per cent per annum in real terms for the entire period. By the 1980s, Singapore had joined the ranks of Hong Kong, South Korea and Taiwan to become one of four newly industrialising countries in Asia. Its per capita income has increased to become the second highest in Asia after that of Japan.

In the 1980s, eventually, due to the government's adoption of a high-wage policy to accelerate the move away from labour-intensive industries and the attraction to high-technology industries, wage bills swelled as the world slipped into an economic slowdown and Singapore slid into a recession. With the new goal of positioning Singapore as a Total Business Centre, the EDB set out to attract international service corporations in the financial, educational, lifestyle, medical, IT and software sectors; identifying personal computer, printed circuit board and disc drive manufacture as important sunrise industries.[43] By working hard to attract investors to these areas, Singapore's and Southeast Asia's first silicon wafer manufacture plant opened in the early 1980s, followed by Apple Computers in 1981 and one for disc drives in 1982. Meanwhile, the Science Park was set up next to the National University of Singapore to stimulate R&D activities by the private sector. The latter half of the 1980s witnessed the emergence of industrial clusters in Singapore which enabled companies to benefit economically from agglomeration effects.[44] A major feature of the industrial policies during this era of growth was the use of cluster strategies to reinforce the strength of the economy and deepen the capabilities of companies. The government took a more proactive role to drive greater R&D, better customer–producer relationships, more innovation, and more extensive networks among others. The direct result of this was the steady increase in share of modern services in GDP from 16 per cent in 1965 to 24 per cent in 1985 and 28 per cent in 2010.[45] One notable industrial cluster is found in One-North neighbourhood of Singapore. One-North, a 200-hectare development, is designed to host a cluster of research facilities and business park space. Built to promote the growth of biomedical sciences, information technology and media, it is well-supported by strong capabilities from private-sector research laboratories which are co-located with public research institutes, tertiary hospitals and universities.

To achieve the goal, the EDB set up EDB Investments, a wholly owned investment arm of EDB, in 1991 to make investments into companies that will grow key industry clusters and promote emergent technologies and innovations. For example, its Technopreneurship Investment Fund has invested in more than 100 partnerships worldwide.[46] Other government-led initiatives include funding Support such as the SPRING Startup Enterprise Development Scheme, the ACE Startups Grant and the Micro Loan Programme among others. SPRING Singapore is an agency under the Ministry of Trade and Industry responsible for helping Singapore enterprises grow and building trust in Singapore products and services. As the enterprise development agency, SPRING works with partners to help enterprises in financing, capability and management development, technology and innovation, and access to markets. The Capability Development Grant under SPRING aims to support SMEs to scale up business capabilities and ensure business sustainability. The grant can be spent on projects like product development, human capital development, business processes enhancements for productivity and business model transformation. Seventy per cent of qualifying project costs such as consultancy, training, certification and equipment costs can be supported by the government.

Unlike Hong Kong, which has transformed into a service-oriented economy almost entirely, Singapore remains strong in several key industries, namely chemicals, electronics and engineering. Singapore's position as a global chemicals hub has grown in tandem with the extensive development of Jurong Island, an integrated complex housing many of the world's leading energy and chemical companies, among them BASF, ExxonMobil, Lanxess, Mitsui Chemicals, Shell and Sumitomo Chemicals.[47] In 2010, the chemicals and chemical products sector contributed SG$38 billion of manufacturing output. The idea of the industrial cluster is also seen in this industrial sector by having the Institute of Chemical and Engineering Sciences, an autonomous national research institute, located on Jurong Island. Another well-established industry in Singapore is electronics. In 2013, manufacturing output in the electronics sector reached SG$79.1 billion, contributing 28 per cent of Singapore's manufacturing output.[48] The electronics industry had a workforce over 79,000. Singapore is still a leading manufacturer of enterprise hard disc drives with Seagate and Hitachi Global Storage Technologies having significant presence, accounting for over 40 per cent of the world's output volume. Singapore's precision engineering is the crucial enabler for other industries as diverse as aerospace, petroleum, medical devices and electronics. The sector began in the 1970s to support the first manufacturing investments. It comprises a range of companies from contract manufacturers to full solution providers, who offer design, prototyping, production and supply chain management capabilities. The sector employed 94,000 people, 22.6 per cent of the total manufacturing workforce, with an output of SG$32 billion in 2014.[49] Nanyang Polytechnic, EDB and SPRING officially opened the Centre for Digital and Precision Engineering in January 2010 to enhance a comprehensive range of capabilities for the sector. Since the 1990s, the city also began leveraging its leadership in these industries to develop the pharmaceutical biotechnology and medical technology sectors. The development of the Biopolis (at One-North) is intended to turn Singapore into a global biomedical sciences hub advancing human healthcare. Phase 1 of the Biopolis comprises a seven-building complex linked by sky bridges and offers a built-up area of 185,000 square metres. It is situated near the National University of Singapore and the National University Hospital.

As of 2016, the manufacturing sector remained the most important contributor of GDP, making up 20 per cent of total.[50] But in the same year the combined business and financial services sector accounted for 28.9 per cent of GDP, exceeding that of manufacturing alone.[51] This illustrates that Singapore's economic structure has been largely diversified and balanced, though there is a trend to move towards services. Singapore was already a thriving regional financial centre since the 1970s.[52] Since the 1960s, Singapore has adopted an outward looking financial development strategy.[53] The government implemented financial sector reforms, opened new financial markets and enacted regulatory and fiscal incentives to attract financial institutions to Singapore. The number of institutions in the financial sector increased from less than 100 in the 1970s to almost 450 in the 1990s. As of August 2017, Singapore's financial sector had 128 commercial banks (five local and 123 foreign) together with hundreds of other types of financial institutions such as insurance companies, stockbroking companies, fund management companies and so on.[54] It is believed that the increase in the number of competitors would force local banks to upgrade their financial products and services, as well as management expertise. As early as the beginning of the twentieth century, the first Chinese bank was established in Singapore.[55] Kwong Yik Bank was founded by Wong Ah Fook in 1903, who was then a leading building contractor and gambier planter. It provided ordinary banking facilities, and arranged for mortgages and loans to its predominantly Chinese clientele. Soon, more Chinese banks were established, such as the Chinese Commercial Bank in 1912, Ho Hong Bank in 1917, the Oversea-Chinese Bank in 1919, the United Chinese Bank in 1935 and Chung Khiaw Bank in 1947. Nowadays, these banks still exist but in another form. The first three merged into the Oversea-Chinese Banking Corporation in 1932 and the United Chinese Bank was renamed as the United Overseas Bank in 1965. These two banks remain amongst the top three banks in Singapore. The game changer came in 1968 when the Development Bank of Singapore (DBS) was incorporated. It remains the largest bank in Singapore. One-third of all initial financial commitments from the bank were in the electrical machinery and petroleum industries.[56] Consequently, this led to the raid expansion of the two industries. The DBS was also an initial step in the development of a colossal web of off-budget government corporations like Singapore Airlines. It was estimated that state-owned corporations, together with statutory boards like the EDB and the Jurong Town Corporation which ran the industrial estates, contributed roughly one-third of GDP in 1984.[57]

Other than funding from the government and the banks, another source of capital for the expanding economy in Singapore is the stock market. The government has encouraged private companies to be converted into public companies, so companies can expand with the help of funds from the general public.[58] Since the colonial time, there was the joint Stock Exchange of Malaysia and Singapore. In May 1973, the Malaysia Government decided to split the joint stock exchange. The Stock Exchange of Singapore was incorporated in the same year as a result. Despite being self-proclaimed as 'Asia's leading and trusted market infrastructure' and featured highly in the Global Financial Centre Index as said before, Singapore's stock exchange is far from successful when compared to its counterparts in Hong Kong, Shanghai and Shenzhen, as discussed in the previous chapter. As of July 2017, its market capitalisation was US$760 billion, just around one-fifth of the size of its three counterparts.[59] Currently, there are more than 700 companies listed there. Around 270 are from overseas, of which more than 100 are from China. Chinese companies listed in Singapore led the local IPO market from 2005 to 2007 before such listings came to a halt in mid-2012.[60] The slowdown is largely attributed to the Chinese inclination to choose Hong Kong over Singapore. However, the Singapore exchange is still one of the most international exchanges globally with around 40 per cent of listed firms coming from outside Singapore.

To conclude, as a newly independent country in 1965 with no natural resources, Singapore faced much uncertainty. The government has always tried to introduce various initiatives to maintain a competitive and business friendly environment in Singapore. From its days as a small and underdeveloped nation, Singapore has clearly emerged from various challenges over the years to transform into one of the most affluent countries in the world today.

Legal institutions

Singapore is known for rule of law. According to the World Justice Project's Rule of Law Index, Singapore is one of the top performers in the 2016 rankings, ranking ninth out of 113 countries worldwide.[61] According to the 2017 World Bank 'Doing Business' report, Singapore, along with New Zealand, are the easiest places in the world to conduct business, partly due to the hassle-free way in which administrative matters are handled.[62] Singapore helps streamline the process of setting up by making it simple to incorporate a company and register for taxes by using the same online form. Forms for construction permits, new workplace safety and healthcare regulations can also be submitted online. In addition, Singapore eased property registration by improving on its computerised system. The roots of Singapore's legal system can be traced back to the English legal system and it has evolved over the years. The sources of law are derived from the Constitution, legislation, subsidiary legislation, and judge-made law. The Constitution is the supreme law of the land and lays down the basic legal framework for the state. Within the Constitution, law is interpreted to include 'written law and any legislation of the United Kingdom or other enactment or instrument whatsoever which is in operation in Singapore and the common law in so far as it is in operation in Singapore and any custom or usage having the force of law in Singapore', illustrating a rather wholesale reception of the colonial legal system.[63]

The government has always adopted a pro-business policy. As discussed in previous chapters, one key aspect perhaps is a functional set of corporate and financial law. The Companies Act of Singapore was first enacted in 1967. This first Act followed closely the provisions contained in the Malaysian Companies Act 1965, as it was considered that Singapore's new law relating to companies should not be different from the legislation in force in Malaysia in order to facilitate trade and commercial intercourse with and within this region.[64] The Malaysian Companies Act 1965 was itself primarily based on the UK Companies Act 1948 and the Australian Uniform Companies Act 1961.[65] Since its enactment, the Act has been amended 18 times.[66] Of these amendments, most were piecemeal responses to specific outdated or problematic aspects of the law, and it was not until the turn of the last century that a comprehensive review of the Act was undertaken.[67] In December 1999, the Company Legislation and Regulatory Framework Committee was appointed to conduct an extensive review of the company law and regulatory framework.[68] The chief objective was to ensure that Singaporean laws were sufficiently modern and flexible to enhance Singapore's competitiveness as a global business centre. To this end, the Committee recommended wide ranging measures to modernise the Act. The subsequent part will principally focus on the legal changes brought about by this arguably most significant review thus far and any subsequent amendments.

It should be noted though that specific types of companies may, in addition to the Companies Act, be regulated by other statutes. For example, when a public company issues securities to the public, they are also regulated by the securities law. In 1973, when the Stock Exchange of Singapore was established, the Securities Industry Act was enacted. Again, this legislation was heavily influenced by Malaysia and it was described as 'identically worded' with the Malaysian legislation.[69] It is understandable, as discussed before, the two countries used to run a joint stock exchange but split in 1973. The Securities Industry Act was enacted to control speculative and manipulation of the stock market and to prevent insider trading. However, the collapse of the Pan-Electric Group of 13 companies in December 1985 caused the Stock Exchange of Singapore and the Stock Exchange of Malaysia to be closed for a few days.[70] The Pan-Electric crisis precipitated a thorough overhaul of the regulatory framework. The Securities Industry Act 1973 was repealed and replaced by the Securities Industry Act 1986. From that point, there was a general tightening up of securities regulation up to the Asian financial crisis in 1997. Since then, there have been changes to the regulatory balance of the market, culminating in the enactment in 2001 of the Securities and Futures Act. The Act has since been the main Singaporean legislation regulating the capital markets and financial investments sector in Singapore.

Furthermore, Singapore has made efforts in building up its corporate governance standards aimed at promoting investor confidence in companies listed on the Singapore Exchange and putting Singapore on the global map as a trusted international financial hub. The Code of Corporate Governance was first issued by the Corporate Governance Committee on 21 March 2001. Like the UK and other jurisdictions which follow its approach, such as Hong Kong, the Code has adopted a 'comply or explain' principle. In other words, compliance with the Code is not mandatory but listed companies are required under the Singapore Exchange Listing Rules to disclose their corporate governance practices and give explanations for deviations from the Code in their annual reports. According to the report from the Committee, faced with the three possible regulatory models to promoting good corporate governance, it has expressly rejected a prescriptive model.[71] In this model, companies are required to adopt specific corporate governance practices. In the view of the Committee, this model is only appropriate in certain circumstances, for example where capital markets are undeveloped, and such an approach is inconsistent with the disclosure-based philosophy to regulation that Singapore was moving toward.[72] Furthermore, a prescriptive model assumes that a 'one size fits all' approach is appropriate, but what is good corporate governance is likely to vary across companies and over time. In contrast, a non-prescriptive approach to corporate governance is probably best exemplified by the approach in the US. In the US, the Securities and Exchange Commission and the various stock exchanges generally do not prescribe corporate governance practices that companies should adopt, although some private sector bodies and major institutional investors have developed codes that embody what they consider to be good corporate governance. On balance, the Committee has decided the balanced approach adopted in markets such as the UK and Canada provide the best way forward for improving corporate governance in Singapore.[73] In 2002, then Deputy Prime Minister and Minister for Finance, Lee Hsien Loong, launched the Council on Corporate Disclosure and Governance. The Chairman and members of the Council were appointed by the Minister for Finance. The Council's composition included representatives from businesses, professional bodies, academic institutions and government. It initiated a review of the Code in May 2004. A revised Code was issued on 14 July 2005. The matter was subsequently passed on to the Corporate Governance Council, under the Monetary Authority of Singapore (MAS). It conducted a comprehensive review of the Code, and submitted its recommendations to MAS on 22 November 2011. MAS issued a revised Code of Corporate Governance on 2 May 2012, the current version as of today.

Other areas of law have not been overlooked by Singapore. Singapore is especially proud of its robust intellectual property regime to ensure that the city remains a preferred location for innovation. It has placed a great deal of commitment into developing a strong domestic regulatory framework to protect intellectual property rights. It is currently rated the best place in Asia and fourth in the world for intellectual property rights protection in the Global Competitiveness Report.[74] All in all, it can be seen that Singapore has been committed to introducing and updating its laws in corporate and financial matters regularly, so that the legal regime can keep up with the ever evolving business environment. The next subsection will consider specifically how the laws serve to protect investors in Singapore.

Quality of the laws

In general, the Company Law Review in 1999 sought to streamline regulatory structures, lower compliance costs and to enlarge the range of business vehicles.[75] For example, considering that private companies remain the principal corporate vehicle for small business and start-ups, the Review recommended that private companies should be allowed to incorporate with a minimum of one shareholder and one director.[76] Also, every company in Singapore shall have at least one director who is ordinarily resident in Singapore and, where the company only has one member, that sole director may also be the sole member of the company.[77] In the past, private companies were required to have a minimum of two shareholders and two directors. This change obviously intends to reduce incorporation and maintenance costs of using the corporate form. This change was also made in line with what had been witnessed in other common law jurisdictions where private companies were permitted to have only one director.[78] Under the Companies Act, any directors of a company must at all times act honestly and use reasonable diligence in the discharge of the duties of his office.[79] Specifically, a director is not allowed to make improper use of any information acquired by virtue of his position as officer or agent of the company to gain an advantage for himself or for any other person or to cause detriment to the company. A breach of this statutory duty will render the director liable both civilly and criminally.[80] Furthermore, a director is generally required to make a disclosure at a directors' meeting if he is interested in a transaction or proposed transaction with the company.[81] Meanwhile, in addition to these two statutory duties, under common law, directors are expected to act bona fide in what they consider is in the best interests of the company, and to avoid conflicts of interest.[82] With some other common law duties, there has been a debate on whether Singapore should follow the UK and extensively codify directors' duties.[83] It has been noted that non-exhaustive statements of directors' duties have long been a feature of the Companies Act in Singapore.[84] Whilst recognising that an exhaustive legislative statement would lend to certainty and accessibility, the Steering Committee for Review of the Companies Act was nonetheless concerned that such a move would inhibit judicial development in a particularly dynamic area of law.[85]

It is worth noting that directors are not acting individually. Decision making is made collectively as a board of directors. The Corporate Governance Code was issued to ensure that there is an effective Board to lead and control the company. The Code recommends that independent directors should be making up at least one-third of the Board.[86] An independent director is one who has no relationship with the company, its related corporations, the majority shareholders and corporate officers. Another mechanism to enhance independence of the board is that there should be a clear division of responsibilities between the leadership of the Board and the executives responsible for managing the company's business.[87] The board chairman and the company CEO should be separate persons to avoid a considerable concentration of power. Furthermore, the board should be divided into committees for more specialised decision making such as remuneration policies, appointment of executives and audit matters.[88] Recent surveys conducted in Singapore, such as the SID-ISCA's Singapore Directorship Report 2014 and the SID-SGX's Board of Directors Survey, have revealed that although companies in Singapore generally abide by the Code, disclosures about remuneration, risk governance, board diversity and sustainability were still lacking comprehensiveness.[89] One of the main concerns lay in remuneration disclosures. Only 31 per cent of listed companies disclosed the precise remuneration of their directors on a named basis when the Corporate Governance Code demands it. The reason behind the reluctance to disclose was confidentiality, so as to prevent poaching of executives and to prevent comparison. Another shortcoming was board diversity. Female representation was below 10 per cent, lagging behind many Asian countries.

Another key aspect of good corporate governance is transparency and disclosure. Currently, all companies are required to prepare accounts in accordance with the Singapore Financial Reporting Standards. All companies must be audited unless the company is one falling under the small company concept.[90] In Singapore, the issue of a prospectus is necessary when there is an offer of securities under the Securities and Futures Act.[91] The contents of a prospectus are governed by the law.[92] Generally, it should include all the information that investors and their professional advisers would reasonably require to make an informed investment decision and other matters prescribed by the Monetary Authority of Singapore (MAS). Specifically, it will stipulate clearly the rights and liabilities attaching to the securities, financial position and performance, and prospects of the issuer. In the event of any false or misleading statement or non-disclosure of a material fact in a prospectus, those persons that were involved in the preparation of the prospectus will be subject to both criminal and civil liabilities. The wrongdoers shall be liable on conviction to a fine not exceeding SG$150,000, or to imprisonment for a term not exceeding two years, or both.[93] Furthermore, the involved parties shall be liable to compensate any person who suffers loss or damage as a result of the false or misleading statement in or omission from the prospectus.[94] Once a company is listed on the stock exchange, it is subject to the continuing disclosure requirements of the stock exchange, as provided in Chapter 7 of the Singapore Stock Exchange's Listing Rules. A listed company must announce any information known to them concerning it or any of its subsidiaries or associated companies which is necessary to avoid the establishment of a false market in the company's securities; or would be likely to materially affect the price or value of its securities.[95] Paragraph 8 of Appendix 7.1 provides a non-exclusive list of matters which are considered to require immediate public announcement.[96] Furthermore, Chapter 9 of the Listing Rules requires listed companies to disclose related-party transactions to guard against the risk of these transactions that may adversely affect the interests of the companies or their shareholders.

There is always a tension between increasing shareholder protection and the resulting burden placed on the businesses. The law reformers in Singapore have also tried to enhance efficiency by the adoption of technology. This strategy was a prominent feature of the 1999 Review of the Companies Act, which resulted in a simpler and cheaper incorporation process via electronic filings, amendments that enabled the passing of shareholder resolutions by electronic communications, as well as provisions for the electronic distribution of notices of meetings and other statutory reports and documents.[97] The 2007 Review also followed this approach by phasing out physical registers kept by companies and migrating to a centralised online register maintained by the Registrar. This is a significant development as it distinguishes Singapore as one of the first jurisdictions in the world to operate a centralised online register for private companies.[98]

Singapore's superior regime in minority shareholder protection is confirmed by the World Bank. According to the Bank's 2017 'Doing Business' report, it is ranked first jointly with New Zealand in the Protecting Minority Investors Index.[99] It is worth noting that Singapore's effort in protecting investors is not a recent phenomenon. At the time when La Porta and colleagues conducted their study towards the new millennium, they already gave the highest score possible to Singapore according to their shareholder right index, putting it in the same league with the UK, US and Hong Kong.[100] However, as said before, there is still a need to look at the enforcement situation so as to form a comprehensive assessment of its legal regime.

Public enforcement

The MAS is the supervisor and regulator of the financial services sector. Meanwhile, it is also the central bank. It was established by the Monetary Authority of Singapore Act of 1970 and began operation on 1 January 1971. Prior to 1970, the various monetary functions associated with a central bank had been performed by several government departments and agencies.[101] For example, the Commissioner of Banking and the Commissioner for Finance Companies had been responsible for the regulation and supervision of banks and finance companies. The Exchange Control Department had overseen all foreign exchange matters, while the Department of Overseas Investment had been in charge of the government's external assets. These government bodies had been directed and coordinated by the Ministry of Finance. As Singapore progressed, the demands of an increasingly complex banking and monetary environment necessitated streamlining the functions to facilitate the development of a more dynamic and coherent policy on monetary matters. In order to regulate and supervise the financial sector, the MAS would exercise authority under the Banking Act of 1970, the Finance Companies Act of 1967 and the Exchange Control Ordinance of 1953 over a wide range of financial matters. The regulatory functions under the Securities Industry Act (1973) were also transferred to MAS in September 1984. Meanwhile, the Accounting and Corporate Regulatory Authority is the body responsible for administering the Companies Act, Business Registration Act, Limited Liability Partnerships Act, Limited Partnerships Act and supervising public accountants in Singapore. In other words, it is the national regulator of business entities, public accountants and corporate service providers in Singapore.[102] Its goal is to ensure good corporate governance, quality corporate financial reporting and high quality audit in the financial and corporate sectors of Singapore. It was made a statutory board on 1 April 2004, following the merger of the then Registry of Companies and Businesses, and the Public Accountants' Board under the Accounting and Corporate Regulatory Authority Act. It can be seen that it has been the practice of Singapore to empower a single regulator to perform multiple functions. It used to be the same in the UK as well. Gordon Brown, then Prime Minister, announced in May 1997 that the responsibilities of financial services regulation in the UK would be merged into a single entity, which was the Financial Services Authority. It was the broadest financial regulator in the world, bringing together nine regulatory bodies.[103] On the one hand, the existence of one single national regulator (or consolidating regulatory bodies into just two or three regulators) is justified by the need for communication, coordination, cooperation and consistency across specialist regulatory bodies which had become increasingly acute and increasingly difficult to manage efficiently.[104] On the other hand, a single regulator would have to operate across very different legal, economic and commercial contexts and this can hamper efficiency.

Indeed, MAS describes capital markets enforcement in Singapore as a three-pronged approach.[105] First, MAS is the integrated regulator and supervisor of the financial services sector. A key component of MAS' regulatory and supervisory mandate involves taking enforcement actions for breaches of laws under its purview. Second, the Commercial Affairs Department (CAD) of the Singapore Police Force is the principal law enforcement agency for the criminal investigation of white-collar crime in Singapore. Third, the three approved exchanges in Singapore, namely, the Singapore Exchange Securities Trading Limited, the Singapore Exchange Derivatives Trading Limited and ICE Futures Singapore are non-government organisations that undertake the role of front-line supervisors of the market and carry out some regulatory functions. In capital markets enforcement, MAS reviews suspected breaches of laws and regulations, for example, under the Securities and Futures Act. Market misconduct offences under Part XII of the Act, including offences of insider trading, market manipulation, making false or misleading disclosures and a failure to provide continuous disclosure. MAS has the power to impose a number of administrative sanctions against listed companies, financial institutions and their representatives such as the suspension or revocation of licences or exemptions, the issuance of prohibition orders, reprimands and warnings, and the offering of composition on non-custodial offences.[106] For more serious offences with a criminal element, the cases are referred to the CAD for investigation. With effect from 17 March 2015, the MAS and CAD will embark on a joint investigations arrangement to optimise investigations into market misconduct offences.[107] Previously each agency would conduct its own investigations with MAS pursuing civil penalty actions and the CAD pursuing criminal prosecutions. With joint investigations, both now jointly investigate all potential market misconduct offences from the outset. It is believed that this arrangement can draw significant synergies from MAS' role as a financial regulator and the police's crime investigation and intelligence capabilities.[108] As for the approved exchanges, they undertake frontline monitoring of trading activities in their respective markets and conduct preliminary assessment of possible misconduct. Suspicious cases are then referred to MAS for review. They are also empowered to take disciplinary action or impose sanctions on exchange members or listed companies for breach of its trading or listing rules.[109]

These are the enforcement procedures and powers of the authorities on paper. As said, the more satisfactory approach to measuring enforcement is to focus on inputs and outputs.[110] In the investigation by Jackson and Roe, Singapore, together with Hong Kong and Luxembourg, were observed to have deep and broad financial markets and devote significant resources to supporting their markets.[111] All three economies had the highest staffing and budgets in 2006.[112] The IOSCO Objectives and Principles of Securities Regulation states that a regulator should have adequate powers, proper resources and the capacity to perform its functions and exercise its powers.[113] According to an assessment by the IMF of Singapore's implementation of this principle in 2013, the IMF was of the opinion that within the annual budget allocation for financial supervision, the

Capital Markets Group of MAS, which has supervisory responsibility for capital markets and capital market intermediaries, received funding appropriate to its responsibilities and the size and complexity of the market.[114] On a headcount basis, the Capital Markets Group appeared to have the necessary resources relative to the other supervisory groups and the scope and size of the various tasks it is required to undertake. In relation to enforcement outputs, according to the IMF, MAS' enforcement statistics indicated that it had a reasonable success rate in the cases it brought. To achieve effective deterrence, there must be public knowledge of MAS' enforcement actions in serious cases of market misconduct. The MAS and CAD regularly publish summaries of the enforcement actions in their annual reports.[115] Also, MAS issues press releases at the conclusion of a civil penalty trial or when a civil penalty settlement has been entered into. In the public interest, MAS may also issue press releases on prosecution or civil penalty actions that the MAS is taking. In addition, MAS also issues press releases on prohibition orders and compositions relating to market misconduct offences. However, reprimands are normally not publicised unless it is in the public interest to do so. Supervisory warnings are also not published. These press releases, which clearly state the penalties imposed, are intended to ensure that market participants and the public are aware of the serious consequences of engaging in market misconduct.[116] Singapore's intensive public enforcement can send a strong signal of their commitment to uphold city's reputation as a trusted financial centre.

Private enforcement

In 1993, Singapore maintained its leading edge on minority shareholder protection by introducing a statutory derivative action. The legislative framework is found in sections 216A and 216B of Singapore's Companies Act, which are modelled on sections 238 to 240 of the Canadian Business Corporations Act.[117] At common law, the shareholder's access to litigation to pursue actions rightly belonging to the company is restricted.[118] This is known as the 'proper plaintiff' rule. As a company has a personality separate from that of its members, a member of the company cannot sue to enforce rights that belong to the company. An exception to this 'proper plaintiff rule' is possible on the ground of a 'fraud on the minority'.[119] However, this exception has failed to address the limitations of shareholders to sue a wronging director, as exemplified in the case *Ting Sing Ning* in Singapore.[120] The introduction of the statutory derivative action in many of jurisdictions has been prompted by the recognition that it is necessary give shareholders a significant role in corporate governance.

The *Ting Sing Ning* case, the leading Singapore case on the common law derivative action, concerned a Hong Kong incorporated company, in which the plaintiff was a minority shareholder and director. At first instance, it was found by the court that the plaintiff did not satisfy the fraud on the minority exception because he could not establish that the wrongdoing directors had 'wrongdoer control'. In the view of Boyle, the issue of wrongdoer control may make common law derivative actions extremely difficult to bring except in the smallest private companies.[121] The rationale for the concept of wrongdoer control is based on the assumption that the company itself would have chosen to sue if not for the wrongdoers being in control. In the Court of Appeal, the decision in the first instance was reversed. The Court of Appeal's analysis of wrongdoer control can be viewed from three perspectives: (1) the percentage of shares held by the wrongdoers; (2) the actual de facto control that the wrongdoers had over the company, specifically over the decision of whether to sue; and (3) whether fully informed independent shareholders (if they existed) would have supported the company pursuing the action. Although it reflects a principled approach in addressing the wrongdoer control issue, the *Ting Sing Ning* case is a good illustration of the difficulties surrounding the common law derivative action.[122]

Singapore was one of the first Commonwealth countries to introduce a statutory derivative action in 1993. New Zealand introduced it in the same year.[123] Not until 1999 and 2006 was it seen in Australia and the UK respectively.[124] As a comparison, Hong Kong as a keen competitor of Singapore and former Commonwealth country, statutory derivative action was only added to its Companies Ordinance in 2004, over ten years later than Singapore.[125] Section 216A of the Companies Act allows a complainant to apply to the court for leave to bring an action in the name of and on behalf of the company, or to intervene in an action to which the company is a party. Most importantly, the section sets out the preconditions to the court granting leave for the bringing of such an action. The court must be satisfied as to three elements.[126] First, the complainant must have given 14 days' notice to the directors of the company of his intention to apply to the court, if the directors of the company do not bring, diligently prosecute or defend or discontinue the action; second, the complainant must act in good faith; and, third, that it appears to be prima facie in the interests of the company that the action be brought, prosecuted, defended or discontinued. Apparently, with the statutory action, shareholders are in a better position to bring a lawsuit against a wrongdoing director. However, there are several shortcomings. First, it is not available for a company which is incorporated in a foreign country. That is why in *Ting Sing Ning* the complainant had to rely on the common law action. Second, it used to be not available for listed companies.[127] The exclusion of listed companies was based on the belief that public listed companies are already monitored by various regulatory authorities and disgruntled shareholders of such companies have an avenue in that they can sell their shares in the open market.[128] This move was described as 'controversial'.[129] To deny the listed shareholder the availability of a statutory derivative action on the basis that he has the option of selling his shares on the market is to ignore the deterrent effect of the provision. Even worse, this may actually provide wrongdoers with a perceived sense of immunity. Third, it has not been widely used, as in the first few years since its enactment, there were only two reported cases in which the action was invoked.[130] Indeed, including common law actions as well, between 1987 and 2010, there were only ten reported cases altogether.[131] This may cast a doubt on whether there is a genuine demand for shareholder lawsuits.

Asian values may serve as an explanation.[132] There is a preference for harmony and consensus as opposed to confrontation and dissent. Furthermore, the costs of any litigation action plays a large part in the decision whether to commence an action. In this regard, in a statutory derivative action, the courts may make orders or interim orders as it thinks fit in the interests of justice, including an order requiring the company to pay reasonable legal fees and disbursements incurred by the complainant in connection with the action.[133] But there is always a risk on the complainant that he may be accountable for these interim costs upon the final disposition of the action.

Other than a derivative action, a shareholder may opt for the oppression remedy under section 216 of the Companies Act. The basic idea behind this remedy is to give a shareholder standing to complain that the affairs of the company were being conducted in a manner that was unfair to him. The difference between sections 216 and 216A is in the sense that the former will offer a personal relief whilst the latter will offer a group relief that any gains will be split between all shareholders in the company. As a result, when a wrong has been done to the company, the most appropriate route is for the plaintiff to commence a derivative action against the wrongdoers. In reality, the potential overlapping of both types of action is recognised in Singapore.[134] The effects of the oppression remedy can be wide-ranging, as the court may, with a view to bringing an end or remedying the matters complained of, make an order as it thinks fit. Such orders may include directing or prohibiting any act or cancelling or varying any transaction or resolution; regulating the conduct of the affairs of the company in future; authorizing civil proceedings to be brought in the name of the company; providing for the purchase of the shares and debentures of the company by other members or holders of debentures or the company itself; or even winding up the company. But a purchase order of the complainant's shares is most common result, rendering the oppression remedy meaningless in the context of a public company, as shareholders can easily sell their shares off in the market. There were a total of 25 reported cases under section 216 between 1987 and 2010.[135] Apparently, the oppression remedy has been more popular among shareholders than derivative action.

In the most drastic situation, the court may wind up a company where it is just and equitable to do so.[136] This is also an important remedy for shareholders as it provides a means for disgruntled shareholders to use the winding up process to disengage from a company. There were a total of 18 reported just and equitable winding up between 1987 and 2010.[137] The emergence in shareholder actions has been a relatively recent phenomenon. In the two decades following Singapore's independence, there were virtually no such actions.[138] Although more and more actions have been witnessed, the number may not be commensurate with the number of business entities in Singapore.[139] Public enforcement, in which Singapore has done well as discussed before, is important to regulate the public listed companies. However, for majority of the companies, which are non-public, private enforcement is far more important by contrast. Unfortunately, like Hong Kong, as well as the UK, private enforcement arguably has not been the major landscape of the regulatory system in Singapore. Needless to say, sparse private enforcement is not necessarily a bad sign. It can be due to good compliance by the companies and their officers, or alternatively, disputes may well be resolved through alternative channels before being escalated into litigations.

Political institutions

According to the Singapore government itself, its system is modelled after the Westminster system in the UK.[140] There are three separate branches. The Legislature or Parliament makes the laws. The Government, comprising Cabinet Ministers and other office-holders, administers the law. The Judiciary interprets the law through the courts. This system is known as the parliamentary representative democratic republic model, where the Prime Minister of Singapore is the Head of Government and the President of Singapore is the Head of State. The Members of Parliament are voted in at regular General Elections. The leader of the political party that secures the majority of seats in Parliament will be asked by the President to become the Prime Minister. The Prime Minister will then select his Ministers from elected MPs to form the Cabinet. As opposed to the UK, which essentially has a two-party system, Singapore does not have a one-party system but instead it has a dominant party system.[141] In dominant party systems, only one party has the capacity to govern. The PAP is one of the world's longest surviving dominant parties, having been elected to power in 1959 and returned to power in every general election since then. In the most recent general election in 2015, the PAP secured a popular vote share of 69.9 per cent taking 83 of the 89 seats available, a rise of 10 per cent from the 60.1 per cent it got in the 2011 election when it took 81 seats.[142] In the 2015 election, for the first time since independence in 1965, all seats were contested.[143] A record eight opposition parties entered the election, including with the Workers' Party, the National Solidarity Party, the Reform Party and the Singapore Democratic Party. The Workers' Party won the remaining six seats. The current parliament has 100 members. Other than elected members, there is a small number of Non-Constituency Members and Nominated Members.[144] Owing to the dominance of the PAP, only three people have ever been Prime Minister. The late Lee Kuan Yew was the first and longest-serving prime minister of Singapore from 1959 to 1990. Lee was succeeded by Goh Chok Tong. Goh retired on 12 August 2004 and was succeeded by Lee Kuan Yew's son Lee Hsien Loong.

Despite different signs of a democracy, such as a parliamentary system of government, elected president and universal suffrage, Singapore is largely an authoritarian state. In the view of Reyes, the PAP's longstanding and undemocratic dominance is particularly interesting because it positions Singapore, among the world's richest countries, in direct opposition to one of the most established models in political science that democracy is a direct effect of economic development.[145] Strangely, in the case of Singapore, it is economic advancement that serves as a 'powerful legitimising factor' of the authoritarian rule.[146] The central idea promoted by the government is that to ensure stability and continuous economic growth it is necessary that community interests be placed above individual ones. It is quite clear that citizens in Singapore enjoy restricted freedom. According to the Freedom House's Freedom in the World rankings, which track the status of political rights and civil liberties, Singapore was ranked as a 4 in each category, giving it the label of only 'Partly Free'.[147] The courts continue to hand down jail terms for critical online speech, with defendants in at least two prominent cases pleading guilty recently. The founders of a news portal that had been closed down in 2015, Ai Takagi and Yang Kaiheng, were sentenced to ten months and eight months in prison in March and June, respectively, after pleading guilty to sedition charges. In September, seventeen-year-old blogger Amos Yee was sentenced to six weeks in prison after pleading guilty to wounding religious feelings. Yee sought political asylum in the US in December 2016. Many believe one reason for Yee's conviction is that he is one of the few Singaporean voices openly criticising Lee Kuan Yew's legacy.[148]

Huff agrees that the economic progress in Singapore contributed to the PAP's acceptance by voters and Singapore's dominant party system.[149] By contrast, almost everywhere else in post-colonial Asia, leaders had political skills associated with their role in independence movements, but little regard for economic considerations. When Milton Friedman looked at Singapore, he remarked that Lee Kuan Yew was a 'benevolent dictator' and drew the lesson that it is possible to combine a free private market economic system with a dictatorial political system.[150] Whilst many dictators gain power with initial promises that they will make their country better for its citizens, most eventually forget citizens' needs and instead focus on their own desires for wealth and recognition. Benevolent dictators remain focused on improving their country and they use their absolute power to do so.[151] Their power becomes a unifying force, rallying people to work for the benefit of their country and to support the dictator's wishes.

Despite being labelled as a dictator, there is no doubt that Lee Kuan Yew was the founder and patriarch of modern Singapore.[152] His greatest achievement was to promote the concept of good governance in Southeast Asia, a region long plagued by corrupt, inefficient governments. As Singapore's prime minister for more than 30 years, he built his small island republic into one of the world's most successful economies. Average per capita income just after independence in 1965 was a mere US$511. By the time Lee resigned as prime minister it had topped US$50,000. His perfectionism, farsightedness, elitism, authoritarianism and intolerance, along with his obsessions with security, cleanliness and order, are reflected in nearly every aspect of modern Singaporean life.[153] After the Second World War, he enrolled at the London School of Economics in 1946 before transferring to Fitzwilliam Hall at Cambridge University in early 1947 to study law. His political awareness grew through involvement with the British Labour Party and participation in London's Malayan Forum (a Malayan students' discussion group), and he turned strongly against colonial rule.[154] Initially working as lawyer, in 1954 a series of political meetings at his house led to the founding of the PAP. When the UK gave Singapore self-government in 1959, Lee became prime minister at the age of 35. He had always backed the idea of a Malaysian Federation linking the island of Singapore with the Malay Peninsula. He argued that an independent Singapore was a 'political, economic and geographical absurdity'.[155] As Singapore lacked natural resources and was economically largely dependent on Malaya, few believed full independence was viable. Lee thus made it a priority to achieve merger with Malaya. The new country, Malaysia, was established in September 1963 with the merger of Malaya, Singapore, Sabah and Sarawak. However, there were tensions, sometimes violent, with Malay hardliners and the federal government over various issues, culminating in Malaysia's expulsion of Singapore in 1965.

Lee was not one to shy away from his economic triumphs for the city state. The second volume of his published memoirs carries the title *From Third World to First: The Singapore Story: 1965–2000*. His main contribution, and the key to his success, was that he understood that in order to put Singapore on a sustainable growth trajectory one needs much more than sound economic policy.[156] Lee built a country whose institutional set-up is unparalleled, including the rule of law, efficient government structures, the continuous fight against corruption and overall stability. He built a Singaporean model of economic development which depended externally on services as much as manufactured exports, with extensive government intervention and planning.[157] Lim identifies two major differences between Singapore's growth model and those of the other Asian economies.[158] The first is the continued dominance of multinationals and government-linked corporations in sectors of the economy that elsewhere have strong domestic private sector participation. The second is the heavy reliance on state-promoted immigration.

As part of its post-independence industrialisation plan, the Singapore government assumed a proactive entrepreneurial role by establishing state enterprises, also known as government-linked companies (GLCs).[159] They existed in key sectors such as manufacturing, finance, trading, transportation, shipbuilding and services. In the late 1960s, the Singapore government created GLCs and statutory boards to spearhead development in various sectors of the economy. GLCs included the Keppel, Sembawang and Jurong Shipyards which were intended to spur the development of Singapore as a major shipbuilding and ship repair centre. The EDB was set up to provide development finance. Neptune Orient Lines was formed to leverage on the city state's strategic location. Joint ventures with foreign investors were also seen. The Singapore Refining Company was a joint venture with Caltex and British Petroleum. The Petrochemical Corporation of Singapore was a joint venture with Shell and a Japanese consortium. In 1974, the government established a limited holding company, Temasek, to manage its investments in GLCs. At that time, 36 companies were transferred to Temasek's control.[160] The 1980s and 1990s also saw the corporatisation of a number of statutory boards into GLCs. It was estimated that in the beginning of the new century, the total number of GLCs was in the hundreds.[161] According to a more updated survey by Mak, in 2015, Temasek still controlled 12 GLCs directly and

18 more indirectly.[162] It was estimated that these 30 GLCs accounted for 30 per cent of total market capitalisation in the Singapore Exchange and 20 per cent share of overall economy.

As early as the 1980s, Lee Kuan Yew already realised the importance of attracting talent from around the world.[163] It was not sufficient to rely on home-grown talent for social development. Singapore focuses on two levels of immigrants: professionals or skilled immigrants with ‘portable skills’, and ordinary workers. In 2007, the government sought to change the pattern of immigration by attracting more immigrants with higher educational qualifications to fill vacancies in private banking, financial institutions and other service industries, and also positions in biotechnology and education.[164] This was a change based on Singapore’s new economic development needs. Unlike its Southeast Asian neighbours, since its independence in 1965, Singapore has embraced multiracialism. This has helped to support an open immigration policy. Lee Kuan Yew once said:

> We are going to be a multiracial nation in Singapore. We will set an example. This is not a Malay nation; this is not a Chinese Nation; this is not an Indian nation. Everyone will have his place equal: language, culture, religion.[165]

The role of multiracialism and multiculturalism in the economic growth of Singapore is to be explored in the next part.

Cultural institutions

According to the Department of Statistics in Singapore, as of 2017, 74.3 per cent of population in Singapore were Chinese, 13.4 per cent Malay, 9.1 per cent Indian (includes Sri Lankan), with other ethic groupings making up the remaining 3.2 per cent of the population.[166] As a result, it is clear that Singapore has a significant Chinese community and the discussions in the two previous chapters about the cultural considerations of Chinese should to a large extent be applicable to the case of Singapore. Many observers have attributed the success of several fast-growing East Asian economies to their common cultural, largely Confucian, values, such as respect for authority, loyalty to good leaders, preference for order, hard work, thrift and emphasis on education, and these factors seem to have worked in Singapore.[167] For example, Lee Kuan Yew said in his book *From Third World to First*:

> Singapore depends on the strength and influence of the family to keep society orderly and maintain a culture of thrift, hard work, filial piety, and respect for elders and for scholarship and for learning. These values make for a productive people and help economic growth.[168]

Lee believed that in Confucian societies the individual exists in the context of the family, extended family, friends and wider society, and that the government cannot and should not take over the role of the family.[169] Therefore, Singapore, and indeed East Asia as a whole, have shied away from the Western approach in which the government tries to fulfil the obligations of the family. Lee was widely regarded as one of the main architects of the Asian values argument.[170] The cultural source of Asian values is most commonly Confucianism.[171] At heart, Confucianism is about people and relationships, and it governs how everyone acts in a traditional Chinese hierarchical society. Similarly, proponents of the Asian Values advocate a view of society that is always hierarchical and tends to stem from emphasising the interdependence and social nature of human beings. In particular, Lee argued for a paternalistic, illiberal state, which is presumed to be strong and stable.[172] He viewed paternalistic government as the necessity for strong measures to achieve economic growth.

The focus on traditional family values is also seen in the commercial sector. According to a survey by NUS Business School's Centre for Governance, Institutions and Organisations on family firms, it was found that they played a key role in Singapore's economy, making up the majority (52 per cent) of companies listed on the Singapore Exchange and representing about 30 per cent of total market capitalisation.[173] They also performed better than non-family firms, enjoying an average of 5 per cent returns on assets, compared to 3 per cent for non-family firms. Like those in Hong Kong, these firms have a hands-on approach to management. For example, it was found in the survey that the board size of family firms was generally smaller than that of non-family firms.[174] There was a median board size of six in family firms in Singapore, as opposed to seven in non-family firms. Also, family firms typically had fewer non-executive directors. The majority of family members that hold directorships in family firms were executive directors. Quite worryingly, many family businesses had low scores on the Governance and Transparency Index, which indicate a lower level of compliance with governance practices compared to non-family firms. As said before, family firms derive benefits such as stability, a long-term orientation and efficient decision-making structures. But at the same time business families should also ensure they maintain a strong and independent element in their boards, which will ultimately contribute to the long-term sustainability of family firms amidst the rising importance of good corporate governance. In another report by KPMG and CPA Australia on differing perspectives in Singapore's family businesses, it is recognised that family businesses do in fact have a unique advantage over non-family owned businesses, such as value-driven organisational structure (stronger sense of belonging), faster decision making (smaller chain of command than complex companies) and a significant home-ground advantage (with a better understanding of Singapore and neighbouring countries).[175] On the other hand, there are challenges, particularly in succession planning, growth and talent retention. As a result, professionalisation of operations becomes a key goal for many family-owned businesses in Singapore. As observed by Tong, large-scale Chinese family businesses, such as the Hong Leong Group, Lee Kim Tah Group and United Overseas Bank Group, to cite some examples, are run very professionally.[176] Hundreds of top- and middle-level staff are now employed to perform operational and technical work. A key feature in large-scale Chinese firms is the rise of a professional class. Despite the rising emphasis on rational business and economic practices and the emergence of a professional class, the basic principles by which the Chinese run their companies may still remain. The Hong Leong Group of companies may illustrate this.[177]

Kwek Hong Png came to Singapore in the late 1920s from China. In 1941, he established Hong Leong Company, which supplied equipment to rubber plantations and traded in building materials. As business grew, the founder invited his three younger brothers to join the firm. The Kwek brothers chose to keep their loans from banks to a minimum, relying on their own resources instead. Hong Leong Group, like many other large Chinese family business groups in Singapore, shows vast diversification in their businesses, including financing, manufacturing, property development and service industries. Despite the large number of firms and the presence of several public companies, however, the control of Hong Leong is still in the hands of the Kwek family. The control of the family business is not diluted by the presence of professionals occupying top positions. These professional managers/executives do not exercise control comparable to core family members because their control is limited to only one section of the group business.

Whilst the Chinese community, as the major ethnic group, and their thinking has been influential in the rise of Singapore, the city state has taken pride in their multiracial and multicultural society and the contributions from other ethnic groups should not be overlooked. In the beginning, British colonial administrators found themselves planning and administering the port city on the basis of ethnic enclaves assigned to the Chinese, Indians, Malays and Europeans.[178] Specific quarters were to be allocated to immigrant groups on the basis of races and their perceived occupations. Europeans resided adjacent to the government centre, the Arabs and Bugis sharing trading and religious interests were placed close to Malay royalty further away, and the majority Chinese and Indians were concentrated in the centre of mercantile activity south of the Singapore River. The local Malays who lived outside of the town limits along the coast and upriver, depending on fishing and cultivation, were largely left alone. The master culture, that is, British or Western culture, was not imposed on the local population, except for its laws and government. In the view of Chan Sek Keong, former Chief Justice of Singapore, this helped to minimise racial and religious conflicts between different groups.[179] On the other hand, different strategies have been used to manage the ready mix of the various ethnic and religious components of Singapore society and made it possible for the different communities to live together in peace.[180] Under the Constitution of Singapore, English, Malay, Mandarin and Tamil are designated the official languages of Singapore, with Malay recognised as the national language, but English is the language of government, of the administration of justice, of trade and commerce, and is the language spoken at all levels of Singapore society.[181] Whilst formally recognising the pre-existing ethnic groups by allowing them to keep their respective languages, the English language has provided all races in Singapore with a common space to develop and nurture shared values and a common identity.[182]

There are currently over 500,000 Malays in Singapore, compared to close to four million Chinese there. While Article 152 of the Singapore Constitution recognises the special position of Malays as the indigenous people of Singapore, resentment at their relative weakness in employment and political terms as well as the perceived favouritism towards ethnic Chinese has continued to create tensions, according to the Minority Rights Group.[183] For example, only 1.5 per cent of university graduates were Malay in 1980, and by the late 1980s their average earnings were about 70 per cent of those of the Chinese majority.[184] Overall, few Malays occupy high-level political or civil service positions. The 2006 parliamentary elections saw the election of 12 Malay MPs under the governing PAP banner, a number which roughly corresponded to the minority's share of the population, though only one Malay sat in the Cabinet of 19 ministers.[185] There were no Malays sitting on the Supreme Court. In a sharp contrast, with a population of just 356,876, fewer than Malays, Indians continue to be well represented overall in political, judicial and some of the higher education and technical fields, generally slightly above their proportion of the population.[186] In 2005, the average monthly income for Indian residents (SG$3,660) exceeded those for all residents (SG$3,500).[187] Both Chinese and Indian earned significantly more than Malays (SG$2,200). In the same year, 25 per cent of Indian residents had a university degree as their highest qualification attained. In contrast the national average was only 17 per cent. Also, Indians have managed to occupy key roles in society. For example, the current Chief Justice, Sundaresh Menon, is of Indian origin. Three past Presidents of Singapore had an Indian origin.[188] However, under the constitutional change in 2016, an election will be reserved for a particular racial group if no-one from that group has been president for five continuous terms.[189] This means that the Presidential Election in 2017 is reserved for candidates from the Malay community. This does not necessarily mean handing more powers to the Malays, as the President of Singapore, as the Head of State, remains largely a ceremonial role, despite the constitution having been amended in 1991 to give this role a few discretionary powers relating to the safeguarding of national reserves and the appointment of key personnel in the public sector and certain government companies.[190] Singapore's society, on the face of it, is multiracial but remains largely dominated by Chinese and to a lesser extent Indians.

Role of market infrastructure

As said, one strategy for the Singapore government to support its economic growth is to attract talents from all over the world, which also serves as an explanation of why it has a multiracial society. Lacking other resources, human resources were and still are seen as the city state's most precious asset. Education was seen, from the beginning, as central to building both the economy and the nation. Its job was to deliver the human capital engine for economic growth. Singapore's education system has evolved over the past 40 years in tandem with the changing economy.[191] In the 1960s, the emphasis was on attracting labour-intensive foreign manufacturing to provide jobs for its low-skilled workforce. In the 1970s and 1980s, a shift to more skill-intensive manufacturing led to an emphasis on technical fields. From the mid-1990s on, Singapore has sought to become a player in the global knowledge economy, encouraging more research- and innovation-intensive industry and seeking to attract scientists and scientific companies from around the globe. As a result, the economic goals of education have given education policy a very pragmatic bent and a strong focus on scientific and technical fields.

At independence, most of Singapore's two million people were illiterate and unskilled.[192] Therefore the focus of this early period was to expand basic education as quickly as possible. Singapore created a national system of public education, with universal primary education attained in 1965 and universal lower secondary by the early 1970s. In January 1979, a new education system was introduced. Singapore moved away from its earlier 'one size fits all' approach to schooling that would create multiple pathways for students in order to produce the more technically skilled labour force needed to achieve the new economic goals. The multiple pathways included three types of high school: (1) academic high schools, which prepared students for college; (2) polytechnic high schools, which focused on advanced occupational and technical training and that could also lead to college; and (3) technical institutes, which focused on occupational and technical training for the lowest fifth of students.[193] More recently, a key instrument as Singapore intentionally navigated towards the global knowledge economy has been the government's Agency for Science, Technology and Research, which provides generous funding for research and aims to attract top scientists and scientific companies.[194] One million foreign nationals with scientific, technical or managerial skills have been encouraged to work in Singapore in international corporations and in higher education. There are currently six publicly funded universities in Singapore, of which the National University of Singapore and Nanyang Technological University are both consistently ranked among top in Asia and even globally. Singapore's literacy rate is now amongst the highest in the world, up from 52.6 per cent in 1960 to 97 per cent in 2016.[195] According to the Ministry of Education of Singapore, the city state has achieved a publicly funded cohort participation rate of 26 per cent.[196] This means that more than one in four students from each Primary One cohort obtained a place in one of Singapore's publicly funded universities. The level is high when compared to Asian jurisdictions such as Hong Kong, Japan, South Korea and Taiwan with a rate of 10–20 per cent, but is low when compared to European countries, with the rate in Nordic countries like Denmark and Finland for example exceeding 50 per cent.[197]

Other than human capital, the need to develop hard infrastructure has not been overlooked. As mentioned before, one of the first initiatives was the development of the Jurong Industrial Estate. Despite being described as a hilly, jungled area mostly covered by crocodile-infested mangrove swamps, Jurong was selected as the location for the first industrial estate of Singapore. Its founding father, then Minister of Finance, Dr Goh Keng Swee's vision for Jurong was to be the birthplace of large-scale industrialisation in order to shift Singapore's economy to higher gears.[198] To jumpstart the area's development, he offered tax incentives and drew in foreign investments. His other achievement was the setting up of the EDB, which has been playing an instrumental role in Singapore's economic development ever since. The Jurong Town Corporation, established in 1968, is the lead agency in Singapore to spearhead the planning, promotion and development of land and space to support the transformation of industries. Thus far, it has developed over 7,000 hectares of industrial land and 4 million square metres of ready-built facilities.[199] Apart from developing Singapore's first industrial township, Jurong Industrial Estate, from swampland, other key projects include a chemical hub in Jurong Island, business and industrial parks such as the Airport Logistics Park of Singapore, International and Changi Business Parks, Seletar Aerospace Park, CleanTech Park, Tuas Biomedical Park and One-North, a cluster for knowledge-based industries with key developments like Biopolis, Fusionopolis and Mediapolis.

Singapore has long been a port city and entrepot trade has been an important economic pillar since the beginning of the colonial era. According to the World Shipping Council, in the past few years, Singapore was the second largest container port in the world, below Shanghai but above Shenzhen.[200] It was also the same in the 1920s. Singapore was again one of the greatest sea-ports in the world according to tonnage entered and cleared, and ranked next below Liverpool.[201] For a long period of time in the nineteenth century, the dock and wharf business was primarily conducted by the Tanjong Pagar Dock Company. In 1905, the colonial government explored the potential of establishing a Habour Board for the purpose of administering the port in Imperial interests. The Tanjong Pagar Dock Company was transformed into the Tanjong Pagar Dock Board. Afterwards, the Straits Settlements Port Ordinance 1912 led to the formation of the Singapore Harbour Board. The new board took over the property and undertakings of the Tanjong Pagar Dock Board from 1 July 1913. The Singapore Harbour Board was then replaced by the Port of Singapore Authority (PSA) when it was formed as a statutory board in 1964. As of today, the PSA is chiefly acting as a port operator and exists as a corporation. It operates a total of 60 berths with a handling capacity of 40 million TEUs yearly at its container terminals in Tanjong Pagar, Keppel, Brani and Pasir Panjang.[202] The regulatory function on the other hand is performed by the Maritime and Port Authority of Singapore, which was established on 2 February 1996. It is responsible for the overall development and growth of the port of Singapore, which includes terminal operators, such as the PSA. Apart from the PSA, another major operator in Singapore is Jurong Port, which began operations in 1965 as a general and bulk cargo port, serving the development needs of Jurong Industrial Estate. The early economic policy of a free port status promulgated by Sir Stamford Raffles allowed unrestricted movement of goods through Singapore, and laid down the foundation of Singapore as one of the most successful and busiest ports in the world. This policy has largely remained. Almost all imports into Singapore enter the country duty-free, with the exception of high excise taxes levied on distilled spirits and wine, tobacco products, motor vehicles and petroleum products.[203] Looking ahead, to cater for the continued growth of the port, the land use and port planners are working together to identify another area suitable for the continued expansion of the port. The older ports in the central city area at Tanjong Pagar, Keppel and Brani are likely to be phased out by 2027.[204] The area is predicted to be redeveloped as an extension to the current downtown area. Provisionally, an area in Tuas has been identified, with a designed capacity of 65 million TEUs, which is double the actual cargo volume handled by Singapore in 2015.[205]

Apart from a world-class port, Singapore also has a world-class airport. Singapore Changi Airport is widely regarded as one of the best airports in the world. Changi has consistently topped the rankings at the World Airport Awards, organised by Skytrax, an aviation research organisation. The 2017 awards, based on the opinions of 13.82 million travellers from 105 countries, saw Changi named the world's best for the fifth consecutive year, beating competition from 555 other airports.[206] It is also one of the busiest airports in the world.[207] The airport serves more than 100 airlines flying to some 380 cities in about 90 countries and territories worldwide. Each week, about 7,000 flights land or depart from Changi, with more than 58.7 million passengers passing through the airport a year. Kallang Airport was Singapore's first purpose-built commercial airport.[208] It was opened on 12 June 1937. Prior to the construction of Kallang Airport, the Seletar military airbase had been used to handle commercial air services. Towards the end of the 1940s, Kallang Airport began to face difficulties coping with the increased air traffic and larger planes. The colonial government decided in 1950 to replace Kallang Airport with a new one at Paya Lebar. Paya Lebar Airport officially opened on 20 August 1955 and served as Singapore's commercial international airport for 26 years until 1981, when it was converted into a military airbase.[209] Despite the expansion work of Paya Lebar Airport, it was becoming clear by early 1970 that the airport was operating at capacity. Passenger and aircraft volume had increased so rapidly that the airport handled 1.7 million passenger movements and 51,000 aircraft movements by 1970. The government decided in 1975 that a new civil airport had to be built on a much larger site, and the location chosen was Changi. That year marked the start of Changi Airport's Phase 1 developments. Costing SG$1 billion, it was the single biggest public project at that time.[210] Changi Airport officially commenced operations in 1981. It started a series of firsts in the world.[211] It is the first to introduce the concept of airport gardens, the first to allow passengers to make free local telephone calls in transit and more. It was also the first time passengers were provided with a completely air-conditioned experience from disembarkation to their taxis as the taxi queues were located indoors. When Changi surpassed its 10 million passenger mark in 1986, construction works for Terminal 2 had been in progress. The new terminal subsequently opened in 1991. A third terminal also opened in 2008. In April 2017 the airport welcomed its one-billionth passenger handled since its opening on 1 July 1981. It is worth noting that Changi is home to Singapore's flag carrier, Singapore Airlines, which is one of the significant GLCs in Singapore. As of 2017, Temasek holds a 55.63 per cent stake in the airline.[212] Its origins can be traced to Malayan Airways Limited, which was formed on 21 October 1937.[213] In 1966, Malaysian Airways Limited became Malaysia-Singapore Airlines. Then in 1972, it separated into two airlines, Malaysian Airline System and Singapore Airlines as they are known today. Like its home airport, Singapore Airlines has received a number of awards, arguably making it the world's most awarded airline. All these point to the fact that Singapore is extremely committed to developing itself into a transportation hub which supports the growth of its economy.

Determinants of future growth

One of the most obvious uncertainties in Singapore has arisen from their loss of Lee Kuan Yew. Lee, Singapore's founding father, leading the city-state for more than three decades, died in 2015 at the age of 91. He was Singapore's first prime minister after independence in 1965, and continued the role until 1990, after which Goh Chok Tong took over until 2004; afterwards Lee Hsien Loong succeeded Goh as prime minister. Lee Kuan Yew continued to serve as Senior Minister under his successor, Goh until 2004, then as Minister Mentor until 2011, under his son Lee Hsien Loong. Such an arrangement reflected the institutionalisation of seniority and also Lee Kuan Yew's continuing influence in Singapore's politics.[214] In 2011, Lee, then Minister Mentor, withdrew from day-to-day governance by quitting his Cabinet post along with Senior Minister, Goh Chok Tong. According to a joint statement from them at that time, they both felt that 'the time has come for a younger generation to carry Singapore forward in a more difficult and complex situation'.[215] Many people believed that 'the complex' situation pointed to that year's general election. In the election, the share of the popular vote for Lee's PAP fell to a historic low of 60.1 per cent. Moreover, amidst Singapore' dominant party system, the opposition Workers' Party took an unprecedented six seats. Some predicted that this might mark the beginnings of an evolution into a two-party system for Singapore over the longer term.[216] This prediction did not materialise in the subsequent election in 2015, at least. As said before, PAP won about 69.9 per cent of the vote in this most recent election, in contrast to the party's worst ever performance in 2011. It was believed that this victory was largely owed to a sense of patriotism inspired by the fiftieth anniversary of independence and respect for the country's independence leader, former premier Lee Kuan Yew, who died in the same year.[217] To what extent Singapore will relinquish or retain Lee's vast legacy to his country remains unclear. What is more clear is that Lee's death might mark a turning point for a country whose destiny so far has been so powerfully shaped by one man.

Despite winning a major election, the beginning of Lee Hsien Loong's era has not been smooth. In July 2017, the younger siblings of Lee Hsien Loong released a seven-page joint statement online and a summary of their case against their elder brother in the dispute over their family home at Oxley Road.[218] In the joint statement, Lee Wei Ling and Lee Hsien Yang gave their side of the story with regard to how the rift with their elder brother came about. They accused the prime minister of being opposed to carrying out their late father's wish that their family home be eventually demolished, rather than becoming a monument. As a result, they claimed that they had lost confidence in their brother as the nation's leader. Authoritarian Singapore has long prided itself on being Southeast Asia's most prosperous and arguably most successful post-colonial nation, and analysts are watching the divisions in the Lee family with intense interest.[219] The family dispute has become intensely vitriolic because of the growing importance of the Lee family brand in Singapore, which had become closely identified with the Singaporean model of professionalism, planning and incorruptibility in public life. The row has been a rare public spectacle of acrimony within Singapore's tightly disciplined First Family and has been highly unusual in a country which is used to swift resolution of public conflicts. The following quote from the joint statement of Lee Wei Ling and Lee Hsien Yang may have summarised the uncertainty of Singapore to a degree:

> Nobody ever doubted that Lee Kuan Yew always held the best interests of Singapore and Singaporeans at heart. He was authentic and spoke his mind. The same cannot be said for our brother, Lee Hsien Loong and his wife, Ho Ching.[220]

This episode has drawn attention to the closely held nature of power in a society where the prime minister is the son of the country's first leader, while his wife Ho Ching is chief executive of the state investor Temasek.[221]

Incidentally, all this has come about when there are signs of slow growth ahead for Singapore economy. Singapore's Trade and Industry Ministry reported in 2016 that the economy grew by just 0.6 per cent in the third quarter, compared with the same period in the previous year.[222] Compared to the previous quarter, the economy contracted by 4.1 per cent, the biggest slump since 2012. Another quarter of negative growth might push Singapore into a technical recession. At the end, Singapore's economy grew by 1.8 per cent for the whole of 2016.[223] It averted a technical recession with a 9.1 per cent quarter-on-quarter growth in the fourth quarter. The economy is expected to grow at a slow place in the near future. Never before has modern Singapore's economy grown below 5 per cent for five years in a row, as it has now since 2012.[224] The Minister for Trade and Industry, Lim Hng Kiang, whilst ruling out an 'outright recession', indicated the possibility that Singapore's economy could see some quarters of negative growth.[225] Weak external demand, tepid growth in major trading partners and the increasingly protectionist mode in the global trading environment, coupled with high operation costs and low productivity domestically are making the prospects challenging for Singapore ahead in the future.[226] The question is whether Singapore's economy can continue to transform as it has done in the past to maintain its global competitiveness in the coming decades. Looking ahead, there are global and regional developments that could disrupt businesses that fail to adapt to the times, but promise gains to those that transform and respond to change effectively.[227] Trade-boosting pacts such as the Trans-Pacific Partnership are faltering during the Trump administration in the US. However, with other opportunities like China's Belt and Road Initiative, what Singapore needs to do is figure out how to help local companies prepare for them.

Concluding remarks

As said in the beginning, Singapore has frequently been compared to Hong Kong. The pattern of their economic growth was very similar before the 1980s and 1990s. Under British colonial rule, both economies took off with entrepot trade, very much thanks to their strategic geographical location, with Singapore as the sea link between India and China, and Hong Kong as the gateway to China. Then in 1950s and 1960s, both economies turned their attention to labour-intensive manufacturing. Afterwards, in the face of more intensive competition from other economies, they were forced to transform into services-oriented economies. It was the point when their economies evolved differently. Hong Kong basically ditched all secondary production and embraced a service-oriented economy. By contrast, like Hong Kong, Singapore also started to place more emphasis on trade and business related services by, for example, developing its financial sector. However, at the same time, Singapore still retained its secondary production and moved up the value chain by shifting to skill-intensive manufacturing and high technology. The result is that Singapore now has a more balanced economy and it has developed notably better than its keen competitor when looking at their GDP data.

It is fair to say that the prosperity of both economies has a British origin. As former British colonies, they were able to attract a considerable volume of trade as the foundation of their later development. Indeed, trade remains an important part of their economies as exemplified by the annual volume of cargo handled by their airports and ports. Meanwhile, another advantage of their British origin is that they were able to come up with a functional and much tested legal framework to support local trade and commercial activities. Both economies managed to retain a common law system, even after their independence or a change of sovereignty. Specifically, their early corporate law systems were borrowed from the British Companies Act, which provided a ready-made system of investor protection to support their economies. Both jurisdictions have consistently reformed their corporate and financial systems afterwards to make sure that they can meet modern business needs. In these reforms, it has been a common practice for the governments to consider the experience in the UK and other Commonwealth countries. To ensure its financial sector can thrive, like Hong Kong, Singapore has put a lot of resources into the public enforcement of law. Again like Hong Kong (and also the UK), private enforcement has not been the major landscape of regulation.

Unlike Hong Kong which was under colonial rule until 1997, Singapore had gained independence much sooner. As a result, clearly the colonial origin of Singapore should only take some of the credit for its success. This success indeed has been largely owed to the visionary leadership provided by Lee Kuan Yew, as the founding father of modern Singapore, and his government. The Singapore government has introduced and formulated a number of initiatives to foster its economic growth. The government has been authoritarian, but has also been described as a 'benevolent dictatorship'. The civil and political rights of citizens may come as an expense but at least the government has managed to focus all their efforts on social welfare and economic growth. Whilst Singapore's society is largely Chinese, its government has managed to embrace multiculturalism to achieve social harmony, in light of the pre-existing ethnic groups before its dependence. Singapore is so committed to economic and social development that Nobel winning economist, Paul Krugman, once said: 'Singapore grew through a mobilisation of resources that would have done Stalin proud.'[228] This apparently points to a conclusion that Singapore's experience can be a mix of Hong Kong's capitalist and China's socialist models. Looking to the future, with the death of Lee Kuan Yew, it is hard to say to what extent his legacy will be retained.

Notes

1 See, for example, Alwyn Young (1992), 'A Tale of Two Cities: Factor Accumulation and Technical Change in Hong Kong and Singapore' in *NBER Macroeconomics Annual*, **7**; K.C. Ho and Alvin So (1997), 'Semi-periphery and Borderland Integration: Singapore and Hong Kong Experiences' in *Political Geography*, **16**; and Jon Quah (1994), 'Controlling corruption in city-states: A Comparative Study of Hong Kong and Singapore' in *Crime, Law and Social Change*, **22**.

2 Data from the World Bank.

3 IMD (2017), 'World Competitiveness Yearbook 2017 Results'. Online. Available at: www.imd.org/wcc/world-competitiveness-center-rankings/competitiveness-2017-rankings-results.

4 Grace Leong (2017), 'Singapore Tops New Ranking of Digital Competitiveness' in *Straits Times* (31 May 2017). In this ranking, Sweden took second place in the new ranking, followed by the US, Finland, Denmark, the Netherlands and Hong Kong.

5 Long Finance (2017), 'The Global Financial Centres Index'. Online. Available at: www.longfinance.net/publications.html.

6 Data from the World Bank.

7 National Library Board of Singapore (2014), 'Archaeology of the Forbidden Hill'. Online. Available at: http://eresources.nlb.gov.sg/history/events/2ebfebad-a4d5-4bbb-bf43-c7db6e30eb7d.

8 National Library Board of Singapore (2014), 'Stamford Raffles's Career and Contributions to Singapore'. Online. Available at: http://eresources.nlb.gov.sg/infopedia/articles/SIP_715_2004-12-15.html.

9 Ibid.

10 National Library Board of Singapore (2017), 'Colonial Port City 1819–1945'. Online. Available at: http://eresources.nlb.gov.sg/history/timeline/1819-1945.

11 Mary Turnbull (2009), *A History of Modern Singapore 1819–2005*, Singapore: NUS Press, p. 34.

12 National Library Board of Singapore (2014), 'First Census of Singapore is Taken'. Online. Available at: http://eresources.nlb.gov.sg/history/events/2fb8948b-5f16-4a7a-8e3c-7a724e1eb6ad.

13 National Library Board of Singapore (2011), 'Formation of the Straits Settlements'. Online. Available at: http://eresources.nlb.gov.sg/history/events/57f1cda6-b5e7-4646-bd4f-14cb08181bfe.

14 Turnbull (2009), op. cit., p. 106.

15 George Bogaars (1955), 'The Effect of the Opening of the Suez Canal on the Trade and Development of Singapore' in *Journal of the Malayan Branch of the Royal Asiatic Society*, **28**, pp. 100–101.
16 Ibid.
17 Lin Ken Wong (1978), 'Singapore: Its Growth as an Entrepot Port, 1819–1941' in *Journal of Southeast Asian Studies*, **9**, p. 64.
18 National Library Board of Singapore (2015), 'Straits Trading Company Limited is Established'. Online. Available at: http://eresources.nlb.gov.sg/history/events/bc8fd0f6-1c2a-4b33-841e-c3a1dffc8cd2.
19 Ibid.
20 National Library Board of Singapore (2011), 'First Rubber Trees are Planted in Singapore'. Online. Available at: http://eresources.nlb.gov.sg/history/events/a8ceea4c-1c8b-4c9a-885c-b85038b39e4c.
21 National Library Board of Singapore (2014), 'Singapore Chamber of Commerce Rubber Association is Formed'. Online. Available at: http://eresources.nlb.gov.sg/history/events/fed06a3a-caee-4120-bf21-9b1eaa428c23.
22 National Library Board of Singapore (2014), 'Establishment of the Post Office Saving Banks'. Online. Available at: http://eresources.nlb.gov.sg/history/events/b1c18cda-b48b-4dd7-8521-ecbd1d445c0b.
23 National Library Board of Singapore (2015), 'Steam Tram Service Begins'. Online. Available at: http://eresources.nlb.gov.sg/history/events/792b7cbe-e877-4978-b6f9-312b4b435c68.
24 Department of Trade and Industry of Great Britain (1945), *The Entrepot Trade of Singapore*, London: Department of Trade and Industry, p. 9.
25 Ibid. p. 13.
26 Wong (1978), op. cit., p. 70.
27 Ibid. p. 81.
28 National Library Board of Singapore (2014), 'Malayan Union is Inaugurated'. Online. Available at: http://eresources.nlb.gov.sg/history/events/e8db672a-3571-4fa3-9df0-220e83ee2a88#3.
29 W.G. Huff (1993), *The Economic Growth of Singapore: Trade and Development in the Twentieth Century*, Cambridge: CUP, p. 278.
30 Ibid. p. 279.
31 Ibid.
32 Ibid. p. 290.
33 National Library Board of Singapore (2014), 'Economic Development Board is Formed'. Online. Available at: http://eresources.nlb.gov.sg/history/events/509d1656-8fc5-405f-8eec-ad058d8a540c.
34 World Bank (2008), 'Singapore Local Economic Development: The Case of the Economic Development Board'. Online. Available at: http://siteresources.worldbank.org/INTLED/Resources/339650-1194284482831/4356163-1211318886634/SingaporeProfile.pdf.
35 Ravi Menon (2015), 'An Economic History of Singapore: 1965–2065' Keynote Address of the Singapore Economic Review Conference. Online. Available at: www.mas.gov.sg/News-and-Publications/Speeches-and-Monetary-Policy-Statements/Speeches/2015/An-Economic-History-of-Singapore.aspx.
36 Ibid.
37 World Bank (2008), op. cit.
38 W.G. Huff (1999), 'Singapore's Economic Development: Four Lessons and some Doubts' in *Oxford Development Studies*, **27**, pp. 38–39.
39 Ibid. p. 39.
40 Poh-Kam Wong (1997), 'Creation of a Regional Hub For Flexible Production' in *Industry and Innovation*, **4**.
41 Menon (2015), op. cit.

42 World Bank (2008), op. cit.
43 Economic Development Board (2016), 'The Eighties'. Online. Available at: www.edb.gov.sg/content/edb/en/why-singapore/about-singapore/our-history/1980s.html.
44 Faizal Yahya (2016), 'Developing High-tech Companies in Singapore' in *Journal of General Management*, **42**, p. 9.
45 Menon (2015), op. cit.
46 World Bank (2008), op. cit.
47 Economic Development Board (2017), 'Chemical Industry in Singapore'. Online. Available: www.edb.gov.sg/content/edb/en/industries/industries/chemicals.html.
48 Economic Development Board (2017), 'Electronics'. Online. Available: www.edb.gov.sg/content/edb/en/industries/industries/electronics.html.
49 Economic Development Board (2017), 'Precision Engineering'. Online. Available: www.edb.gov.sg/content/edb/en/industries/industries/precision-engineering.html.
50 Department of Statistics of Singapore (2017), 'Share of GDP by Industry'. Online. Available at: www.singstat.gov.sg/statistics/visualising-data/charts/share-of-gdp-by-industry.
51 Compared to 15 years ago in 2001, manufacturing accounted for 24.9 per cent of the GDP and combined business and financial services accounted for 22.2 per cent.
52 Menon (2015), op. cit.
53 Denis Hew (2005), 'Singapore as a Regional Financial Centre' in Donna Vandenbrink and Denis Hew (eds), *Capital Markets in Asia: Changing Roles for Economic Development*, Singapore: Institute of Southeast Asian Studies.
54 Monetary Authority of Singapore (2017), 'Number of Financial Institutions and Relevant Organisations in Singapore'. Online. Available at: https://masnetsvc.mas.gov.sg/FID.html.
55 National Library Board of Singapore (2014), 'Kwong Yik Bank is Founded'. Online. Available at: http://eresources.nlb.gov.sg/history/events/d79189ba-007c-4581-88ea-f33214266c8a.
56 Young (1992), op. cit.
57 Ibid.
58 Sheng-Yi Lee (1990), *The Monetary and Banking Development of Singapore and Malaysia*, Singapore: NUS Press, p. 94.
59 Data from the World Federation of Exchanges.
60 CNBC (2017), 'More Chinese firms are saying goodbye to Singapore's stock market'. Online. Available at: www.cnbc.com/2017/04/27/more-chinese-firms-are-saying-goodbye-to-singapores-stock-market.html.
61 World Justice Project (2016), 'WJP Rule of Law Index 2016'. Online. Available at: https://worldjusticeproject.org/our-work/wjp-rule-law-index/wjp-rule-law-index-2016.
62 World Bank (2017), 'Doing Business'. Online. Available at: www.doingbusiness.org.
63 Constitution of the Republic of Singapore, art. 2.
64 The Explanatory Statement to the Companies Bill 1966 (Singapore).
65 Aiman Mohd-Sulaiman and Shanthy Rachagan (2017), 'Company Law and Corporate Governance in Malaysia' in Roman Tomasic (ed.), *Routledge Handbook of Corporate Law*, Abingdon: Routledge.
66 The latest is the Companies (Amendment) Act 2017.
67 Pey Woan Lee and Christopher Chen (2016), 'Modernising Company Law: The Singapore Experience' in *Company and Securities Law Journal*, **34**.
68 The result of this review led to the Companies Act (Cap 50, 2006 Rev Ed).
69 Mark Gillen and Pitman Potter (2000), 'The Convergence of Securities Law in Asia' in Gerry Ferguson and Douglas Johnston (eds), *Asia-Pacific Legal Development*, Vancouver: UBC Press, p. 44.
70 Lee (1990), op. cit., p. 94.

71 Corporate Governance Committee (2001), 'Report of the Committee and Code of Corporate Governance'. Online. Available at: www.mas.gov.sg/~/media/MAS/Regulations%20and%20Financial%20Stability/Regulatory%20and%20Supervisory%20Framework/Corporate%20Governance%20of%20Listed%20Companies/corfinalrpt.pdf.
72 Ibid. para. 10.
73 Ibid. para. 13.
74 World Economic Forum (2016), 'Global Competitiveness Report 2015–2016'. Online. Available at: www3.weforum.org/docs/gcr/2015-2016/Global_Competitiveness_Report_2015-2016.pdf.
75 Lee and Chen (2016), op. cit.
76 Companies Act (Cap 50, 2006 Rev Ed), s. 20A.
77 Ibid. s. 145.
78 Australian Corporations Act 2001, s. 201A(1); UK Companies Act 1985, s. 282(3); and the New Zealand Companies Act 1993, s. 150.
79 Companies Act (Cap 50, 2006 Rev Ed), s. 157.
80 Ibid. s. 157(3). The wrongdoing director is liable to the company for any profit made by him or for any damage suffered by the company as a result of the breach. Also, breach of the duty is a criminal offence. If found guilty, the wrongdoer is liable to a fine not exceeding SG$5,000 or to imprisonment for a term not exceeding twelve months. There was a proposal to decriminalise the offence, but the Company Law Steering Committee found it appropriate to retain the current position so as not to send the wrong signal. The Steering Committee was concerned that decriminalisation may encourage misconduct. See Ministry of Finance (2011), 'Report of the Steering Committee for Review of the Companies Act'. Online. Available at: www.acra.gov.sg/uploadedFiles/Content/Publications/Public_Consultation/SCReportComplete28Jul.pdf.
81 Companies Act (Cap 50, 2006 Rev Ed), s. 156.
82 *Mutual Life and Insurance Co of New York* v. *Rank Organisation Ltd* [1985] BCLC 11; *Regal (Hastings)* v. *Gulliver* [1967] 1 AC 134. For the cases in Singapore, see for example, *ECRC Land Pte Ltd* v. *Wing On Ho Christopher* [2004] 1 SLR 105; *Chew Kong Huat* v. *Ricwil (Singapore) Pte Ltd* [2000] 1 SLR 385.
83 UK Companies Act 2006, ss. 171–177.
84 Lee and Chen (2016), op. cit.
85 Ministry of Finance (2011), op. cit., para. 115.
86 Code of Corporate Governance 2012, s. 2.1.
87 Code of Corporate Governance 2012, Principle 3.
88 Code of Corporate Governance 2012, Principles 4, 7 and 12.
89 Joyce Koh and Annabelle Yip (2015), 'The Evolution of Corporate Governance in Singapore' in Singapore Institute of Directors (ed.), *Board Room Matters Volume II*, Singapore: Singapore Institute of Directors.
90 A company qualifies as a small company if: (a) it is a private company in the financial year in question; and (b) it meets at least 2 of 3 following criteria for immediate past two consecutive financial years: (i) total annual revenue less than SG$10m; (ii) total assets less than SG$10m; (iii) number of employees less 50. Under section 18 of Companies Act (Cap 50, 2006 Rev Ed), a private company is one with restriction on the right to transfer its shares, and with no more than 50 members.
91 Securities and Futures Act (Cap 289), s. 240.
92 Ibid. s. 243.
93 Ibid. s. 253.
94 Ibid. s. 254.
95 Rule 703 of the Listing Rules.
96 There are 17 items in the list, including a merger or acquisition, purchase or sale of a significant asset, significant litigation and so on.

97 Lee and Chen (2016), op. cit.
98 Ibid.
99 World Bank (2017), op. cit.
100 Rafael La Porta *et al.* (1998), 'Law and Finance' in *Journal of Political Economy*, **106**.
101 National Library Board of Singapore (2014), 'Establishment of the Monetary Authority of Singapore'. Online. Available at: http://eresources.nlb.gov.sg/history/events/c7b1b413-f920-4df7-bc0d-c91ebccb3640. See also, Monetary Authority of Singapore (2016), 'Overview'. Online. Available at: www.mas.gov.sg/about-mas/overview.aspx.
102 Accounting and Corporate Regulatory Authority (2014), 'About ACRA'. Online. Available at: www.acra.gov.sg/About_ACRA.
103 Clive Briault (2000), 'The Rationale for a Single National Financial Services Regulator' in World Bank (ed.), *European Union Accession Opportunities and Risks in Central European Finances*, Washington D.C.: World Bank, p. 211. These nine bodies were the Securities and Investments Board, the Personal Investment Authority, the Investment Management Regulatory Organisation, the Securities and Futures Authority, the Supervision and Surveillance Division of the Bank of England, the Building Societies Commission, the Insurance Directorate of the Department of Trade and Industry, the Friendly Societies Commission, and the Registrar of Friendly Societies.
104 Ibid. p. 216.
105 Monetary Authority of Singapore (2016), 'Capital Markets Enforcement'. Online. Available at: www.mas.gov.sg/~/media/MAS/News%20and%20Publications/Mono graphs%20and%20Information%20Papers/MAS%20Capital%20Markets%20Enforcement.pdf.
106 Ibid. pp. 7–8.
107 Ibid. p. 8.
108 Ibid. p. 9.
109 For example, Chapter 14 of the Listing Rules of the Singapore Stock Exchange outlines the disciplinary and appeals procedures, and enforcement powers of the exchange.
110 John Coffee (2007), 'Law and the Market: The Impact of Enforcement' in *University of Pennsylvania Law Review*, **156**.
111 Howell Jackson and Mark Roe (2009), 'Public and Private Enforcement of Securities Laws: Resource-based Evidence' in *Journal of Financial Economics*, **93**.
112 For example, the direct staff per million of population ratio in Singapore was 88.28, compared to 58.47 in Hong Kong and 314.43 in Luxembourg. See ibid.
113 The IOSCO Objectives and Principles of Securities Regulation, Principle 3.
114 International Monetary Fund (2013), 'Singapore: Detailed Assessment of Implementation on the IOSCO Objectives and Principles of Securities Regulation'. Online. Available at: www.imf.org/external/pubs/ft/scr/2013/cr13344.pdf.
115 Monetary Authority of Singapore (2016), op. cit., p. 27.
116 Ibid.
117 Meng Seng Wee and Dan Puchniak (2012), 'Derivative Actions in Singapore' in Dan Puchniak *et al.* (eds), *The Derivative Action in Asia*, Cambridge: CUP, p. 330.
118 *Foss* v. *Harbottle* (1843) 2 Hare 461.
119 A.J. Boyle (2002), *Minority Shareholders' Remedies*, Cambridge: CUP, pp. 25–26; and *Burland* v. *Earle* [1902] AC 83.
120 *Ting Sing Ning* v. *Ting Chek Swee* [2008] 1 SLR 197. See Wee and Puchniak (2012), op. cit., p. 333.
121 Boyle (2002), op. cit., p. 29.
122 Wee and Puchniak (2012), op. cit., p. 335.
123 New Zealand's Companies Act 1993, ss. 165–168.

124 Part 2F.1A of the Australian Corporations Act 2001 and the UK's Companies Act 2006, ss. 260–264.
125 See the relevant discussion in the previous chapter of this book.
126 Pearlie Choo (2001), 'The Statutory Derivative Action in Singapore – A Critical and Comparative Examination' in *Bond Law Review*, **13**.
127 Companies Act (Cap 50, 2006 Rev Ed), s. 216A(1). Here, a company was defined to mean a company other than a company that is listed on the securities exchange in Singapore. But this definition was removed by the Companies (Amendment) Act 2014, meaning a statutory derivative action is now available to public companies as well.
128 Wee and Puchniak (2012), op. cit., p. 338.
129 Choo (2001), op. cit., pp. 81–82.
130 Ibid. p. 64.
131 Wee and Puchniak (2012), op. cit., p. 360.
132 Wee and Puchniak (2012), op. cit., p. 352.
133 Companies Act (Cap 50, 2006 Rev Ed), s. 216A(5)(c).
134 Choo (2001), op. cit., p. 88.
135 Wee and Puchniak (2012), op. cit., p. 360.
136 Companies Act (Cap 50, 2006 Rev Ed), s. 254(1)(i).
137 Wee and Puchniak (2012), op. cit., p. 355.
138 Ibid. p. 354.
139 As of the end of 2016, there were over 300,000 companies in Singapore. Statistics from the Accounting and Corporate Regulatory Authority.
140 Parliament of Singapore (2017), 'System of Government'. Online. Available at: www.parliament.gov.sg/about-us/structure/system-of-government.
141 Diane Mauzy and Robert Milne (2002), *Singapore Politics under the People's Action Party*, Abingdon: Routledge, p. 38.
142 Sumiko Tan (2015), 'GE2015: PAP Vote Share Increases to 69.9%, Party Wins 83 of 89 Seats including WP-held Punggol East' in *Straits Times* (12 September 2015).
143 Ibid.
144 Up to nine Non-Constituency Members of Parliament from the opposition political parties can be appointed. This is to ensure that there will be a minimum number of opposition representatives in Parliament and that views other than the government's can be expressed in Parliament. Also, a constitutional provision for the appointment of up to nine Nominated Members of Parliament was made in 1990 to ensure a wide representation of community views in Parliament. Their appointment is intended to contribute independent and non-partisan views.
145 Sebastian Reyes (2015), 'Singapore's Stubborn Authoritarianism' in *Harvard Political Review* (29 September 2015).
146 Mauzy and Milne (2002), op. cit., p. 128.
147 Freedom House (2017), 'Freedom in the World 2017'. Online. Available at: https://freedomhouse.org/report/freedom-world/2017/singapore.
148 BBC (2015), 'Amos Yee: The Boy who Criticised Lee Kuan Yew'. Online. Available at: www.bbc.co.uk/news/world-asia-32604122.
149 Huff (1993), op. cit., p. 359.
150 Ibid.
151 Hal Marcovitz (2011), *Dictatorships*, North Mankato: Essential Library, p. 79.
152 John Burton *et al.* (2015), 'Lee Kuan Yew, Singapore's Founding Father, 1923–2015' in *Financial Times* (22 March 2015).
153 Ibid.
154 National Library Board of Singapore (2015), 'Lee Kuan Yew'. Online. Available at: http://eresources.nlb.gov.sg/infopedia/articles/SIP_2013-03-18_164023.html.
155 Burton *et al.* (2015), op. cit.
156 BBC (2015), 'How Lee Kuan Yew Engineered Singapore's Economic Miracle'. Online. Available at: www.bbc.co.uk/news/business-32028693.

157 W.G. Huff (1995), 'What is the Singapore Model of Economic Development?' in *Cambridge Journal of Economics*, **19**.
158 Linda Lim (2008), 'Singapore's Economic Growth Model – Too Much or Too Little?' Paper for the Singapore Economic Policy Conference. Online. Available at: www.fas.nus.edu.sg/ecs/scape/doc/24Oct08/Linda%20Lim.pdf.
159 Carlos Ramirez and Lung Hui Tan (2003), 'Singapore, Inc. Versus the Private Sector: Are Government-linked Companies Different?' IMF Working Paper WP/03/156. Online. Available at: www.imf.org/external/pubs/ft/wp/2003/wp03156.pdf.
160 Ibid.
161 Ibid.
162 Yuen Teen Mak (2015), 'Governance of Government-Linked Companies in Singapore for the EU Asia' Presentation in Corporate Governance Dialogue. Online. Available at: http://law.nus.edu.sg/ewbclb/events/EACG_Dialogue_Conference 2015/pdfs/mak_gglcs_slides.pdf.
163 Hong Liu and Huimei Zhang (2017), 'Lee Kuan Yew's Thoughts on Talent and Singapore's Development Strategy' in Chen-Ning Yang *et al.* (eds), *Lee Kuan Yew through the Eyes of Chinese Scholars*, Singapore: World Scientific, p. 101.
164 Ibid. 106.
165 Ibid. pp. 103–104.
166 Department of Statistics of Singapore (2017), 'Population and Population Structure'. Online. Available at: www.singstat.gov.sg/statistics/browse-by-theme/population-and-population-structure.
167 Chwee Huat Tan (1989), 'Confucianism and Nation Building in Singapore' in *International Journal of Social Economics*, **16**.
168 Quoted in Justin Moyer (2015), 'How Lee Kuan Yew Made Singapore Strong: Family Values' in *Washington Post* (23 March 2015).
169 Ibid.
170 Michael Barr (2000), 'Lee Kuan Yew and the "Asian Values" Debate' in *Asian Studies Review*, **24**.
171 Ibid. p. 311.
172 Ibid. p. 312.
173 Marleen Dieleman (2011), 'Drawing a Portrait of Family Firm Governance in Singapore'. Online. Available at: https://bschool.nus.edu.sg/Portals/0/images/CGIO/Report/CGIO%20-%20FBN%20Asia%20Family%20Business%20Report.pdf.
174 Ibid.
175 KPMG and CPA Australia (2017), 'Two Sides of a Coin: Differing Perspectives in Singapore's Family Business'. Online. Available at: https://assets.kpmg.com/content/dam/kpmg/sg/pdf/2017/03/two-sides-of-a-coin.pdf.
176 Chee Kiong Tong (2014), 'Centripetal Authority, Differentiated Networks: The Social Organization of Chinese Firms in Singapore' in Chee Kiong Tong (ed.), *Rethinking Guanxi and Trust in Chinese Business Networks*, Singapore: Springer, p. 32.
177 Ibid. pp. 32–35.
178 Kwen Fee Lian (2016), 'Multiculturalism in Singapore: Concept and Practice' in Kwen Fee Lian (ed.), *Multiculturalism, Migration, and the Politics of Identity in Singapore*, Singapore: Springer, p. 12.
179 Sek Keong Chan (2013), 'Multiculturalism in Singapore' in *Singapore Academy of Law Journal*, **25**, p. 87.
180 Ibid.
181 Constitution of Singapore, art. 153A.
182 Ibid.
183 Minority Rights Group International (2017), 'Singapore – Malays'. Online. Available at: http://minorityrights.org/minorities/malays.

184 Ibid.
185 Ibid.
186 Minority Rights Group International (2017), 'Singapore – Indians'. Online. Available at: http://minorityrights.org/minorities/indians-3.
187 Department of Statistics of Singapore (2006), 'Key Indicators of the Resident Population'. Online. Available at: https://web.archive.org/web/20070919204403/http://www.singstat.gov.sg/pubn/popn/ghsr1/indicators.pdf.
188 They were Yusof Ishak, C.V. Devan Nair and S.R. Nathan.
189 Zakir Hussain (2016), 'Constitutional Commission Report Released; Key Changes Proposed to Elected Presidency' in *Straits Times* (7 September 2016).
190 The Istana of Singapore (2013), 'Roles and Responsibilities'. Online. Available at: www.istana.gov.sg/roles-and-responsibilities.
191 OECD (2011), 'Singapore: Rapid Improvement Followed by Strong Performance' in OECD (ed.) *Lessons from. PISA for the United States*, Paris: OECD Publishing, p. 161.
192 Ibid.
193 Ibid. p. 162.
194 Ibid.
195 Department of Statistics of Singapore (2017), 'Education, Language Spoken and Literacy'. Online. Available at: www.tablebuilder.singstat.gov.sg/publicfacing/createDataTable.action?refId=967.
196 Ministry of Education of Singapore (2016), 'Singapore's University Landscape'. Online. Available at: www.moe.gov.sg/news/committee-on-university-education-pathways-beyond-2015/singapore-university-landscape#footnote-1.
197 Ibid.
198 Diwakar Kaushik (2012), 'Evolution of Industrial Landscape in Singapore' Paper for the 48th ISOCARP Congress. Online. Available at: www.isocarp.net/Data/case_studies/2108.pdf.
199 Jurong Town Corporation (2017), 'Overview'. Online. Available at: www.jtc.gov.sg/about-us/Pages/default.aspx.
200 World Shipping Council (2016), 'Top 50 World Container Ports'. Online. Available at: www.worldshipping.org/about-the-industry/global-trade/top-50-world-container-ports.
201 Anon (1922), *A Short History of the Port of Singapore*, Singapore: Fraser & Neave.
202 Port of Singapore Authority (2017), 'About Us'. Online. Available at: www.singaporepsa.com/about-us.
203 Department of Commerce of the US (2017), 'Singapore: Trade Regulations, Customs and Standards'. Online. Available at: http://2016.export.gov/singapore/doingbusinessinsingapore/traderegulationscustomsandstandards/index.asp.
204 Kai Yeng Wong and W. Chng (2016), 'Singapore: A Port City – the Case of Port Development and its Impact on the City' Paper for the 15th World Conferences Cities and Ports. Online. Available at: www.clc.gov.sg/documents/books/research-workshop/2016/Rotterdam-Port-and-the-City-Heart-of-Innovation-Presentation-Paper.pdf.
205 Ibid.
206 Skytrax (2017), 'The 2017 World Airport Awards: Methodology'. Online. Available at: www.worldairportawards.com/Awards/awards_methodology.html.
207 Changi Airport (2017), 'Traffic Statistics'. Online. Available at: www.changiairport.com/corporate/about-us/traffic-statistics.html.
208 National Library Board of Singapore (2015), 'Kallang Airport is Opened'. Online. Available at: http://eresources.nlb.gov.sg/history/events/1f7c688e-c520-4e68-a16b-7b02b250603c.
209 National Library Board of Singapore (2014), 'Paya Lebar Airport'. Online. Available at: http://eresources.nlb.gov.sg/infopedia/articles/SIP_130_2005-01-22.html.

210 Changi Airport (2017), 'Our Story'. Online. Available at: www.changiairport.com/corporate/about-us/our-story.html.
211 Ibid.
212 Singapore Airlines (2017), 'Stock and Shareholding Information'. Online. Available at: www.singaporeair.com/en_UK/us/about-us/information-for-investors/shareholding-info.
213 Singapore Airlines (2017), 'Our Heritage'. Online. Available at: www.singaporeair.com/en_UK/us/flying-withus/our-story/our-heritage.
214 Kristina Göransson (2009), *The Binding Tie: Chinese Intergenerational Relations in Modern Singapore*, Honolulu: University of Hawaii Press, p. 73.
215 Neel Chowdhury (2011), 'Why Lee Kuan Yew, Modern Singapore's Founding Father, Stepped Down' in *Time* (19 May 2011).
216 Ibid.
217 BBC (2015), 'Singapore Election: Governing Party Secures Decisive Win'. Online. Available at: www.bbc.co.uk/news/world-asia-34205869.
218 Wei Ling Lee and Hsien Yang Lee (2017), 'Oxley Road: Lee Hsien Yang, Lee Wei Ling will Stop Posting Evidence on Social Media – Full Text of Statement' in *Straits Times* (6 July 2017).
219 Jeevan Vasagar (2017), 'Singapore's First Family Feud over "Big Brother"' in *Financial Times* (14 June 2017).
220 CNN (2017), 'Singapore Prime Minister Lee Hsien Loong Publicly Denounced by Siblings'. Online. Available at: http://edition.cnn.com/2017/06/14/asia/singapore-lee-kuan-yew-children-no-confidence-lee-hsien-loong/index.html.
221 Vasagar (2017), op. cit.
222 Yan Min Chia (2016), 'Economists Slash Singapore GDP Forecasts for 2016, 2017 after Disappointing Q3 Data' in *Straits Times* (14 October 2016).
223 Weilun Soon (2017), 'Quick takes: Singapore Economy Dodges Tech Recession but still in Slow Motion' in *Business Times* (3 January 2017).
224 Fiona Chan (2016), 'Slow Growth is Here to Stay' in *Straits Times* (20 November 2016).
225 Siew Ying Wong (2016), 'Government does not Expect 'Outright Recession' for Singapore' in *Straits Times* (11 October 2016).
226 Chia (2016), op. cit.
227 Khee Giap Tan and Beng Kai Tan (2017), 'Transform or Risk New Normal of Low, Slow Growth' in *Straits Times* (18 January 2017).
228 Paul Krugman (1994), 'The Myth of Asia's Miracle' in *Foreign Affairs*, **73**, p. 70.

References

Accounting and Corporate Regulatory Authority (2014), 'About ACRA'. Online. Available at: www.acra.gov.sg/About_ACRA.

Anon (1922), *A Short History of the Port of Singapore*, Singapore: Fraser & Neave.

Barr, Michael (2000), 'Lee Kuan Yew and the "Asian Values" Debate' in *Asian Studies Review*, **24**.

BBC (2015), 'Amos Yee: The Boy who Criticised Lee Kuan Yew'. Online. Available at: www.bbc.co.uk/news/world-asia-32604122.

BBC (2015), 'How Lee Kuan Yew Engineered Singapore's Economic Miracle'. Online. Available at: www.bbc.co.uk/news/business-32028693.

BBC (2015), 'Singapore Election: Governing Party Secures Decisive Win'. Online. Available at: www.bbc.co.uk/news/world-asia-34205869.

Bogaars, George (1955), 'The Effect of the Opening of the Suez Canal on the Trade and Development of Singapore' in *Journal of the Malayan Branch of the Royal Asiatic Society*, **28**.

Boyle, A.J. (2002), *Minority Shareholders' Remedies*, Cambridge: CUP.

Briault, Clive (2000), 'The Rationale for a Single National Financial Services Regulator' in World Bank (ed.), *European Union Accession Opportunities and Risks in Central European Finances*, Washington D.C.: World Bank.

Burton, John; Montagnon, Peter; Brown, Kevin; and Grant, Jeremy (2015), 'Lee Kuan Yew, Singapore's Founding Father, 1923–2015' in *Financial Times* (22 March 2015).

Chan, Fiona (2016), 'Slow Growth is Here to Stay' in *Straits Times* (20 November 2016).

Chan, Sek Keong (2013), 'Multiculturalism in Singapore' in *Singapore Academy of Law Journal*, **25**.

Changi Airport (2017), 'Traffic Statistics'. Online. Available at: www.changiairport.com/corporate/about-us/traffic-statistics.html.

Changi Airport (2017), 'Our Story'. Online. Available at: www.changiairport.com/corporate/about-us/our-story.html.

Chia, Yan Min (2016), 'Economists Slash Singapore GDP Forecasts for 2016, 2017 after Disappointing Q3 Data' in *Straits Times* (14 October 2016).

Choo, Pearlie (2001), 'The Statutory Derivative Action in Singapore – A Critical and Comparative Examination' in *Bond Law Review*, **13**.

Chowdhury, Neel (2011), 'Why Lee Kuan Yew, Modern Singapore's Founding Father, Stepped Down' in *Time* (19 May 2011).

CNBC (2017), 'More Chinese firms are saying goodbye to Singapore's stock market'. Online. Available at: www.cnbc.com/2017/04/27/more-chinese-firms-are-saying-goodbye-to-singapores-stock-market.html.

CNN (2017), 'Singapore Prime Minister Lee Hsien Loong Publicly Denounced by Siblings'. Online. Available at: http://edition.cnn.com/2017/06/14/asia/singapore-lee-kuan-yew-children-no-confidence-lee-hsien-loong/index.html.

Coffee, John (2007), 'Law and the Market: The Impact of Enforcement' in *University of Pennsylvania Law Review*, **156**.

Corporate Governance Committee (2001), 'Report of the Committee and Code of Corporate Governance'. Online. Available at: www.mas.gov.sg/~/media/MAS/Regulations%20and%20Financial%20Stability/Regulatory%20and%20Supervisory%20Framework/Corporate%20Governance%20of%20Listed%20Companies/corfinalrpt.pdf.

Department of Commerce of the US (2017), 'Singapore: Trade Regulations, Customs and Standards'. Online. Available at: http://2016.export.gov/singapore/doingbusinessinsingapore/traderegulationscustomsandstandards/index.asp.

Department of Statistics of Singapore (2006), 'Key Indicators of the Resident Population'. Online. Available at: https://web.archive.org/web/20070919204403/www.singstat.gov.sg/pubn/popn/ghsr1/indicators.pdf.

Department of Statistics of Singapore (2017), 'Share of GDP by Industry'. Online. Available at: www.singstat.gov.sg/statistics/visualising-data/charts/share-of-gdp-by-industry.

Department of Statistics of Singapore (2017), 'Population and Population Structure'. Online. Available at: www.singstat.gov.sg/statistics/browse-by-theme/population-and-population-structure.

Department of Statistics of Singapore (2017), 'Education, Language Spoken and Literacy'. Online. Available at: www.tablebuilder.singstat.gov.sg/publicfacing/createDataTable.action?refId=967.

Department of Trade and Industry of Great Britain (1945), *The Entrepot trade of Singapore*, London: Department of Trade and Industry.

Dieleman, Marleen (2011), 'Drawing a Portrait of Family Firm Governance in Singapore'. Online. Available at: https://bschool.nus.edu.sg/Portals/0/images/CGIO/Report/CGIO%20-%20FBN%20Asia%20Family%20Business%20Report.pdf.

Economic Development Board (2016), 'The Eighties'. Online. Available at: www.edb.gov.sg/content/edb/en/why-singapore/about-singapore/our-history/1980s.html.

Economic Development Board (2017), 'Chemical Industry in Singapore'. Online. Available: www.edb.gov.sg/content/edb/en/industries/industries/chemicals.html.

Economic Development Board (2017), 'Electronics'. Online. Available: www.edb.gov.sg/content/edb/en/industries/industries/electronics.html.

Economic Development Board (2017), 'Precision Engineering'. Online. Available: www.edb.gov.sg/content/edb/en/industries/industries/precision-engineering.html.

Freedom House (2017), 'Freedom in the World 2017'. Online. Available at: https://freedomhouse.org/report/freedom-world/2017/singapore.

Gillen, Mark and Potter, Pitman (2000), 'The Convergence of Securities Law in Asia' in Gerry Ferguson and Douglas Johnston (eds), *Asia-Pacific Legal Development*, Vancouver: UBC Press.

Göransson, Kristina (2009), *The Binding Tie: Chinese Intergenerational Relations in Modern Singapore*, Honolulu: University of Hawaii Press.

Hew, Denis (2005), 'Singapore as a Regional Financial Centre' in Donna Vandenbrink and Denis Hew (eds), *Capital Markets in Asia: Changing Roles for Economic Development*, Singapore: Institute of Southeast Asian Studies.

Ho, K.C. and So, Alvin (1997), 'Semi-periphery and Borderland Integration: Singapore and Hong Kong Experiences' in *Political Geography*, **16**.

Huff, W.G. (1993), *The Economic Growth of Singapore: Trade and Development in the Twentieth Century*, Cambridge: CUP.

Huff, W.G. (1995), 'What is the Singapore Model of Economic Development?' in *Cambridge Journal of Economics*, **19**.

Huff, W.G. (1999), 'Singapore's Economic Development: Four Lessons and some Doubts' in *Oxford Development Studies*, **27**.

Hussain, Zakir (2016), 'Constitutional Commission Report Released; Key Changes Proposed to Elected Presidency' in *Straits Times* (7 September 2016).

IMD (2017), 'World Competitiveness Yearbook 2017 Results'. Online. Available at: www.imd.org/wcc/world-competitiveness-center-rankings/competitiveness-2017-rankings-results.

International Monetary Fund (2013), 'Singapore: Detailed Assessment of Implementation on the IOSCO Objectives and Principles of Securities Regulation'. Online. Available at: www.imf.org/external/pubs/ft/scr/2013/cr13344.pdf.

The Istana of Singapore (2013), 'Roles and Responsibilities'. Online. Available at: www.istana.gov.sg/roles-and-responsibilities.

Jackson, Howell and Roe, Mark (2009), 'Public and Private Enforcement of Securities Laws: Resource-based Evidence' in *Journal of Financial Economics*, **93**.

Jurong Town Corporation (2017), 'Overview'. Online. Available at: www.jtc.gov.sg/about-us/Pages/default.aspx.

Kaushik, Diwakar (2012), 'Evolution of Industrial Landscape in Singapore' Paper for the 48th ISOCARP Congress. Online. Available at: www.isocarp.net/Data/case_studies/2108.pdf.

Koh, Joyce and Yip, Annabelle (2015), 'The Evolution of Corporate Governance in Singapore' in Singapore Institute of Directors (ed.), *Board Room Matters Volume II*, Singapore: Singapore Institute of Directors.

KPMG and CPA Australia (2017), 'Two Sides of a Coin: Differing Perspectives in Singapore's Family Business'. Online. Available at: https://assets.kpmg.com/content/dam/kpmg/sg/pdf/2017/03/two-sides-of-a-coin.pdf.

Krugman, Paul (1994), 'The Myth of Asia's Miracle' in *Foreign Affairs*, **73**.

La Porta, Rafael; Lopez-de-Silane, Florencio; Shleifer, Andrei; and Vishny, Robert (1998), 'Law and Finance' in *Journal of Political Economy*, **106**.

Lee, Pey Woan and Chen, Christopher (2016), 'Modernising Company Law: The Singapore Experience' in *Company and Securities Law Journal*, **34**.

Lee, Sheng-Yi (1990), *The Monetary and Banking Development of Singapore and Malaysia*, Singapore: NUS Press.

Lee, Wei Ling and Lee, Hsien Yang (2017), 'Oxley Road: Lee Hsien Yang, Lee Wei Ling will Stop Posting Evidence on Social Media – Full Text of Statement' in *Straits Times* (6 July 2017).

Leong, Grace (2017), 'Singapore Tops New Ranking of Digital Competitiveness' in *Straits Times* (31 May 2017).

Lian, Kwen Fee (2016), 'Multiculturalism in Singapore: Concept and Practice' in Kwen Fee Lian (ed.), *Multiculturalism, Migration, and the Politics of Identity in Singapore*, Singapore: Springer.

Lim, Linda (2008), 'Singapore's Economic Growth Model – Too Much or Too Little?' Paper for the Singapore Economic Policy Conference. Online. Available at: www.fas.nus.edu.sg/ecs/scape/doc/24Oct08/Linda%20Lim.pdf.

Liu, Hong and Zhang, Huimei (2017), 'Lee Kuan Yew's Thoughts on Talent and Singapore's Development Strategy' in Chen-Ning Yang; Ying-Shih Yu; and Gungwu Wang (eds), *Lee Kuan Yew Through the Eyes of Chinese Scholars*, Singapore: World Scientific.

Long Finance (2017), 'The Global Financial Centres Index'. Online. Available at: www.longfinance.net/publications.html.

Mak, Yuen Teen (2015), 'Governance of Government-Linked Companies in Singapore for the EU Asia' Presentation in Corporate Governance Dialogue. Online. Available at: http://law.nus.edu.sg/ewbclb/events/EACG_Dialogue_Conference2015/pdfs/mak_gglcs_slides.pdf.

Marcovitz, Hal (2011), *Dictatorships*, North Mankato: Essential Library.

Mauzy, Diane and Milne, Robert (2002), *Singapore Politics under the People's Action Party*, Abingdon: Routledge.

Menon, Ravi (2015), 'An Economic History of Singapore: 1965–2065' Keynote Address of the Singapore Economic Review Conference. Online. Available at: www.mas.gov.sg/News-and-Publications/Speeches-and-Monetary-Policy-Statements/Speeches/2015/An-Economic-History-of-Singapore.aspx.

Ministry of Education of Singapore (2016), 'Singapore's University Landscape'. Online. Available at: www.moe.gov.sg/news/committee-on-university-education-pathways-beyond-2015/singapore-university-landscape#footnote-1.

Ministry of Finance (2011), 'Report of the Steering Committee for Review of the Companies Act'. Online. Available at: www.acra.gov.sg/uploadedFiles/Content/Publications/Public_Consultation/SCReportComplete28Jul.pdf.

Minority Rights Group International (2017), 'Singapore – Malays'. Online. Available at: http://minorityrights.org/minorities/malays.

Minority Rights Group International (2017), 'Singapore – Indians'. Online. Available at: http://minorityrights.org/minorities/indians-3.

Mohd-Sulaiman, Aiman and Rachagan, Shanthy (2017), 'Company Law and Corporate Governance in Malaysia' in Roman Tomasic (ed.), *Routledge Handbook of Corporate Law*, Abingdon: Routledge.

Monetary Authority of Singapore (2016), 'Overview'. Online. Available at: www.mas.gov.sg/about-mas/overview.aspx.

Monetary Authority of Singapore (2016), 'Capital Markets Enforcement'. Online. Available at: www.mas.gov.sg/~/media/MAS/News%20and%20Publications/Monographs%20and%20Information%20Papers/MAS%20Capital%20Markets%20Enforcement.pdf.

Monetary Authority of Singapore (2017), 'Number of Financial Institutions and Relevant Organisations in Singapore'. Online. Available at: https://masnetsvc.mas.gov.sg/FID.html.

Moyer, Justin (2015), 'How Lee Kuan Yew Made Singapore Strong: Family Values' in *Washington Post* (23 March 2015).

National Library Board of Singapore (2011), 'Formation of the Straits Settlements'. Online. Available at: http://eresources.nlb.gov.sg/history/events/57f1cda6-b5e7-4646-bd4f-14cb08181bfe.

National Library Board of Singapore (2011), 'First Rubber Trees are Planted in Singapore'. Online. Available at: http://eresources.nlb.gov.sg/history/events/a8ceea4c-1c8b-4c9a-885c-b85038b39e4c.

National Library Board of Singapore (2014), 'Archaeology of the Forbidden Hill'. Online. Available at: http://eresources.nlb.gov.sg/history/events/2ebfebad-a4d5-4bbb-bf43-c7db6e30eb7d.

National Library Board of Singapore (2014), 'Stamford Raffles's Career and Contributions to Singapore'. Online. Available at: http://eresources.nlb.gov.sg/infopedia/articles/SIP_715_2004-12-15.html.

National Library Board of Singapore (2014), 'First Census of Singapore is Taken'. Online. Available at: http://eresources.nlb.gov.sg/history/events/2fb8948b-5f16-4a7a-8e3c-7a724e1eb6ad.

National Library Board of Singapore (2014), 'Singapore Chamber of Commerce Rubber Association is Formed'. Online. Available at: http://eresources.nlb.gov.sg/history/events/fed06a3a-caee-4120-bf21-9b1eaa428c23.

National Library Board of Singapore (2014), 'Establishment of the Post Office Saving Banks'. Online. Available at: http://eresources.nlb.gov.sg/history/events/b1c18cda-b48b-4dd7-8521-ecbd1d445c0b.

National Library Board of Singapore (2014), 'Malayan Union is Inaugurated'. Online. Available at: http://eresources.nlb.gov.sg/history/events/e8db672a-3571-4fa3-9df0-220e83ee2a88#3.

National Library Board of Singapore (2014), 'Economic Development Board is Formed'. Online. Available at: http://eresources.nlb.gov.sg/history/events/509d1656-8fc5-405f-8eec-ad058d8a540c.

National Library Board of Singapore (2014), 'Kwong Yik Bank is Founded'. Online. Available at: http://eresources.nlb.gov.sg/history/events/d79189ba-007c-4581-88ea-f33214266c8a.

National Library Board of Singapore (2014), 'Establishment of the Monetary Authority of Singapore'. Online. Available at: http://eresources.nlb.gov.sg/history/events/c7b1b413-f920-4df7-bc0d-c91ebccb3640.

National Library Board of Singapore (2014), 'Paya Lebar Airport'. Online. Available at: http://eresources.nlb.gov.sg/infopedia/articles/SIP_130_2005-01-22.html.

National Library Board of Singapore (2015), 'Straits Trading Company Limited is Established'. Online. Available at: http://eresources.nlb.gov.sg/history/events/bc8fd0f6-1c2a-4b33-841e-c3a1dffc8cd2.

National Library Board of Singapore (2015), 'Steam Tram Service Begins'. Online. Available at: http://eresources.nlb.gov.sg/history/events/792b7cbe-e877-4978-b6f9-312b4b435c68.

National Library Board of Singapore (2015), 'Lee Kuan Yew'. Online. Available at: http://eresources.nlb.gov.sg/infopedia/articles/SIP_2013-03-18_164023.html.

National Library Board of Singapore (2015), 'Kallang Airport is Opened'. Online. Available at: http://eresources.nlb.gov.sg/history/events/1f7c688e-c520-4e68-a16b-7b02b250603c.

National Library Board of Singapore (2017), 'Colonial Port City 1819–1945'. Online. Available at: http://eresources.nlb.gov.sg/history/timeline/1819-1945.

OECD (2011), 'Singapore: Rapid Improvement Followed by Strong Performance' in OECD (ed.) *Lessons from. PISA for the United States*, Paris: OECD Publishing.

Parliament of Singapore (2017), 'System of Government'. Online. Available at: www.parliament.gov.sg/about-us/structure/system-of-government.

Port of Singapore Authority (2017), 'About Us'. Online. Available at: www.singaporepsa.com/about-us.

Quah, Jon (1994), 'Controlling corruption in city-states: A Comparative Study of Hong Kong and Singapore' in *Crime, Law and Social Change*, **22**.

Ramirez, Carlos and Tan, Lung Hui (2003), 'Singapore, Inc. Versus the Private Sector: Are Government-linked Companies Different' IMF Working Paper WP/03/156. Online. Available at: www.imf.org/external/pubs/ft/wp/2003/wp03156.pdf.

Reyes, Sebastian (2015), 'Singapore's Stubborn Authoritarianism' in *Harvard Political Review* (29 September 2015).

Singapore Airlines (2017), 'Stock and Shareholding Information'. Online. Available at: www.singaporeair.com/en_UK/us/about-us/information-for-investors/shareholding-info.

Singapore Airlines (2017), 'Our Heritage'. Online. Available at: www.singaporeair.com/en_UK/us/flying-withus/our-story/our-heritage.

Skytrax (2017), 'The 2017 World Airport Awards: Methodology'. Online. Available at: www.worldairportawards.com/Awards/awards_methodology.html.

Soon, Weilun (2017), 'Quick takes: Singapore Economy Dodges Tech Recession but still in Slow Motion' in *Business Times* (3 January 2017).

Tan, Chwee Huat (1989), 'Confucianism and Nation Building in Singapore' in *International Journal of Social Economics*, **16**.

Tan, Khee Giap and Tan, Beng Kai (2017), 'Transform or Risk New Normal of Low, Slow Growth' in *Straits Times* (18 January 2017).

Tan, Sumiko (2015), 'GE2015: PAP Vote Share Increases to 69.9%, Party Wins 83 of 89 Seats including WP-held Punggol East' in *Straits Times* (12 September 2015).

Tong, Chee Kiong (2014), 'Centripetal Authority, Differentiated Networks: The Social Organization of Chinese Firms in Singapore' in Chee Kiong Tong (ed.), *Rethinking Guanxi and Trust in Chinese Business Networks*, Singapore: Springer.

Turnbull, Mary (2009), *A History of Modern Singapore 1819–2005*, Singapore: NUS Press.

Vasagar, Jeevan (2017), 'Singapore's First Family Feud over "Big Brother"' in *Financial Times* (14 June 2017).

Wee, Meng Seng and Puchniak, Dan (2012), 'Derivative Actions in Singapore' in Dan Puchniak *et al.* (eds), *The Derivative Action in Asia*, Cambridge: CUP.

Wong, Kai Yeng and Chng, W. (2016), 'Singapore: A Port City – the Case of Port Development and its Impact on the City' Paper for the 15th World Conferences Cities and Ports. Online. Available at: www.clc.gov.sg/documents/books/research-workshop/2016/Rotterdam-Port-and-the-City-Heart-of-Innovation-Presentation-Paper.pdf.

Wong, Lin Ken (1978), 'Singapore: Its Growth as an Entrepot Port, 1819–1941' in *Journal of Southeast Asian Studies*, **9**.

Wong, Siew Ying (2016), 'Government does not Expect "Outright Recession" for Singapore' in *Straits Times* (11 October 2016).

Wong, Poh-Kam (1997), 'Creation of a Regional Hub For Flexible Production' in *Industry and Innovation*, **4**.

World Bank (2008), 'Singapore Local Economic Development: The Case of the Economic Development Board'. Online. Available at: http://siteresources.worldbank.org/INTLED/Resources/339650-1194284482831/4356163-1211318886634/Singapore Profile.pdf.

World Bank (2017), 'Doing Business'. Online. Available at: www.doingbusiness.org.

World Economic Forum (2016), 'Global Competitiveness Report 2015–2016'. Online. Available at: www3.weforum.org/docs/gcr/2015-2016/Global_Competitiveness_Report_2015-2016.pdf.

World Justice Project (2016), 'WJP Rule of Law Index 2016'. Online. Available at: https://worldjusticeproject.org/our-work/wjp-rule-law-index/wjp-rule-law-index-2016.

World Shipping Council (2016), 'Top 50 World Container Ports'. Online. Available at: www.worldshipping.org/about-the-industry/global-trade/top-50-world-container-ports.

Yahya, Faizal (2016), 'Developing High-tech Companies in Singapore' in *Journal of General Management*, 42.

Young, Alwyn (1992), 'A Tale of Two Cities: Factor Accumulation and Technical Change in Hong Kong and Singapore' in *NBER Macroeconomics Annual*, **7**.

6 Malaysia

In the previous chapter, the institutional conditions of Singapore were assessed. There is a close connection between Malaysia and Singapore. Singapore was part of Malaysia briefly before the city state's independence. Since its independence, Singapore has become one of the most successful experiences of development in the world. In sharp contrast, Malaysia remains a developing country. Indeed, Malaysia shares some common characteristics with Singapore and Hong Kong. They all are former British colonies and have managed to inherit some institutional advantages left behind during the colonial era, notably a legal system based on common law. However, clearly in terms of economic development, Malaysia has not been performing as well as Singapore and Hong Kong. There must be some institutional differences which may account for their varying degree of development. Following on the previous three chapters looking at the stories of China, Hong Kong and Singapore, this chapter will move the discussion onto Malaysia. Like the previous three chapters, with the help of the analytical framework laid down in Chapter 2, this chapter will first provide an overview of Malaysia's economic development both before and after its independence. Afterwards, it will examine the legal, political, cultural and other institutional conditions of the country one by one, before presenting a conclusion at the end. This chapter is the last of the four largely parallel chapters which explore the institutional conditions of the economies selected by this book, namely, China, Hong Kong, Singapore and Malaysia.

Economic growth of Malaysia

Compared to the previous three economies studied, the economic growth of Malaysia has been relatively lacklustre. China is the second largest economy in the world measured by GDP, and is substantially larger than the other three.[1] On the other hand, the GDP figures of Hong Kong, Singapore and Malaysia are roughly similar.[2] However, after taking their population into account, the story is different. Hong Kong and Singapore have the highest GDP per capita level in the region whilst that of Malaysia is only comparable to China (see Figure 6.1). According to the IMF's 'World Economic Outlook' report, only Hong Kong and Singapore are considered as advanced economies, whilst Malaysia and China are

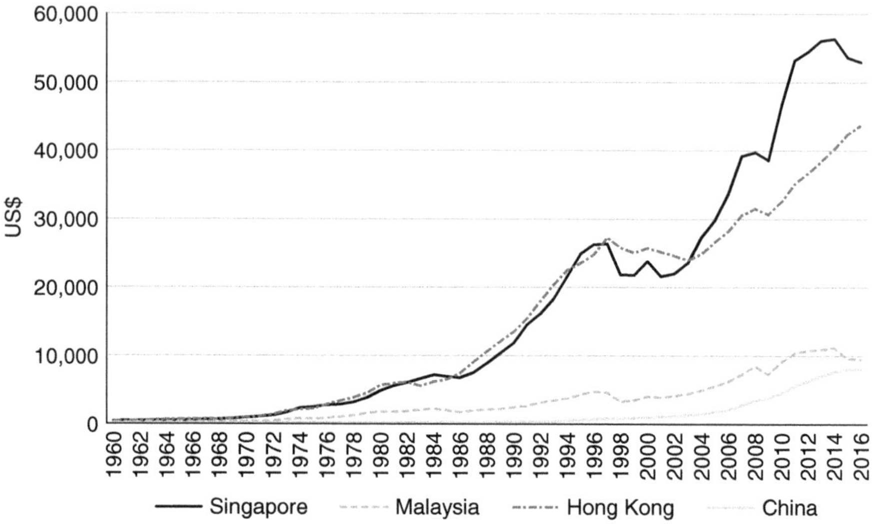

Figure 6.1 Comparative GDP per capita growth of Malaysia, China, Hong Kong and Singapore (US$).

Source: World Bank.

considered as developing economies.[3] However, this is not to say Malaysia has been doing badly. It still has a notable higher GDP per capita level when compared to surrounding economies (see Figure 6.2). It is described as 'a highly open, upper-middle income economy' by the World Bank and there is prospect for it 'to secure a lasting place among the ranks of high-income economies'.[4] Malaysia was one of 13 countries identified by the World Bank's Commission on Growth and Development in its Growth Report to have recorded average growth of more than 7 per cent per year for 25 years or more.[5] Economic growth was inclusive, as Malaysia also succeeded in nearly eradicating poverty. From an economy dominated by the production of raw natural resource materials, such as tin and rubber, even as recently as the 1970s, Malaysia today has a diversified economy and has become a leading exporter of electrical appliances, electronic parts and components, palm oil and natural gas. The Malaysian government has tried their best to create a business-friendly environment for businesses to operate in. These efforts have been affirmed in the 2017 World Bank's 'Doing Business' report, which ranked the country the twenty-third best place in the world to conduct business.[6] The World Bank's competitiveness criteria in the 'Doing Business' ranking include ease of starting a business, licensing approvals, tax administration efficiency and ease of cross-border trading. In particular, investors accessing the Malaysian market may benefit from the country's strong investor protection policies, which have been affirmed by the country's third place in the report in relation to minority investor protection.[7] Apart from the

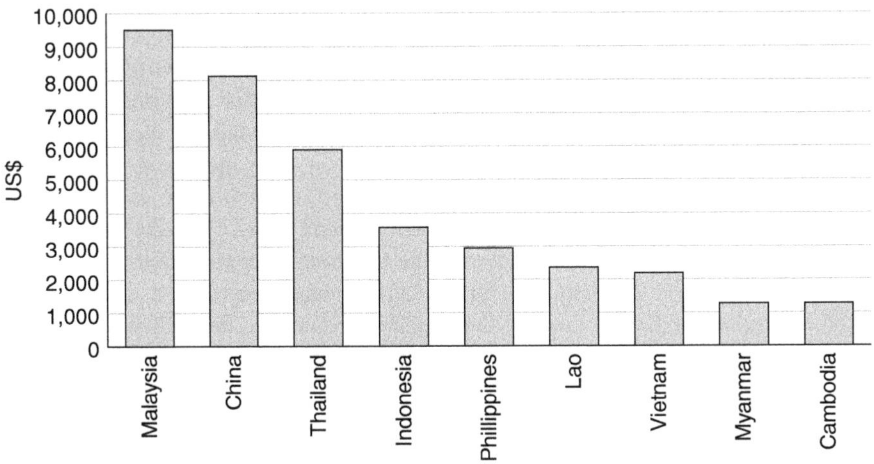

Figure 6.2 Comparative GDP per capita of selected Asian economies in 2016 (US$).
Source: World Bank.

World Bank, the World Economic Forum placed Malaysia twenty-fifth out of 138 countries ranked for competitiveness in its 'Global Competitiveness Report 2016–2017'.[8] This put Malaysia ahead of other nearby competitors such as South Korea (twenty-sixth), China (twenty-eighth), Thailand (thirty-fourth) and Indonesia (forty-first). The report especially ranked Malaysia highly for its goods market efficiency and financial market development.

Growth before independence

On 31 August 1957 the Federation of Malaya became an independent nation. The Malaysia Agreement, under which North Borneo, Sarawak and Singapore would become states in the new Federation of Malaysia, was signed in 1963 by the UK, Malaya, North Borneo, Sarawak and Singapore. The Federation of Malaysia came into being on 16 September 1963, with Singapore subsequently leaving the Federation as discussed in the previous chapter. Before the country's independence, Penang, Malacca[9] and Singapore were ruled directly by Britain as the Straits Settlements for over a century. Other parts of Malaysia, such as Sabah and Sarawak, became British protectorates during that period.

In prehistoric times, the region was inhabited by aboriginal people.[10] Formerly North Borneo, Sabah may have been inhabited since 7000 BCE. Sarawak was likely to have been inhabited from about 5000 BCE. The first settlers in the Malay Peninsula were believed to have arrived from south China much later. Around the beginning of the first century, Indian traders began settling in Kedah and along the west coast of the peninsula. The Javanese controlled the peninsula around 1330–50. The port of Malacca was founded in the fifteenth century. Its rulers converted to Islam and traded with Muslim merchants. Malacca at its foundation was no more than a small fishing village, but within a decade or so the population soared to around 6,000 and at the time of the Portuguese conquest (1511) was estimated at up to 100,000.[11] A century later, the Portuguese were driven out by the Dutch in alliance with the Sultan of Johor. The peninsula then became a Malay kingdom ruled by Johor. The Straits of Malacca was an integral part of the international sea route linking the East with the West. Since their occupation of Malacca in 1641, the Dutch aspired to establish it as a base that could tap the trade covering the India–Straits–China route.[12] On the other hand, the English at that time did not have a port that could support their trade in the Straits. Thus, a new English base in the Straits was seen to be a necessity. In 1786 the Sultan of Kedah granted the island of Penang to the British East India Company for use as a trading post. Less than a decade later, the British took Malacca from the Dutch. Trade was a leading sector in this period. Total shipping arrivals at Malacca practically tripled between 1761 and 1785.[13] The proportion of English and Portuguese vessels increased, but were far surpassed by Chinese, Malay and Bugis shipping. Throughout these centuries, the main commodities sought after were generally pepper, spices, gold, tin and forest products, such as rattan and aromatic woods, from the Southeast Asian regions.[14] In return, there was the demand for cloth, opium and various manufactured products from India and China.

Despite being largely overshadowed by the opening of Singapore in 1819, the ports of Penang and Malacca experienced some rapid growth upon the discovery of rich deposits of tin ore in Sungei Ujoing, and several other districts in Selangor and Perak. Exports of tin from the peninsula increased from 2,400 tonnes in the early 1840s, to around 6,600 tonnes in the 1850s and 8,650 tonnes in the 1860s.[15] From April 1867 the three strategically located port cities of Penang, Malacca and Singapore came to be ruled directly as the British Crown Colony of the Straits Settlements, having earlier been controlled as one administrative unit by the British East India Company. Each of the three Straits Settlements had free port status, meaning that shipping and cargo could enter and leave without taxation. Meanwhile, rapid growth of the tin trade from around the mid-nineteenth century had brought with it an influx of Chinese labour to the tin-producing west-coast states of Perak, Selangor and Negri Sembilan. Intense rivalry among Chinese rival business and social groups intersected with the political strife between local Malay rulers. Trade was disrupted as tensions escalated into widespread unrest in the decade before the signing of the Pangkor Treaty.[16] The British, responding to the Straits Settlements trading community who were financing the mines, intervened to safeguard and strengthen their commercial interests in lands that they perceived to be rich in natural resources. This led to the signing of the Pangkor Treaty.[17] Signed on 20 January 1874, the Pangkor Treaty provided for the appointment of a British Resident to advise the Sultan of Perak in all matters affecting the general administration, including maintaining peace and security, overseeing the collection of revenue from taxation and encouraging economic development. James Birch was appointed the first

Resident of Perak. Andrew Clarke as Governor of the Straits Settlements subsequently negotiated similar arrangements in Selangor and Negeri Sembilan. The Straits Settlements benefited from the intensified development of the Malay States under British protection.[18] In 1895, the Federated Malay States, combining the three neighbouring states of Negri Sembilan, Selangor and Perak on the western side of the peninsula, and Pahang on the eastern side, formally came into existence through the Treaty of Federation, with Kuala Lumpur designated as the administrative capital of the four British protected states. The four northern and eastern Malay states, Kedah, Perlis, Trengganu and Kelantan, together with Johore, in the south of the peninsula, remained outside of the Federated Malay States. In contrast with the Federated Malay States, the Unfederated Malay States were more autonomous with their rulers enjoying some political discretion and they were not administered collectively.[19] Each had a British Advisor in its administration. Within the Unfederated Malay States, apart from Johore which was more developed, other states were heavily rural and predominantly Malay in population composition, with employment being overwhelmingly concentrated in traditional agriculture and fishing.

There was not much growth in either export or import values until the early 1880s, and then there was a sustained upsurge until 1900.[20] A boom in tin and rubber production was the main constituent. Whilst tin mining had existed for centuries, it was the agricultural sector which came to the forefront at this time. The cultivation of rubber-yielding trees became commercially attractive as a raw material for new industries in the West, notably for tyres for the booming automobile industry, especially in the US. The boom reached vast proportions as the rubber price reached record heights in 1910. Growth was affected between 1910 and 1915 during the outbreak of war in Europe. However, by 1921 the rubber acreage in Malaysia (mostly in the peninsula) had reached 935,000 hectares and output stood at 50 per cent of world production.[21] The larger estates, mainly British-owned, were financed through British-registered public joint stock companies. For example, between 1903 and 1912 some 260 companies were registered to operate in Malaya.[22] By contrast, Chinese planters for the most part preferred to form private partnerships to operate estates which were on average smaller. After the war, the international economy experienced a resurgence brining a period of overall growth in Malaysian export volumes at an annual average rate well above that of its Southeast Asian neighbours until the Great Depression in 1929.[23] The next decade ended with the outbreak of another war in Europe in 1939. Except in this year, when there was a rush to build up stocks of strategic raw materials, thereby boosting export output and earnings, trade in this decade generally had been below the level at the onset of the Great Depression.[24] Malaysia had very few secondary industries before the Second World War. The little that did appear was connected mainly with the processing of the primary exports, rubber and tin, together with limited production of manufactured goods for the domestic market.

During the Japanese occupation, exports were to consist only of what was required for the Japanese economy. Production of tin fell to at most one-third of the 1940 level by 1943, continued to drop to a mere 3,000 tonnes in 1945, around the level of the mid-nineteenth century.[25] Similarly, for rubber, between 1942 and 1945, a total of some 168,000 tonnes were shipped from the peninsula, equivalent to about 30 per cent of output in 1940 alone.[26] After the Japanese occupation, the Straits Settlements were dissolved. Penang and Malacca were then grouped with the Unfederated Malay States and the Federated Malay States to form the Malayan Union on 1 April 1946. Singapore was left out of the Malayan Union and became a separate crown colony due to its economic and strategic importance as a free port and naval base. The creation of the Malayan Union, which involved the surrender of Malay sovereignty over the Malay states and the extension of citizenship to immigrant communities, was perceived as detrimental to Malay political standing and prestige.[27] Faced with intense Malay resistance, the British entered into confidential consultations with Malay leaders that eventually led to the replacement of the Malayan Union with the Federation of Malaya on 1 February 1948.

It was estimated that the gross national product (GNP) of the Federation was three times that of Singapore between 1949 and 1955.[28] There was an 'unusually high proportion' of the national product in exports and the wide fluctuations in GNP during the period corresponded fairly closely to the world market conditions for rubber and tin, illustrating the economy's continued reliance on the two commodities.[29] It was estimated that rubber accounted for about 60 per cent of the value of total exports, with tin making up of 20 per cent, coming second to rubber. The pattern of industrial development at this point consisted of a wide variety of small and relatively simple industrial organisations. The Federation government realised the importance of developing secondary industries in order to create jobs for an unusually fast growing working population and for absorbing the impact of fluctuations in the fortunes of rubber and tin by diversifying the economy.[30] As a result, the government established a special Division for Industrial Development which operated within the Ministry of Commerce and Industry with a view to shaping and implementing an industrial development policy with substantial inducements to private domestic and foreign enterprises. It is worth noting that at that time, a large part of the commercial agriculture, mining, trading and banking activities were carried on with British enterprise and capital.[31] With only a few exceptions, the capital, management and labour of industrial enterprises were Chinese, operating mainly on a family basis. As a result, levels of technical equipment and working efficiency varied greatly and industrial ventures started and closed down at a fast rate.

Post-independence economy

When Malaysia gained independence in 1957, the country was considered to be one of the relatively prosperous countries in Asia. The level of per capita incomes there at that time was the third highest in Asia, after Japan and Singapore.[32] Also, by 1956, Malaysia took over the position of the largest rubber producer, overtaking its neighbouring country, Indonesia. Leaders of the newly independent government were very committed in their objective to implement the diversification policy as well as the strengthening of existing activities, especially to modernise the rubber planting industry. Three public agencies, namely, the Rubber Industry Smallholder Development Authority, Federal Land Development Authority, and Federal Land Consolidation and Rehabilitation Authority, were established to foster the industry and more efficient agricultural land use, especially in the rural areas. As a consequence of the government's efforts, the level of rubber output increased from just 0.6 million tonnes in 1951, to 0.7 million tonnes in 1960 and to 1.2 million tonnes in 1970.[33] At its peak, rubber production reached 1.6 million tonnes in the middle of the 1970s. Meanwhile, the industrial sector in the economy was expanded gradually. In 1947 the industrial sector contributed only 5.7 per cent to GDP, rising to 6.3 per cent of GDP in 1957, 9 per cent in 1960 and 12.2 per cent in 1970.[34] The policy to develop the industrial sectors can be grouped into the following measures: (1) to develop general infrastructures such as improving the road-network, improving the seaport and airport facilities, and to enhance communication and energy capacities; (2) to provide fiscal and financial incentives both to local and foreign investors; (3) to provide land areas for the development of industries and to develop industrial estates and free-trade zones areas; and (4) to expand educational facilities so that more skilled and educated manpower could be provided.

Since gaining independence in 1957, Malaysia's economy has been growing at an average rate of 6 per cent per year between 1957 until 1970.[35] However, the benefits of the rapid growth rate were not equally distributed among its people. In 1970, the poverty rate amongst the ethnic Malays was high (65 per cent) compared to other ethnic groups, namely the Chinese (26 per cent) and Indians (39 per cent).[36] Tension between the native Malay population and the more economically powerful Chinese population erupted into violence in 1969. Fist fights broke out between a group of Malays and Chinese bystanders who taunted them, which then escalated into bottle and stone throwing. The Malays burned cars and shops, killed and looted in the Chinese areas. The violence quickly spread throughout the city. Over the next few days, hundreds of people were killed. The riot resulted in the New Economic Policy (NEP), which aimed to eradicate poverty for all Malaysians as well as reduce and subsequently eliminate identification of race by economic function and geographical location.

It is worth noting that the Malaysian development policies have been clearly spelt out in five-year development plans called the Malaysia Plan that emphasises growth with equity in the context of a multi-racial society. The first Malaysia Plan came out in 1966 and covered the period 1966–70. The latest one, the Eleventh Malaysia Plan, covers the period 2016–20. Prior to the first Malaysia Plan, there had indeed been three economic plans. The first plan was for the period 1950–55. The second was for 1956–60, officially known as Malaya's First Five-Year Plan. The Second Five-Year Plan was for 1961–65. In the early plans, the only target was in public investment. Only in Malaya's Second Five-Year Plan was a full-scale attempt at national economic planning seen.[37] Initial efforts by the government to reduce poverty were through a package of rural development programmes as stated in the First Malaysia Plan (1966–70). However, these programmes were not successful as evidenced by the racial riot in 1969. As a result, the NEP was formulated in the Second Malaysia Plan (1971–75) with a specific goal of eradicating absolute poverty. The implementation of NEP continued through until the Fifth Malaysia Plan (1986–90).

Prior to 1970, Malaysia's development policy was primarily aimed at promoting growth with a strong emphasis on the export market. Although the economy grew very rapidly during this period at an annual average of 6 per cent, there was insufficient emphasis on distributional aspects, resulting in socio-economic imbalances among the ethnic groups with negative social consequences in the form of a racial riot in 1969. The NEP underscored the importance of achieving socio-economic goals alongside pursuing economic growth objectives as a way of creating harmony and unity in a nation with many ethnic and religious groups. According to Drabble, the major strategies contained in the NEP were: (1) continued rural development, principally through land schemes, to commercialise peasant agriculture; (2) the promotion of manufacturing industry, especially export-oriented industrialisation; (3) regional development to even out the large disparities between different areas; and (4) ancillary policies involving preferential treatment for Bumiputeras, the majority Malay ethnic group.[38] The implementation of these strategies to eradicate poverty and restructure the society resulted in certain observable improvements by 1990.[39] For example, the poverty rate declined from 49.3 per cent in 1970 to 16.5 per cent in 1990. In terms of corporate equity restructuring, 63.3 per cent of corporate equity in Malaysia was owned by foreigners in 1970, while the Bumiputeras owned 2.4 per cent. The NEP set a restructuring target of 30:40:30, where by 1990 the holdings of the Bumiputeras should reach 30 per cent, other Malaysians 40 per cent and foreigners 30 per cent. In 1990, the Bumiputera share of equity amounted to 19.3 per cent of total corporate equity share and the holdings of other Malaysians reached 46.8 per cent and 33.9 per cent for foreign holdings. The target was not reached, but the result might have represented a significant extent of wealth redistribution. On the other hand, according to an assessment by the US government in the 1980s, despite the apparent increasing ownership of corporate equity by the Bumiputeras, most of the shares were held in government trust agencies.[40] More worryingly, the NEP provided opportunities for some people to turn the government's policies to their own advantage.[41] This occurred through the establishment of so-called 'Ali Baba companies' that misrepresented Bumiputera participation. Ali Baba companies were primarily Chinese-owned enterprises that paid Bumiputeras a fee for the use of their names on the board of directors or ownership roster in order to appear to be in compliance with the NEP guidelines of 30 per cent Bumiputera participation.

In relation to industrial promotion, earlier, the Incentive Act of 1958 to promote import-substitution helped small- and medium-scale industries expand substantially through the 1960s.[42] Malay small- and medium-sized enterprises focused on handicrafts, batik, furniture, motor and food processing. These products were generally not for export but were consumed domestically. Most of these industries were operated by the ethnic Chinese. Hence, under the NEP, to counterbalance the predominance of the Chinese entrepreneurs in commerce and industry, the Malaysian government instead chose to extend substantially state-run large enterprises. Creation of the Heavy Industries Corporation of Malaysia (HICOM) in 1980 marked the launching of a fully state-owned heavy industry in Malaysia. HICOM aimed at a long-term programme to radically transform the national economy from being highly dependent upon commodities. Consequently, industrial points throughout the Malay Peninsula were set up: steel in Trengganu, cement in Kedah, motorcycle engine manufacturing plants in Penang, Kedah and Selangor, shipbuilding in Sabah, petrochemical plants in both Sabah and Sarawak, as well as a car-making project in Shah Alam. Out of the Federal government's investment fund for the manufacturing sector, HICOM receives an overwhelming proportion of 76 per cent for the Fifth Malaysia Plan period (1986–90).[43] Furthermore, with 96 industrial estates and 8 free trade zones, there were an increasing presence of foreign industries.[44] Japan, Taiwan and Singapore were the major sources of foreign investment, accounting for over half of the total amount in the 1980s. Malaysia managed to move up the technological ladder as a result of the investment and technology transfer from the more advanced economies. In the 1980s, the agriculture sector contributed only 1 per cent of national growth compared to 2.1 per cent from manufacturing and 3 per cent from services.[45] The leading sub-sectors in services were wholesale and retail trade, and hotels and restaurants which accounted for about 11.1 per cent of GDP, and finance, insurance, real estate and business services which contributed approximately 9.8 per cent of GDP in 1990.[46]

The New Development Policy (NDP) succeeded the NEP when it came to an end in 1990. The NDP has as its main goal the 'Vision 2020' program, by which Malaysia intends to become fully developed. It emphasised science and technology and, therefore, a further development of human resources, including a productive and disciplined workforce to meet the challenges of an industrial society. Both the NDP and Vision 2020 have built on the NEP; however, they have added new dimensions to cope with globalisation, including the need to attract foreign direct investment and enhance technology transfer, shifting the emphasis from focusing on agriculture to manufacturing, and from manufacturing of basic to more sophisticated commodities.[47] The NDP programmes included loan schemes for small-scale agricultural and commercial development, land consolidation and rehabilitation programmes, commercialisation of farms, agricultural productivity enhancement projects, provision and improvement of services for the urban poor, and efforts to promote employment opportunities in manufacturing, construction and other urban-based industries.[48] Vision 2020 was launched by Mahathir Mohamad, then Prime Minister in 1990. In spite of the fact that the NDP (1991–2000) was subsequently replaced by the National Vision Policy (NVP) and then the New Economic Model (NEM), Vision 2020 has remained an overarching development goal for the nation. The main emphasis of the Vision is economically related. To realise the Vision, it was envisaged that an annual growth rate of 7 per cent is required, which means that GDP has to be doubled every ten years.

The successor of the NDP, the NVP (2001–10), was operated through the Third Outline Perspective Plan. In essence, according to the Malaysian government, the NVP 'represents the consolidation of all past development efforts and is aimed at establishing a united, progressive and prosperous Malaysia that lives in harmony and engages in full and fair partnership.'[49] It recognised that overall growth of GDP in the preceding five-year period had been positive although the Asian financial crisis had caused the economy to contract by 7.4 per cent in 1998.[50] The main thrust of NVP was that the private sector would spearhead economic growth, while the public sector would provide the enabling environment and ensure the achievement of the socio-economic objectives. Key strategies of NVP include a knowledge-based economy, human resource development and the shift of the key economic sectors towards more efficient production processes and high value-added activities.[51]

Recognising that Vision 2020 is not achievable without more radical economic, social and government transformation, the Malaysia government introduced the NEM in 2010, which was accompanied by an Economic Transformation Programme (ETP) so as to propel Malaysia to being an advanced nation with inclusiveness and sustainability in line with the goals set forth in Vision 2020. There were various indicators pointing to the need for radical reforms.[52] Inequality remained high, even with a reduction in the Gini coefficient from 50 per cent in 1970s. In the mid-1990s, in the run-up to the 1997 Asian financial crisis, Malaysia's GDP grew at an average rate greater than 9 per cent annually. Since 1997, however, Malaysia's GDP growth rate has practically halved. The 2008 global financial crisis depressed it further. Investment was 40 per cent of GDP in Malaysia in the mid-1990s. Since 1997 it has steadily fallen, reaching just 20 per cent of GDP right before the 2008 global financial crisis. Malaysia's export structure has focused mainly on electrical and electronics products and on primary commodities such as petroleum and palm oil. A large majority of the industries continue to focus only on assembly operations, being unable to make a breakthrough to new higher value-added products. The goal of the ETP is to elevate the country to developed-nation status by 2020, targeting GNI per capita of US$15,000 (meanwhile the actual figure was US$9,850 in 2016). It seeks to attract US$444 billion in investments which would, in turn, create 3.3 million new jobs. Accordingly, the ETP identified 12 National Key Economic Areas, representing economic sectors which account for significant contributions to GNI.[53]

The ETP identified Greater Kuala Lumpur/Klang Valley, a geographical location, along with 11 sectors of industries and services as key economic areas. The development of Malaysia's capital Kuala Lumpur so far has not been discussed. In Drabble's view, Malaysia's economic core had for a long period of time lain in Singapore.[54] Kuala Lumpur grew rapidly from the end of the nineteenth century to become the administrative centre of the Federated Malay States. Nonetheless, even prior to independence in 1957, Kuala Lumpur remained essentially 'a provincial town overshadowed by Singapore'.[55] Meanwhile, another former Straits Settlement, Penang, though declining in its share of population, developed as the centre of an industrial area in the 1980s.[56] Similarly, Malacca was revived as a centre of light industry. In 1972, Kuala Lumpur was given city status and two years later became a separate Federal Territory. Its early rise was attributed to a combination of industrialisation and 'bureaucratisation' owing to the concentration of government employees.[57] Under the NEP, urban development has been skewed towards the so-called 'Western corridor' of the Malay Peninsula and around Kuala Lumpur in particular.[58] By the early 1970s, Klang Valley, including the four Selangor state districts of Gombak, Klang, Petaling and Hulu Langat, was recognised as a coherent urban planning region. Nowadays, Kuala Lumpur is a commercial and financial hub for the country. There are some 2,000 international companies that have grown their Asia operations from the national capital, including Shell, Citibank, Huawei, Vale, Schlumberger, Toshiba, AECOM and Worley Parsons.[59] All leading financial institutions in Malaysia are headquartered in Kuala Lumpur, including Maybank, CIMB, Public Bank, RHB and Hong Leong. Kuala Lumpur is also home to one of the two stock exchanges in the country, Bursa Malaysia. The history of the exchange can be traced back to 1930 when the first formal securities business organisation was established in Malaysia, the Singapore Stockbrokers' Association, which changed its name to the Malayan Stockbrokers' Association in 1937.[60] The Malayan Stock Exchange was established in 1960 with trading rooms in both Singapore and Kuala Lumpur and the public trading of shares commenced. In 1973, the exchange was divided into the Kuala Lumpur Stock Exchange Berhad and the Stock Exchange of Singapore with the cessation of currency interchangeability between Malaysia and Singapore. The former was renamed as Bursa Malaysia in 2004. It is worth noting that by 2000 Bursa Malaysia had been the only stock exchange in Malaysia until the Labuan Financial Exchange was launched in that year.[61] Today, it is one of the largest bourses in ASEAN and is home to more than 900 listed companies.[62] One new dimension of the financial sector in Kuala Lumpur is the vision to become an international Islamic financial centre. Islamic finance has existed in the country for decades. In 2006, the Malaysia International Islamic Financial Centre initiative was launched. Kuala Lumpur is now widely regarded as a global hub for Islamic finance, alongside Dubai.[63] The Malaysian capital has a reputation for efficient regulation of Islamic finance and a huge domestic market for local-currency Islamic bonds. Malaysia had the second largest global share Islamic finance banking assets in 2015, just after Saudi Arabia but above UAE.[64] In the same year, Malaysia accounted for 54 per cent (US$175 billion) of the total Islamic bonds (*sukuk*) outstanding globally.[65]

Legal institutions

As discussed before, the quality of the legal regime to protect minority investors in Malaysia is well recognised and is placed third in the world according to the World Bank's 'Doing Business' report.[66] The primary legislation to provide this protection is the Companies Act 2016. Its predecessor was the Companies Act

1965, which was based on the UK Companies Act 1948 and the Australian Uniform Companies Act 1961.[67] The Act used to be administered by the Registrar of Companies. There is now the Companies Commission of Malaysia, which was established by the Companies Commission of Malaysia Act 2001. The main activity of the Commission is to serve as an agency to incorporate companies and register businesses as well as to provide company and business information to the public. At the same time, it has taken the initiative to review Malaysian corporate law under its Corporate Law Reform Programme. For this programme, the Commission has established a committee called the Corporate Law Reform Committee (CLRC) pursuant to sections 17 and 19 of the Companies Commission of Malaysia Act 2001. The Committee, established on 17 December 2003, together with the Commission aims to provide a regulatory framework which is conducive for companies and businesses to operate. After over more than three decades since its enactment, the Commission recognised the need to review the Companies Act 1965 to reflect the current and future needs of the business environment. Accordingly, the CLRC was tasked to undertake a fundamental review of the Companies Act 1965 in order to propose amendments that are necessary for corporate and business activities to function in line with international standards of good corporate governance. It was felt that although there were various laws and statutes that might affect a company's business operations, the primary source of company law and the main statute on company law that determines the company's formation, the rules governing the relationship between participants in companies (shareholders, directors and other officers of the company, and sometimes employees) and between the company and its participants (in particular, rules relating to share capital, members rights, directors' duties and other matters relating to the management of companies) and termination of a company was the Companies Act 1965. The work of the Committee eventually led to the Companies Act 2016. According to the Committee, one approach of the reform was to consider law reform initiatives conducted internationally, notably the UK Company Law Review,[68] with adaptation and refinement to suit the Malaysian corporate and business environment.[69]

Similarly, the greater part of the securities law of Malaysia (and indeed also Singapore) was modelled on British and Australian laws.[70] The current law is the Capital Markets and Services Act 2007 (last amended in 2015), which is a consolidation of the Securities Industry Act 1983 and Futures Industry Act 1993. The Act seeks to regulate and to provide for matters relating to the activities, markets and intermediaries in the capital markets. The predecessor of the Securities Industry Act 1983 was the Securities Industry Act 1973, which was a response to a major change in the Malaysian securities market when the Stock Exchange of Malaysia and Singapore was formally split into two separate exchanges.[71] Until 1993, Malaysia had no dedicated securities commission to enforce the Act. Various bodies regulated different aspects of the capital market including the Capital Issues Committee, the Registrar of Companies, the Panel on Takeovers and Mergers, the Foreign Investment Committee and the Kuala Lumpur Stock Exchange.[72] On 1 March 1993, the Securities Commission was established pursuant to the Securities Commission Act 1993, as a single regulatory authority to oversee the capital market.

Another important aspect of the regulation is corporate governance. Codes of conduct and codes of best practices as well as self-regulation are now considered as complementary to statutory regulation. The Malaysian Code on Corporate Governance was first introduced in 2000 against the backdrop of the Asian Financial Crisis in order to strengthen the corporate governance framework and increase investor's confidence. The Code was reviewed in 2007 and 2012 to ensure that it was aligned with globally recognised best practices and standards. The current version is the Malaysian Code on Corporate Governance 2017. Like other laws, the Code has drawn from the UK experience set out in the Hampel Report.[73] In the previous codes, a 'comply or explain' approach, as introduced first by the UK, was adopted. Under this approach, a listed company must ensure that its board of directors provides a narrative statement of its corporate governance practices with reference to the Malaysian Code on Corporate Governance in its annual report.[74] In making the corporate governance statement, the listed company must describe that it has applied the principles set out in the Code, or alternatively explain reasons for not following them. One important change introduced by the new Code is the introduction of the 'Comprehend, Apply and Report' (CARE) approach in respect of a public listed company's adherence to the practices in the new Code.[75] Under the new approach, on top of the information required under a 'comply or explain' approach, in the event of non-compliance, the listed company must disclose the alternative practice and how the application of the practice achieves the intended outcome.

Quality of the laws

The overriding objective of the company law review was twofold: first, to create a legal and regulatory structure that will facilitate business; and, second, to promote accountability and protection of corporate directors and members taking into account the interest of other stakeholders, in line with international standards.[76] Some specific concerns included the compliance cost in general and in particular for private companies. The CLRC sought to streamline company formation and simplify the reporting obligations to ease the administrative burdens imposed upon companies. In this regard, the Committee wanted to draw on particularly the experience of the UK Company Law Review and the Singapore Company Legislation and Regulatory Framework Committee.[77] Another concern was the relationship between various corporate participants and directors' accountability. The Committee took note of two main approaches in the corporate governance debate, namely the shareholder theory and the stakeholder theory. The shareholder theory considers that directors have a duty to consider shareholders' interests in company management, whilst the stakeholder theory allows, or requires, directors to consider the interests of other persons who are involved in a company's management, for example creditors and employees. The CLRC indicated that they would be guided by the shareholder theory whilst taking account of the interests of other stakeholders.[78] As discussed, the Companies Act 1965 was modelled upon the Australian Uniform Companies Act 1961, together with other English company law principles. The Committee was very concerned that many of these provisions were over 150 years old which might no longer be in agreement with how businesses operate in the present day.[79] It was observed that Commonwealth countries, notably Canada, Australia, New Zealand and Singapore, that once had placed great reliance on the traditional English company law model, have also chosen to abandon some aspects of English company law when reforming their respective corporate law. In the view of Dato' K.C. Vohrah, Chairman of the CLRC, 'the Companies Act 1965 comprises 374 numbing sections lost in a wilderness of obscure subsections and nine accompanying schedules'.[80] An update was therefore much needed.

As said, one of the core objectives of the Corporate Law Reform Programme is to make the law and regulations conducive to business. The concern lies in the blanket application of companies' legislation to all companies, regardless of size and structure, imposing burdens on smaller companies.[81] The Companies Act 1965 prescribed the same minimum membership requirements for all companies. At least two members were required to form a company.[82] In practice, this was not a problem as it is possible to structure a company in such a way that in substance the entire economic interest and control is vested in one single person through the use of a nominee shareholder, who basically owns only one share. However, in the company law reform, the CLRC recommended that the law allows the formation of a single member company.[83] They believed that individual entrepreneurs to limit liability would promote the spirit of entrepreneurship especially amongst small businesses. This change is indeed in line with what has been witnessed in other jurisdictions.[84] Furthermore, it is now easier to incorporate a company in terms of the formalities involved. Previously, persons intending to incorporate a company must lodge with the Registrar a package of documents.[85] The Committee believed that the information contained in various documents should be consolidated into a single form. At the same time, the incorporation process should be expedited by using electronic means. The new incorporation process can now be done online through the Companies Commission of Malaysia's MyCoID portal. A single electronic template replaces the various forms previously required for incorporation.[86] Furthermore, under Section 255(3) of the new Act, the Companies Registrar has the power to exempt certain categories of private companies from having to appoint an auditor for a financial year. However, the Registrar has yet to make use of this power and so for now, the audit requirement is still mandatory for all companies.

One core aim of company law is to address the agency problem within a company, so as to ensure the directors of a company will perform their duties honestly and diligently. The Companies Act 1965 included a statutory prescription of a director's duty in this regard.[87] However, the statutory provision was silent with respect to the care and skill that is expected of a director when carrying out his stewardship function. Traditionally, a subjective standard of care has been imposed by the common law in the English case of *Re City Equitable*

Fire Insurance.[88] The CLRC has noted that there had been case law development in other Commonwealth jurisdictions where the trend was moving towards imposing an objective standard of care and skill on a company director.[89] The advantage of a subjective test is flexibility, but at the same time there is no minimum objective standard required of the directors. One legislative option is to introduce a dual test of an objective and subjective standard, as seen in the UK.[90] In response to the recommendation from the Committee, it is now required that a director of a company must exercise reasonable care, skill and diligence with (1) the knowledge, skill and experience which may reasonably be expected of a director having the same responsibilities (objective standard); and (2) any additional knowledge, skill and experience which the director in fact has (subjective standard).[91] Another move to clarify the extent of duties and liabilities of directors is the codification of the business judgement rule. The CLRC acknowledged the need of a clear statement in law in relation to the directors' responsibilities and protection/immunity given to reasonably diligent directors in the exercise of their duties as directors.[92] Company directors may be insulated from liabilities when they make a business decision in good faith, for proper purpose and in the interest of the company.[93]

A growing concern in corporate governance has been the rise of executive pay, especially after the global financial crisis. The Companies Act 1965 did not contain any specific provision as to the manner of quantum of any remuneration to directors. Like other important decisions of the company, the issue of remuneration is to be determined by shareholders at the general meeting. The disclosure of the terms of employment and directors' remuneration is found in the notes to the accounts laid before the shareholders at the annual general meeting.[94] However, there is no need for the accounts to be approved. In light of the observation that several jurisdictions require approval of directors' remuneration, the CLRC was of the view that Malaysia should follow the practice.[95] Under the new Act, the remuneration and benefits of directors of public companies, listed companies and subsidiaries of listed companies must be approved by shareholders at general meeting.[96] In the case of private companies, the remuneration of directors may be approved by the board of directors. On the other hand, in light of the rise of corporate social responsibility, one legal trend around the world is to recognise the interests of stakeholders in company law.[97] The Companies Act 1965 placed emphasis on the shareholders theory where directors' duty and accountability are concerned. The law required company directors to act in the interest of the company and interest of the company is usually taken to mean the collective interest of the company's shareholders or at least the interest of the majority of the company's shareholders.[98] However, the CLRC was of the view that social obligations of the company should not be incorporated in the new Act.[99] Indeed, the Companies Act 1965 already contained provisions empowering company directors to establish and support various facilities to benefit employees and past employees and their various dependents.[100] Accordingly, the new Act, similar to its predecessor, does not pay much attention to the relationship between a company and its stakeholders such as employees and creditors.

Apart from the Companies Act, the corporate governance code in Malaysia also has a role in raising the standards of how a company is run. For example, according to the code of 2017, at least half of the board of directors should comprise independent directors.[101] This is to be contrasted with the code of 2012 which required that only in cases where the chairman of the company is not an independent director, the board had to comprise a majority of independent directors.[102] The World Bank made assessments on the corporate governance in Malaysia in 2005 and 2012.[103] In the view of the World Bank, Malaysia is a large and robust capital market which is underpinned by a well-developed legal and regulatory framework and strong institutions, including the Securities Commission, Companies Commission of Malaysia, Bank Negara Malaysia (the central bank) and Bursa Malaysia. Corporate governance reform has been a priority in Malaysia since the 1997 financial crisis. The regulators have all been active in enforcing laws and regulations and building their capacities and resources to do so. In 2012, the World Bank criticised that the Companies Act 1965 was 'decades old', but obviously Malaysia acted swiftly to introduce a new Act in 2016.[104] Furthermore, companies comply with many of the corporate governance provisions and report on their compliance. The World Bank observed that most directors were non-executive directors, and typically at least one-third of the board were considered independent of management and major shareholders.[105] Whilst the performance of Malaysia in the World Bank's 'Doing Business' report has already been acknowledged in this chapter, the investor protection regime in Malaysia has also been recognised in academic study. Shareholder protection in 30 countries between 1990 and 2013 was coded by the Centre for Business Research at the University of Cambridge.[106] The top countries in 1990 were Malaysia, France, the US, the UK and Japan. Of the top five countries of 1990, only France, Malaysia and the UK were still at the top in 2013. This surely illustrates Malaysia's consistent commitment to their legal and regulatory framework, and this framework has been comparable, if not better than, some of the most developed economies in the world for a long time.

Public enforcement

Generally speaking, company law is an area of private law that will rarely attract criminal liabilities. However, there are certain exceptions. One example is a breach of the directors' duty to act in good faith.[107] The case of *Marchesi* v. *Barnes*[108] is accepted as the definitive case in interpreting this statutory duty where a director is required to act 'bone fide in the interests of the company in the performance of functions attaching to the office of a director'. As decided in *Marchesi*, there is criminal liability for the contravention of the section only if the director is aware that he is not acting in the best interest of the company. This requires a proof of mental element of dishonesty. A possible defence is that the wrongdoing director has 'acted honestly and reasonably'.[109] During the reform of the Companies Act 1965, the CLRC reviewed the use of criminal, civil and administrative sanctions by the regulators.[110] They were of the view that criminal sanctions for the contravention of directors' duties should be imposed where the contravention is accompanied by fraud or dishonesty. Where there is no such fraud or dishonesty, the contravention should not be criminalised and in this case the regulator should be empowered to bring civil penalty proceedings instead. One notable change in the new Act is that it imposes heavier fines and longer terms of imprisonment on directors for breaches. For example, a false and misleading statement made by the directors can result in up to a ten-year imprisonment or up to a RM3 million fine, or both, upon conviction.[111] The RM3 million fine is a 100-fold increase from the fine of RM30,000 under the Companies Act 1965 and this serves as a stronger deterrent against improper behaviour and practices by directors.

The landscape of public enforcement in Malaysia involves various regulatory instruments and enforcers. These may include but are not limited to the Capital Markets and Services Act 2007 administered by the Securities Commission, the Companies Act 2016 administered by the Companies Commission of Malaysia, the Banking and Financial Institutions Act 1989 administered by Bank Negara Malaysia, the Penal Code which is enforced by the Police, and the Malaysian Anti-Corruption Commission Act 2009 which is enforced by the Malaysian Anti-Corruption Commission. The stock exchange, Bursa Malaysia, is responsible for ensuring compliance with its Listing Requirements by listed companies. In the view of the World Bank, all these regulators have clear areas of authority and there are no notable gaps in the enforcement framework.[112] Meanwhile, there are areas of overlap, and the various bodies do seek to cooperate. The Companies Commission Malaysia is well resourced and more active in enforcement than company registrars in many other countries.[113] The commission is self-financed with fees, which it splits with the national budget. It has about 400 personnel in the enforcement department, including 15 prosecution officers attached to the headquarters and 2 prosecution officers in each state. Likewise, the Securities Commission (SC) is well resourced, with a 2010 budget of RM136 million (around US$45 million). It has 450 professional staff, out of 670 staff in total.[114] The SC has been 'largely free from scandal and has a positive reputation in the eyes of market participants'.[115] As for the Bursa, it is a locally listed, profit-making company (since its demutualisation in 2004), with about RM300 million (around US$100 million) in revenue and a RM180 million budget.[116] This is used to support a number of departments and professional staff engaged in enforcement and ensuring companies comply with Listing Requirements.

While the exchange is primarily responsible for ensuring that publicly listed companies comply with the listing requirements, the SC carries out risk-focused surveillance on those listed companies to ensure compliance with securities laws. The attention is centred on their corporate conduct and disclosures with the objective of detecting suspicious corporate transgressions and enhancing the quality and reliability of financial statements. According to the SC, they seek to utilise the full suite of enforcement tools available, including leveraging their wide supervisory powers for a more targeted and pre-emptive approach to enforcement.[117] To combat market misconduct, the securities law in Malaysia (indeed also true for Singapore) has chosen an almost word-for-word adoption of the general anti-fraud rule in US Rule 10b-5.[118] The Capital Markets and Services Act 2007 provides that it is unlawful for any person directly or indirectly to: (1) use any device, scheme or artifice to defraud; (2) engage in any act, practice or course of business which operates or would operate as a fraud or deceit upon any person; or (3) make any untrue statement of a material fact or to omit to state a material fact which is necessary in order to make the statements, in the light of the circumstances under which they were made, not misleading.[119] A person who commits this offence will be punished, on conviction, with imprisonment for a term not exceeding ten years and a fine of not less than RM1 million.[120] Furthermore, insider trading is prohibited.[121] The penalty of the offence of insider trading is the same as the use of manipulative and deceptive devices.[122] Apart from criminal measures, the SC's powers include administrative actions, such as warning letters, public reprimands, fines, and the suspension and removal of licenses.[123] It may also issue directives to comply with relevant securities law and regulation. The commission may also initiate civil actions in court, including against directors and controlling shareholders in listed companies, and may collect damages on behalf of shareholders.[124]

The commitment of the regulators to combat market misconduct can be measured by enforcement output. There had not been a single securities market regulator before the SC was established. The idea of having a central authority to regulate and develop the capital market was seen in the sixth Malaysia Plan in 1990. Finally on 1 March 1993, the SC came into being, with four Divisions divided into 14 departments. Enforcement actions were seen in its first year of operation when three public reprimands were issued.[125] Furthermore, in this first year, the Investigation and Enforcement Department referred nine cases of illegal short selling to the Public Prosecutor for further action.[126] Out of the nine cases referred, five cases were prosecuted with fines ranging from RM10,000 to RM100,000. Over the years, more and more enforcement actions have been seen from the Commission. Between 2004 and 2006, Sulaiman observed that several companies in Malaysia had been involved in financial misreporting or misstatements probes by the securities market regulators.[127] In his view, in this period, financial misreporting in relation to public companies was largely left to the securities regulator to enforce, in contrast to shareholders' suits which were common in certain jurisdictions.[128] From 2007 to 2011, the SC took over 130 administrative actions, 51 civil actions and initiated 45 prosecutions.[129] They also issued dozens of warning letters each year for minor issues. These enforcement actions covered a range of offenses, including provision of false and misleading information, and failure to comply with rules on takeovers and other securities regulation requirements. They were taken against directors and controlling shareholders in listed companies as well as market intermediaries. However, there may be evidence to suggest that the Commission is stepping up enforcement and deterrence by using more criminal actions. For example, in 2015, there were 220 criminal charges laid, compared to only 41 administrative actions in the year.[130] Indeed, in 2014, there were only three administrative actions in the whole year. This is apparently consistent with the view of Mohamed Sadique and colleagues that fraud is a serious threat to businesses, specifically to investors, in Malaysia.[131] There is a need for a tougher stance in public enforcement to address the problem.

Private enforcement

In the case of weak economic incentive for private parties to sue and limited access to information support action by private parties, as seen above, regulators may be compelled to step into the shoes of private individuals seeking recourse through the court systems. The SC calls it 'quasi-public enforcement', as it is a public regulator which initiates a private civil action on behalf of the victims.[132] There are some very recent examples of how it can be used to achieve justice. On 26 July 2017, the Commission filed a civil suit against Kheng-Chew Yeow, Paulene Chee and Yee-Chee Tan.[133] The three individuals were charged for their alleged involvement in insider trading in relation to the proposed merger of Kencana Petroleum and SapuraCrest Petroleum Bhd in 2011. In the lawsuit, the Commission sought, among others, an order that Yeow and Chee severally pay the sum of RM2,326,980, being three times the difference of the price of securities in concern, an order that Tan pay the sum of RM452,280 for the same reason, and an order for a civil penalty of RM1 million against Yeow, Paulene Chee and Tan severally, among others. On 15 August 2017, the High Court recorded a Consent Judgment between the SC and the three Defendants granting the orders which were sought by the SC. In another case, the Commission filed a civil suit against Tee-Jin Koh, Thiam-Seong Koh and Hui-Sim Koh for insider trading involving the shares of Axis Inc Bhd, a garment manufacturing firm that was delisted in November 2010.[134] In this case, the SC sought, among others, a payment of the sum of RM7 million in total, together with a civil penalty of RM1 million for each of the accused.

In theory, a person who suffers loss or damages by reason of, or by relying on, the conduct of another person who has committed, for example, the offence of insider trading, may recover the amount of loss or damages by instituting civil proceedings against the other person.[135] However, according to Sulaiman, there has not been any case brought by investors or shareholders under the Capital Markets and Services Act 2007 (or the former Securities Industry Act 1983).[136] Malaysian investors have not taken an active stance in bringing investor-related civil proceedings and instead have relied on the regulators to initiate legal proceedings. On other hand, shareholders can consider bringing an action under the Companies Act. Any member or debenture holder of a company may apply to the Court for an order on the ground that the affairs of the company are being conducted or the powers of the directors are being exercised in a manner oppressive to one or more of the members or debenture holder.[137] Remedies under this oppression petition include an order to: (1) direct or prohibit any act or cancel or vary any transaction or resolution; (2) regulate the conduct of the affairs of the company in the future; (3) provide for the purchase of the shares or debentures of the company by other members or debenture holders of the company or by the company itself; (4) in the case of a purchase of shares by the company, provide for a reduction accordingly of capital of the company; or (5) provide that the company be wound up. It can be seen that this petition is almost the same as the one in the UK and the equivalent in Hong Kong and Singapore.[138] However, as observed by Salim and Lawton, the oppression remedy was designed with the smaller private company in mind rather than the public quoted corporation, and its use in the latter context has not been very successful in the large majority of cases in either the UK or Malaysia.[139]

Alternatively, shareholders may consider bringing a derivative action. In Malaysia, the statutory derivative action was introduced in 2007.[140] In a derivative action, a person is entitled to bring a proceeding on behalf of and in the name of the company, as an exception to the common law rule in *Foss* v. *Harbottle*.[141] In Malaysia the range of persons who can bring a derivative action is fairly broad, including a member, a former member, a director and the Registrar.[142] This is to be contrasted with the UK, where a derivative action is available only to existing members, and with Singapore where it is available to any person in the discretion of the court.[143] As discussed in the previous chapter, in Singapore, a statutory derivative action used to be not available to public companies. There has been no such restriction in Malaysia. One critique by Salim and Kaur on the statutory derivative action is that the idea and purpose of the provision is not easily understood without a basic understanding of the common law derivative action and reference to foreign legislation and case law.[144] The law is silent on what a derivative action is and the circumstances when it can be brought; it gives only vague guidance on when leave is or is not to be granted and when the court can make an order for costs. Further, the preservation of the common law derivative action made it even more confusing for many.[145]

According to the investigation by Chen, there were 32 decisions involving shareholders' derivative actions from 2008 to 2015.[146] However, 24 out of the 32 cases (75 per cent) of cases failed in the initial stages. This may illustrate the limitations in the Malaysian statutory derivative action in facilitating easier access to redress for breaches of directors' duties. Comparatively, there were six reported and unreported cases involving derivative actions during 1999–2006.[147] It is clear that since the introduction of the statutory derivative action in 2007, the number of derivative actions has increased substantially. In the reform of the Companies Act, the CLRC has expressed their concern regarding the potential abuse of the litigation.[148] One safeguard is a notice requirement to provide the company time to address the applicant's concerns prior to the proceedings. In Malaysia, the complainant should give the company notice of at least 30 days before the commencement of the proceedings of his or her intention to bring a statutory derivative action.[149] Another safeguard will be to set out more clearly criteria for allowing an action. However, even in the absence of safeguards, there are issues of cost and the free-rider problem which should act as disincentives to potential complainants.[150] This is consistent with the discussions in the previous chapters that Hong Kong, Singapore and the UK similarly are not strong in private enforcement.

Political institutions

Malaysia is a parliamentary democracy with a federal constitutional monarch, the Yang di-Pertuan Agong, as head of state.[151] This monarch is chosen for a five-year term from among their own number by the nine hereditary rulers of the Malay Peninsula. The nine hereditary states are Perlis, Negeri Sembilan, Kedah, Perak, Johor, Selangor, Pahang, Terengganu and Kelantan. The head of state in the four states that do not have hereditary rulers, namely Malacca, Pulau Pinang, Sabah and Sarawak, is the Yang di-Pertuan Negeri, or governor, and is appointed by the Yang di-Pertuan Agong for a four-year term. The current King is Sultan Muhammad V, the fifteenth Yang di-Pertuan Agong, from the state of Kelantan. Parliament is the highest legislative body in Malaysia. It consists of the King as the Head of State, the Senate and the House of Representatives.[152] Article 55 of the Federal Constitution stipulates that only the King can summon for Parliament to be in session. The King also has the absolute power to prorogue or dissolve the Parliament. Apart from this, the role is largely ceremonial in nature.

The Senate (*Dewan Negara* in Malay) consists of 70 members. The membership of the Senate is made up of two categories: 26 members elected to represent 13 states (each state represented by two members); 44 members appointed by the King on the advice of the Prime Minister. The Senate is the upper house of the parliament. Except for financial and fiscal matters, they have the power to initiate and amend legislation. Once a legislative bill is passed by the one house it is forwarded to the other house. The lower house, the House of Representatives (*Dewan Rakyat* in Malay) has 222 elected members and each member represents a Parliamentary Constituency. A General Election is held every five years to elect members of the House of Representatives. Parties with the most elected members can form a federal government to rule the country. The next general election is due in August 2018. However, it can come earlier than that when the current Prime Minister requests the King to dissolve Parliament. In the last election in 2013, Barisan Nasional coalition won 133 of the 222 parliamentary seats and the current Prime Minister Najib Razak managed to stay in power.[153] Najib Razak's predecessor was Abdullah Ahmad Badawi who served from 2003 to 2009. Before that, the prime minister was Mahathir Mohamad, longest-serving holder of that office from 1981 to 2003. In 2003, the Malaysian Government declared Mahathir to be the 'Father of Modern Malaysia' in recognition of his contribution in turning Malaysia into a modern, advanced and industrialised nation.[154]

The major political party in the Barisan Nasional coalition is the United Malays National Organisation (UMNO). Each of Malaysia's six Prime Ministers has been an UMNO member. The Barisan has never been defeated in a general election. Because of its usual large majority of seats and firm party discipline, the Parliament is regarded as weak.[155] Government-introduced bills usually pass as a matter of course, while other bills are seldom successful. The opposition parties have little power. The Malaysian political leadership has been practising a father-leadership style since its independence in 1957. Tun Abdul Rahman, the first Prime Minister and Father of Malaysia who fought against the British for independence, was said to be 'a classic case of the iron hand within the velvet glove'.[156] Mahathir has continued this style of leadership. From his perspective, Asian leaders should assume and assert true leadership, seizing the initiative in terms of ideas and thoughts and getting their people's respect.[157] His view was that some countries may suffer from too much democracy. According to him, governments are not necessarily undemocratic because the government party remains in power for so long. He argued that if the people choose the same party and the same leader, it is the people's democratic right to do so. He also cited China's Deng Xiaoping as a successful undemocratic leader who took China into a modern era.

Mahathir's role in Malaysia's economic development is arguably as important as Deng's role to China, and Lee Kuan Yew's to Singapore. The country's national car manufacturer, Proton, was established by Mahathir in 1983, a year after he assumed the premiership. He saw it as a catalyst to promote industrialisation in an economy that heavily relied on commodities.[158] Right from the start, Mahathir took a very hands-on approach in Proton's operation. When he retired in 2003, he was made an adviser and then chairman of the company, a position he held until 2016. He reportedly 'cried' over the sale of Proton to Chinese automaker Zhejiang Geely in 2017.[159] Proton is widely regarded as an iconic national brand of Malaysia. The company becomes 'a source of national pride and the centrepiece of a bold strategy by Mahathir, for more than two decades, to turn his country into an industrialised powerhouse equal to Asian Tigers like South Korea and Taiwan'.[160] Malaysia's success under the leadership of Mahathir has been in diversifying away from the export of palm oil and rubber.[161] In the early 1980s, Mahathir launched Malaysia's Heavy Industries Policy with the establishment of HICOM. This policy amounted to a shift in pre-Mahathir industrialisation policy, which concentrated on processing imported raw materials and assembling imported components.[162] HICOM have shaped Mahathir's grand industrialisation strategy by setting up companies, incorporated in an Industrial Development Master Plan. One notable project undertaken by HICOM is Proton. When Mahathir took office, FDI inflow into Malaysia was concentrated in the manufacturing sector catering for domestic needs.[163] Subsequently, the bulk of FDI moved from manufacturing to heavy industries.

One critique of Mahathir's regime is that he has provided political stability but papered over ethnic divisions.[164] The notion of 'Bangsa Malaysia' was officially introduced by Mahathir in 1991, as part of the package in his Vision 2020 project. In short, it is an attempt to bring together the diverse ethnic group and varying perceptions into one united Malaysian nation. There are three essential elements.[165] First, people should be able to identify themselves with the country. This calls for undivided loyalty and a sense of patriotism towards Malaysia as a country. Second, people should speak *Bahasa Malaysia*, referring to one common language as means of communication among Malaysians. Third, people should accept the Constitution. The Constitution of Malaysia sets out key fundamentals of the country, including the democratic system of electing the government, the federal structure of the political system, the rights of the people, the rule of law, constitutional monarchy, Malay as the national language, Islam as the official religion and so on. Inter-racial harmony has been repeatedly appearing on the agenda of the Malaysian governments led by different prime ministers. No-one will forget the riot in 1969 which prompted the government to introduce the NEP. The riot was directly connected to the General Election held in that year, in which the ruling party lost many seats to the opposition and the parties tried to win voters by making racist attacks on one another. As of 2016, the total population of Malaysia was estimated at 31.7 million, with the majority of them ethnic Bumiputeras (68.6 per cent), followed by Chinese (23.4 per cent), Indians (7 per cent) and others (1 per cent).[166]

The formation of the existing ethnic structure and ethnicised mindset in Malaysia is inseparable from the past legacy of British colonial rule.[167] The British rulers expanded the number of Chinese and Indian immigrants; created an artificial occupational segregation on ethnic lines (Malays in agriculture, the Chinese in commerce; and Indians in plantations); reinforced a sense of inter-ethnic divisions; and, thus, prevented any kind of solidarity among these major ethnic groups. In the Malaysian Constitution, Article 153 provides ‘special rights’ to Malays in education, business and the public service, and these rights are to be safeguarded by the Yang di-Pertuan Agong. These constitutionally guaranteed special rights became a major source of discontent among both Malays and non-Malays; whereas Malays considered it insufficient, non-Malays took it as a discriminatory measure.[168] The NEP further expanded the Malay special rights in investment, capital ownership and education. Hence, the state tried to play its role in managing ethnic tensions by expanding the interests of Malays as a dominant ethnic group rather than mediating the interests of all ethnic communities. The state provided different rationales for ethnic preferential policies.[169] Under British rule, the colonial policy makers tried to justify these preferential policies in the name of ensuring the welfare of the Malay rulers and their subjects and preserving the traditional way of Malay lifestyle disrupted by the immigrant communities and cultures. During the current post-colonial period, the agenda of preferential policies has been advocated by the state on the ground that these policies would assist the economically disadvantaged Malay population, eliminate rural (mostly Malay) poverty and reduce interethnic income inequalities.

The ethnic preferential policy is also practiced in the domain of economics and business in Malaysia. One aspect is land ownership. During colonial rule, the Malay Reservation Act that designated certain areas as Malay Reservation Land, which allowed only Malays to own, lease, and mortgage land in such designated areas. After independence, as discussed, the NEP aimed to raise Malay ownership and participation in industrial and commercial activities to 30 per cent by 1990. The Industrial Coordination Act was introduced, which required that any non-Malay firm with capital and reserves funds worth more than RM250,000 and more than 25 employees must demonstrate at least 30 per cent of Bumiputera equity ownership or participation to get business licenses approved or renewed. The state could deny any non-Malay firm a license if it failed to satisfy this requirement. Furthermore, the government has created institutions such as the Bumiputera Commercial and Industrial Community, Majlis Amanah Rakyat, Bank Bumiputra, Perbadanan Nasional Berhad and the State Economic Development Corporations to provide credit and technical assistance to Malay business entrepreneurs.[170] With other benefits such as discounts on property prices and special tax incentives, the government manged to nurture a number of Malay tycoons who could compete with their Chinese counterparts, as part of the special rights given to Malays as the rightful owners of the national economy in reference to their indigenous status.[171] As a result of the government's efforts, Bumiputera participation in the secondary and tertiary sectors expanded rapidly, reaching 30.5 per cent and 40.5 per cent respectively in 1990, up from 12.1 per cent and 21.7 per cent respectively in 1970.[172] As discussed before, Bumiputera corporate equity of around 20 per cent in 1990 (as opposed to 30 per cent) might perhaps be one of the rare cases that fell well below the target of the NEP.[173]

The NEP may be successful from a social point of view. However, some believe that 'promoting Malay supremacy makes for unsound economics'.[174] When Prime Minister Najib Razak came to power in 2009, he convened a group of economists to devise a new economic plan. The panel recommended replacing the existing racial preferences with need-based policies that would help any Malaysians, regardless of ethnicity, at the bottom 40 per cent of the population in terms of household income. This plan was subsequently dropped owing to political opposition. According to Chin, market discipline, transparency and good governance are falling by the wayside in the name of Malay supremacy.[175]

Cultural institutions

Pretty much like Singapore, Malaysia is a multi-racial country but with Bumiputeras as the major ethnic group. The term 'bumiputera' is not found in the Federal Constitution. The Constitution uses the term 'Malay' to describe this ethnic group who 'profess the religion of Islam, habitually speak the Malay language and conform to Malay custom'.[176] According to this definition, a Bumiputera must be at the same time a Muslim. According to the 2010 census, Islam was the most widely professed religion in Malaysia with the proportion of 61.3 per cent.[177] As a multi-racial nation, other religions embraced were Buddhism (19.8 per cent), Christianity (9.2 per cent) and Hinduism (6.3 per cent). The Constitution recognises Islam as the national religion, but at the same time allows other religions to be practised.[178] Article 11 of the Constitution further confirms freedom of religion. Malaysia is an essentially Islamic country and therefore, unlike Singapore and Hong Kong, it does not have a pure common law system. Its system is based on the English system but with distinct characteristics in the form of Islamic religious courts and two separate High Courts for the Peninsula and for the Borneo states.[179] Malaysia's civil court structure is broadly the same with other common law jurisdictions. Meanwhile, the Islamic courts exist side by side in a dual court structure. The matters dealt with by the two courts are mutually exclusive. As recognised by the Constitution, the civil courts have no jurisdiction in respect of any matter within the jurisdiction of the Islamic courts.[180] The general jurisdiction of the Islamic courts is expressly provided for in the Constitution under Article 74(2) and List II, Schedule 9.[181] In other words, they have jurisdiction over 'Islamic law and personal and family law of persons professing the religion of Islam', which includes *inter alia*, matters such as betrothal, marriage, divorce, legitimacy, dowry, maintenance, adoption, succession, religious endowments. As stated in the Constitution, Islamic law is a state law matter.[182] Earlier discussions in this chapter regarding the legal institutions of Malaysia are a federal matter. As a result, the Islamic legal tradition of Malaysia should have little relevance in the context of this book.

As discussed in the previous section, the dividing nature of the differentiation of 'Bumiputera' and 'Non-Bumiputera' among the people of Malaysia has dichotomised the society. The Malay ruling elites used the Malay language and Malay culture as the means to foster Malay dominance. There are two important implications.[183] First, the usage of the Malay language and cultural symbols is the basis of national representation and unity. Second, the Malay ruling elites seek to establish Malay nationalism and Malay cultural hegemony to legitimise their governance. Article 152 of the Constitution states that the national language in Malaysia is the Malay language ('Bahasa Malaysia' in Malay). However, no person will be prohibited from using other languages as recognised by the same constitutional provision. As a result, despite the Malay language being the language of formal instruction in schools, colleges and universities, English is widely used in both formal and informal communication and Mandarin is widely used by the Chinese community.[184] Within the Indian community, Tamil and Telegu are commonly used.

Some people may describe Malays as 'economically backward', 'stupid', 'lazy', 'used to the easy life', 'living off the fat of the land' and so on.[185] This is believed to be connected to the traditional culture of Malay sultans, and the feudal culture of misused power and complacency, which were present in early NEP-era entrepreneurs. Their mentality was that wealth and economic opportunities are either deserved or easily acquired through political or royal patronage. This may also be connected to a religious view that *takdir* (fate) and *rezeki* (livelihood) are predetermined by Allah.[186] Abdullah and colleagues seek to identify factors leading to success and failure of Bumiputera entrepreneurs.[187] Their study confirmed that eight factors are vital to the success of Bumiputera entrepreneurs: advancement drive, achievement orientation, commitment, decision-making ability, managing risk, tenacity, networking and optimism. As for the factors leading to the failure of Bumiputera entrepreneurs, inability to compete, lack of competency and capital, customer-related problems, employee-related problems, unfavourable economic conditions, bureaucracy, supplier discrimination and negative community attitudes were found to be crucial. According to Hamidon, despite the government's concerted efforts and initiatives, Malay entrepreneurship is still lacking.[188] While the government has been successful in helping more Malays to become entrepreneurs, their numbers are still small compared with the Chinese entrepreneurs and their sustainability and competitiveness are well below the other races. Hamidon attributes this to the privileges enjoyed by the Malays which make them complacent and more dependent on the government.[189] He also argues that culture may have played a role with the lack of achievement in the entrepreneurial activities by the Malays. Quite like the Chinese society, Malays are known as a collective society and are generally taught to value community well-being above the individual's. They value family traditions and put others above themselves, and are taught to be polite, courteous and respectful of elders.

According to a study by Fontaine and Richardson, which investigates the cultural values of 324 employees working in various industries throughout the Malay Peninsula, they find few significant differences in cultural values between ethnic groups.[190] Storz argues that the core values of the Chinese and Malays are derived from Confucianism and the *budi* complex[191] respectively, and both share similarities.[192] According to Tham, the ethical system of the Malays is encapsulated in the *budi* complex.[193] In his view, it is the essence of their social relationships. It formulates norms of individual and social behaviour. The way an individual should feel and think about himself or herself and others is guided by the *budi* complex. The Malay and Chinese views of self as derived from the *budi* complex and Confucianism is essentially one that is socially constructed by others – their definitions, their approval, their acceptance.[194] The self is dependent on the perceptions of others. The Malay and Chinese view of self is collective and socially contextualised based on commonality and connectedness. As a result, values which focus on reciprocity and mutuality are manifested in business attitudes and practices.[195] The Malay and the Chinese would find it more important to focus on the social and relational aspects of the business transaction rather than simply on the facts of the business.

Despite being favoured by the NEP, the Malay have not really reversed the domination of the commercial community by the Chinese. It is estimated that the Chinese control around 70 per cent of national income through mainly family-run enterprises.[196] Their grip on the real-estate sector is particularly strong. Around 75 per cent of office blocks are believed to be in the hands of Chinese. Furthermore, the Chinese contribution to state revenues is immense. They pay around 90 per cent of total income tax while accounting for 60 per cent of gross domestic product.[197] Indeed, 80 per cent of the top 40 richest Malaysians were ethnic Chinese in 2012.[198] Sugar trader and owner of world's largest palm oil listed company, Wilmar International, Robert Kuok was the richest, with a net worth of RM30.28 billion. As of 2017, Kuok remains Malaysia's wealthiest person.[199] Kuok made it to the top of the list for the twelfth straight year. Other notable Chinese Malaysian billionaires include Leng Chan Quek of the Hong Leong Group, and Kok Thay Lim of Genting Group. The only two non-Chinese on the 2017 list were Ananda Krishnan of Aircel, a telecommunications company, who has an Indian origin, and Mokhtar Albukhary, owner of

Albukhary Group of companies, a diversified business group, who is a Malay. In the view of Koon, Kuok's business activities resemble certain representative characteristics of Chinese entrepreneurship: (1) its organising principles are derived from Confucian values; (2) its synergy and dynamism come from family owned businesses; (3) it grows more rapidly with political patronage; and (4) the most successful Chinese companies have become transnational corporations that are constantly upgrading their technological and management bases.[200] Kuok is fluent in his mother tongue of the Fuzhou dialect, literate in both Mandarin and Malay, but most articulate in English. This enabled him to manipulate a complex multicultural environment. Further, the role played by the Malaysian state and opportunities offered by a fast-changing regional environment have been equally important to his success. After securing a near monopoly in sugar trading and refining in Malaysia in the early 1960s, he has earned the title of Malaysia's Sugar King. Today, he presides over a family business empire that spans the Shangri-La hotel chain to logistics to being the world's biggest processor of palm oil.

According to Sia, considerable interest has been shown in the relationship between Kuok and his brothers and prominent members of the Malaysian government both at the State and Federal levels.[201] Kuok's success was attributed to his cultivation of civil servants who later would fill top Government positions. For example, Kuok met Lee Kuan Yew of Singapore in 1941 as students at Raffles College in pre-war Singapore.[202] School and college days gave Kuok some of the most enviable connections.[203] Apart from Lee, among his schoolmates were two Prime Ministers of Malaysia. It was the ability of Kuok to understand government needs and work with government institutions and policies that allowed his company to grow rapidly. However, at the same time, it is worth noting that the government in Malaysia has not been very transparent to work with. A recent article published by *Time* magazine listed the top five countries said to be the most corrupt.[204] In the list were Brazil, South Africa, China, Russia and Malaysia. Malaysia was listed in the second spot of world corruption, behind Brazil. This perhaps agrees with a point made in a previous chapter that it is difficult to draw a clear line between *guanxi* and corruption. There is no exception in Malaysia, given the resemblance between the Malay and Chinese cultural values.

Role of market infrastructure

As discussed in previous chapters, one common characteristic of China, Hong Kong and Singapore is that they have the largest ports in the world. As discussed before in this chapter, Penang and Malacca used to be two crucial links in the trade between India and China. Their importance has declined over the years. Today, more than 90 per cent of the country's trade is by sea via Malaysia's seven international ports, namely Penang Port, Port Klang, Johor Port, Port of Tanjung Pelepas, Kuantan Port and Kemaman Port in the Malay Peninsula and Bintulu Port in Sarawak.[205] According to the World Shipping Council, among these ports, Port Klang is the largest in the country, and the twelfth in the world.[206] Port Klang is situated on the west coast of the Peninsula, about 40 kilometres from the capital city, Kuala Lumpur. Its proximity to the greater Klang Valley – the commercial and industrial hub of the country as well as the country's most populous region – ensures that the port plays a pivotal role in the economic development of the country.[207] Port Klang Authority is a statutory corporation established on 1 July 1963. In tandem with the Government policy to infuse private sector management and discipline in various Government-owned/controlled undertakings in the country, the first privatisation of a major port facility took place in Port Klang. In 1986 the container terminal facilities operated by Port Klang Authority were privatised to Klang Container Terminal Berhad. Whilst still maintaining a 20 per cent equity in the company, the Authority has taken on an enhanced role of a trade facilitator, regulator and landlord. Port Klang is subdivided into three terminals which are known as Northport, Southpoint and Westport. The terminals at Port Klang have a total capacity of 130.5 million TEUs.[208] As of 2015, the amount of cargo handled was 11.89 million TEUs.

Privatisation of Port Klang was just a small part of Mahathir's plan of industrialisation. He was also keen to invest in infrastructure, as a catalyst for the rest of the economy.[209] These infrastructure projects include: the North-South Expressway; Kuala Lumpur International Airport; Petronas Twin Towers; Putrajaya, the new administrative capital; Proton, a car maker; Perwaja, the national steel corporation; Cyberjaya, the multimedia super corridor; and so on. The North-South Expressway is the longest expressway in Malaysia, with a total length of 772 kilometres running from Bukit KayuHitam in Kedah near the Malaysia-Thai border to Johor Bahru at the southern portion of Peninsular Malaysia. The expressway links many major cities and towns in western Peninsular Malaysia, acting as the backbone of the west coast of the Peninsula. The expressway is aimed at providing major economic benefits to Malaysia by increasing industrial productivity, facilitating access to ports and airports and promoting domestic tourism.[210]

Another notable project during Mahathir's era was the construction of the Kuala Lumpur International Airport. Situated in the Sepang district, the airport is approximately 50 kilometres from the capital city, Kuala Lumpur. Surrounded by four main cities, it was not intended to serve Kuala Lumpur only, but also Shah Alam, Seremban and Malacca. It began its operations in June 1998, and today the airport is capable of handling 35 million passengers and 1.2 million tonnes of cargo a year.[211] The purpose-built second terminal dedicated for low-cost carriers, known as klia2, is built with the initial capacity to accommodate up to 45 million passengers annually and is designed to allow expansion for future air travel growth trends and airlines' operational models.[212] This new terminal was officially opened on 2 May 2014. The project is to be developed in three phases (of which the first two are completed), building up to a final capacity of 100 million passengers per annum. The project was intended to relieve the strain on the pre-existing Sultan Abdul Aziz Shah Airport, which was Kuala Lumpur's main airport from 1965 to 1998. When the Sultan Abdul Aziz Shah Airport opened in 1965, the runway was the longest in Southeast Asia at 3,700 metres long. This has now been superseded by the Kuala Lumpur International Airport where the runway is 4,124 metres. In 2016, the old airport handled 2.8 million passengers and 36,146 tonnes of cargo, compared to 52 million passengers and 642,558 tonnes of cargo by the new airport (two terminals combined).[213] In 1991, when then Prime Minister, Mahathir, launched an ambitious plan to make the country a fully developed industrial nation by 2020, the airport was regarded as part of a new national infrastructure development that would enhance the country's potential to become a regional hub and an international gateway.[214]

Another highlight of Mahathir's projects is certainly the Petronas Twin Towers. Soaring to a height of 451.9 metres, the 88-storey twin structure is Kuala Lumpur's iconic landmark. Twin Towers is inspired by Mahathir's vision for Malaysia to be a global player.[215] According to Mahathir, 'as an internationally recognised landmark, [the Twin Towers] symbolise the courage, ingenuity, initiative, and determination, energy, confidence, optimism, advancement and zest of a nation.'[216] There is certainly a reason for the Malaysians to be proud, as the Twin Towers were once the tallest building in the world from 1998 to 2004, and is still the world's tallest twin structure.

Industries in Malaysia are mainly located in over 200 industrial estates or parks and 14 Free Industrial Zones developed throughout the country.[217] These Zones are export processing zones which have been developed to cater to the needs of export-oriented industries. Companies in the Zones are allowed duty free imports of raw materials, components, parts, machinery and equipment directly required in the manufacturing process. Specialised parks have been developed in Malaysia to cater to the needs of specific industries. Examples of these parks are the Technology Park Malaysia in Bukit Jalil, Kuala Lumpur and the Kulim Hi-Tech Park in the northern state of Kedah which cater to technology-intensive industries and R&D activities. One recent example of these specialised parks is perhaps the Tun Razak Exchange, formerly known as 1Malaysia Development Berhad (1MDB) Real Estate. The Tun Razak Exchange, which is wholly owned by the Malaysian Ministry of Finance, is an iconic 70-acre development in the heart of Kuala Lumpur that is seeking to become a leading centre for international finance and business. It is part of the country's ETP which aims to strengthen Kuala Lumpur's role as the country's financial capital, by the creation of a central business environment for financial services firms, multinational companies and supporting ancillary businesses.[218] This development is in line with Kuala Lumpur's vision to become a leader in Islamic Finance. Since Malaysia's first Islamic bank was opened in 1983, it has now become the world leader in *sukuk* issuances as previously discussed. The city is certainly on course to attain its goal. The Tun Razak Exchange according to some is poised to catalyse Malaysia's growing prominence in global finance and leverage its existing dominance in Islamic finance.[219]

However, the Tun Razak Exchange project has come with a major controversy surrounding it. It is believed that more than US$1 billion entered Malaysia

Prime Minister Najib Razak's personal bank accounts, much of it from state investment 1MDB, the government backing behind the project.[220] The scandal has caused a political crisis in Malaysia and threatens to end years of one-party rule in the country. Another concern is whether there is sufficient human capital to support the project. Wiranto, an economist at Oversea-Chinese Banking Corporation in Singapore, believes that Malaysia has an advantage in Islamic finance through its development of infrastructure as well as the human capital skillset and legal workforce.[221] Malaysia published almost a third of all research papers on Islamic finance from 2011 to 2013, the most of any country, and has the most Islamic scholars in the world.[222] The supply of the legal workforce has had a close connection with the colonial root of Malaysia. The Malaysian Bar is a creature of statute established under the Advocates and Solicitors' Ordinance 1947 which was subsequently replaced by the Legal Profession Act 1976. The legal profession in Malaysia is a fused one in which each advocate and solicitor is automatically a member of the Malaysian Bar so long as he/she holds a valid Practising Certificate.[223] As of 2017, there are 16,524 legal practitioners in Malaysia, compared to 13,672 in 2011. As part of the English common law system, Malaysia recognised 66 universities in the UK and their respective law courses as part of the qualification requirements with a view of admission to the Malaysian Bar.[224] Degrees from Australia and New Zealand are also recognised, further increasing the number of potential lawyers. However, as recognised by the Malaysian Bar, Malaysia is not a hub for legal services in the region.[225] The best minds are more interested in practising in other jurisdictions where the work and pay is better.

Other than lawyers, a leading financial centre requires the support of financial professionals including accountants. According to the IMF, foreign banks have been in Malaysia for over a century and all commercial banks have to be locally incorporated.[226] The longest established banks are the UK ones, HSBC and Standard Chartered. The UK banks have extensive branch networks, as do the two Singaporean banks, Oversea-Chinese Banking Corporation and United Overseas Bank. Citibank is the other foreign commercial bank with a significant presence. Overall, foreign banks hold around 20 per cent of the assets and deposits of the banking system.[227] Foreign financial institutions might exert competitive pressures on domestic ones so as to enhance the quality of the sector. As for the accounting sector, the Malaysian Institute of Accountants is the competent authority under the Accountants Act 1967 to regulate the profession. Under Part II of the First Schedule of the Accountants Act 1967, the membership of ten overseas accounting bodies, including those in the UK, Ireland, Australia, New Zealand, Canada and India, is recognised in Malaysia. This means that there are various options to practice in Malaysia as an accountant. With the country's vision to strengthen its financial sector, there is obviously a demand for more accountants. As of 2016, there were 32,000 accountants registered with the Malaysian Institute of Accountants.[228] Meanwhile, the government has set a target to increase the number of accountants to 60,000 by 2020. This clearly shows that the government acknowledges the importance of talents, in addition to infrastructure, in order for the country to develop into a high-income economy.

Determinants of future growth

Initially an economy dominated by the production of raw natural resource materials, such as tin and rubber, Malaysia today has a diversified economy and has become a leading exporter of electrical appliances, electronic parts and components, palm oil and natural gas. After the Asian financial crisis of 1997–98, Malaysia continued to post solid growth rates, averaging 5.5 per cent per year from 2000 to 2008. Malaysia was hit by the global financial crisis in 2008 but recovered rapidly, posting growth rates averaging 5.7 per cent since 2010. Vision 2020, launched in 1991, sets out nine challenges Malaysia has had to meet to become a fully developed country by 2020.[229] In more specific terms, to qualify for 'developed nation' status, Malaysia must achieve a gross national income (GNI) per capita of US$15,000. Malaysia's GNI per capita dropped from US$10,345 in 2013 to US$8,821 in 2016, leaving the grand target well out of reach. In light of some of the challenges in Vision 2020, Malaysia may have made some good progress. In relation to a fair and equitable distribution of the wealth, less than 1 per cent of Malaysian households live in extreme poverty, and the government's focus has shifted toward addressing the well-being of the poorest 40 per cent of the population. For example, from 2009 to 2014 the real average household incomes of this underprivileged group grew at 11.9 per cent per year, compared to 7.9 per cent for the total population of Malaysia, thus narrowing income disparities. In contrast, the recent 1MDB scandal may not help Malaysia to become a fully moral and ethical society, another challenge laid down in Vision 2020. Apart from raising questions about the government's transparency, the scandal surrounding 1MDB has also impacted Malaysia's currency and business environment.[230]

According to the World Bank, the potential risks to Malaysia's economic growth are primarily external ones, stemming from threats of trade protectionism in the US fiscal stimulus and trade policies, and from the impacts of potential fluctuations in global commodity prices.[231] Likewise, the IMF agrees that, internally, the authorities are implementing structural reforms on a wide front in support of Malaysia's goal of achieving high-income status by 2020.[232] Continued investment in infrastructure and in research and development can help spur home-grown innovation and increase incomes. Together with improvements in the quality of education, these efforts can help raise labour productivity, support higher sustainable growth and foster a more inclusive society. Koen and colleagues have made a comprehensive appraisal regarding what the regime has done well and less well so far.[233] On education, they recognise that Malaysia's education policy has long focused on inclusiveness, and access to education has improved significantly in recent years. Education has reached near-universal levels in Malaysia, with primary education enrolment at around 98 per cent in 2015 and pre-school and secondary education enrolment at around 95 per cent and 89 per cent respectively.[234] As a result, increasing the quality of education is critical to boosting human capital development and workforce productivity, increasing the availability of skilled workers and improving Malaysia's attractiveness to investment in higher value-added activities. Furthermore, sustainable long-term growth will increasingly depend on the contribution of innovation-driven productivity gains rather than increasing factor inputs. Innovation will be key for competitiveness in international markets and participation in global value chains, improvements in the quality of products and processes, and technology-driven enhancements of living standards.[235] As Minister of Science, Technology and Innovation, Datuk Seri Madius Tangau, said in 2016, 'Science, Technology and Innovation is the driver of Malaysia's new economy and the nation's competitiveness will very much rely on how ideation is translated into reality.'[236] One recent policy initiative in this direction is the formation of the National Science Council. Its inaugural meeting was held on 27 January 2016. It is supposed to be in charge of the overall Science, Technology and Innovation agenda. However, the OECD notes that the council is advisory in nature, and since the mandate of this council is not available, it is not known what its connection will be with other existing initiatives to foster this area of growth.[237]

Despite being highly regarded for its regulatory framework in relation to companies, Koen and colleagues have critiqued the Malaysian business environment for small to medium enterprises.[238] They indicate that these enterprises accounted for 97 per cent of total business establishments in the 2011 economic census, but only 36 per cent of GDP in 2015, below the 50 per cent of GDP average for high-income countries.[239] This demonstrates that the labour productivity of small to medium enterprises is low compared to both their counterparts in other countries and large companies in Malaysia. Regulatory reform facilitating firm entry and exit would help improve their performance. As discussed before, helping smaller companies was one of the major aims of the reform of the Companies Act 2016. Other than the measures already discussed, reviewing the corporate insolvency regime was also a focus of the CLRC.[240] Trade, investment and regional integration have been essential to Malaysia's development and provide increasingly important leverage for productivity enhancing structural reforms.[241] Malaysia is geopolitically well situated to benefit from ongoing efforts to increase the regional connectivity of trade, investment, people and markets. The free trade area under the ASEAN Economic Community, the once hopeful Trans-Pacific Partnership and the One Belt One Road initiative should present numerous business opportunities to large and small companies alike.

Concluding remarks

Since the time as Straits Settlements, Malaysia's development has been largely overshadowed by Singapore.[242] Out of the three colonial ports of Singapore, Penang and Malacca, Singapore was the more developed. After the country's independence, the roadmap of economic development has been largely set out by the Malaysia Plan. Initially, the country's economy relied on the export of commodities such as tin and rubber. The Malaysia Plan sought to transform the country into a manufacturing economy. Today, the country is a leading exporter of electrical appliances, electronic parts and components. There has been an emergence of heavy industries with the establishment of HICOM in 1980. For example, Proton, a car maker in Malaysia, has essentially become a national pride. One characteristic of the economic reform in Malaysia is that it also carries a social mission of wealth redistribution. Bumiputeras, the majority Malay ethnic group, have managed to receive different preferential policies under the NEP. One notable example is the national target of 30:40:30 in corporate equity division. It was intended that by 1990, the holdings of the Bumiputeras should reach 30 per cent, other Malaysians 40 per cent and foreigners 30 per cent. Such an arrangement clearly has the social objective to elevate the supposedly underprivileged ethnic majority group, as opposed to achieving an economically efficient outcome. Towards the end of the NEP, then Prime Minister Mahathir introduced Vision 2020, which has then been integrated into subsequent economic plans such as the NDP. Vision 2020 aims to set out the pathway for Malaysia to reach the status of a developed nation, more specifically, achieving a GNI per capita of US$15,000. With a GNI per capita of US$8,821 in 2016, it seems very unlikely that Malaysia will meet its Vision 2020 goal.

As a former British colony like Singapore and Hong Kong, immediately after its independence, Malaysia managed to draw on a functional regulatory framework for companies essentially based on the UK Companies Act 1948. Its Companies Act 1965 has provided a remarkable level of investor protection and the regime has been regarded highly by, for example, the World Bank and the Cambridge Centre for Business Research. The country's new Companies Act 2016 has built on the success of its predecessor and incorporated new measures to ensure that Malaysia continues to provide a conducive and competitive business environment. In addition to good laws, the regulators in Malaysia are well resourced and active in enforcement. The situation is pretty much like the one in Singapore and Hong Kong, where public enforcement is strong enough to fill the void of private enforcement. Malaysian investors have not been keen to commence litigations to safeguard their own interests.

Politically, the major problem in Malaysia has been inter-racial conflicts. The NEP was a direct result of a riot in 1969 which prompted the government to place more concerns on socio-economic imbalances among the ethnic groups. As a result, the NEP underscored the importance of achieving socio-economic goals alongside pursuing economic growth objectives. However, it may be doubtful whether both set of goals and objectives can be achieved at the same time. For example, as said, a designated ratio of corporate ownership between different ethnic groups may lack a clear economic and business rationale. Furthermore, the perception of corruption remains quite high in Malaysia (at least relative to Singapore and Hong Kong), as evidenced by the 1MDB scandal recently. Culturally, Chinese entrepreneurs have been very successful in Malaysia and this follows from the previous point of whether it makes any economic sense to favour Malay entrepreneurs at the expense of their Chinese counterparts. However, despite having to take various social considerations into account, the Malaysian government is committed to economic development. Infrastructure projects like the North-South Expressway and the Kuala Lumpur International Airport have served to provide better transportation links to support business activities and economic growth. In summary, economic growth in Malaysia has not been the strongest, but it has been inclusive with the simultaneous aim to curtail poverty and reduce income inequalities. Future growth may perhaps hinge on whether the government can manage different, potentially conflicting, goals well.

Notes

1 As of 2016, the three largest economies in the world were the US, China and Japan with GDP at US$18.57 trillion, US$11.2 trillion and US$4.94 trillion respectively. Data from the World Bank.

2 As of 2016, the GDP of Hong Kong, Singapore and Malaysia were US$320.9 billion, US$297 billion and US$296.4 billion respectively. They were ranked at 32th, 36th and 37th respectively amongst 195 economies in the world. Data from the World Bank.

3 International Monetary Fund (2015), 'World Economic Outlook'. Online. Available at: www.imf.org/external/pubs/ft/weo/2015/01/pdf/text.pdf. It is worth noting that both Hong Kong and Singapore had been considered developing countries until the 1990s.

4 World Bank (2017), 'Malaysia: Overview'. Online. Available at: www.worldbank.org/en/country/malaysia/overview. The World Bank has classified its 189 member countries, and all other economies with populations of more than 30,000 into several notable groups. The groups, divided according to gross national income (GNI) per capita in 2015, are: low income, US$1,025 or less; lower middle income, US$1,026–4,035; upper middle income, US$4,036–12,475; and high income, US$12,476 or more.

5 Commission on Growth and Development of the World Bank (2008), 'The Growth Report: Strategies for Sustained Growth and Inclusive Development'. Online. Available at: https://openknowledge.worldbank.org/handle/10986/6507.

6 World Bank (2017), 'Doing Business Report: Malaysia'. Online. Available at: www.doingbusiness.org/data/exploreeconomies/malaysia.

7 Ibid.

8 World Economic Forum (2017), 'Global Competitiveness Report 2016–2017'. Online. Available at: www3.weforum.org/docs/GCR2016-2017/05FullReport/TheGlobalCompetitivenessReport2016-2017_FINAL.pdf.

9 The name 'Malacca' is commonly used in English. However, the name is 'Melaka' in the local Malaysian language, Bahasa Malaysia. In 2017, the Malaysian state government called for standardising the use of the name 'Melaka'. Anon (2017), '"Malacca" now known as "Melaka": State government' in *Straits Times* (3 May 2017).

10 The Commonwealth (2017), 'Malaysia: History'. Online. Available at: http://thecommonwealth.org/our-member-countries/malaysia/history.

11 John Drabble (2000), *An Economic History of Malaysia, c.1800–1990*, Basingstoke: Macmillan, p. 10.

12 Nordin Hussin (2006), *Trade and Society in the Straits of Melaka*, Copenhagen: NIAS Press, p. 13.

13 Drabble (2000), op. cit., pp. 19–20.
14 Hussin (2006), op. cit., p. 13.
15 Drabble (2000), op. cit., pp. 32–33.
16 National Library Board of Singapore (2014), 'Pangkor Treaty is Signed'. Online. Available at: http://eresources.nlb.gov.sg/history/events/07f0aaea-4348-4e34-947e-69448be4407f#2.
17 Ibid.
18 Ibid.
19 Asia-Europe Institute (2017), 'Economic History of Malaysia'. Online. Available at: www.ehm.my/about/history-of-malaysia.
20 Drabble (2000), op. cit., p. 37.
21 Ibid. p. 53.
22 Ibid. p. 57.
23 Ibid. p. 124.
24 Ibid. p. 126.
25 Ibid. p. 150.
26 Ibid.
27 National Library Board of Singapore (2014), 'Malayan Union is Inaugurated'. Online. Available at: http://eresources.nlb.gov.sg/history/events/e8db672a-3571-4fa3-9df0-220e83ee2a88.
28 International Bank for Reconstruction and Development (1958), 'The Economy of the Federation of Malaya'. Online. Available at: http://documents.worldbank.org/curated/en/867961468045084833/Malaya-The-economy-of-the-federation-of-Malaya.
29 Ibid.
30 Ibid.
31 Ibid.
32 Sadono Sukirno (2004), 'Growth and Transformation of the Malaysian Economy'. Online. Available at: www.ekonomikerakyatan.ugm.ac.id/My%20Web/sembul20_1.htm.
33 Ibid.
34 Ibid.
35 Mohammed Yusoff *et al.* (2000), 'Globalisation, Economic Policy, and Equity: The Case of Malaysia' OECD Conference Background Paper. Online. Available at: www.oecd.org/countries/malaysia/2682426.pdf.
36 Ibid.
37 Institute of World Current Affairs (1962), 'Planning for Economic Development in Malaya'. Online. Available at: www.icwa.org/wp-content/uploads/2015/09/GDN-17.pdf.
38 Drabble (2000), op. cit., p. 197.
39 Economic Planning Unit of Malaysia (2013), 'New Economic Policy'. Online. Available at: www.epu.gov.my/en/development-policies/new-economic-policy.
40 Central Intelligence Agency (1985), 'Malaysia's Unfulfilled Promise: The New Economic Policy in Arrears'. Online. Available at: www.cia.gov/library/readingroom/docs/CIA-RDP90T01298R000200200001-0.pdf.
41 Ibid.
42 Tai Chee Wong (1990), 'Industrial Development, the New Economic Policy in Malaysia, and the International Division of Labour' in *ASEAN Economic Bulletin*, 7, p. 107.
43 Ibid. pp. 107–108.
44 Ibid. p. 108.
45 Drabble (2000), op. cit., p. 211.
46 Vijayakumari Kanapath (2003), 'Services Sector Development in Malaysia: Education and Health as Alternate Sources of Growth' AT120 Research Conference paper.

Online. Available at: www.nomurafoundation.or.jp/en/wordpress/wp-content/uploads/2014/09/20030220-21_Vijayakumari_Kanapathy.pdf.

47 Mahmoud Safy Mahmoud and Hoda Mitkee (2017), 'Malaysia's Vision 2020 and the Role of leadership in Economic Development' in *Asian Social Science*, **13**, p. 51.

48 Normaliza Abdul Manaf and Kamarulazizi Ibrahim (2017), 'Poverty Reduction for Sustainable Development: Malaysia's Evidence-Based Solutions' in *Global Journal of Social Sciences Studies*, **3**, p. 32.

49 Economic Planning Unit of Malaysia (2001), 'The Eighth Malaysia Plan'. Online. Available at: www.epu.gov.my/sites/default/files/Bab%201%20-%20Objektif%20Dasar.pdf.

50 Ibid.

51 Manaf and Ibrahim (2017), op. cit., p. 32.

52 National Economic Advisory Council (2010), 'New Economic Model for Malaysia'. Online. Available at: www.epu.gov.my/sites/default/files/nem.pdf.

53 These 12 areas are: Greater Kuala Lumpur/Klang Valley; oil, gas and energy; financial services; wholesale and retail; palm oil and rubber; tourism; electrical and electronics; business services; communications content and infrastructure; education; agriculture; and healthcare.

54 Drabble (2000), op. cit., p. 292.

55 Tim Bunnell *et al.* (2002), 'Kuala Lumpur Metropolitan Area: A Globalizing City–Region' in *Cities*, **19**, p. 358.

56 Drabble (2000), op. cit., p. 193.

57 Bunnell *et al.* (2002), op. cit., p. 358.

58 Ibid. pp. 358–359.

59 Elaine Deng (2012), 'Multinationals Choose Greater Kuala Lumpur and Klang Valley as Asia Base' in *South China Morning Post* (24 September 2012).

60 Bursa Malaysia (2017), 'Corporate History'. Online. Available at: www.bursamalaysia.com/corporate/about-us/corporate-history.

61 The Labuan Federal Territory of Malaysia was designated as an international financial centre in 1990.

62 Bursa Malaysia (2017), 'Overview'. Online. Available at: www.bursamalaysia.com/corporate/about-us/overview.

63 Bernardo Vizcaino (2013), 'Analysis: London, Dubai, Kuala Lumpur in Three-way Fight for Islamic Finance Crown' in *Reuters* (12 November 2013). Online. Available at: www.reuters.com/article/us-islamic-finance-competition-analysis/analysis-london-dubai-kuala-lumpur-in-three-way-fight-for-islamic-finance-crown-idUSBRE9AB0LZ20131112.

64 World Economic Forum (2015), 'These are the Top 9 Countries for Islamic Finance'. Online. Available at: www.weforum.org/agenda/2015/07/top-9-countries-islamic-finance.

65 Vincent Koen *et al.* (2017), 'Malaysia's Economic Success Story and Challenges' OECD Economics Department Working Papers No. 1369. Online. Available at: www.oecd.org/eco/Malaysia-s-economic-success-story-and-challenges.pdf.

66 World Bank (2017), op. cit.

67 Philip Koh (2005), 'Corporate Governance in Malaysia: Reforms in Light of Post-1998 Crisis' in Khai Leong Ho (ed.), *Reforming Corporate Governance in Southeast Asia: Economics, Politics, and Regulations*, Singapore: ISEAS Publishing, p. 103.

68 Company Law Review Steering Group (1998), 'Modern Company Law for a Competitive Economy'. Online. Available at: http://webarchive.nationalarchives.gov.uk/20121101191751/www.bis.gov.uk/files/file23283.pdf.

69 Companies Commission of Malaysia (2017), 'Corporate Law Reform Committee: Scope'. Online. Available at: www.ssm.com.my/en/clrc/scope.

70 Mark Gillen and Pitman Potter (2000), 'The Convergence of Securities Law in Asia' in Gerry Ferguson and Douglas Johnston (eds), *Asia-Pacific Legal Development*, Vancouver: UBC Press, pp. 42–43.

71 Sau Ngan Wong and Shanthi Kandiah (2008), 'Financial Sector Legal Developments' in Kwame Jomo and Sau Ngan Wong (eds), *Law, Institutions and Malaysian Economic Development*, Singapore: NUS Press, pp. 96–97.
72 Ibid. 98.
73 Malaysian Code on Corporate Governance 2007, para. 2.2.
74 Listing Requirements of Bursa Malaysia, para. 15.26.
75 Malaysian Code on Corporate Governance 2017, para. 3.1.
76 Companies Commission of Malaysia (2017), op. cit.
77 Ibid.
78 Ibid.
79 Anil Josh (2005), 'An Insight to Corporate Law Reform in Malaysia' Corporate Law Reform Committee Paper. Online. Available at: www.ssm.com.my/files/clrc/articles/CLRCArt1.pdf.
80 Ibid. p. 5.
81 Corporate Law Reform Committee (2007), 'A Consultative Document on Creating a Conducive Legal and Regulatory Framework for Business'. Online. Available at: www.ssm.com.my/files/clrc/consultation_documents/cd7.pdf.
82 Companies Act 1965, s. 14(1).
83 Corporate Law Reform Committee (2007), op. cit., para. 8.7; Companies Act 2016, s. 9.
84 For example, Singapore, and this has been discussed in the relevant part in the previous Chapter.
85 Companies Act 1965, s. 16. The documentary requirements included memorandum and articles of association of the company; a declaration of compliance a declaration by each director; a cover letter; and a copy of the company name approval.
86 Section 14 of the Companies Act 2016 contains provisions regarding the information required in an application.
87 Companies Act 1965, s. 132(1).
88 [1925] Ch 407.
89 Corporate Law Reform Committee (2006), 'A Consultative Document on Clarifying and Reformulating the Directors' Role and Duties'. Online. Available at: www.ssm.com.my/files/clrc/consultation_documents/cd5.pdf.
90 UK Companies Act 2006, s. 174.
91 Companies Act 2016, s. 213(2).
92 Corporate Law Reform Committee (2006), op. cit., para. 3.18.
93 Companies Act 2016, s. 214.
94 Companies Act 1965, Ninth Schedule; Companies Act 2016, s. 249(4) and Fifth Schedule.
95 Corporate Law Reform Committee (2006), op. cit., paras. 1.34–1.38.
96 Companies Act 2016, s. 230.
97 See the adoption of the Enlightened Shareholder Value approach in Section 172 of the UK Companies Act 2006.
98 *Greenhalgh* v. *Arderne Cinemas Ltd (No 2)* [1951] Ch 286.
99 Corporate Law Reform Committee (2006), op. cit., para. 4.7.
100 Companies Act 1965, Third Schedule.
101 Malaysian Code on Corporate Governance 2017, para. 4.1.
102 Malaysian Code on Corporate Governance 2012, Recommendation 3.5.
103 World Bank (2012), 'The 2012 Corporate Governance ROSC for Malaysia'. Online. Available at: https://openknowledge.worldbank.org/bitstream/handle/10986/20446/908220ROSC0Box0laysia0201200PUBLIC0.pdf?sequence=1&isAllowed=y.
104 Ibid. p. 5.
105 Ibid. p. 2.
106 Mathias Siems (2016), 'CBR Extended Shareholder Protection Index'. Online. Available at: www.repository.cam.ac.uk/bitstream/handle/1810/256566/cbr-spi-30-

countries-codebook-and-methodology.pdf?sequence=9&isAllowed=y. See also Dionysia Katelouzou and Mathias Siems (2015), 'Disappearing Paradigms in Shareholder Protection: Leximetric Evidence for 30 Countries, 1990–2013' in *Journal of Corporate Law Studies*, **15**.

107 Companies Act 1965, s. 132(1); Companies Act 2016, s. 213(1).
108 [1970] VR 434.
109 Companies Act 2016, s. 581(1).
110 Corporate Law Reform Committee (2007), 'A Consultative Document on the Review of Criminal, Civil and Administrative Sanctions in the Companies Act 1965'. Online. Available at: www.ssm.com.my/files/clrc/consultation_documents/cd11.pdf.
111 Companies Act 2016, s. 591.
112 World Bank (2012), op. cit., p. 13.
113 Ibid.
114 Ibid. p. 15.
115 Ibid. p. 16.
116 Ibid.
117 Securities Commission Malaysia (2015), 'Regulatory Philosophy' Online. Available at: www.sc.com.my/wp-content/uploads/eng/html/aboutUs/scRegulatoryPhilosophy_150305.pdf.
118 Gillen and Potter (2000), op. cit., p. 43.
119 Capital Markets and Services Act 2007, s. 179.
120 Ibid. s. 182.
121 Ibid. s. 188.
122 Ibid. s. 188(4).
123 Ibid. s. 220.
124 Ibid. ss. 200 and 201(6).
125 Ishaque Qureshit (1995), 'Regulatory Mechanisms of Securities Trading in Malaysia' in *Pacific Rim Law and Policy Journal*, **4**, pp. 655–656.
126 Ibid. p. 659. See also Securities Industry Act 1983, s. 41(1).
127 Aiman Sulaiman (2008), 'Financial Misreporting and Securities Fraud – Public and Private Enforcement' in *Australian Journal of Corporate Law*, **22**.
128 Ibid. p. 32.
129 World Bank (2012), op. cit., p. 15.
130 Securities Commission Malaysia (2017), 'Enforcement Statistics'. Online. Available at: www.sc.com.my/enforcement/enforcement-statistics.
131 Raziah Bi Mohamed Sadique *et al.* (2010), 'Corporate Fraud: An Analysis of Malaysian Securities Commission Enforcement Releases' in *International Journal of Social, Behavioral, Educational, Economic, Business and Industrial Engineering*, **4**, p. 1188.
132 Securities Commission Malaysia (2011), *Corporate Governance Blueprint 2011*, Kuala Lumpur: Securities Commission Malaysia, pp. 65–66.
133 *Securities Commission Malaysia* v. *Yeow Kheng Chew and others* (High Court of Malaya at Kuala Lumpur: WA-22NCC-300–07/2017).
134 Securities Commission Malaysia (2017), 'Civil Actions and Regulatory Settlements'. Online. Available at: www.sc.com.my/post_archive/civil-action-in-2017.
135 Capital Markets and Services Act 2007, s. 201(1).
136 Sulaiman (2008), op. cit., p. 45.
137 Companies Act 2016, s. 346.
138 UK Companies Act 2006, s. 994 and the relevant discussions in previous chapters about Hong Kong and Singapore.
139 Mohammad Salim and Philip Lawton (2008), 'The Law in a Post-Colonial State: The Shareholders' Oppression Remedy in Malaysia' in *Global Jurist*, **8**, p. 20.
140 Companies Act 1965, s. 181A-E; Companies Act 2016, s. 347.
141 (1843) 2 Hare 461.

142 Mohammad Salim and Deborah Kaur (2012), 'The Statutory Derivative Action in Malaysia' in *Bond Law Review*, **24**, pp. 132–133.
143 UK Companies Act 2006, s. 260(1); Singapore Companies Act (Cap 50, 2006 Rev Ed), s. 216A(1)(c).
144 Salim and Kaur (2012), op. cit., p. 155.
145 Note this critique is no longer true as under section 347(3) the Companies Act 2016, 'the right of any person to bring, intervene in, defend or discontinue any proceedings on behalf of a company at common law is abrogated.'.
146 Vivian Chen (2017), 'The Statutory Derivative Action in Malaysia: Comparison with an Australian Judicial Approach' in *Asian Journal of Comparative Law*, **12**.
147 Ibid.
148 Corporate Law Reform Committee (2007), 'A Consultative Document on Members' Rights and Remedies'. Online. Available at: www.ssm.com.my/files/clrc/consultation_documents/cd6.pdf.
149 Companies Act 2016, s. 348(2).
150 Salim and Kaur (2012), op. cit., p. 125.
151 The Commonwealth (2017), op. cit.
152 Parliament of Malaysia (2016), 'General Information'. Online. Available at: www.parlimen.gov.my/yang-di-pertuan-agong.html?uweb=yg&.
153 BBC (2013), 'Malaysia Vote: PM Najib Razak's Barisan Nasional wins'. Online. Available at: www.bbc.co.uk/news/world-asia-22422172.
154 Office of the Prime Minister Malaysia (2014), 'Tun Dr. Mahathir Mohamad'. Online. Available at: www.pmo.gov.my/home.php?menu=page&page=1645.
155 Diane Mauzy and R.S. Milne (1999), *Malaysian Politics under Mahathir*, Abingdon: Routledge, p. 2.
156 Patrick Low (2013), *Leading Successfully in Asia*, Heidelberg: Springer, p. 243.
157 Ibid.
158 Kyodo (2017), '"My Child is Lost": Mahathir Bemoans Sale of Proton to Chinese' in *South China Morning Post* (25 May 2017).
159 Ibid.
160 Matthew Campbell and En Han Choong (2017), 'Malaysia Eyes Sale of Proton as Mahathir's Auto Dream Dies' in *Bloomberg* (16 May 2017). Online. Available at: www.bloomberg.com/news/articles/2017-05-16/malaysia-eyes-sale-of-proton-as-mahathir-s-auto-power-dream-dies.
161 BBC (2003), 'Mahathir's Economic Legacy'. Online. Available at: http://news.bbc.co.uk/1/hi/business/3151942.stm.
162 Karminder Dhillon (2009), *Malaysian Foreign Policy in the Mahathir Era, 1981–2003: Dilemmas of Development*, Singapore: NUS Press, p. 97.
163 Ibid.
164 BBC (2003), op. cit.
165 Mohamed Ishak (2006), 'Tun Dr. Mahathir and the Notion of "Bangsa Malaysia"' in *Journal of international Studies*, **2006**.
166 Department of Statistics Malaysia (2016), 'Current Population Estimates, Malaysia, 2014–2016'. Online. Available at: www.dosm.gov.my/v1/index.php?r=column/ctheme&menu_id=L0pheU43NWJwRWVSZklWdzQ4TlhUUT09&bul_id=OWlxdEVoYlJCS0hUZzJyRUcvZEYxZz09.
167 Shamsul Haque (2003), 'The Role of the State in Managing Ethnic Tensions in Malaysia' in *American Behavior Scientist*, **47**, p. 244.
168 Ibid. p. 245.
169 Ibid.
170 Ibid. p. 248.
171 Ibid.
172 Rajah Rasiah and Ishak Shari (2001), 'Market, Government and Malaysia's New Economic Policy' in *Cambridge Journal of Economics*, **25**, p. 61.

173 Ibid.
174 James Chin (2015), 'The Costs of Malay Supremacy' in *New York Times* (27 August 2015).
175 Ibid.
176 Constitution of Malaysia, art. 160.
177 Department of Statistics Malaysia (2011), 'Population Distribution and Basic Demographic Characteristic Report 2010'. Online. Available at: www.dosm.gov.my/v1/index.php?r=column/ctheme&menu_id=L0pheU43NWJwRWVSZklWdzQ4TlhUUT09&bul_id=MDMxdHZjWTk1SjFzTzNkRXYzcVZjdz09.
178 Constitution of Malaysia, art. 3.
179 Yvonne Tew (2011), 'The Malaysian Legal System: A Tale of Two Courts' in *Commonwealth Judicial Journal*, **19**.
180 Constitution of Malaysia, art. 121(1A).
181 Tew (2011), op. cit., p. 5.
182 Constitution of Malaysia, art. 3.
183 Yat Ming Loo (2013), *Architecture and Urban Form in Kuala Lumpur*, Abingdon: Routledge, p. 28.
184 Dunston Ayudurai *et al.* (2002), 'Malaysia' in Michael Zanko (ed.), *The Handbook of Human Resource Management Policies and Practices in Asia-Pacific Economies*, Cheltenham: Edward Elgar, p. 442.
185 Patricia Sloane (1999), *Islam, Modernity and Entrepreneurship among the Malays*, Basingstoke: Palgrave Macmillan, p. 78.
186 Joel Kahn (2006), *Other Malays: Nationalism and Cosmopolitanism in the Modern Malay World*, Honolulu: University of Hawaii Press, p. 90.
187 Firdaus Abdullah *et al.* (2009), 'Developing a Framework of Success of Bumiputera entrepreneurs' in *Journal of Enterprising Communities: People and Places in the Global Economy*, **3**.
188 Syahira Hamidon (2014), *The Development of Malay Entrepreneurship in Malaysia*, Kuala Lumpur: Institut Terjemahan and Buku Malaysia, p. 2.
189 Ibid.
190 Rodrigue Fontaine and Stanley Richardson (2005), 'Cultural Values in Malaysia: Chinese, Malays and Indians Compared' in *Cross Cultural Management*, **12**.
191 It is a term used to describe an individual mental set that guides one's behaviour in Malay culture. See H.M. Dahlan (1991), 'Local Values in Intercultural Management' in *Malaysian Management Review*, **26**.
192 Moni Lai Storz (1999), 'Malay and Chinese Values Underlying the Malaysian Business Culture' in *International Journal of Intercultural Relations*, **23**.
193 Seong Chee Tham (1971), 'Tradition, Values and Society among the Malays' in *Review of Southeast Asian Studies*, **4**.
194 Storz (1999), op. cit., pp. 123–124.
195 Ibid.
196 Selywn Parker (2013), 'Malaysia's Waning Political Monopoly' in *World Finance* (5 July 2013). Online. Available at: www.worldfinance.com/special-reports/malaysias-waning-political-monopoly.
197 Ibid.
198 China Daily (2012), '80% of 40 Richest Malaysia are Ethnic Chinese' in *China Daily* (3 February 2012).
199 New Straits Times (2017), 'Malaysia's Top 10 Richest People on Forbes List' in *New Straits Times* (2 March 2017).
200 Heng Pek Koon (1997), 'Robert Kuok and the Chinese Business Network in Eastern Asia: A Study in Sino-Capitalism' in Timothy Brook and Hy Luong (eds.), *Culture and Economy: The Shaping of Capitalism in Eastern Asia*, Ann Arbor: University of Michigan Press, p. 156.
201 Irene Sia (1995), 'Robert Kuok: Taipan Incorporated' in *Jati Journal of Southeast Asian Studies*, **1**, p. 57.

202 Xueying Li (2015), 'Remembering Lee Kuan Yew: "The Greatest Chinese outside Mainland China"' in *Straits Times* (25 March 2015).
203 Sia (1995), op. cit., p. 65.
204 Ian Bremmer (2016), 'These 5 Facts Explain the State of Global Corruption' in *Time* (17 March 2016).
205 Malaysian Investment Development Authority (2017), 'Developed Infrastructure'. Online. Available at: www.mida.gov.my/home/developed-infrastructure/posts.
206 World Shipping Council (2017), 'Top 50 World Container Ports'. Online. Available at: www.worldshipping.org/about-the-industry/global-trade/top-50-world-container-ports.
207 Port Klang Authority (2012), 'Background'. Online. Available at: www.pka.gov.my/index.php/en/about-us-/port-klang-authority-/background-.html.
208 Ibid.
209 James Chin and Joern Dosch (2015), 'The Strongman: An Introduction' in James Chin and Joern Dosch (eds), *Malaysia Post-Mahathir: A Decade of Change*, Singapore: Marshall Cavendish.
210 Tony Merna and Cyrus Njiru (2002), *Financing Infrastructure Projects*, London: Thomas Telford, p. 112.
211 Kuala Lumpur International Airport (2017), 'About KLIA'. Online. Available at: www.klia.com.my/index.php?m=airport&c=info&id=1&aid=1.
212 Kuala Lumpur International Airport (2017), 'About klia2'. Online. Available at: www.klia.com.my/index.php?m=airport&c=info&id=3&aid=2.
213 Malaysia Airports (2017), 'Skypark Terminal Sultan Abdul Aziz Shah Airport'. Online. Available at: www.malaysiaairports.com.my/?m=business&c=business_about&id=38.
214 Hanif Kara (2007), 'Kuala Lumpur International Airport' Archnet Review Report 2554.MAL. Online. Available at: https://archnet.org/system/publications/contents/1566/original/FLS1809.pdf?1384750483.
215 Petronas Twin Towers (2015), 'Overview'. Online. Available at: www.petronastwintowers.com.my/about#petronas_TwinTowers.
216 Ibid.
217 Malaysian Investment Development Authority (2017), op. cit.
218 Tun Razak Exchange (2017), 'About Tun Razak Exchange'. Online. Available at: http://trx.my/about-tun-razak-exchange.
219 Islamic Finance News (2016), 'Malaysia Catalyses Financial Centre Ambitions with Tun Razak Exchange' in *Islamic Finance News* (31 March 2016). Online. Available at: www.islamicfinancenews.com/malaysia-catalyzes-financial-center-ambitions-with-tun-razak-exchange.html.
220 Yantoultra Ngui *et al.*, (2016), 'Malaysian Leader Najib Razak Promised Openness, but Dissent Over 1MDB Stifled' in *Wall Street Journal* (30 December 2016).
221 Islamic Finance News (2016), op. cit.
222 Ibid.
223 The Malaysian Bar (2008), 'About Us'. Online. Available at: www.malaysianbar.org.my/bar_council.html.
224 The Legal Profession Qualifying Board Malaysia (1999), 'New List of Recognised Law Degrees (LL.B.) from the United Kingdom'. Online. Available at: www.lpqb.org.my/index.php?option=com_content&view=article&id=96&Itemid=77.
225 The Malaysian Bar (2012), '"Unattractive" Legal Profession'. Online. Available at: www.malaysianbar.org.my/national_young_lawyers/unattractive_legal_profession.html.
226 International Monetary Fund (2014), 'Malaysia: Financial Sector Assessment Program Banking System Spillovers – Technical Note'. Online. Available at: www.imf.org/en/Publications/CR/Issues/2016/12/31/Malaysia-Financial-Sector-Assessment-Program-Banking-System-Spillovers-Technical-Note-41475.

227 Ibid.
228 Rozana Sani (2016), 'More than Numbers' in *New Straits Times* (1 September 2016).
229 These nine challenges are: (1) establishing a united Malaysian nation made up of one Bangsa Malaysia (Malaysian Race); (2) creating a psychologically liberated, secure and developed Malaysian society; (3) fostering and developing a mature democratic society; (4) establishing a fully moral and ethical society; establishing a matured liberal and tolerant society; (6) establishing a scientific and progressive society; (7) establishing a fully caring society; (8); ensuring an economically just society, in which there is a fair and equitable distribution of the wealth of the nation; (9) establishing a prosperous society with an economy that is fully competitive, dynamic, robust and resilient.
230 CNBC (2015), 'How the 1MDB Scandal Impacts Malaysia'. Online. Available at: www.cnbc.com/video/2015/07/28/how-the-1mdb-scandal-impacts-malaysia.html.
231 World Bank (2017), 'Malaysia Economic Monitor June 2017: Data for Development'. Online. Available at: www.worldbank.org/en/country/malaysia/publication/malaysia-economic-monitor-june-2017-data-for-development.
232 International Monetary Fund (2015), 'IMF Survey: Favorable Prospects for Malaysia's Diversified Economy'. Online. Available at: www.imf.org/en/News/Articles/2015/09/28/04/53/socar030315c.
233 Koen *et al.* (2017), op. cit.
234 Ibid. p. 26.
235 Ibid. p. 27.
236 Ministry of Science, Technology and Innovation (2016), 'PM's Strong Leadership Paving Clearer Directions to Nation's STI Advancement'. Online. Available at: www.mosti.gov.my/wp-content/uploads/2017/03/PRESS-RELEASE-PMS-STRONG-LEADERSHIP-PAVING-CLEARER-DIRECTIONS-TO-NATIONS-STI-ADVANCEMENT.pdf.
237 OECD (2016), *OECD Reviews of Innovation Policy: Malaysia 2016*, Paris: OECD, p. 158.
238 Koen *et al.* (2017), op. cit., p. 32.
239 Ibid.
240 Corporate Law Reform Committee (2007), 'A Consultative Document on Corporate Insolvency, Rehabilitation and Charges'. Online. Available at: www.ssm.com.my/en/clrc/consultation-document/cd10.
241 Koen *et al.* (2017), op. cit., p. 32.
242 Drabble (2000), op. cit., p. 292.

References

Abdul Manaf, Normaliza and Ibrahim, Kamarulazizi (2017), 'Poverty Reduction for Sustainable Development: Malaysia's Evidence-Based Solutions' in *Global Journal of Social Sciences Studies*, **3**.

Abdullah, Firdaus; Hamali, Jamil; Deen, Abdul Rahman; Saban, Gluma; Abg Abdurahman, Abg Zainoren, (2009), 'Developing a Framework of Success of Bumiputera entrepreneurs' in *Journal of Enterprising Communities: People and Places in the Global Economy*, **3**.

Anon (2017), '"Malacca" now known as "Melaka": State government' in *Straits Times* (3 May 2017).

Asia-Europe Institute (2017), 'Economic History of Malaysia'. Online. Available at: www.ehm.my/about/history-of-malaysia.

Ayudurai, Dunston; Yahaya, Siti Rohani; and Zainuddin, Sharifuddin (2002), 'Malaysia' in Michael Zanko (ed.), *The Handbook of Human Resource Management Policies and Practices in Asia-Pacific Economies*, Cheltenham: Edward Elgar.

BBC (2003), 'Mahathir's Economic Legacy'. Online. Available at: http://news.bbc.co.uk/1/hi/business/3151942.stm.

BBC (2013), 'Malaysia Vote: PM Najib Razak's Barisan Nasional wins'. Online. Available at: www.bbc.co.uk/news/world-asia-22422172.

Bremmer, Ian (2016), 'These 5 Facts Explain the State of Global Corruption' in *Time* (17 March 2016).

Bunnell, Tim; Barter, P.; and Morshidi, S. (2002), 'Kuala Lumpur Metropolitan Area: A Globalizing City–Region' in *Cities*, **19**.

Bursa Malaysia (2017), 'Corporate History'. Online. Available at: www.bursamalaysia.com/corporate/about-us/corporate-history.

Bursa Malaysia (2017), 'Overview'. Online. Available at: www.bursamalaysia.com/corporate/about-us/overview.

Campbell, Matthew and Choong, En Han (2017), 'Malaysia Eyes Sale of Proton as Mahathir's Auto Dream Dies' in *Bloomberg* (16 May 2017). Online. Available at: www.bloomberg.com/news/articles/2017-05-16/malaysia-eyes-sale-of-proton-as-mahathir-s-auto-power-dream-dies.

Central Intelligence Agency (1985), 'Malaysia's Unfulfilled Promise: The New Economic Policy in Arrears'. Online. Available at: www.cia.gov/library/readingroom/docs/CIA-RDP90T01298R000200200001-0.pdf.

Chen, Vivian (2017), 'The Statutory Derivative Action in Malaysia: Comparison with an Australian Judicial Approach' in *Asian Journal of Comparative Law*, **12**.

Chin, James (2015), 'The Costs of Malay Supremacy' in *New York Times* (27 August 2015).

Chin, James and Dosch, Joern (2015), 'The Strongman: An Introduction' in James Chin and Joern Dosch (eds), *Malaysia Post-Mahathir: A Decade of Change*, Singapore: Marshall Cavendish.

China Daily (2012), '80% of 40 Richest Malaysia are Ethnic Chinese' in *China Daily* (3 February 2012).

CNBC (2015), 'How the 1MDB Scandal Impacts Malaysia'. Online. Available at: www.cnbc.com/video/2015/07/28/how-the-1mdb-scandal-impacts-malaysia.html.

Commission on Growth and Development of the World Bank (2008), 'The Growth Report: Strategies for Sustained Growth and Inclusive Development'. Online. Available at: https://openknowledge.worldbank.org/handle/10986/6507.

The Commonwealth (2017), 'Malaysia: Constitution and Politics'. Online. Available at: http://thecommonwealth.org/our-member-countries/malaysia/constitution-politics.

Companies Commission of Malaysia (2017), 'Corporate Law Reform Committee: Scope'. Online. Available at: www.ssm.com.my/en/clrc/scope.

Corporate Law Reform Committee (2006), 'A Consultative Document on Clarifying and Reformulating the Directors' Role and Duties'. Online. Available at: www.ssm.com.my/files/clrc/consultation_documents/cd5.pdf.

Corporate Law Reform Committee (2007), 'A Consultative Document on Creating a Conducive Legal and Regulatory Framework for Business'. Online. Available at: www.ssm.com.my/files/clrc/consultation_documents/cd7.pdf.

Corporate Law Reform Committee (2007), 'A Consultative Document on the Review of Criminal, Civil and Administrative Sanctions in the Companies Act 1965'. Online. Available at: www.ssm.com.my/files/clrc/consultation_documents/cd11.pdf.

Corporate Law Reform Committee (2007), 'A Consultative Document on Members' Rights and Remedies'. Online. Available at: www.ssm.com.my/files/clrc/consultation_documents/cd6.pdf.

Corporate Law Reform Committee (2007), 'A Consultative Document on Corporate Insolvency, Rehabilitation and Charges'. Online. Available at: www.ssm.com.my/en/clrc/consultation-document/cd10.

Company Law Review Steering Group (1998), 'Modern Company Law for a Competitive Economy'. Online. Available at: http://webarchive.nationalarchives.gov.uk/20121101191751/www.bis.gov.uk/files/file23283.pdf.

The Commonwealth (2017), 'Malaysia: History'. Online. Available at: http://thecommonwealth.org/our-member-countries/malaysia/history.

Dahlan, H.M. (1991), 'Local Values in Intercultural Management' in *Malaysian Management Review*, **26**.

Deng, Elaine (2012), 'Multinationals Choose Greater Kuala Lumpur and Klang Valley as Asia Base' in *South China Morning Post* (24 September 2012).

Department of Statistics Malaysia (2011), 'Population Distribution and Basic Demographic Characteristic Report 2010'. Online. Available at: www.dosm.gov.my/v1/index.php?r=column/ctheme&menu_id=L0pheU43NWJwRWVSZklWdzQ4TlhUUT09&bul_id=MDMxdHZjWTk1SjFzTzNkRXYzcVZjdz09.

Department of Statistics Malaysia (2016), 'Current Population Estimates, Malaysia, 2014–2016'. Online. Available at: www.dosm.gov.my/v1/index.php?r=column/ctheme&menu_id=L0pheU43NWJwRWVSZklWdzQ4TlhUUT09&bul_id=OWlxdEVoYlJCS0hUZzJyRUcvZEYxZz09.

Dhillon, Karminder (2009), *Malaysian Foreign Policy in the Mahathir Era, 1981–2003: Dilemmas of Development*, Singapore: NUS Press.

Drabble, John (2000), *An Economic History of Malaysia, c.1800–1990*, Basingstoke: Macmillan.

Economic Planning Unit of Malaysia (2001), 'The Eighth Malaysia Plan'. Online. Available at: www.epu.gov.my/sites/default/files/Bab%201%20-%20Objektif%20Dasar.pdf.

Economic Planning Unit of Malaysia (2013), 'New Economic Policy'. Online. Available at: www.epu.gov.my/en/development-policies/new-economic-policy.

Fontaine, Rodrigue and Richardson, Stanley (2005), 'Cultural Values in Malaysia: Chinese, Malays and Indians Compared' in *Cross Cultural Management*, **12**.

Gillen, Mark and Potter, Pitman (2000), 'The Convergence of Securities Law in Asia' in Gerry Ferguson and Douglas Johnston (eds), *Asia-Pacific Legal Development*, Vancouver: UBC Press.

Hamidon, Syahira (2014), *The Development of Malay Entrepreneurship in Malaysia*, Kuala Lumpur:Institut Terjemahan and Buku Malaysia.

Haque, Shamsul (2003), 'The Role of the State in Managing Ethnic Tensions in Malaysia' in *American Behavior Scientist*, **47**.

Hussin, Nordin (2006), *Trade and Society in the Straits of Melaka*, Copenhagen: NIAS Press.

Institute of World Current Affairs (1962), 'Planning for Economic Development in Malaya'. Online. Available at: www.icwa.org/wp-content/uploads/2015/09/GDN-17.pdf.

International Bank for Reconstruction and Development (1958), 'The Economy of the Federation of Malaya'. Online. Available at: http://documents.worldbank.org/curated/en/867961468045084833/Malaya-The-economy-of-the-federation-of-Malaya.

International Monetary Fund (2014), 'Malaysia: Financial Sector Assessment Program Banking System Spillovers – Technical Note'. Online. Available at: www.imf.org/en/Publications/CR/Issues/2016/12/31/Malaysia-Financial-Sector-Assessment-Program-Banking-System-Spillovers-Technical-Note-41475.

International Monetary Fund (2015), 'World Economic Outlook'. Online. Available at: www.imf.org/external/pubs/ft/weo/2015/01/pdf/text.pdf.

International Monetary Fund (2015), 'IMF Survey: Favorable Prospects for Malaysia's Diversified Economy'. Online. Available at: www.imf.org/en/News/Articles/2015/09/28/04/53/socar030315c.

Ishak, Mohamed (2006), 'Tun Dr. Mahathir and the Notion of 'Bangsa Malaysia' in *Journal of international Studies*, **2006**.

Islamic Finance News (2016), 'Malaysia Catalyses Financial Centre Ambitions with Tun Razak Exchange' in *Islamic Finance News* (31 March 2016). Online. Available at: www.islamicfinancenews.com/malaysia-catalyzes-financial-center-ambitions-with-tun-razak-exchange.html.

Josh, Anil (2005), 'An Insight to Corporate Law Reform in Malaysia' Corporate Law Reform Committee Paper. Online. Available at: www.ssm.com.my/files/clrc/articles/CLRCArt1.pdf.

Kahn, Joel (2006), *Other Malays: Nationalism and Cosmopolitanism in the Modern Malay World*, Honolulu: University of Hawaii Press.

Kanapath, Vijayakumari (2003), 'Services Sector Development in Malaysia: Education and Health as Alternate Sources of Growth' AT120 Research Conference paper. Online. Available at: www.nomurafoundation.or.jp/en/wordpress/wp-content/uploads/2014/09/20030220-21_Vijayakumari_Kanapathy.pdf.

Kara, Hanif (2007), 'Kuala Lumpur International Airport' Archnet Review Report 2554. MAL. Online. Available at: https://archnet.org/system/publications/contents/1566/original/FLS1809.pdf?1384750483.

Katelouzou, Dionysia and Siems, Mathias (2015), 'Disappearing Paradigms in Shareholder Protection: Leximetric Evidence for 30 Countries, 1990–2013' in *Journal of Corporate Law Studies*, **15**.

Koen, Vincent; Asada, Hidekatsu; Nixon, Stewart; Rahuman, Mohamed; Mohd Arif, A.Z. (2017), 'Malaysia's Economic Success Story and Challenges' OECD Economics Department Working Papers No. 1369. Online. Available at: www.oecd.org/eco/Malaysia-s-economic-success-story-and-challenges.pdf.

Koh, Philip (2005), 'Corporate Governance in Malaysia: Reforms in Light of Post-1998 Crisis' in Khai Leong Ho (ed.), *Reforming Corporate Governance in Southeast Asia: Economics, Politics, and Regulations*, Singapore: ISEAS Publishing.

Koon, Heng Pek (1997), 'Robert Kuok and the Chinese Business Network in Eastern Asia: A Study in Sino-Capitalism' in Timothy Brook and Hy Luong (eds.), *Culture and Economy: The Shaping of Capitalism in Eastern Asia*, Ann Arbor: University of Michigan Press.

Kuala Lumpur International Airport (2017), 'About KLIA'. Online. Available at: www.klia.com.my/index.php?m=airport&c=info&id=1&aid=1.

Kuala Lumpur International Airport (2017), 'About klia2'. Online. Available at: www.klia.com.my/index.php?m=airport&c=info&id=3&aid=2.

Kyodo (2017), '"My Child is Lost": Mahathir Bemoans Sale of Proton to Chinese' in *South China Morning Post* (25 May 2017).

The Legal Profession Qualifying Board Malaysia (1999), 'New List of Recognised Law Degrees (LL.B.) from the United Kingdom'. Online. Available at: www.lpqb.org.my/index.php?option=com_content&view=article&id=96&Itemid=77.

Li, Xueying (2015), 'Remembering Lee Kuan Yew: "The Greatest Chinese outside Mainland China"' in *Straits Times* (25 March 2015).

Loo, Yat Ming (2013), *Architecture and Urban Form in Kuala Lumpur*, Abingdon: Routledge.

Low, Patrick (2013), *Leading Successfully in Asia*, Heidelberg: Springer.

Mahmoud, Mahmoud Safy and Mitkee, Hoda (2017), 'Malaysia's Vision 2020 and the Role of leadership in Economic Development' in *Asian Social Science*, **13**.

Malaysia Airports (2017), 'Skypark Terminal Sultan Abdul Aziz Shah Airport'. Online. Available at: www.malaysiaairports.com.my/?m=business&c=business_about&id=38.

The Malaysian Bar (2008), 'About Us'. Online. Available at: www.malaysianbar.org.my/bar_council.html.

The Malaysian Bar (2012), 'Unattractive' Legal Profession'. Online. Available at: www.malaysianbar.org.my/national_young_lawyers/unattractive_legal_profession.html.

Malaysian Investment Development Authority (2017), 'Developed Infrastructure'. Online. Available at: www.mida.gov.my/home/developed-infrastructure/posts.

Mauzy, Diane and Milne, R.S. (1999), *Malaysian Politics under Mahathir*, Abingdon: Routledge.

Merna, Tony and Njiru, Cyrus (2002), *Financing Infrastructure Projects*, London: Thomas Telford.

Ministry of Science, Technology and Innovation (2016), 'PM's Strong Leadership Paving Clearer Directions to Nation's STI Advancement'. Online. Available at: www.mosti.gov.my/wp-content/uploads/2017/03/PRESS-RELEASE-PMS-STRONG-LEADERSHIP-PAVING-CLEARER-DIRECTIONS-TO-NATIONS-STI-ADVANCEMENT.pdf.

Mohamed Sadique, Raziah Bi; Roudaki, Jamal; Clark, Murray; and Alias, Norhayati (2010), 'Corporate Fraud: An Analysis of Malaysian Securities Commission Enforcement Releases' in *International Journal of Social, Behavioral, Educational, Economic, Business and Industrial Engineering*, **4**.

National Economic Advisory Council (2010), 'New Economic Model for Malaysia'. Online. Available at: www.epu.gov.my/sites/default/files/nem.pdf.

National Library Board of Singapore (2014), 'Pangkor Treaty is Signed'. Online. Available at: http://eresources.nlb.gov.sg/history/events/07f0aaea-4348-4e34-947e-69448be4407f#2.

National Library Board of Singapore (2014), 'Malayan Union is Inaugurated'. Online. Available at: http://eresources.nlb.gov.sg/history/events/e8db672a-3571-4fa3-9df0-220e83ee2a88.

New Straits Times (2017), 'Malaysia's Top 10 Richest People on Forbes List' in *New Straits Times* (2 March 2017).

Ngui, Yantoultra; Fernandez, Celine and; Barta, Patrick (2016), 'Malaysian Leader Najib Razak Promised Openness, but Dissent Over 1MDB Stifled' in *Wall Street Journal* (30 December 2016).

OECD (2016), *OECD Reviews of Innovation Policy: Malaysia 2016*, Paris: OECD.

Office of the Prime Minister Malaysia (2014), 'Tun Dr. Mahathir Mohamad'. Online. Available at: www.pmo.gov.my/home.php?menu=page&page=1645.

Parker, Selywn (2013), 'Malaysia's Waning Political Monopoly' in *World Finance* (5 July 2013). Online. Available at: www.worldfinance.com/special-reports/malaysias-waning-political-monopoly.

Parliament of Malaysia (2016), 'General Information'. Online. Available at: www.parlimen.gov.my/yang-di-pertuan-agong.html?uweb=yg&.

Petronas Twin Towers (2015), 'Overview'. Online. Available at: www.petronastwintowers.com.my/about#petronas_TwinTowers.

Port Klang Authority (2012), 'Background'. Online. Available at: www.pka.gov.my/index.php/en/about-us-/port-klang-authority-/background-.html.

Qureshit, Ishaque (1995), 'Regulatory Mechanisms of Securities Trading in Malaysia' in *Pacific Rim Law and Policy Journal*, **4**.

Rasiah, Rajah and Shari, Ishak (2001), 'Market, Government and Malaysia's New Economic Policy' in *Cambridge Journal of Economics*, **25**.

Salim, Mohammad and Lawton, Philip (2008), 'The Law in a Post-Colonial State: The Shareholders' Oppression Remedy in Malaysia' in *Global Jurist*, **8**.

Salim, Mohammad and Kaur, Deborah (2012), 'The Statutory Derivative Action in Malaysia' in *Bond Law Review*, **24**.

Sani, Rozana (2016), 'More than Numbers' in *New Straits Times* (1 September 2016).

Securities Commission Malaysia (2011), *Corporate Governance Blueprint 2011*, Kuala Lumpur: Securities Commission Malaysia.

Securities Commission Malaysia (2015), 'Regulatory Philosophy' Online. Available at: www.sc.com.my/wp-content/uploads/eng/html/aboutUs/scRegulatoryPhilosophy_150305.pdf.

Securities Commission Malaysia (2017), 'Enforcement Statistics'. Online. Available at: www.sc.com.my/enforcement/enforcement-statistics.

Securities Commission Malaysia (2017), 'Civil Actions and Regulatory Settlements'. Online. Available at: www.sc.com.my/post_archive/civil-action-in-2017.

Sia, Irene (1995), 'Robert Kuok: Taipan Incorporated' in *Jati Journal of Southeast Asian Studies*, **1**.

Siems, Mathias (2016), 'CBR Extended Shareholder Protection Index'. Online. Available at: www.repository.cam.ac.uk/bitstream/handle/1810/256566/cbr-spi-30-countries-codebook-and-methodology.pdf?sequence=9&isAllowed=y.

Sloane, Patricia (1999), *Islam, Modernity and Entrepreneurship among the Malays*, Basingstoke: Palgrave Macmillan.

Storz, Moni Lai (1999), 'Malay and Chinese Values Underlying the Malaysian Business Culture' in *International Journal of Intercultural Relations*, **23**.

Sukirno, Sadono (2004), 'Growth and Transformation of the Malaysian Economy'. Online. Available at: www.ekonomikerakyatan.ugm.ac.id/My%20Web/sembul20_1.htm.

Sulaiman, Aiman (2008), 'Financial Misreporting and Securities Fraud – Public and Private Enforcement' in *Australian Journal of Corporate Law*, **22**.

Tew, Yvonne (2011), 'The Malaysian Legal System: A Tale of Two Courts' in *Commonwealth Judicial Journal*, **19**.

Tham, Seong Chee (1971), 'Tradition, Values and Society among the Malays' in *Review of Southeast Asian Studies*, **4**.

Tun Razak Exchange (2017), 'About Tun Razak Exchange'. Online. Available at: http://trx.my/about-tun-razak-exchange.

Vizcaino, Bernardo (2013), 'Analysis: London, Dubai, Kuala Lumpur in Three-way Fight for Islamic Finance Crown' in *Reuters* (12 November 2013). Online. Available at: www.reuters.com/article/us-islamic-finance-competition-analysis/analysis-london-dubai-kuala-lumpur-in-three-way-fight-for-islamic-finance-crown-idUSBRE9AB0LZ20131112.

Wong, Sau Ngan and Kandiah, Shanthi (2008), 'Financial Sector Legal Developments' in Kwame Jomo and Sau Ngan Wong (eds), *Law, Institutions and Malaysian Economic Development*, Singapore: NUS Press.

Wong, Tai Chee (1990), 'Industrial Development, the New Economic Policy in Malaysia, and the International Division of Labour' in *ASEAN Economic Bulletin*, **7**.

World Bank (2012), 'The 2012 Corporate Governance ROSC for Malaysia'. Online. Available at: https://openknowledge.worldbank.org/bitstream/handle/10986/20446/908220ROSC0Box0laysia0201200PUBLIC0.pdf?sequence=1&isAllowed=y.

World Bank (2017), 'Malaysia: Overview'. Online. Available at: www.worldbank.org/en/country/malaysia/overview.

World Bank (2017), 'Doing Business Report: Malaysia'. Online. Available at: www.doingbusiness.org/data/exploreeconomies/malaysia.

World Bank (2017), 'Malaysia Economic Monitor June 2017: Data for Development'. Online. Available at: www.worldbank.org/en/country/malaysia/publication/malaysia-economic-monitor-june-2017-data-for-development.

World Economic Forum (2015), 'These are the Top 9 Countries for Islamic Finance'. Online. Available at: www.weforum.org/agenda/2015/07/top-9-countries-islamic-finance.

World Economic Forum (2017), 'Global Competitiveness Report 2016–2017'. Online. Available at: www3.weforum.org/docs/GCR2016-2017/05FullReport/TheGlobalCompetitivenessReport2016-2017_FINAL.pdf.

World Shipping Council (2017), 'Top 50 World Container Ports'. Online. Available at: www.worldshipping.org/about-the-industry/global-trade/top-50-world-container-ports.

Yusoff, Mohammed; Abu Hasan, Fauziah; and Abdul Jalil, Suhaila (2000), 'Globalisation, Economic Policy, and Equity: The Case of Malaysia' OECD Conference Background Paper. Online. Available at: www.oecd.org/countries/malaysia/2682426.pdf.

7 Globalisation, regionalism and interdependence of economies

The global financial crisis trigged by the US subprime mortgage crisis in the summer of 2007 spread rapidly to all parts of the world. While the developed nations fell into the worst global economic recession since the Great Depression of the 1930s, most Asian countries did not suffer to the same extent from the effects of the financial crisis. Even after that, the impact on the region overall was less severe than on the rest of the world.[1] Yet, it is certainly not true to say that Asia was totally immune from the crisis as the region was pummelled by the sharp drop in external demand from the developed countries. But most countries bounced back relatively quickly. Prior to the global financial crisis, the 'decoupling thesis' was popular among some Asian investors and policymakers.[2] The thesis argued that Asian economies could rely on intra-Asia trade and achieve rapid growth regardless of the performance of the US economy. However, the credit crunch cast doubt on such a thesis as every Asian country was somehow dragged into growth recession by the US crisis.[3]

Surprisingly, however, most Asian economies, especially China, Hong Kong and Singapore, were able to recover quickly in the aftermath of crisis.[4] A number of factors explain why these Asian economies performed better than their Western counterparts. First, they had limited exposure to the subprime-related financial derivatives.[5] Second, their dependence on foreign borrowing has declined since 1997 and this had minimised their exposure to financial stress emanating from the advanced economies. Third, their financial institutions and systems had been rebuilt after the Asian financial crisis. The banking systems are generally much healthier in the light of asset quality, profitability, capital adequacy and low non-performing loan ratio.[6] Last but not least, a closer trade connection among Asian countries with a high relevance to China's growth strengthens their resistance to the financial tsunami, which is also the main focus of this chapter. The chapter is organised into two major sections after this introduction. The first section explores China as a driving engine to the economic growth of the world and Asia in particular. This section is further divided into three subsections which use Hong Kong, Singapore and Malaysia as three case countries to examine the role of China in Asian economies, in particular after the global financial crisis, in terms of bilateral trade, foreign direct investment (FDI) and economic cooperation. The second section proceeds to examine the world trading system and explores why economies are looking beyond the World Trade Organisation (WTO) as a multilateral trade platform and going for alternative arrangements such as the Association of Southeast Asian Nations (ASEAN), Trans-Pacific Partnership (TPP) and China's One Belt One Road (OBOR) initiative, all of which may play an influential role in the future grow of Asia.

Rise of China as engine of global and Asian growth

From a historical perspective, Maddison has provided a detailed analysis of the development of the Chinese economy over the past millennium.[7] He concluded that Chinese per capita income was higher than that of Europe from the tenth to the early fifteenth century and it was the world's biggest economy for several centuries before falling into decline. Maddison even predicted that China's open-door policy in 1978 was likely to resume its normal position as the world's top economy by 2015. Maddison's prediction has turned into reality. In 2010, China overtook Japan as the second largest economy in the world and in 2011 it had a share of about 15 per cent of world GDP and 21 per cent of world population.[8] China's GDP had maintained a robust growth with an average annual rate of appropriately 10 per cent for a few decades, despite a slowdown in recent years. China's National Bureau of Statistics reported that the economy's growth in the first half-year of 2015 had slowed down to 7 per cent, the slowest growth in six years.[9] The IMF now projects that growth between 2017 and 2021 for China is expected to average 6.4 per cent, compared to 6.0 per cent in 2016.[10] In retrospect Japan, Taiwan and South Korea also had their extended growth periods for a quarter of century before slowing down as China is now showing, despite the different economic approaches.[11]

But will the rising China be another US? The answer is probably negative due to Chinese cultural uniqueness and the careful controls over its ideology and society by the Beijing government to enable stability and harmony, but not American-style freedom.[12] This can be portrayed by the 'China Dream' put forth by Chinese President Xi Jinping.[13] The China Dream has been a Communist party ambition since Mao took power in 1949, which is to build a moderately prosperous society and realise national rejuvenation. Under such an ideology, a new policy was launched in the Central Conference on Work Relating to Foreign Affairs held in Beijing on 28–29 November 2015, led by President Xi Jinping and Premier Li Keqiang and with all the top leaders of China. In view of the fact that China overtook the US as the largest trading partner for 124 countries in 2012,[14] the new policy is to develop a distinctive diplomatic approach befitting its role as a major country. Instead of leaning one-sidedly on the US and EU, China is going to stress good political relations at the expense of economic gain in order to improve relations and diminish fear of relentless economic competition from China. The new Asian Infrastructure Investment Bank initiated by China is part of this policy.

While the 'China threat' discourse is frequently posed by politicians against China, many commentators believe that the world could gain benefits from the rise of China.[15] Its international economic influence can be better illustrated by its role in the global commodity market. China consumes more than half of the world's iron ore and more than 30 per cent of the world's aluminium and zinc.[16] China espouses a strongly 'neo-mercantilist' foreign economic policy, based on securing natural resources – energy, minerals and food.[17] Its strong domestic demand is the driving force behind the global commodity market. According to the IMF, there is a positive linkage between the growth of China and the world economy.[18] A 1 per cent point rise in China's growth could increase emerging market economies' growth by about 0.1 per cent, and 0.4 per cent point of the US's growth. The positive effect tends to build over time, as the trade of those emerging markets will get a further boost, highlighting China's relevance for global commodity market.

From 1990 to 2013, China's share of world GDP rose sharply from 3.8 per cent to 15.4 per cent (Figure 7.1). Given the central role of trade and openness in the expansion of China's economy, its trade had also experienced a similarly rapid growth. The share of China's trade in total world imports and exports also significantly increased four-times in two decades.[19] In the context of Asia, Figure 7.2 illustrates that China's share of emerging and developing Asia's GDP rose from 36.4 per cent in 1990 to 68.3 per cent in 2013. During the same period, its impacts on the five founding members of ASEAN were even more obvious, rising from 130.9 per cent to 456.2 per cent in the light of the share of GDP. For the developed Asian economies, it is found that a decade of China's growth has increased GDP per capita by about 17 per cent.[20] Likewise, China's trade accounted for nearly 40 per cent of the region's total imports and exports recently.[21] Those values represent a significant contribution to regional growth. The sources of such growth are mainly from improvements in trade.[22] The Asian economies benefit from higher export prices to the Chinese market. Moreover, the lower relative import prices,

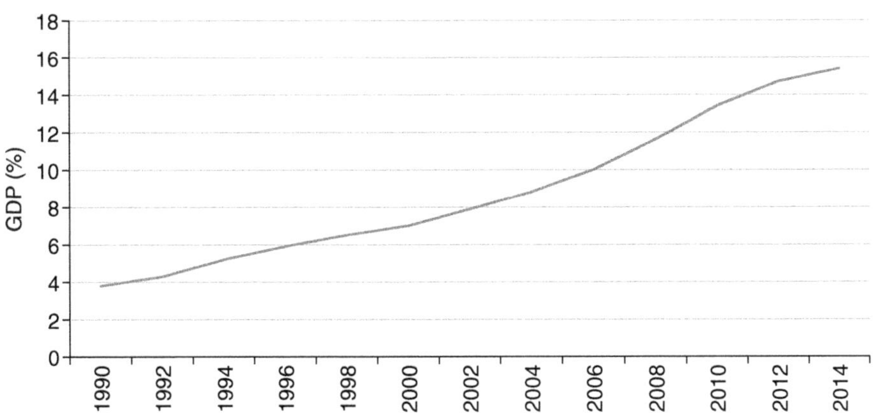

Figure 7.1 Share of China in world GDP (%).

Source: IMF.

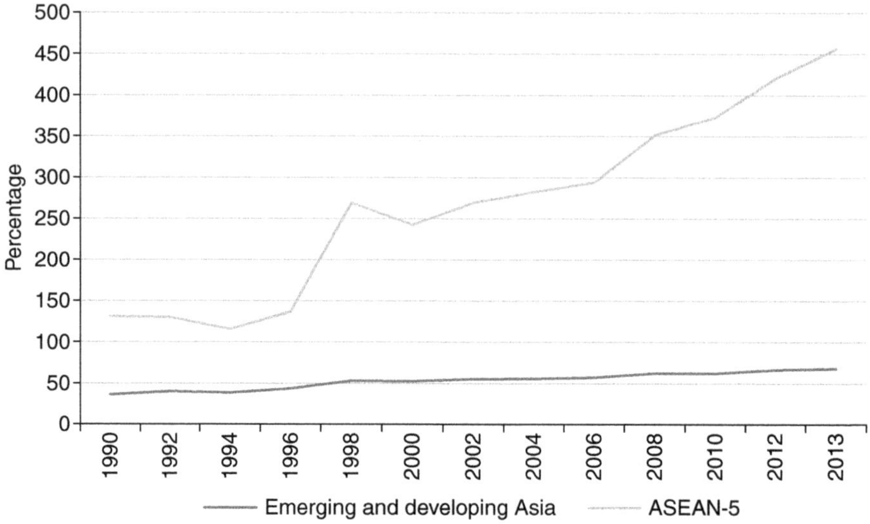

Figure 7.2 Share of China in GDP in emerging and developing Asia and in ASEAN-5 (%).

Source: IMF.

Note

Emerging and developing Asia includes 29 countries while ASEAN-5 consists of Indonesia, Malaysia, Philippines, Thailand and Vietnam.

particularly from imports of Chinese durable goods, induce substantial accumulation of machinery and equipment capital.

In recent years, China has been the biggest trade partner of ASEAN. Their bilateral trade reached US$319.5 billion in 2012, with a proportion of 12.9 per cent of total ASEAN trade.[23] In the field of FDI, China ranked fifth in the top ten sources of FDI inflows into ASEAN with an amount of direct investment of US$14 billion in 2010–12, following the EU, ASEAN, Japan and the US. The impacts of the rising China on Asian economies are profound. A richer China can pull up its neighbours by providing a huge market for goods, a source of millions of tourists, profitable investment opportunities, demand for financial and other services in which China lags behind, and countless other mutually beneficial activities.[24] Specifically speaking, first, China contributes to the global markets by importing intermediate inputs from elsewhere, especially emerging Asia, to produce goods for developed countries.[25] Second, China's investment-oriented growth can boost commodity-exporting emerging market economies via higher commodity demand and prices. Third, China can support growth of the other economies through higher FDI flows into them.[26] The following subsections will proceed to consider what role China plays in the growth of Asian neighbourhoods, in particular during their recovery in the post-financial crisis era, in light of its bilateral trade relations with the three other economies studied by this book as an illustration.

China and Hong Kong

Since Hong Kong's reunification with China in 1997, Hong Kong has become a Special Administrative Region of China under the ideology 'One Country, Two Systems'. Their close relationship was described by Edgar Cheng, the former Chairman of the Council of the Stock Exchange of Hong Kong as follows:

> Hong Kong's success as a global centre in the long term will, however, be closely bound up with our success in becoming not just a 'window on China and China's window on the world', but the main international financial centre of a China which will be part of the world market.[27]

Various factors are attributable to the Chinese government's economic support to Hong Kong. First, a politically stable and economically prosperous Hong Kong is important for China to showcase the 'One Country, Two Systems' formula that it hopes to sell to Taiwan.[28] Also, while the Taiwan question looms larger, Beijing is likely to provide more economic support to Hong Kong in order to relieve the pressure from the electoral protest.[29] Second, China's long-term grand strategy is to build a 'Greater Financial System' based on enhanced economic integration within the entire Greater China area.[30] Third, Hong Kong remains vital to China's economy as foreign companies often use Hong Kong as their staging post for investing in China.[31] For this purpose, Beijing cannot afford to let Hong Kong lose its global competitiveness in financial and banking markets.

Trade

Hong Kong and mainland China have maintained a close trading relationship with each other for many years. On the one hand, in the past decade, China was Hong Kong's largest destination of re-exports and supplier of imports, on average accounting for 49.8 per cent and 45.7 per cent of Hong Kong's total re-exports and imports respectively.[32] Since 2005, China had replaced the US to become the largest destination of Hong Kong's domestic exports. On the other hand, Hong Kong has also played an important role in the external trade with China, accounting for 36 per cent on average of total domestic exports over the last decade. As illustrated in Table 7.1, domestic exports to China decreased from HK$37.9 billion to HK$24.8 billion during 2004 to 2013. Despite the notable growth in the year of 2005, domestic exports to China have shown an overall downward trend since 2006, particularly in 2008 and 2009, mainly attributable to the weak external demand as the result of the global financial crisis.

In 2013, the value of Hong Kong's total merchandise trade reached HK$7,620.4 billion or appropriately 359 per cent of GDP in that year.[33] The value of exports was HK$3,559.7 billion, accounting for 168 per cent of GDP. Among those export countries, the mainland was Hong Kong's largest domestic

Table 7.1 Merchandise trade between Hong Kong with Mainland China, 2004–13 (HK$100 million)

Type of trade	*2004*	*2005*	*2006*	*2007*	*2008*	*2009*	*2010*	*2011*	*2012*	*2013*
Domestic export	379 (+3.1)	446 (+17.8)	403 (–9.8)	406 (+0.8)	348 (–14.4)	267 (–23.3)	312 (+17.1)	307 (–1.7)	260 (–15.2)	248 (–4.8)
Re–exports	8,506 (+20.5)	9,680 (+13.8)	11,159 (+15.3)	12,677 (+13.6)	13,357 (+5.4)	12,366 (–7.4)	15,670 (+26.7)	17,167 (+9.6)	18,317 (+6.7)	19,245 (+5.1)
Imports	9,183 (+16.9)	10,493 (+14.3)	11,930 (+13.7)	13,297 (+11.5)	14,107 (+6.1)	12,494 (–11.4)	15,298 (+22.4)	16,968 (+10.9)	18,409 (+8.5)	19,421 (+5.5)

Source: Hong Kong Census and Statistics Department.

Note
Figures in parentheses denote year-on-year percentage changes.

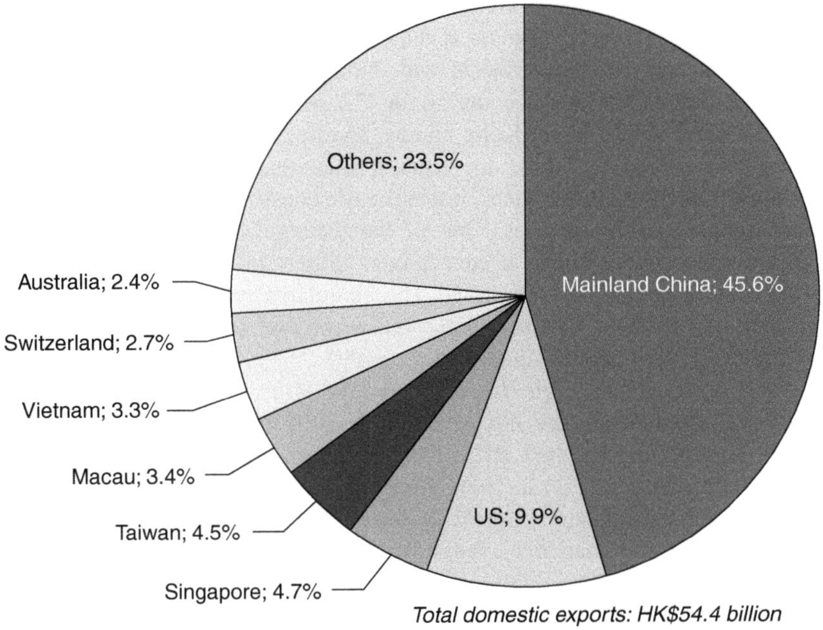

Figure 7.3 Hong Kong's domestic exports by main destination, 2013.

Source: Trade and Industry Department of Hong Kong.

export market, followed by the US and Singapore. The mainland absorbed HK$24.8 billion worth of goods, or 45.6 per cent of the total domestic exports in 2013 (Figure 7.3). By contrast, Hong Kong's re-exports to China registered a year-on-year increase except the period of the credit crunch. The value of Hong Kong's re-exports to China climbed substantially from HK$850.6 billion in 2004 to HK$1,924.5 billion in 2013, representing an average annual growth of 10.9 per cent over the period. Performance was particularly outstanding in 2004 and 2010 with annual growth rates of 20.5 per cent and 26.7 per cent respectively. However, due to the global economic downturn, the year of 2009 witnessed a slight drop on re-exports. Likewise, the change in the value of Hong Kong's imports from the mainland was mostly promising in the last decade, with the only negative growth of –11.4 per cent recorded in 2009. The value of Hong Kong's imports from the mainland increased substantially from HK$918.3 billion in 2004 to HK$1942.1 billion in 2013, representing an average annual growth rate of 9.8 per cent.

FDI

Apart from being each other's biggest trading partner, the mainland and Hong Kong are also each other's largest source of FDI. This reflects the close economic links between the two economies. In Table 7.2, the mainland was the biggest recipient for Hong Kong's direct investment outflow, with a share of 41.3 per cent of the total outward direct investment at the end of 2012. By 2013, the mainland had approved nearly 360,000 projects with Hong Kong investment, involving HK$5,158.9 billion in total and accounting for 47.7 per cent of the mainland's total FDI.[34] In the early 1980s, Hong Kong mainly invested in China's real estate and hotels, and later in industry.[35] Over the years, it has extended to other sectors such as retail trade, tourist-related services, infrastructure construction and various business and communication services. One of the distinguishing characteristics of Hong Kong's investment is that it concentrates largely on Guangdong Province due to their close geographic proximity. The cumulative value of Hong Kong's realised direct investment in Guangdong was estimated at HK$1,557.7 billion, accounting for 61.9 per cent of Guangdong's total.[36]

Similarly, as shown in Table 7.3, the mainland is also Hong Kong's largest source of realised FDI. In the five years from 2008 to 2012, the total direct investment from China reached HK$11,682.6 billion, accounting for 36.4 per cent of the total inflow of FDI in Hong Kong in the same period. It was clearly ahead of British Virgin Islands, Bermuda, the Netherlands and the US. According to the Census and Statistics Department of Hong Kong, investment and holding, real estate, professional and business services attracted the largest amount of the total FDI in 2012, at HK$4,976.8 billion.[37] This was followed by banking, import/export, wholesale and retail trades at HK$925.7 billion and HK$800.1 billion respectively. However, 'round-tripping' FDI may boost the statistics of trade and investment between China and Hong Kong.[38] Money sent offshore resulting from the overstatement of imports will return to China as FDI from a foreign entity, and then these funds return in new forms to Hong Kong. Official estimates of this type of FDI by the Chinese Government are not available, but others have suggested that such flows may account for up to 25 per cent of the total inflows.[39] Likewise, Singapore also has significant round-tripping Chinese FDI. Motives for China's round-tripping FDI are not only tax advantages and fiscal incentives,[40] but also related to the safety and risk management of capital.[41]

Table 7.2 Top five destinations of Hong Kong's direct investment abroad, 2008–12 (HK$ billion)

Country	*2008*	*2009*	*2010*	*2011*	*2012*
China	2,624.6	2,731.5	2,499.4	3,019.1	3,217.4
British Virgin Islands	845.9	938.8	2,805.4	3,177.9	3,178.5
Bermuda	79.1	188.3	183.0	231.8	295.5
UK	74.3	87.2	191.7	210.7	214.3
Cayman Islands	40.8	31.3	33.1	57.2	140.7
Total	4,106.7	4,497.5	6,464.2	7,416.7	7,795.8

Source: Census and Statistics Department, Hong Kong.

Table 7.3 Top five sources of FDI in Hong Kong, 2008–12

Country	*2008*	*2009*	*2010*	*2011*	*2012*
China	1,694.2	2,193.0	2,467.4	2,636.7	2,691.3
British Virgin Islands	1,579.8	1,876.9	1,725.6	1,928.4	2,288.2
Bermuda	327.2	412.3	504.4	595.1	606.4
Netherlands	309.7	383.6	464.6	514.4	555.4
US	216.1	295.4	219.0	306.5	277.8
Total	4,980.5	6,077.8	6,325.0	7,046.6	7,628.7

Source: Census and Statistics Department, Hong Kong.

Economic cooperation after the global financial crisis

As an integral part of the international nexus, Hong Kong was quite exposed to the global downturn due to its heavy dependence on external trade and financial services. Its economic growth was down to 2.5 per cent in 2008 from 6.4 per cent in 2007, and then further dropped to a lowest level of –2.5 per cent in 2009 since 1999.[42] The stock market had seen a sharp decline, with the Hang Seng index plunging 48 per cent from a year before, unseen since 1974. Total export also dropped by 21.8 per cent year-on-year in January 2009.[43] However, Hong Kong recovered impressively from the global recession and quickly bounced back to the pre-crisis level with GDP growth rate of 6.8 per cent in 2010. According to the WTO, several crucial reasons can explain why Hong Kong has recovered fairly quickly.[44] First, the economy's resilience to external shocks is also underpinned by the flexibility of its wages and prices, which is especially important as the Hong Kong dollar remains pegged to the US dollar. Hong Kong's flexibility in wages is due to the lack of strong labour organisations and in prices being exposed to the world market for a long period.[45] But flexible wages were replaced by a universal statutory minimum wage in Hong Kong in 2011 to relieve income inequality.[46] Second, Hong Kong's prudent regulation has shielded it from the worst effects of the global financial tsunami. Last but also most importantly, it is mainly owing to China's strong recovery and its closer economic relationship with Hong Kong.

When the international financial crisis broke out in 2008, the mainland government was highly concerned about its impact on Hong Kong. In December of that year, it introduced 14 policies in seven areas to support Hong Kong's financial stability and economic development.[47] In the meantime, in December 2008, the Beijing government set out a Framework programme to establish the Pearl River Delta as one of the world's most competitive regions by 2020.[48] Under the Framework, the central government vowed to 'solidify' Hong Kong's position as a premier international centre for finance, trade, maritime, logistics and high value-added services. All these policies played a positive role in boosting confidence, strengthening capability to defuse risks and stimulating the economic recovery of Hong Kong. In January 2009, the central government launched more policies, including the signing of a RMB200 billion currency swap agreement by the People's Bank of China with the Hong Kong Monetary Authority.[49] As of 2013, a total of 216 Hong Kong banks joined the RMB clearing platform, and the amount of cross-border RMB settlement in Hong Kong reached RMB3.84 trillion, accounting for 82.9 per cent of the total cross-border RMB settlement of China.[50] The balance of Hong Kong's RMB customer deposits and depository receipts reached RMB1 trillion. Hong Kong has become the world's largest offshore RMB trading centre.

In addition, the mainland has offered and promised more future, non-reciprocal economic concessions to Hong Kong. Through a series of agreements under the Closer Economic Partnership Arrangement (CEPA) between Hong Kong and the mainland,[51] the mainland has unilaterally given WTO-plus market access treatment to the service providers from Hong Kong, in addition to zero tariffs for all imports of goods from Hong Kong. Between 2004 and 2013, the two economies have signed ten supplements to broaden and enrich the content of CEPA. The recent Supplement X to CEPA signed on 29 August 2013 provides for a total of 73 new measures on trade in services, adding the total number of such measures to 403 since CEPA took effect in 2003. Since 2013, four new agreements have been signed, covering areas such as services, investment and economic and technical cooperation.[52]

The impacts of CEPA are far-reaching. At the domestic level, the CEPA offers peculiar benefits to Hong Kong's financial sector. For example, the recognition of the qualification of Hong Kong securities professionals for the purpose of practising on the mainland extends the professional activities of Hong Kong's securities industry to one of the major markets in the world.[53] Furthermore, the measures in relation to banking, securities and insurance envisaged in CEPA would tremendously strengthen Hong Kong's position versus other global finance centres by relocating financial resources from the mainland to Hong Kong.[54] In addition, an important innovation in CEPA is the establishment of the category of 'Hong Kong service supplier' in Annex 5 of Supplement X. That is, to qualify for the CEPA benefits, a company must be duly incorporated in Hong Kong and have engaged in substantive business operations for three to five years, pay profit tax, have a business premise, and employ 50 per cent or more of its staff in Hong Kong. In essence, this measure compels international services to set up a substantial commercial presence in Hong Kong should they plan to enjoy the preferential treatment offered under CEPA. This will undoubtedly bring international investors to Hong Kong to strengthen the city's financial sector. At the international level, these market opportunities are also available to companies of any nationality based in Hong Kong. Under CEPA's trade and investment facilitation agenda both sides have undertaken, inter alia, to improve the transparency of laws and regulations, and the protection of intellectual property rights. Therefore, CEPA may bring benefits to the broader WTO membership.[55]

With closer economic cooperation between mainland China and Hong Kong, a subsequent question will arise: will Hong Kong be replaced by Shanghai? Many worry that legalising Shanghai as an international financial centre in the State Council's regulation will lead to the demise of Hong Kong.[56] But Huang and Yeung argue that Hong Kong and Shanghai coexisted in the last century.[57] 'Shangkong' (a partnership between Shanghai and Hong Kong) with their distinct appeal can achieve better results together than on their own and compete with the established centres of New York and London.[58]

China and Singapore

In Kim's view, Singapore–China relations can be described as 'economy in command'.[59] Geostrategic considerations are important calculations in Singapore–China policies, although earlier Singapore favoured the Soviet Union over China in seeking international alignments in the wake of its own loss of position in Indonesia.[60] Survival was of paramount concern and Singapore's China policy was a function of both domestic needs and external imperatives. Bilateral trade between Singapore and China has been flourishing since the two countries established diplomatic relations in 1990. Since 1997, China has been Singapore's top foreign investment destination.[61] The entry of China into the WTO and the start of the China–ASEAN tariff reduction plan in 2005 have further opened up the Chinese market. This provides more opportunities for Singapore to improve its bilateral trade relationship with China.

Trade

As demonstrated in Table 7.4, China has been a top-five Singapore trading partner since 2008, covering about one-tenth of Singaporean trade. In 2012, China ranked second in the main destinations of Singapore's merchandise exports, accounting for 10.8 per cent, behind Malaysia (12.3 per cent), but imports from China slightly declined. Due to geographical imperatives described as a 'lips and teeth' relationship, Malaysia and Indonesia are also Singapore's main trading partners.[62] In 2013 Singapore's total trade reached SG$980.2 billion, lower than the previous year's achievement of SG$984.9 billion. Total exports expanded marginally by 0.6 per cent in 2013 while imports declined by 1.6 per cent in the same period.[63] Singapore's bilateral trade with China has been increasing steadily over the years. China became Singapore's largest trading partner in 2013, with bilateral trade increasing 11 per cent from the previous year to SG$113.5 billion, surpassing Malaysia.[64] Trade in services largely contributed to Singapore's external trade. A proportion of trade in services to Singapore's GDP in 2012 was 87.6 per cent, reflecting its growing importance to Singapore's.[65] Transport, travel and business management services accounted for the bulk of Singapore's international trade in services.

FDI

Singapore has traditionally been a major recipient of FDI, third in the region after China and Hong Kong.[66] It seems set to remain an attractive destination for foreign investors, with its business environment still one of the most attractive in

Table 7.4 Trade with top five trading partners, 2008–12 (SG$ million and % of total)

Country	*2008*		*2009*		*2010*		*2011*		*2012*	
	Export	*Import*	*Export*	*Import*	*Export*	*Import*	*Export*	*Import*	*Export*	*Import*
Total	476,762	450,893	391,118	356,299	478,841	423,222	514,741	459,665	510,329	474,554
% of total										
Malaysia	12.1	11.9	11.5	11.6	11.9	11.7	12.2	10.7	12.3	10.6
EU	10.4	12.3	9.6	13.8	10.0	12.3	9.6	12.6	8.9	12.6
China	9.2	10.6	9.7	10.5	10.3	10.8	10.4	10.4	10.8	10.3
US	7.1	11.8	6.6	11.9	6.5	11.5	5.5	10.8	5.4	10.2
Indonesia	10.6	5.5	9.7	5.8	9.4	5.4	10.4	5.3	10.6	5.3

Source: Department of Statistics Singapore.

the world. Table 7.5 illustrates the top five sources of FDI in Singapore by region in 2008–12. The US retained its position as Singapore's top source country of FDI, followed by the Netherlands, British Virgin Island, Japan and the UK. Though China was out of the league, the investment from China rose to SG$14.2 billion in 2012, increasing more than three-fold from 2008.

On the other hand, Table 7.6 shows the top five destinations into which Singapore's direct investment outflowed in 2008–12. Singapore's stock of direct investment overseas reached SG$462.71 billion in 2012, with an increase of 48 per cent from 2008. Financial and insurance services, manufacturing and real estate were the sectors favoured by Singapore investors. Collectively, these sectors attracted about three-quarters of the direct investment abroad. China continued to be the most popular investment region for Singaporean investors, receiving SG$90.5 billion and accounting for 19.6 per cent of Singapore's total outward direct investment in 2012. Singapore's investment projects in China came from sectors such as infrastructure services, environmental services, aviation, healthcare services and logistics.[67] These were areas in which Singapore-based companies wield strong capabilities. Apart from China, other major destinations of Singapore's direct investment were the UK, Hong Kong, Australia and Indonesia.

Table 7.5 Top five sources of FDI in Singapore, 2008–12 (SG$ million)

Country/region	*2008*	*2009*	*2010*	*2011*	*2012*
US	52,758	58,969	67,162	74,666	106,513
Netherlands	61,001	61,512	60,547	69,373	72,723
British Virgin Islands	38,754	39,678	50,116	55,892	59,391
Japan	50,446	50,515	53,577	53,722	59,128
UK	47,569	49,499	48,947	55,654	48,437
China	4,424	9,726	14,029	13,597	14,217
Total	510,585	574,699	626,383	678,909	746,690

Source: Department of Statistics Singapore.

Table 7.6 Top five destinations of Singapore's direct investment abroad, 2008–12 (SG$ million)

Country/region	*2008*	*2009*	*2010*	*2011*	*2012*
China	54,476	62,245	72,434	85,598	90,545
UK	19,925	32,492	39,502	37,255	43,159
Hong Kong	20,054	23,425	25,008	38,903	39,169
Australia	18,122	23,107	33,323	35,339	38,260
Indonesia	22,327	28,162	31,343	34,876	37,252
Total	312,381	372,253	429,363	446,372	462,710

Source: Department of Statistics Singapore.

Economic cooperation after the global financial crisis

When the global financial tsunami came, Singapore was the first Southeast Asian country to step into recession with a dramatic drop in GDP from 9 per cent to 1.7 per cent in 2007–08.[68] However two years later, Singapore's economy bounced back and reached the peak at a record rate of 14.7 per cent in 2010.[69] The quick recovery was driven by a surge in manufacturing activity, resilient exports and stellar performance in tourism-related sectors, a part of which was contributed by the trade with China. While developed countries still live in the shadow of the financial crisis, such a crisis has been turned into a development opportunity for some Asian countries. The year 2009 was a symbolic one for Singapore–China bilateral economic cooperation. Singapore facilitated SG$2 billion of overseas sales and SG$1.2 billion of overseas investment into China by Singapore-based companies.[70] In the meantime, Singapore has set up seven bilateral councils with China co-chaired by both sides' government leaders, underlining the significance both countries place on deepening economic engagement.

In response to the global crisis, the Monetary Authority of Singapore (MAS) established a three-year China–Singapore currency swap arrangement of RMB150 billion with the People's Bank of China (PBOC) on 23 July 2010, to promote bilateral trade and direct investment for the economic development of the two countries.[71] This RMB/SGD swap facility allows the Authority to provide RMB liquidity to financial institutions for trade and financial stability purposes. In addition, the Industrial and Commercial Bank of China's Singapore branch launched RMB clearing services in Singapore in May 2013. This followed the signing of a memorandum of understanding between the MAS and the PBOC on RMB business cooperation. Together, the collaboration between MAS and the Chinese central bank and financial authorities will deepen financial and economic cooperation between China and Singapore, and strengthen regional financial markets.

Singapore–China economic cooperation is even enhanced by the Sino-Singaporean Free Trade Agreement (CSFTA) which was signed on 23 October 2008. According to the Agreement, Singapore pledged to rescind the tariffs on all its imported goods from China from 1 January 2009; and China pledged to realise zero tariff policy on 97.1 per cent of its imported goods from Singapore before 1 January 2012. Besides, the two sides have made commitments higher than those to WTO in the fields of trade in services such as medical care, education and accounting. The CSFTA is the first comprehensive bilateral FTA concluded by China with an Asian country, covering areas ranging from commodity trade and trade in services to customs procedures as well as dispute settlements. Meanwhile, as all the nations across the globe are coping with the financial turbulence, the signing of the Agreement is conducive to maintaining the two nations' trade and economic stability and growth, and will make active contributions to maintaining the world economic stability and promoting trade liberalisation.

Furthermore, as Singapore is one of the ASEAN members, the Singapore–China relation has been covered by the ASEAN-China Free Trade Agreement (ACFTA). Why is Singapore-China going towards the route of bilateral trade agreement

(BTA)? The general view is that there are several perceived benefits from entering into a BTA, apart from gaining greater market access, and lowering business costs by reduction of tariff barriers.[72] First, BTAs that involve economic partnership agreements are comprehensive and involve deeper liberalisation beyond tariff reduction. BTAs can serve as a 'testing ground' for negotiating complex issues bilaterally, and set a precedent for negotiating them multilaterally among a larger group of countries. Second, it is believed that legal provisions of the BTAs can lock in policy reforms, particularly in service and investment which are otherwise difficult to undertake at the multilateral level. Third, BTAs could provide a positive signal towards enhancing economic and strategic cooperation, and address regional security concerns.

China and Malaysia

Although Malaysia established diplomatic relations with China in 1974, their economic relations can be traced back to a few centuries ago. Currently, their economic ties are even stronger, as Malaysia has been China's top trading partner within ASEAN for five consecutive years since 2008, with bilateral trade hitting a record high of nearly RM203.3 billion in 2013.[73] As of the end of 2013, mutual actual investment reached RM22.2 billion, covering more than 5,000 programmes.[74] Malaysia will become the third Asian country after Japan and South Korea, whose bilateral trade with China exceeds RM300 billion in a few years. Malaysia was China's eighth largest trading partner, sixth largest source of imports and eleventh largest export destination in 2013.[75]

Trade

Malaysia's trade ties with China have grown faster than those with the rest of the world, particularly since the Asian financial crisis in 1997–98.[76] The expansion in trade with China is attributed largely to China's success in integrating into the regional and international production networks including product design, supply of inputs, production and distribution.[77] From Table 7.7, the trade between the two economies had been steadily increasing from RM100.88 billion in 2006 to

Table 7.7 Bilateral trade between Malaysia and China, 2009–13 (RM billion)

Year	*Total trade*	*Total exports*	*Total imports*
2006	100.88	42.62	58.26
2007	117.75	53.04	64.71
2008	130.06	63.21	66.85
2009	128.27	67.24	61.03
2010	147.03	80.60	66.43
2011	167.22	91.25	75.97
2012	180.61	88.75	91.86
2013	203.23	96.97	106.26

Source: Department of Statistics Malaysia.

RM203.2 billion in 2013, except for a slight decline in 2009. But also in 2009, China overtook Singapore as Malaysia's major trading partner, accounting for 12.9 per cent of total trade. The trade growth between the two parties is positive at the level of approximately 10 per cent on a year-on-year basis. In 2013, Malaysia–China trade totalled RM203.32 billion, accounting for 14.8 per cent of total Malaysian trade in that year, and a more than six-fold increase compared with that of a decade ago. Exports to China were valued at RM97.17 billion in 2013, contributing 13.5 per cent of total exports, an increase of 9 per cent compared to the previous year. An increase in exports was due to a surge in electrical and electronic products, palm oil and palm oil-based products, refined petroleum products and chemical products. From China's perspective, Malaysia was ranked its eighth largest trading partner. Imports from China rose by 15.9 per cent to RM106.47 billion or 16.4 per cent of Malaysia's total imports in 2013.[78] China was Malaysia's largest import source with manufactured goods accounting for over 90 per cent of total imports.

Malaysia's trade mainly focuses on the Asian market. Its trade with Asia in 2012 increased by 4.1 per cent to reach RM938.65 billion and contributed to 71.7 per cent of Malaysia's global trade.[79] ASEAN accounted for more than one-quarter share of its total trade. The growth in trade is attributed to acceleration in intra-ASEAN trade as well as FTAs signed with trading partners within Asia. China remained the biggest trading partner with Malaysia in 2013, followed by Singapore, Japan and the EU (Figure 7.4). Despite the mounting fears that China

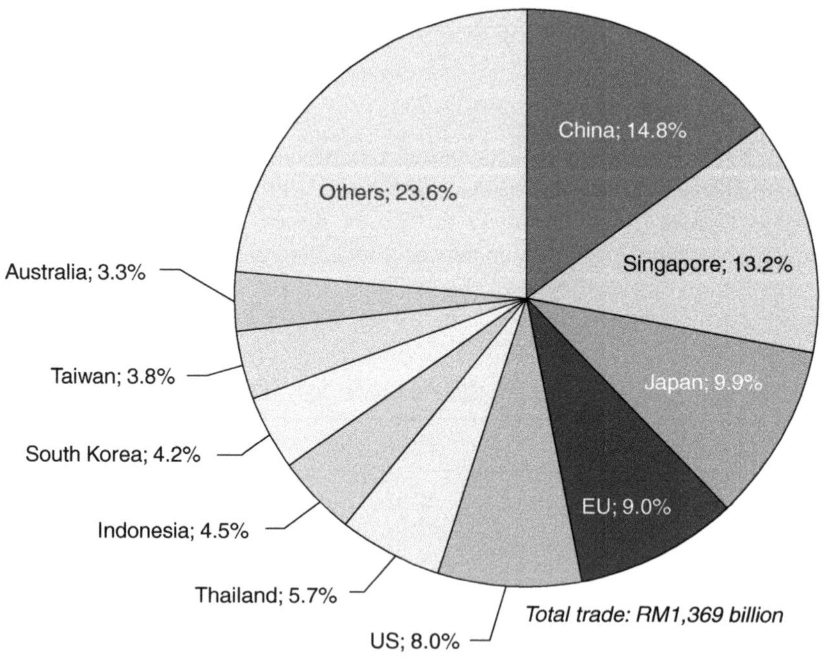

Figure 7.4 Total trade by major countries, 2013 (% of total trade).

Source: Department of Statistics of Malaysia.

would compete with Malaysia to become a more favourable investment location in Asia, trade with China is important for Malaysia to tap directly into the Chinese domestic market and to gain market access indirectly in advanced markets outside the region. China has become a regional production base, importing intermediate goods for further processing and export to developed countries as well as the world's most important consumer market. Therefore, in the long run, the benefits from trade with China overcome the fears of competition.

FDI

Historically, Malaysia relied heavily on FDI for her economic expansion and industrial upgrading. Table 7.8 shows the FDI inflows to Malaysia for the period 2008–13. The top five sources of foreign investment were Japan (21.13 per cent), US (17.78 per cent), Singapore (9.08 per cent), Republic of Korea (8.19 per cent) and Hong Kong (7.17 per cent). China was the seventh largest foreign investor in Malaysia in this period. The investment from China stood just below the Netherlands and surpassed Germany, Taiwan and Indonesia. But the amount of Chinese investment increased more than nine-fold from RM162.2 million in 2009 to RM1,977.8 million in 2012, or 11 per cent of total foreign investment in Malaysia (Table 7.8).

The statistics published by the Malaysia Investment Development Authority show that the number of approved projects dropped from 542 in 2009 to 470 in 2012.[80] By contrast, the China-involved projects increased by 35.3 per cent to 23 per cent in the same period. Compared to ASEAN countries, FDI from China to Malaysia was second only to Singapore and well ahead of the third largest ASEAN source of FDI (i.e. Indonesia). Investments from China were involved in the following industries: electrical and electronic products, chemical products, wood and wood products, non-metallic mineral products, machinery manufacturing, food manufacturing and plastic products manufacturing.

Economic cooperation after the global financial crisis

In response to the recent economic tsunami, the Malaysian government introduced several policy measures to mitigate the adverse impact of the global downturn, and to prevent the economy from slipping into an economic recession. On the external front, the stabilisation and subsequent gradual recovery in the global economy, especially China, benefits Malaysia. Malaysia's exports to Asia in 2009 increased to 49.3 per cent (2008: 45.7 per cent), with exports to China increasing to 12.2 per cent (2008: 9.5 per cent), while exports to advanced economies, including the US, EU and Japan, declined to 31.6 per cent in the same year (2008: 34.6 per cent).[81] Bank Negara Malaysia and the PBOC entered into a bilateral currency swap arrangement to promote bilateral trade and investment in early 2008 with the objective of promoting and facilitating trade settlement in local currency between the two countries. The arrangement was renewed in

Table 7.8 Main sources of FDI to Malaysia, 2009–13 (RM million)

Country	*2009*	*2010*	*2011*	*2012*	*2013**	*Total*
US	2,345.0	11,738.6	2,509.0	295.8	5,239.5	22,127.9 (17.78%)
Australia	323.1	68.6	290.5	150.1	103.5	935.8 (0.75%)
China	162.2	639.5	1,194.2	1,977.8	1,501.6	5,475.3 (4.40%)
Hong Kong	5,315.7	2,766.5	394.9	90.9	359.3	8,927.3 (7.17%)
Indonesia	2.2	12.7	692.5	85.7	214.0	1,007.1 (0.81%)
Japan	7,041.4	4,029.4	10,101.8	2,792.9	2,325.0	26,290.5 (21.13%)
Germany	425.0	1,936.7	1,951.2	693.3	253.0	5,259.2 (4.23%)
Netherlands	479.7	934.6	1,010.0	834.8	2,302.4	5,561.5 (4.47%)
Republic of Korea	455.5	199.2	5,185.1	1,637.0	2,721.8	10,198.6 (8.19%)
Singapore	1,992.5	2,156.7	2,477.7	2,214.6	2,457.0	11,298.5 (9.08%)
Taiwan	716.1	1,255.9	1,394.4	171.6	88.7	3,626.7 (2.91%)
Others	2,886.3	3,318.2	6,947.4	9,974.6	614.0	23,740.5 (19.08%)
Total	22,144.7	29,056.6	34,148.9	20,919.0	18,179.9	124,449.1 (100%)

Source: Malaysia Ministry of Finance.

Note
* January–July 2013.

February 2012. As at 31 December 2013, the Bank's total commitment under the Currency Swap Arrangement was RM90 billion.[82]

A broader Malaysia–China economic relationship is categorised in the ACFTA. The ACFTA is a free trade area among the ten member states of the ASEAN and China and the largest free trade area in terms of population and third largest in terms of nominal GDP. ASEAN–China cooperation has brought a new type of intra-Asian regional cooperation with China, which reflects China's commitment to good-neighbour diplomacy.[83] In the view of Kwek and Tham, ACFTA brings opportunities and challenges at the same time to Malaysia.[84] For Malaysia, ACFTA is seen as having the potential to accelerate the development of economic relations between her and China, and the economic growth of the two countries. The FTA will bring business and trade between the two countries to a new height and also benefit the banking industry which serves as a bridge of economic promotion and trade development.[85]

Lowering the tariff barriers under the ACFTA will increase the market access for Malaysian companies to enter China's market. Malaysian companies could seize the opportunities accorded by this agreement to identify the potential customs duty savings arising from the margin of preference between the most-favoured nation tariff rate and the lower preferential ACFTA tariff rate. Indeed, the Malaysian business community is actively making use of the preferences accorded under ACFTA to export to China. The utilisation of preferential certificates of origin (COO) under ACFTA has been increasing. Under the ACFTA, a total of 47,097 preferential COOs were issued in 2011 valued at US$6.85 billion compared to US$1.04 billion (9,650 COOs) in 2006.[86] However, meanwhile, the ACFTA also drives competition for Malaysia. It pushes Malaysia's producer to out-compete fellow members of ASEAN for a slice of China's market. The trade structure of the ASEAN countries, especially among the older ASEAN-4 (Indonesia, Malaysia, the Philippines and Thailand), is similar and fundamentally competitive, with a high percentage of exports as well as of imports in machinery and transport equipment.[87] Despite the lower tariffs in Malaysia, the reductions of tariffs under the ACFTA are based on reciprocity and hence Malaysian companies will also face heightened competition in the home market. Producers for the home market will therefore have to enhance their competiveness and be less dependent on the home market alone.[88]

The formation of ACFTA has further increased Malaysia's investment opportunity in China. China's large market, abundant human resources and low production cost in combination may provide great opportunity for Malaysian companies to invest there. With rising labour costs and shortage of workers in the domestic market, Malaysia is no longer a cost-competitive location for labour-intensive operations, and this will lead to the option for labour-intensive manufacturers to relocate to cheaper-cost countries like China and Vietnam.[89] In the meantime, China has been working actively with Malaysia to build a model for cooperation in Southeast Asia, with two joint China-Malaysia industrial parks being built in Qinzhou, Guangxi Zhuang autonomous region, and Kuantan, the largest city on Malaysia's eastern coast. The establishment of the Malaysia-

China Kuantan Industrial Park is a bilateral project which is expected to strengthen the bilateral trade and economic ties between the two countries. The Industrial Park is the first bilateral project to be accorded national-level status and is projected to attract RM7.5 billion worth of domestic and foreign investments, as well as create 5,500 jobs by 2020.[90]

Transcontinental and regional cooperation: lessons from ASEAN, TPP and OBOR

According to Acemoglu, there is a large empirical literature on the impact of trade on growth.[91] The effect of trade on growth has attracted much academic and policy attention. Most economists believe that trade promotes growth, and there is both micro and macro evidence consistent with that belief. Some studies find a positive correlation between openness to international trade and economic growth.[92] According to the WTO, the experience of world trade and economic growth since the Second World War also supports the economic case for an open trading system.[93] Tariffs on industrial products have fallen steeply and now average less than 5 per cent in industrial countries. During the first 25 years after the war, world economic growth averaged about 5 per cent per year, a high rate that was partly the result of lower trade barriers. World trade grew even faster, averaging about 8 per cent during the period. The principle of 'comparative advantage' dating back to classical economist David Ricardo contends that countries prosper first by taking advantage of their assets in order to concentrate on what they can produce best, and then by trading these products for products that other countries produce best.[94]

The WTO is the international organisation for liberalising trade. It was established on 1 January 1995 by the Marrakesh Agreement. Before its establishment, the General Agreement on Tariffs and Trade (GATT) provided the rules for much of world trade from 1948 to 1994. The first round of trade negotiations in Havana, Cuba, in 1947 resulted in a package of trade rules and 45,000 tariff concessions affecting US$10 billion of trade, about one fifth of the world's total.[95] Originally in 1947, only 23 countries were involved. When the negotiation took place in Tokyo during the 1970s, there were 102 countries participating. Nowadays, as of 2016, the WTO has 164 member countries. In the WTO, when countries agree to open their markets for goods or services, they 'bind' their commitments. For goods, these bindings amount to ceilings on customs tariff rates. One of the achievements of the Uruguay Round of multilateral trade talks starting in the 1980s was to increase the amount of trade under binding commitments (see Table 7.9). A promise of not raising a trade barrier can enhance the predictability of trade.

The role of the WTO has been three-fold.[96] First, it is a set of rules. At its heart are the WTO agreements, negotiated and signed by the bulk of the world's trading nations. These documents provide the legal ground-rules for international commerce. Two fundamental principles form the foundation of the multilateral trading system, the first of which is the Most-Favoured-Nation requirement.[97]

Table 7.9 Percentages of tariffs bound before and after the Uruguay Round

	Before	*After*
Developed countries	78	99
Developing countries	21	73
Transition economies	73	98

Source: WTO.

Under the WTO agreements, countries cannot normally discriminate between their trading partners. If a member grants a fellow WTO member state a special favour (such as a lower customs duty rate for one of their products), this member has to extend the same for all other members. Second is the National Treatment requirement.[98] Imported and locally produced goods should be treated equally, at least after the foreign goods have entered the market. The same should apply to foreign and domestic services, and to foreign and local trademarks, copyrights and patents. Other than a set of rules, the WTO is also a negotiating forum, where member governments try to sort out the trade problems they face with each other. Finally, the WTO is dispute settler. Trade relations often involve conflicting interests. There is a dispute settlement process written into the WTO agreements, with a view to providing an impartial procedure based on an agreed legal foundation to settle disputes.[99]

There were certain changes in the global environment which undermined GATT's credibility and effectiveness, and catalysed the formation of the WTO.[100] Despite GATT's success in reducing tariffs to a lower level, in light of a series of economic recessions in the 1970s and early 1980s, governments started to devise other forms of protection for sectors facing increased foreign competition. High rates of unemployment and constant factory closures led governments in Western Europe and North America to seek bilateral market-sharing arrangements with competitors and to embark on a subsidies race to maintain their hold on agricultural trade. The creation of the WTO was intended to be a response to all these development. However, according to Van den Bossche and Zdouc, the challenges facing the WTO and the multilateral trading system remains multiple and formidable.[101] According to them, for the potential of international trade to be realised, there must be: (1) good governance at the national level; (2) a further reduction of trade barriers; (3) more development aid; and (4) better international cooperation and global governance of economic globalisation and international trade. One notable development has been the proliferation of bilateral, plurilateral and regional trade agreements. According to Lester and colleagues, since the establishment of the WTO, the number of these agreements has grown rapidly.[102] There were only 124 of them during the GATT years, while the succeeding ten years of the WTO saw an additional 196.

These agreements, collectively known as Regional Trade Agreements (RTAs) to the WTO, are reciprocal preferential trade agreements between two or more partners. Following the notification of the RTA between Mongolia and Japan in

June 2016, all WTO members now have at least one RTA in force.[103] As of June 2017, there are 445 RTAs currently in force.[104] Non-discrimination among trading partners is one of the core principles of the WTO. However, RTAs constitute one of the exemptions and are authorised under the WTO, subject to a set of rules. In line with these rules, and also recognising the need to enhance transparency and increase understanding of RTAs' impact on interests of WTO members, the WTO will gather information on RTAs. Members participating in new negotiations aimed at the conclusion of an RTA are asked to inform the WTO Secretariat of such negotiations. Members which are parties to a newly signed RTA are also asked to send to the Secretariat information on the RTA. Well known examples of RTAs include the EU, the North American Free Trade Agreement, the ASEAN, the Andean Community, the Common Market of the Caribbean and the Economic Community of West African States. The WTO acknowledges that many WTO Members continue to be involved in new RTA negotiations.[105] This includes negotiations in the Asia-Pacific Region for a TPP Agreement, currently between 12 parties; in Asia between ASEAN members and six other WTO Members with which ASEAN has agreements in force (the Regional Comprehensive Partnership Agreement); the Pacific Alliance in Latin America currently between Chile, Colombia, Mexico and Peru; and the Tripartite Agreement between parties in Africa.

It has been argued that deeper economic integration can be accomplished by these RTAs.[106] First, they can be negotiated much faster than the multilateral process. The rise of RTAs is a natural response to the painfully slow progress of the current Doha Round of negotiation under the WTO. The talks, which began in 2001 and were originally supposed to conclude in 2005, are still ongoing. Commentators attribute this failure to the fact that neither developed economies like the US and the EU nor developing countries like China and India were willing or able to make fundamental concessions.[107] Second, it is felt that RTAs can catalyse multilateralism by establishing prototypes for liberalisation in a wide range of trading areas.[108] On the other hand, it is argued that RTAs have the potential to threaten the sustainability of the multilateral trading system, as RTAs by their very nature are inimical to the non-discriminatory principles of the WTO.[109] Some even question the relevance of the WTO, amidst the rise of RTAs, as some of them like the TPP and Transatlantic Trade and Investment Partnership are 'mega-regional' trade negotiations representing an attempt to pioneer new rules among like-minded countries, as an alternative to the existing WTO.[110] The following subsections will proceed to look at some of these RTAs, both existing and proposed, namely, ASEAN, TPP and OBOR, which are important in the context of this book.

ASEAN

ASEAN was established on 8 August 1967 in Bangkok, Thailand, with the signing of the ASEAN Declaration (Bangkok Declaration) by the founding members, namely Indonesia, Malaysia, Philippines, Singapore and Thailand.

Brunei then joined on 7 January 1984, Vietnam on 28 July 1995, Laos and Myanmar on 23 July 1997 and Cambodia on 30 April 1999, making up the ten member states of ASEAN today. For their comparative economic conditions, see Table 7.10. It can be seen that the ten members have a varying degree of development. Singapore and Brunei are the most affluent economies, with Malaysia and Thailand in the middle of the league, and the rest rather less developed, when one considers their GDP per capita. However, in terms of the overall size of the economy, Indonesia and Thailand are indeed the largest in light of their GDP. For about 25 years from 1970 to 1995, ASEAN's GDP grew at an average annual rate of 7 per cent.[111] Today, ASEAN has a total market of about 635 million people and a combined GDP of more than US$2.5 trillion, being the sixth largest economy in the world.

Over the years, ASEAN's overall trade grew from US$10 billion in 1967 to US$2.27 trillion in 2015.[112] With its combined trade value, ASEAN is one of the largest trading entities in the world together with the EU, US, China and Japan. After the past few decades, there have been different lines of ASEAN economic cooperation. Cooperation in trade and investment began with the introduction of the ASEAN Preferential Tariff Arrangement (PTA) in 1977 and would eventually culminate in the attainment of the ASEAN Free Trade Area. Under this arrangement, an ASEAN-based importer will pay a lower tariff rate on a product if it originated from another ASEAN Member Country than if the same product were obtained from a non-ASEAN source. Then in 1992, an agreement concerning the formation of the ASEAN Free Trade Area (AFTA) was signed by the original six ASEAN member states (ASEAN-6): Brunei, Indonesia, Malaysia, the Philippines, Singapore and Thailand. The AFTA now entails all ten members. At the heart of the AFTA is the Common Effective Preferential Tariff (CEPT) scheme. The CEPT goes further than the original Preferential Tariff Arrangement in different ways so as to move ASEAN to its goal of a free trade area.[113] Hence the CEPT requires that the tariff rates of those products included in the scheme ultimately be reduced to 0.5 per cent. The Preferential Tariff

Table 7.10 Comparative economic indicators of ASEAN members, 2015

Country	*GDP (US$ million)*	*GDP per capita (US$)*
Brunei	12,909	30,942
Cambodia	18,463	1,198
Indonesia	857,603	3,357
Laos	12,639	1,831
Malaysia	294,389	9,656
Myanmar	65,391	1,246
Philippines	289,503	2,850
Singapore	291,938	52,744
Thailand	395,726	5,737
Vietnam	193,407	2,109

Source: ASEAN.

Arrangement does not require a reduction of tariffs of this magnitude. It only requires that, whatever tariff rates are applied by an ASEAN country on imports from the rest of the world, a margin of preference be given to ASEAN partners. The number of products included in the CEPT is also much larger than that covered in the Preferential Tariff Arrangement. The CEPT also includes provisions for the elimination of quantitative restrictions, non-tariff barriers and other cross-border measures.

According to ASEAN, more than 99 per cent of the products in the CEPT list of ASEAN-6 have been brought down to the 0.5 per cent tariff range, meaning that the AFTA has now been virtually established.[114] Meanwhile, newer joiners have been working to bring down tariff of products in accordance with the CEPT. Further, following the signing of the Protocol to Amend the CEPT-AFTA Agreement for the Elimination of Import Duties on 30 January 2003, ASEAN-6 has committed to eliminating tariffs on 60 per cent of their products in the CEPT list. The average tariff for ASEAN-6 under the CEPT Scheme is now down to 1.51 per cent from 12.76 per cent when the tariff cutting exercise started in 1993.[115] It is worth noting that ASEAN is not only inward-looking. In 2016, the value of trade in goods within ASEAN amounted to US$276 billion, as opposed to the value of extra-ASEAN trade at US$874 billion.[116] ASEAN has entered into a number of free trade agreements with other Asian nations that are now radically altering the global sourcing and manufacturing landscape.[117] For example, it has the ACFTA with China to reduce tariffs on nearly 8,000 product categories, or 90 per cent of imported goods, to zero. These favourable terms have taken effect between China and ASEAN-6. ASEAN has a similar agreement with India to reduce tariffs on 90 per cent of all traded goods between ASEAN and India, abolishing import-export duties on over 4,000 products. These two agreements have the collective impact of making ASEAN the strategic hub for global sourcing and manufacturing.[118] With ASEAN's own middle-class consumer base of 150 million, this market alone, then coupled with China and India's 250 million each, represents a total middle-class consumer market with complete free trade of some 650 million people. In addition, ASEAN has a combined FTA with Australia and New Zealand, known as the ASEAN Australia New Zealand FTA. The Agreement, which was signed in 2009, has 18 chapters and four annexes, covering various aspects of trade in goods, services and investment, as well as competition and intellectual property rights. It seeks to eliminate at least 90 per cent of all tariff lines within specified timelines, as well as lowering barriers to trade in services to allow greater market access. Along similar lines, an FTA between ASEAN and South Korea was established in 2010, with another one with Japan in the process of negotiation.

Economic cooperation is not restricted to trade only.[119] Cooperation in finance and banking within ASEAN is aimed at promoting the development of capital markets, free movement of capital and other financial resources, including further liberalisation of the use of ASEAN currencies in trade and investments. The ASEAN Ministerial Understanding on Finance Cooperation also covers the areas of banking, customs matters, insurance matters, taxation and public finance, monetary policy cooperation and human resource development in the area of financial services. Cooperation in industry started with the implementation of the ASEAN Industrial Projects in 1976, followed by the ASEAN Industrial Joint Venture Scheme introduced in 1983 and the Brand-to-Brand Complementation scheme of 1988. In 1996, the ASEAN Industrial Cooperation Scheme was adopted to replace the earlier schemes. The scheme seeks to promote joint manufacturing industrial activities between ASEAN-based companies. The establishment of the ASEAN Economic Community (AEC) in 2015 is a wider initiative to promote regional economic integration. For example, according to the AEC Blueprint 2025, among other objectives, the AEC seeks to be a highly integrated and cohesive economy, where there is seamless movement of goods, services, investment, capital and skilled labour within ASEAN in order to enhance ASEAN's trade and production networks, as well as to establish a more unified market for its firms and consumers.[120]

According to Chia, within ASEAN, while tariff elimination had largely been on schedule, there were difficulties with removal of non-tariff barriers and services and investment liberalisation.[121] The AEC is pursuing something akin to what came to be known as the four freedoms in the context of European integration – freedom of movement of goods, services, capital and labour. Low casts doubt on its future.[122] One challenge is the development divide between established and new members, amid the drive to embed an ASEAN identity in the population, and language. Furthermore, unlike the EU, there are no plans for strong centralised institutions, or a more powerful secretariat. Enforcement mechanisms are undeveloped. Similar to the view of Chia, Low believes that generally not enough has been done to separate the legitimate public policy objectives of non-tariff measures from a desire to protect local interests.[123] The end result is that in the field of services, for example, ASEAN economies are among the most closed in some sectors. Despite the objectives set out in their Blueprint 2025, the future of the AEC is inevitably surrounded by complexities and uncertainties. Meanwhile, the achievement of ASEAN so far is undeniable when the World Economic Forum referred to it as 'one of the success stories of modern economics'.[124]

TPP

US President Donald Trump signed a statement formally abandoning the TPP in January 2017.[125] It was once the most anticipated trade deal in the world. The concluded TPP Agreement was signed in February 2016. As the largest regional trade accord in history, it would have set new terms for trade and business investment among the US and 11 other Pacific Rim nations, namely Australia, Brunei, Canada, Chile, Japan, Malaysia, Mexico, New Zealand, Peru, Singapore and Vietnam. This group of nations has an annual GDP of nearly US$28 trillion that represents roughly 40 per cent of global GDP and one-third of world trade.[126] It was a hallmark achievement for the Obama administration, who had pushed for a more notable presence of the US in the Pacific Rim. It is believed that the goal was to bind Pacific nations closer through lower tariffs while also serving as a buttress against China's growing regional influence.[127] Following the US withdrawal, it is officially claimed that the US would push for bilateral trade agreements instead in the future.

TPP participants belong to various multilateral, regional and bilateral trade and economic agreements.[128] For example, all TPP countries are members of WTO, with Vietnam joining most recently in 2007. In addition, TPP countries have a number of bilateral and regional FTAs in effect. The US has FTAs with 20 countries, including six TPP participants (Australia, Canada, Chile, Mexico, Peru and Singapore). ASEAN is another major regional economic partnership that includes a number of TPP countries. Furthermore, TPP participants are part of a broader network of international partnerships within the Asia-Pacific. The Asia-Pacific Economic Cooperation (APEC) forum is a primary vehicle for broader regional interaction on trade and economic issues in the Asia-Pacific region. Indeed, negotiations for the TPP were initially started in the form of the Trans-Pacific Strategic Economic Partnership, involving New Zealand, Chile and Singapore, which was launched alongside the summit of APEC. Unlike ASEAN which has already created a free trade area among its members, APEC itself does not negotiate trade agreements. It only regards itself as a facilitator of these agreements. APEC's 21 member economies, including all TPP countries, are home to around 2.8 billion people and represent approximately 59 per cent of world GDP and 49 per cent of world trade in 2015.[129]

The TPP as a free trade agreement, if successfully implemented, will deepen economic ties between its members by opening up trade in goods and services, boosting investment flows and promoting closer links across a range of economic policy and regulatory issues.[130] It consists of 30 chapters of provisions. Schedules and annexes are attached to the chapters of the Agreement related to goods and services trade, investment, government procurement and temporary entry of business persons. In terms of trade in goods, TPP countries agree to eliminate and reduce tariffs and non-tariff barriers on industrial goods, and to eliminate or reduce tariffs and other restrictive policies on agricultural goods. In relation to trade in services, the countries accept these obligations to widen market access on a 'negative-list basis', meaning that their markets are fully open to services suppliers from TPP countries, except where they have taken an exception in the annexes attached to the agreement. In relation to investment, the TPP requires non-discriminatory investment policies and protections that assure basic rule-of-law protections.

While the trade deal is aimed at liberalising commerce across the countries, not all of countries, industries and sectors involved will benefit as much as others.[131] It is estimated that some of the world's biggest car manufacturers based in Japan, such as Toyota and Honda, would benefit from getting cheaper access to the US, which is its biggest export market. Likewise, US vehicle exports would also grow if car tariffs as high as 70 per cent in growing emerging markets such as Vietnam were removed. Also, major food exporting countries such as Australia and New Zealand would benefit from the move to reduce or eliminate of tariffs on agricultural products. On the other hand, several labour groups are worried the deal would result in jobs leaving developed economies such as the US and being sent to countries with lower wages and less strict labour laws.[132] In particular for Singapore, TPP may represent an important market and production base for Singapore businesses. According to their Ministry of Trade and Industry, in 2013 TPP partners accounted for almost 30 per cent of Singapore's total goods trade.[133] Likewise, investors from TPP countries contributed 30 per cent of foreign direct investment in Singapore. Meanwhile, it is worth noting that Singapore already has existing FTAs with nine of its 11 TPP partners. In other words, the TPP establishes a new trading relationship only with Canada and Mexico for Singapore. As for Malaysia, TPP will provide preferential access for goods and services from Malaysia into four new markets, namely the US, Canada, Mexico and Peru, in light of the country's existing free trade arrangements. Their Ministry of International Trade and Industry has hoped that Malaysian exporters will gain competitive advantage over regional competitors in exporting products such as electrical and electronics, chemical products, palm oil products, rubber products, wood products, textiles as well as automotive parts and components.[134]

Given that countries negotiating the TPP are all members of both the WTO and trade agreements, it is fair to ask what would actually be the economic benefits of concluding this deal. According to Paul Krugman, the TPP is 'no big deal'.[135] According to him, there is not much more protectionism to eliminate. Average US tariff rates have fallen by two-thirds since 1960. Opponents of the TPP portray the trade deal as a huge plot, suggesting that it would destroy national sovereignty and transfer all the power to corporations.[136] Indeed, for non-participants like China, PBOC predicted that the TPP would shave off an estimated 2.2 per cent from the country's GDP.[137] The manufacturing sector in China is expected to be hardest hit by increased competition from neighbouring economies which are members of the pact. This, in turn, would trim the growth of Hong Kong's export trade, which consists mainly of re-exports to and from the mainland. The spillover effect of declining trade activities could have a far-reaching impact on other services sectors. This includes trade financing, cargo handling and logistics. Whilst the future of the TPP now is so uncertain following the US's withdrawal, the remaining participants are trying to salvage the deal.[138] New Zealand, for example, believes that the agreement is very well balanced and needs little renegotiation for it to proceed. On the other hand, Malaysia has said if the TPP is to proceed without its biggest economy, it should be renegotiated. Some nations like New Zealand, Australia and Japan have been pushing for the deal to continue, but Malaysia was less keen to proceed. The demise of the TPP has prompted people to look at other alternatives, mostly being championed by China, such as the Regional Comprehensive Economic Partnership which includes Southeast Asian countries, as well as Japan, South Korea, Australia, New Zealand and India, as well as the One Belt, One Road initiative. As commented by US Senator John McCain, '[US withdrawal from the TPP] will create an opening for China to rewrite the economic rules'.[139]

OBOR

Tang provides a thoughtful comparison between TPP and OBOR in light of an expectation that the latter can match up against the former.[140] Regarding the objective, the TPP was a cornerstone of the Obama administration's plan to revive trade and implement higher standards for trading rules in the Pacific region. On the other hand, the OBOR initiative was launched by Beijing to promote trade and investment along old trade routes involving over 60 countries, as opposed to 12 in the TPP. The vast majority are developing countries in dire need of money and aid from China. Therefore, China is throwing a lot of institutional support behind the initiative, including creating the Asian Infrastructure Investment Bank and the Silk Road Fund, to ease deals. Regarding the rules, the TPP is far more comprehensive and stricter than standards set within the WTO. Beyond wide cuts in tariffs, the agreement sets new regulations to govern online commerce, the treatment of foreign investors, stricter intellectual property protection, tighter labour laws and an agreement for neutrality regarding state-owned enterprises. In sharp contrast, OBOR is based upon projects, not rules. China has made connectivity and infrastructure as the top priorities. Many projects such as rail links have been arranged through negotiations with other nations and are usually funded with Chinese money.

When Chinese President Xi Jinping visited Central Asia and Southeast Asia in September and October of 2013, he raised the initiative of jointly building the Silk Road Economic Belt and the Twenty-First-Century Maritime Silk Road (hence the name, One Belt One Road). According to the State Council of China, OBOR can help promote the economic prosperity of the countries along the routes and regional economic cooperation, strengthen exchanges and mutual learning between different civilisations, and promote world peace and development.[141] The Silk Road Economic Belt focuses on bringing together China, Central Asia, Russia and Europe (the Baltic); linking China with the Persian Gulf and the Mediterranean Sea through Central Asia and West Asia; and connecting China with Southeast Asia, South Asia and the Indian Ocean. Meanwhile, the Twenty-First-Century Maritime Silk Road is designed to go from China's coast to Europe through the South China Sea and the Indian Ocean in one route, and from China's coast through the South China Sea to the South Pacific in the other.

On land, the initiative will focus on jointly building a new Eurasian Land Bridge and developing the China–Mongolia–Russia, China–Central Asia–West Asia and China–Indochina Peninsula economic corridors by taking advantage of international transport routes, relying on core cities along the Belt and Road and using key economic industrial parks as cooperation platforms. At sea, it will focus on jointly building smooth, secure and efficient transport routes connecting major sea ports along the Belt and Road. The China–Pakistan Economic Corridor and the Bangladesh–China–India–Myanmar Economic Corridor are closely related to the Belt and Road Initiative, and therefore require closer cooperation and greater progress.

Spanning over 60 countries, it is estimated that the initiative includes more than half of the world's population, 75 per cent of known energy resources and 40 per cent of world gross domestic product.[142] The economic and infrastructure developments in countries along the OBOR route are mixed. At present, there are: nine low-income economies; 16 lower-middle-income economies; 14 upper-middle-income economies; and 7 high-income economies along OBOR.[143] Thus, gaps in transport infrastructure may hamper trade and investment flows to the OBOR region. It is estimated that improving the transport network and trade facilitation in countries along the OBOR route could raise the GDP growth in Central, West and South Asia ranging from 0.1 to 0.7 percentage points.[144] It could also contribute to an increase in welfare from about US$6 billion to about US$100 billion. The total exports of countries in the OBOR could also increase by about US$5 billion to US$135 billion.[145] The distribution of benefits arising from OBOR may not be equal, with some countries benefitting more than others. China is expected to gain a lot from it, but some countries such as Mongolia or Pakistan, and sub-regions such as Central Asia and Southeast Asia, stand to gain significant benefit as well.

For example, China Communications Construction Group alone has notched up US$40 billion of contracts and built 10,320 kilometres of road, 95 deepwater ports, ten airports, 152 bridges and 2,080 railways in OBOR countries.[146] As for Hong Kong, in light of the fact that all the infrastructure in OBOR requires investment, the Trade and Development Council of Hong Kong expects the city to exploit a considerable array of opportunities in financing, project risk/quality management, infrastructure and real estate services, as well as several other related fields.[147] Similarly, Singapore seeks to play a role in three key areas of the OBOR initiative: connectivity, transport, finance services and trade.[148] Singapore companies have developed expertise across the infrastructure value chain including master-planning, engineering design, procurement, construction and operations. Many have also engaged in OBOR-related projects. For example, recently, Charisma Energy and Sunseap were awarded a contract to build a 140-megawatt solar farm in India while a home-grown water company has won multiple desalination projects in Middle East in the last two years. Malaysia is also hopeful that it will be 'one of greatest beneficiaries of OBOR'.[149] The construction of a new deep-sea port as part of the RM43 billion Melaka Gateway project, jointly developed by local and Chinese firms, serves notice that the country plans to make itself a key part of the initiative.

Despite all the potential benefits, there are also some risks involved. Singapore is particularly concerned about the political and financial risks of infrastructure projects in developing countries along the Belt and Road.[150] Companies are urged to closely monitor geopolitical developments of the regional infrastructure projects that they are pursuing. A recently concluded UN Economic and Social Commission for Asia and the Pacific Study has warned of financial risks in countries in south and central Asia where China's announced investment value under OBOR is high compared to the relative size of the economy of the recipient country.[151] Behind OBOR is a lending programme of unprecedented breadth to help finance the construction of ports, roads and rail links. As the project grows, so do the risks to lenders and borrowers, all of whom might be tangled in projects 'where commercial logic and demand for roads and bridges are subordinate to political considerations'.[152] It remains uncertain whether future project returns will be sufficient to fully cover repayments of the loans, thereby endangering the sustainability of the whole project.

Concluding remarks

China's experience during its reform period was characterised as an 'economic miracle'. The average growth rate of 10 per cent over a period of 30 years was indeed unprecedented despite a slight slowdown in recent years. As previously discussed, the expansion of China's role in the world trading system has been remarkable, with its overall share in world GDP rising from 3.8 per cent in 1990 to 15.4 per cent in 2013 (Figure 7.1 above). While China's integration into the global trading system is likely to benefit both the global and regional economies, there will no doubt be some short-run distributional effects across countries. China's performance and trade expansion have led to concerns about the competition pressure in the world export market for labour-intensive products and in attraction of FDI. Before China's emergence, Asian countries enjoyed a good inflow of FDI from developed countries and easy access to the markets of developed economies. With China's joining the competition, both previously enjoyed benefits shrank.[153]

On the other hand, however, the opportunities are arising for Asian countries. This is evidenced by China's central role in the regional trade and investment. In the three Asian economies – Hong Kong, Singapore and Malaysia – China is their top trading partner and one of the main sources of FDI, as well as the main recipient of direct investment abroad. China's rapidly expanding trade volume has become a major engine of growth in the Asian region, largely because of primary products imports and processing trade. A greater share of FDI in Asia going to China, and strong capital outflows from China to the region also contribute to the economic growth of both sides.

After the global financial crisis, China and Asian countries have strengthened their cooperation with one another in order to counter recession. They actively promote economic ties in the form of bilateral agreements (i.e. CSFTA between Singapore and China), partnership agreements (i.e. CEPA between Hong Kong and China), free trade areas (i.e. ASEAN–China FTA), as well as government-led projects and policy measures. Such initiatives represent a set of huge opportunities for both sides to increase their cooperation in the areas of trade, investment and infrastructure development, thereby helping them recover from the economic downturn. Beijing has expanded its influence as a major economic and political force in the region and a locomotive for economic recovery and future opportunity. In view of the fact that China is now the largest trading partner for a large number of countries, China's power and ambition have grown by shifting its strategy into taking on a greater leadership role in the world. This is exemplified by the withdrawal of the US from the TPP and the consequential shift of attention to the China's OBOR initiative.

Notes

1 Cedric Tille (201), 'Sailing through the Storm? Capital Flows in Asia during the Crisis' in *Pacific Economic Review*, **17**; Morris Goldstein and Daniel Xie (2009), 'The Impact of the Financial Crisis on Emerging Asia' Paper of Federal Reserve Bank of San Francisco's Conference on Asia and the Global Financial Crisis. Online. Available at: https://pdfs.semanticscholar.org/fbc0/dd85bd71387fa9dc-9c12d28bf6f420aa89b6.pdf.
2 Yiping Huang, (2011), 'Will China Become an Engine of Growth for the Region?' in Lok Sang Ho and John Wong (eds), *APEC and the Rise of China*, Singapore: World Scientific.
3 Masahiro Kawai (2009), 'The Impact of the Global Financial Crisis on Asia and Asia's Reponses' Asian Development Bank Institute Conference paper. Online. Available at: www.ifw-kiel.de/konfer/2009/masahiro-kawai.
4 Ravi Balakrishnan *et al.* (2009), 'The Transmission of Financial Stress from Advanced to Emerging Economies' IMF Working Paper No. 09/133. Online. Available at: www.imf.org/en/Publications/WP/Issues/2016/12/31/The-Transmission-of-Financial-Stress-from-Advanced-to-Emerging-Economies-23039.
5 Jikon Lai (2012), *Financial Crisis and Institutional Change in East Asia*, Basingstoke: Palgrave Macmillan.
6 Philip Turner (2007), 'Are Banking Systems in East Asia Stronger?' in *Asian Economic Policy Review*, **2**.
7 Angus Maddison (2007), *Chinese Economic Performance in the Long Run*, Paris: OECD.
8 Huang (2011), op. cit.
9 National Bureau of Statistics of China (2015), 'China's Economy Showed Moderate but Steady Growth'. Online. Available at: www.stats.gov.cn/english/PressRelease/201507/t20150715_1214964.html.
10 International Monetary Fund (2017), 'China's Economic Outlook in Six Charts'. Online. Available at: www.imf.org/en/News/Articles/2017/08/09/NA081517-China-Economic-Outlook-in-Six-Charts.
11 Joe Studwell (2013), *How Asia Works: Success and Failure in the World's Most Dynamic Region*, New York: Profile Books.
12 Michael Pillsbury (2015), *The Hundred-Year Marathon: China's Secret Strategy to Replace America as the Global Superpower*, New York: Henry Holt, pp. 10–12; and Mario Cavolo (2014), *China: The Big Lie? The Truth of Trillions in a Culture of Cash*, San Francisco: Long River Press, p. 155.
13 For more clarification on the China Dream, see China Daily (2014), 'Background: Connotations of Chinese Dream' in *China Daily* (5 March 2014). Online Available at: www.chinadaily.com.cn/china/2014npcandcppcc/2014-03/05/content_17324203.htm.
14 China Briefing (2013), 'China Passes US to Become World's Largest Trading Nation'. Online. Available at: www.china-briefing.com/news/2013/02/12/china-becomes-worlds-largest-trading-nation-passes-u-s.html.
15 Regarding the China Threat theory, see Bill Gertz (2010), *The China Threat: How the People's Republic Targets America*, Washington, D.C: Regnery; for the opponents, see for example, Yong Deng (2006), 'Reputation and the Security Dilemma: China Reacts to the China Threat Theory' in Alastair Johnston and Robert Ross (eds), *New Directions in the Study of China's Foreign Policy*, Stanford: Stanford University Press, pp. 186–214.

16 Huang (2011), op. cit.
17 Timothy Beardson (2013), *Stumbling Giant: The Threats to China's Future*, New Haven: Yale University Press, p. 384.
18 International Monetary Fund (2014), 'World Economic Outlook.' Online. Available at: www.imf.org/external/Pubs/ft/weo/2014/01.
19 Donghyun Park and Kwanho Shin (2009), 'Can Trade with the People's Republic of China be an Engine of Growth for Developing Asia?' ADB Economic Working Paper Series No. 172. Online. Available at: www.adb.org/sites/default/files/publication/28256/economics-wp172.pdf.
20 Peter Robertson and Jessica Xu (2010), 'In China's Wake: Has Asia Gained from China's Growth?' Economics Discussion Paper. Online. Available at: www.otago.ac.nz/economics/news/seminars/otago078865111111111111.pdf.
21 Park and Shin (2009), op. cit.
22 Robertson and Xu (2010), op. cit.
23 Statistics from ASEAN.
24 Park and Shin (2009), op. cit.
25 International Monetary Fund (2014), op. cit.
26 Era Dabla-Norris *et al.* (2012), 'Spillovers to Low-Income Countries: Importance of Systemic Emerging Markets' IMF Working Paper No. 12/49. Online. Available at: www.imf.org/external/pubs/ft/wp/2012/wp1249.pdf.
27 Edgar Cheng (2002), 'China's Horse in a Global Race – Positioning the Hong Kong Securities Market' in Securities and Futures Commission (ed.), *Securities Regulation in Hong Kong*, Hong Kong: Securities and Futures Commission, pp. 380–381.
28 Jiangyu Wang (2004), 'China's Regional Trade Agreements: The Law, Geopolitics, and Impact on the Multilateral Trading System' in *Singapore Year Book of International Law*, **8**.
29 Ben Blanchard and Donny Kwok (2015), 'Hong Kong Leader Extends Economic Olive Branch after Veto' in *Reuters* (19 June 2015). Online. Available at: www.reuters.com/article/us-hongkong-politics/hong-kong-leader-extends-economic-olive-branch-after-veto-idUSKBN0OZ09R20150619.
30 Paola Subacchi *et al.* (2012), 'Shifting Capital: The Rise of Financial Centres in Greater China' Chatham House Report. Online. Available at: www.chathamhouse.org/publications/papers/view/183257.
31 Economist (2014), 'Why Hong Kong Remains Vital to China's Economy' in *Economist* (30 September 2014).
32 Hong Kong Monthly Digest of Statistics (2013), 'Trade between Hong Kong and the Mainland of China'. Online. Available at: www.censtatd.gov.hk/hkstat/sub/sp230.jsp?productCode=FA100252.
33 Hong Kong Trade and Industry Department (2013), 'The Mainland of China and Hong Kong Special Administrative Regime: Some Important Facts'. Online. Available at: www.tid.gov.hk/english/aboutus/publications/factsheet/china.html.
34 State Council of China (2014), 'White Paper: The Practice of the 'One Country, Two Systems' Policy in the Hong Kong Special Administrative Region'. Online. Available at: www.china.org.cn/government/whitepaper/node_7207387.htm.
35 Junjian Cao (2015), *The Chinese Real Estate Market: Development, Regulation and Investment*, Abingdon: Routledge, p. 111.
36 State Council of China (2014), op. cit.
37 Hong Kong Census and Statistics Department (2012), 'External Direct Investment Statistics of Hong Kong'. Online. Available at: www.censtatd.gov.hk/hkstat/sub/sp260.jsp?productCode=B1040003.
38 Hung-Gay Fung *et al.* (2011), 'Reported Trade Figure Discrepancy, Regulatory Arbitrage, and Round-tripping: Evidence from the China-Hong Kong Trade Data' in *Journal of International Business Studies*, **42**.

39 UNCTAD (2007), 'Rising FDI into China: The Facts behind the Numbers' Investment Brief No. 2 2007. Online. Available at: http://unctad.org/en/Docs/iteiiamisc20075_en.pdf.

40 China provides many preferential policies to attract foreign direct investment, including low tax rates, favourable land use rights, convenient administrative support, and even favourable financial services from domestic and foreign financial institutions.

41 Xiao Geng (2004), 'Round-Tripping Foreign Direct Investment in the People's Republic of China' ADBI Research Policy Brief No. 10. Online. Available at: www.adb.org/sites/default/files/publication/157279/adbi-rpb10.pdf 10.

42 Data from the World Bank.

43 Yang Zhang and Sarah Tong (2009), 'Hong Kong's Economy in the Financial Crisis' EAI Background Brief No. 448. Online. Available at: www.eai.nus.edu.sg/publications/files/BB448.pdf.

44 World Trade Organisation (2010), 'Trade Policy Review: Report by the Secretariat Hong Kong' Document WT/TPR/S/241.

45 Tony Yu (2007), *Entrepreneurship and Economic Development in Hong Kong*, Abingdon: Routledge.

46 The Minimum Wage Ordinance (Cap. 608) is an ordinance enacted by the Legislative Council of Hong Kong to introduce a minimum wage in Hong Kong in July 2010. The executive branch proposed a minimum wage of HK$28 per hour in November 2010. It came into effect on 1 May 2011.

47 Seven areas include (1) strengthen cooperation in the financial services sector; (2) expedite infrastructure projects related to Hong Kong; (3) economic cooperation between Hong Kong and the Pearl River Delta; (4) alleviate difficulties faced by Hong Kong SMEs; (5) expand individual visit scheme; (6) open up mainland service industries to Hong Kong providers; (7) other such as the safe and steady supply of food, water, electricity and gas etc to Hong Kong.

48 National Development and Reform Commission (2008), 'The Outline of the Plan for the Reform and Development of the Pearl River Delta (2008–2020)'. Online. Available at: www.newsgd.com/specials/PRD/default.htm.

49 Hong Kong Monetary Authority (2009), 'People's Bank of China and Hong Kong Monetary Authority Sign Currency Swap Agreement'. Online. Available at: www.hkma.gov.hk/eng/key-information/press-releases/2009/20090120-4.shtml.

50 State Council of China (2014), op. cit.

51 The CEPA framework agreement was signed on 29 June 2003.

52 They are: Agreement between the Mainland and Hong Kong on Achieving Basic Liberalisation of Trade in Services in Guangdong (signed on 18 December 2014); Agreement on Trade in Services (signed on 27 November 2015); Investment Agreement (signed on 28 June 2017); Agreement on Economic and Technical Cooperation (signed on 28 June 2017).

53 Matthew Harrison (2004), 'The Implications of CEPA for the Hong Kong Securities Industry' SFC Quarterly Bulletin 55. Online. Available at: www.sfc.hk/web/doc/EN/research/research/extpaper04%20(eng).pdf.

54 David Donald (2014), A *Financial Centre for Two Empires: Hong Kong's Corporate, Securities and Tax Laws in Its Transition from Britain to China*, Cambridge: CUP.

55 World Trade Organisation (2010), op. cit.

56 *The Opinions on Boosting Development of Modern Service and Advanced Manufacture Industry and Establishing International Financial and Shipping Centre in Shanghai* was issued by China's State Council on 14 April 2009.

57 Flora Huang and Horace Yeung (2014), *Chinese Companies and the Hong Kong Stock Market*, Abingdon: Routledge, pp. 202–207.

58 Jeffrey Garten (2009), 'From NyLon to Shangkong' in *Financial Times* (10 May 2009).

59 Poon Kim Shee (2005), 'Singapore-China Special Economic Relations: In Search of Business Opportunities' in *Ritsumeikan International Affairs*, **3**.
60 Michael Leifer (2000), *Singapore's Foreign Policy: Coping with Vulnerability*, Abingdon: Routledge, p. 122.
61 Teng Siow Song (2009), 'FTAs, China, the ASEAN Charter and the ASEAN Economic Community' in Kok Kheng Yeoh (ed.), *China-ASEAN Relations: Economic Engagement and Policy Reform*, Kuala Lumpur: University of Malaysia Press.
62 Shee (2005), op. cit.
63 International Enterprise Singapore (2014), 'Review of 2013 Trade Performance' Online. Available at: www.iesingapore.gov.sg/Media-Centre/Media-Releases/2014/2/Review-of-2013-Trade-Performance.
64 China Daily (2014), 'China No1 Trade Partner of Singapore in 2013' in *China Daily* (20 February 2014).
65 Department of Statistics Singapore (2012), 'Singapore's International Trade in Services 2012'. Online. Available at: www.singstat.gov.sg/statistics/browse_by_theme/trade.html.
66 World Trade Organisation (2008), 'Trade Policy Review: Report by the Secretariat Singapore' Document WT/TPR/S/202.
67 Internatioal Enterprise Singapore (2010), 'Annual Report 2008/2009'. Online available at: www.iesingapore.gov.sg/Publications/Publications/Annual-Reports.
68 Shandre Thangavelu *et al.* (2009), 'FDI, Growth and Financial Crisis: The Experience of Selected Asian Countries' in *World Economy*, **32**.
69 Flora Huang, (2014), 'The Rising of Asian Values and the Financial Crisis: The Cases of Hong Kong, Malaysia and Singapore' in Georges Depeyrot (ed.), *When Orient and Occident Meet*, Wetteren: Moneta.
70 International Enterprise Singapore (2011), 'Annual Report 2009/2010'. Online. Available at: www.iesingapore.gov.sg/Publications/Publications/Annual-Reports.
71 Monetary Authority of Singapore (2014), 'Annual Report 2012/2013'. Online. Available at: www.mas.gov.sg/About-MAS/Reporting/Annual-Reports.aspx.
72 Rahul Sen (2008), 'Bilateral Trade and Economic Cooperation Agreements in ASEAN: Implications for Asian Economic Integration' in Amita Batra (ed.), *Preferential Trading Agreement in Asia towards an Asian Economic Community*, New Delhi: Academic Foundation.
73 Yongkun Luo (2013), 'Strategic Cooperation can Boost Bilateral Relations' in *China Daily* (4 October 2013).
74 Ibid.
75 Malaysia Ministry of International Trade and Industry (2014), 'Weekly Bulletin Volume 293'. Online. Available at: www.miti.gov.my/index.php/pages/view/3367.
76 Yi Li (2006), 'An Analysis of Recent Sino-Malaysian Trade Relations' in Kok-Kheng Yeoh and Hou Kok Chung (eds), *China and Malaysia in a Globalizing World: Bilateral Relations, Regional Imperatives and Domestic Challenges*, Kuala Lumpur: Institute of China Studies.
77 Evelyn Devadason (2009), 'Malaysia-China Network Trade: A Note on Product Upgrading' *in Journal of Contemporary Asia*, **39**.
78 Malaysia Ministry of International Trade and Industry (2014), op. cit.
79 Malaysia External Trade Development Corporation (2013), 'Annual Report 2012'. Online. Available at: www.matrade.gov.my/en/about-matrade/matrade-network/worldwide-offices/389-annual-reports.
80 Malaysia Investment Development Authority (2013), 'Malaysia Investment Performance Report 2012'. Online. Available at: www.mida.gov.my/env3/uploads/PerformanceReport/2012/MIPR2012_ENG.pdf.
81 Bank Negara Malaysia (2010), 'Annual Report 2009'. Online. Available at: www.bnm.gov.my/index.php?ch=en_press&pg=en_press_all&ac=2015&lang=en.n

82 Bank Negara Malaysia (2014), 'Annual Report 2013'. Online. Available at: www.bnm.gov.my/index.php?ch=en_press&pg=en_press_all&ac=2982.
83 Rafael Leal-Arcas (2011), 'China's Economic Rise and Regional Trade' in Lok Sang Ho and John Wong (eds), *APEC and the Rise of China*, Singapore: World Scientific.
84 Kian Teng Kwek and Siew Yean Tham (2007), 'Trade between Malaysia and China: Opportunities and Challenges for Growth' in Kok-Kheng Yeoh and Evelyn Devadason (eds), *Emerging Trading Nation in an Integrating World: Global Impacts and Domestic Challenges of China's Economic Reform*, Kuala Lumpur: Institution of China Studies.
85 Kok-Kheng Yeoh *et al.* (2011), 'The Role of China in Asia-Pacific Trade Framework in the Context of APEC' in Lok Sang Ho and John Wong (eds), *APEC and the Rise of China*, Singapore: World Scientific.
86 Malaysia South-South Association (2012), 'Ministry of International Trade and Industry ASEAN-China Free Trade Agreement (ACFTA): A Right Decision at the Right Time'. Online. Available at: www.massa.net.my/ministry-of-international-trade-and-industry-asean-china-free-trade-agreement-acfta-a-right-decision-at-the-right-time.
87 Wai-Heng Loke (2009), 'East Asia and Southeast Asia: Similarity in Trade Structures' Singapore Economic Review Conference Paper. Online. Available at: http://eprints.um.edu.my/11188.
88 Kwek and Tham (2007), op. cit.
89 Yeoh *et al.* (2011), op. cit.
90 Malaysia Investment Development Authority (2013), op. cit.
91 Daron Acemoglu (2009), *Introduction to Modern Economic Growth*, Princeton: Princeton University Press, p. 686.
92 See for example, David Dollar (1992), 'Outward-Oriented Developing Economies Really Do Grow More Rapidly: Evidence from 95 LDCs, 1976–1985' in *Economic Development and Cultural Change*, **40**; and Jeffrey Sachs and Andrew Warner (1995), 'Economic Reform and the Process of Global Integration' in *Brookings Papers on Economic Activity*, **26**.
93 World Trade Organisation (2015), *Understanding the WTO*, Geneva: WTO, p. 13.
94 See for example, Rüdiger Dornbusch *et al.* (1977), 'Comparative Advantage, Trade, and Payments in a Ricardian Model with a Continuum of Goods' in *American Economic Review*, **67**.
95 World Trade Organisation (2015), op. cit., p. 15.
96 Ibid. pp. 9–10.
97 GATT, art. 1.
98 GATT, art. 3.
99 The process is chiefly governed by the Understanding on Rules and Procedures Governing the Settlement of Disputes, contained in Annex 2 of the Marrakesh Agreement.
100 World Trade Organisation (2015), op. cit., p. 17.
101 Peter Van den Bossche and Werner Zdouc (2013), *The Law and Policy of the World Trade Organisation*, Cambridge: CUP, p. 1017.
102 Simon Lester *et al.* (2012), *World Trade Law*, Oxford: Hart, p. 331.
103 World Trade Organisation (2017), 'Regional Trade Agreements'. Online. Available at: www.wto.org/english/tratop_e/region_e/region_e.htm.
104 Ibid.
105 Ibid.
106 Lester *et al.* (2012), op. cit., p. 332.
107 Editorial (2016), 'Global Trade after the Failure of the Doha Round' in *New York Times* (1 January 2016).
108 Lester *et al.* (2012), op. cit., p. 333.

109 Ibid. 334.
110 World Economic Forum (2015), 'What is the Future of the WTO?' Online. Available at: www.weforum.org/agenda/2015/09/how-can-the-wto-remain-relevant.
111 ASEAN (2012), 'Economic Achievement'. Online. Available at: http://asean.org/?static_post=economic-achievement.
112 Data from ASEAN.
113 ASEAN (2012a), 'Questions and Answers on the CEPT'. Online. Available at: http://asean.org/?static_post=qusestions-and-answers-on-the-cept.
114 Ibid.
115 Ibid.
116 Data from ASEAN.
117 Chris Devonshire-Ellis (2014), 'Understanding ASEAN's Free Trade Agreements' in *ASEAN Briefing* (13 February 2014).
118 Ibid.
119 ASEAN (2012), op. cit.
120 ASEAN (2015), 'ASEAN Economic Community Blueprint 2025'. Online. Available at: www.asean.org/wp-content/uploads/images/2015/November/aec-page/AEC-Blueprint-2025-FINAL.pdf.
121 Siow Yue Chia (2013), 'The ASEAN Economic Community: Progress, Challenges, and Prospects' ADBI Working Paper 440. Online. Available at: www.econstor.eu/bitstream/10419/101189/1/770509193.pdf.
122 Patrick Low (2016), 'Asean Economic Community Faces Numerous Challenges' in *South China Morning Post* (6 January 2016).
123 Ibid.
124 World Economic Forum (2016), 'The ASEAN Economic Community: What You Need to Know'. Online. Available at: www.weforum.org/agenda/2016/05/asean-economic-community-what-you-need-to-know.
125 Kevin Granville (2017), 'What Is TPP? Behind the Trade Deal that Died' in *New York Times* (23 January 2017).
126 Ibid.
127 Ibid.
128 Brock Williams (2013), 'Trans-Pacific Partnership (TPP) Countries: Comparative Trade and Economic Analysis' Congressional Research Service Paper. Online. Available at: http://digitalcommons.ilr.cornell.edu/cgi/viewcontent.cgi?article=2020&context=key_workplace.
129 Asia-Pacific Economic Cooperation (2015), 'Achievements and Benefits'. Online. Available at: www.apec.org/About-Us/About-APEC/Achievements-and-Benefits.
130 For a quick overview of key features of the TPP, see Office of the United States Trade Representative (2015), 'Summary of the Trans-Pacific Partnership Agreement'. Online. Available at: https://ustr.gov/about-us/policy-offices/press-office/press-releases/2015/october/summary-trans-pacific-partnership.
131 BBC (2015), 'TPP Trade Deal: Who are the Winners and Losers?'. Online. Available at: www.bbc.co.uk/news/business-34451423.
132 Ibid.
133 Ministry of Trade and Industry Singapore (2015), 'Trans Pacific Partnership Free Trade Agreement: 7 Things You Should Know'. Online. Available at: www.mti.gov.sg/MTIInsights/SiteAssets/Pages/TPP/Seven%20things%20you%20should%20know%20about%20the%20TPP%20(Final).pdf.
134 Ministry of International Trade and Industry Malaysia (2016), 'TPP FAQs'. Online. Available at: http://fta.miti.gov.my/index.php/pages/view/258.
135 Paul Krugman (2014), 'No Big Deal' in *New York Times* (27 February 2014).
136 Ibid.
137 Peter Liang (2015), 'TPP to have Major Impact on HK' in *China Daily* (15 October 2015).

138 Rosalind Mathieson and Haslinda Amin (2017), 'New Zealand Splits with Malaysia over Reworking TPP without US' in *Bloomberg* (22 May 2017). Online. Available at: www.bloomberg.com/news/articles/2017-05-22/new-zealand-splits-with-malaysia-over-reworking-tpp-without-u-s.
139 Bloomberg (2017), 'Why Trump's Withdrawal from the TPP is a Boon for China' in *South China Morning Post* (24 January 2017).
140 Frank Tang (2017), 'How does China's "One Belt, One Road" Match up against the TPP?' in *South China Morning Post* (24 January 2017).
141 National Development and Reform Commission, Ministry of Foreign Affairs, and Ministry of Commerce of the People's Republic of China (2015), 'Action Plan on the Belt and Road Initiative'. Online. Available at: http://english.gov.cn/archive/publications/2015/03/30/content_281475080249035.htm.
142 Wade Shepard (2016), 'China's One Belt, One Road Plan Covers more than Half of the Population, 75 per cent of Energy Resources and 40 per cent of World's GDP' in *South China Morning Post* (21 June 2016).
143 James Villafuerte *et al.* (2017), 'The One Belt, One Road Initiative: Impact on Trade and Growth' 19th Annual Conference on Global Economic Analysis Paper. Online. Available at: www.gtap.agecon.purdue.edu/resources/download/8280.pdf.
144 Ibid.
145 Ibid.
146 Shu Zhang and Matthew Miller (2017), 'Behind China's Silk Road Vision: Cheap Funds, Heavy Debt, Growing Risk' in *Reuters* (15 May 2017). Online. Available at: http://in.reuters.com/article/china-silk-road-finance/behind-chinas-silk-road-vision-cheap-funds-heavy-debt-growing-risk-idINKCN18B0XY.
147 Hong Kong Trade and Development Council (2015), '"One Belt, One Road" Initiative: The Implications for Hong Kong'. Online. Available at: http://economists-pick-research.hktdc.com/business-news/article/Research-Articles/One-Belt-One-Road-Initiative-The-Implications-for-Hong-Kong/rp/en/1/1X000000/1X0A23WV.htm.
148 International Enterprise Singapore (2017), 'China's Belt and Road Initiative (BRI): What it Means for Singapore Companies' in *IE Insights* (September 2017).
149 John Teo (2017), 'Malaysia One of Greatest Beneficiaries of OBOR' in *New Straits Times* (16 May 2017).
150 International Enterprise Singapore (2017), op. cit.
151 Dipanjan Roy Chaudhury (2017), 'UN Warns about Financial Risks in China's One Belt One Road Project' in *Economic Times* (25 May 2017).
152 Don Weinland (2017), 'China Warned of Risk to Banks from One Belt, One Road Initiative' in *Financial Times* (26 January 2017).
153 Yunhua Liu (2009), 'Facing the Challenge of Rising China: Singapore's Responses' in *Journal of Policy Modeling*, **29**.

References

Acemoglu, Daron (2009), *Introduction to Modern Economic Growth*, Princeton: Princeton University Press.

ASEAN (2012), 'Economic Achievement'. Online. Available at: http://asean.org/?static_post=economic-achievement.

ASEAN (2012a), 'Questions and Answers on the CEPT'. Online. Available at: http://asean.org/?static_post=qusestions-and-answers-on-the-cept.

ASEAN (2015), 'ASEAN Economic Community Blueprint 2025'. Online. Available at: www.asean.org/wp-content/uploads/images/2015/November/aec-page/AEC-Blueprint-2025-FINAL.pdf.

Asia-Pacific Economic Cooperation (2015), 'Achievements and Benefits'. Online. Available at: www.apec.org/About-Us/About-APEC/Achievements-and-Benefits.

Balakrishnan, Ravi; Danninger, Stephan; Tytell, Irina; Elekdag, Selim (2009), 'The Transmission of Financial Stress from Advanced to Emerging Economies' IMF Working Paper No. 09/133. Online. Available at: www.imf.org/en/Publications/WP/Issues/2016/12/31/The-Transmission-of-Financial-Stress-from-Advanced-to-Emerging-Economies-23039.

Bank Negara Malaysia (2010), 'Annual Report 2009'. Online. Available at: www.bnm.gov.my/index.php?ch=en_press&pg=en_press_all&ac=2015&lang=en.

Bank Negara Malaysia (2014), 'Annual Report 2013'. Online. Available at: www.bnm.gov.my/index.php?ch=en_press&pg=en_press_all&ac=2982.

BBC (2015), 'TPP Trade Deal: Who are the Winners and Losers?'. Online. Available at: www.bbc.co.uk/news/business-34451423.

Beardson, Timothy (2013), *Stumbling Giant: The Threats to China's Future*, New Haven: Yale University Press.

Blanchard, Ben and Kwok, Donny (2015), 'Hong Kong Leader Extends Economic Olive Branch after Veto' in *Reuters* (19 June 2015). Online. Available at: www.reuters.com/article/us-hongkong-politics/hong-kong-leader-extends-economic-olive-branch-after-veto-idUSKBN0OZ09R20150619.

Bloomberg (2017), 'Why Trump's Withdrawal from the TPP is a Boon for China' in *South China Morning Post* (24 January 2017).

Cao, Junjian (2015), *The Chinese Real Estate Market: Development, Regulation and Investment*, Abingdon: Routledge.

Chaudhury, Dipanjan Roy (2017), 'UN Warns about Financial Risks in China's One Belt One Road Project' in *Economic Times* (25 May 2017).

Cavolo, Mario (2014), *China: The Big Lie? The Truth of Trillions in a Culture of Cash*, San Francisco: Long River Press.

Cheng, Edgar (2002), 'China's Horse in a Global Race – Positioning the Hong Kong Securities Market' in Securities and Futures Commission (ed.), *Securities Regulation in Hong Kong*, Hong Kong: Securities and Futures Commission.

Chia, Siow Yue (2013), 'The ASEAN Economic Community: Progress, Challenges, and Prospects' ADBI Working Paper 440. Online. Available at: www.econstor.eu/bitstream/10419/101189/1/770509193.pdf.

China Briefing (2013), 'China Passes US to Become World's Largest Trading Nation'. Online. Available at: www.china-briefing.com/news/2013/02/12/china-becomes-worlds-largest-trading-nation-passes-u-s.html.

China Daily (2014), 'Background: Connotations of Chinese Dream' in *China Daily* (5 March 2014). Online Available at: www.chinadaily.com.cn/china/2014npcandcppcc/2014-03/05/content_17324203.htm.

China Daily (2014), 'China No1 Trade Partner of Singapore in 2013' in *China Daily* (20 February 2014).

Dabla-Norris, Era; Espinoza, Raphael; and Jahan, Sarwat (2012), 'Spillovers to Low-Income Countries: Importance of Systemic Emerging Markets' IMF Working Paper No. 12/49. Online. Available at: www.imf.org/external/pubs/ft/wp/2012/wp1249.pdf.

Deng, Yong (2006), 'Reputation and the Security Dilemma: China Reacts to the China Threat Theory' in Alastair Johnston and Robert Ross (eds), *New Directions in the Study of China's Foreign Policy*, Stanford: Stanford University Press.

Department of Statistics Singapore (2012), 'Singapore's International Trade in Services 2012'. Online. Available at: www.singstat.gov.sg/statistics/browse_by_theme/trade.html.

Devadason, Evelyn (2009), 'Malaysia-China Network Trade: A Note on Product Upgrading' *in Journal of Contemporary Asia*, **39**.

Devonshire-Ellis, Chris (2014), 'Understanding ASEAN's Free Trade Agreements' in *ASEAN Briefing* (13 February 2014).

Dollar, David (1992), 'Outward-Oriented Developing Economies Really Do Grow More Rapidly: Evidence from 95 LDCs, 1976–1985' in *Economic Development and Cultural Change*, **40**.

Donald, David (2014), A *Financial Centre for Two Empires: Hong Kong's Corporate, Securities and Tax Laws in Its Transition from Britain to China*, Cambridge: CUP.

Dornbusch, Rüdiger; Fischer, S.; and Samuelson, P.A. (1977), 'Comparative Advantage, Trade, and Payments in a Ricardian Model with a Continuum of Goods' in *American Economic Review*, **67**.

Economist (2014), 'Why Hong Kong Remains Vital to China's Economy' in *Economist* (30 September 2014).

Editorial (2016), 'Global Trade after the Failure of the Doha Round' in *New York Times* (1 January 2016).

Fung, Hung-Gay; Yau, Jot; Zhang, Gaiyan (2011), 'Reported Trade Figure Discrepancy, Regulatory Arbitrage, and Round-tripping: Evidence from the China-Hong Kong Trade Data' in *Journal of International Business Studies*, **42**.

Garten, Jeffrey (2009), 'From NyLon to Shangkong' in *Financial Times* (10 May 2009).

Geng, Xiao (2004), 'Round-Tripping Foreign Direct Investment in the People's Republic of China' ADBI Research Policy Brief No. 10. Online. Available at: www.adb.org/sites/default/files/publication/157279/adbi-rpb10.pdf 10.

Gertz, Bill (2010), *The China Threat: How the People's Republic Targets America*, Washington, D.C: Regnery.

Goldstein, Morris and Xie, Daniel (2009), 'The Impact of the Financial Crisis on Emerging Asia' Paper of Federal Reserve Bank of San Francisco's Conference on Asia and the Global Financial Crisis. Online. Available at: https://pdfs.semanticscholar.org/fbc0/dd85bd71387fa9dc9c12d28bf6f420aa89b6.pdf.

Granville, Kevin (2017), 'What Is TPP? Behind the Trade Deal that Died' in *New York Times* (23 January 2017).

Harrison, Matthew (2004), 'The Implications of CEPA for the Hong Kong Securities Industry' SFC Quarterly Bulletin 55. Online. Available at: www.sfc.hk/web/doc/EN/research/research/extpaper04%20(eng).pdf.

Hong Kong Census and Statistics Department (2012), 'External Direct Investment Statistics of Hong Kong'. Online. Available at: www.censtatd.gov.hk/hkstat/sub/sp260.jsp?productCode=B1040003.

Hong Kong Monetary Authority (2009), 'People's Bank of China and Hong Kong Monetary Authority Sign Currency Swap Agreement'. Online. Available at: www.hkma.gov.hk/eng/key-information/press-releases/2009/20090120-4.shtml.

Hong Kong Monthly Digest of Statistics (2013), 'Trade between Hong Kong and the Mainland of China'. Online. Available at: www.censtatd.gov.hk/hkstat/sub/sp230.jsp?productCode=FA100252.

Hong Kong Trade and Development Council (2015), '"One Belt, One Road" Initiative: The Implications for Hong Kong'. Online. Available at: http://economists-pick-research.hktdc.com/business-news/article/Research-Articles/One-Belt-One-Road-Initiative-The-Implications-for-Hong-Kong/rp/en/1/1X000000/1X0A23WV.htm.

Hong Kong Trade and Industry Department (2013), 'The Mainland of China and Hong Kong Special Administrative Regime: Some Important Facts'. Online. Available at: www.tid.gov.hk/english/aboutus/publications/factsheet/china.html.

Huang, Flora (2014), 'The Rising of Asian Values and the Financial Crisis: The Cases of Hong Kong, Malaysia and Singapore' in Georges Depeyrot (ed.), *When Orient and Occident Meet*, Wetteren: Moneta.

Huang, Flora and Yeung, Horace (2014), *Chinese Companies and the Hong Kong Stock Market*, Abingdon: Routledge.

Huang, Yiping (2011), 'Will China Become an Engine of Growth for the Region' in Lok Sang Ho and John Wong (eds), *APEC and the Rise of China*, Singapore: World Scientific.

International Enterprise Singapore (2010), 'Annual Report 2008/2009'. Online available at: www.iesingapore.gov.sg/Publications/Publications/Annual-Reports.

International Enterprise Singapore (2011), 'Annual Report 2009/2010'. Online. Available at: www.iesingapore.gov.sg/Publications/Publications/Annual-Reports.

International Enterprise Singapore (2014), 'Review of 2013 Trade Performance' Online. Available at: www.iesingapore.gov.sg/Media-Centre/Media-Releases/2014/2/Review-of-2013-Trade-Performance.

International Enterprise Singapore (2017), 'China's Belt and Road Initiative (BRI): What it means for Singapore companies' in *IE Insights* (September 2017).

International Monetary Fund (2014), 'World Economic Outlook.' Online. Available at: www.imf.org/external/Pubs/ft/weo/2014/01.

International Monetary Fund (2017), 'China's Economic Outlook in Six Charts'. Online. Available at: www.imf.org/en/News/Articles/2017/08/09/NA081517-China-Economic-Outlook-in-Six-Charts.

Kawai, Masahiro (2009), 'The Impact of the Global Financial Crisis on Asia and Asia's Reponses' Asian Development Bank Institute Conference paper. Online. Available at: www.ifw-kiel.de/konfer/2009/masahiro-kawai.

Krugman, Paul (2014), 'No Big Deal' in *New York Times* (27 February 2014).

Kwek, Kian Teng and Tham, Siew Yean (2007), 'Trade between Malaysia and China: Opportunities and Challenges for Growth' in Kok-Kheng Yeoh and Evelyn Devadason (eds), *Emerging Trading Nation in an Integrating World: Global Impacts and Domestic Challenges of China's Economic Reform*, Kuala Lumpur: Institution of China Studies.

Lai, Jikon (2012), *Financial Crisis and Institutional Change in East Asia*, Basingstoke: Palgrave Macmillan.

Leal-Arcas, Rafael (2011), 'China's Economic Rise and Regional Trade' in Lok Sang Ho and John Wong (eds), *APEC and the Rise of China*, Singapore: World Scientific.

Leifer, Michael (2000), *Singapore's Foreign Policy: Coping with Vulnerability*, Abingdon: Routledge.

Lester, Simon; Mercurio, Bryan; and Davies, Arwel (2012), *World Trade Law*, Oxford: Hart.

Li, Yi (2006), 'An Analysis of Recent Sino-Malaysian Trade Relations' in Kok-Kheng Yeoh and Hou Kok Chung (eds), *China and Malaysia in a Globalizing World: Bilateral Relations, Regional Imperatives and Domestic Challenges*, Kuala Lumpur: Institute of China Studies.

Liang, Peter (2015), 'TPP to have Major Impact on HK' in *China Daily* (15 October 2015).

Liu, Yunhua (2009), 'Facing the Challenge of Rising China: Singapore's Responses' in *Journal of Policy Modeling*, **29**.

Loke, Wai-Heng (2009), 'East Asia and Southeast Asia: Similarity in Trade Structures' Singapore Economic Review Conference Paper. Online. Available at: http://eprints.um.edu.my/11188.

Low, Partick (2016), 'Asean Economic Community Faces Numerous Challenges' in *South China Morning Post* (6 January 2016).

Luo, Yongkun (2013), 'Strategic Cooperation can Boost Bilateral Relations' in *China Daily* (4 October 2013).

Maddison, Angus (2007), *Chinese Economic Performance in the Long Run*, Paris: OECD.

Malaysia External Trade Development Corporation (2013), 'Annual Report 2012'. Online. Available at: www.matrade.gov.my/en/about-matrade/matrade-network/worldwide-offices/389-annual-reports.

Malaysia Investment Development Authority (2013), 'Malaysia Investment Performance Report 2012'. Online. Available at: www.mida.gov.my/env3/uploads/Performance Report/2012/MIPR2012_ENG.pdf.

Malaysia Ministry of International Trade and Industry (2014), 'Weekly Bulletin Volume 293'. Online. Available at: www.miti.gov.my/index.php/pages/view/3367.

Malaysia South-South Association (2012), 'Ministry of International Trade and Industry ASEAN-China Free Trade Agreement (ACFTA): A Right Decision at the Right Time'. Online. Available at: www.massa.net.my/ministry-of-international-trade-and-industry-asean-china-free-trade-agreement-acfta-a-right-decision-at-the-right-time.

Mathieson, Rosalind and Amin, Haslinda (2017), 'New Zealand Splits with Malaysia over Reworking TPP without US' in *Bloomberg* (22 May 2017). Online. Available at: www.bloomberg.com/news/articles/2017-05-22/new-zealand-splits-with-malaysia-over-reworking-tpp-without-u-s.

Ministry of International Trade and Industry Malaysia (2016), 'TPP FAQs'. Online. Available at: http://fta.miti.gov.my/index.php/pages/view/258.

Ministry of Trade and Industry Singapore (2015), 'Trans Pacific Partnership Free Trade Agreement: 7 Things You Should Know'. Online. Available at: www.mti.gov.sg/MTI Insights/SiteAssets/Pages/TPP/Seven%20things%20you%20should%20know%20about%20the%20TPP%20(Final).pdf.

Monetary Authority of Singapore (2014), 'Annual Report 2012/2013'. Online. Available at: www.mas.gov.sg/About-MAS/Reporting/Annual-Reports.aspx.

National Bureau of Statistics of China (2015), 'China's Economy Showed Moderate but Steady Growth'. Online. Available at: www.stats.gov.cn/english/PressRelease/201507/t20150715_1214964.html.

National Development and Reform Commission (2008), 'The Outline of the Plan for the Reform and Development of the Pearl River Delta (2008–2020)'. Online. Available at: www.newsgd.com/specials/PRD/default.htm.

National Development and Reform Commission, Ministry of Foreign Affairs, and Ministry of Commerce of the People's Republic of China (2015), 'Action Plan on the Belt and Road Initiative'. Online. Available at: http://english.gov.cn/archive/publications/2015/03/30/content_281475080249035.htm.

Office of the United States Trade Representative (2015), 'Summary of the Trans-Pacific Partnership Agreement'. Online. Available at: https://ustr.gov/about-us/policy-offices/press-office/press-releases/2015/october/summary-trans-pacific-partnership.

Park, Donghyun and Shin, Kwanho (2009), 'Can Trade with the People's Republic of China be an Engine of Growth for Developing Asia?' ADB Economic Working Paper Series No. 172. Online. Available at: www.adb.org/sites/default/files/publication/28256/economics-wp172.pdf.

Pillsbury, Michael (2015), *The Hundred-Year Marathon: China's Secret Strategy to Replace America as the Global Superpower*, New York: Henry Holt.

Robertson, Peter and Xu, Jessica (2010), 'In China's Wake: Has Asia Gained from China's Growth?' Economics Discussion Paper. Online. Available at: www.otago.ac.nz/economics/news/seminars/otago078865111111111111.pdf.

Sachs, Jeffrey and Warner, Andrew (1995), 'Economic Reform and the Process of Global Integration' in *Brookings Papers on Economic Activity*, **26**.

Sen, Rahul (2008), 'Bilateral Trade and Economic Cooperation Agreements in ASEAN: Implications for Asian Economic Integration' in Amita Batra (ed.), *Preferential Trading Agreement in Asia towards an Asian Economic Community*, New Delhi: Academic Foundation.

Shee, Poon Kim (2005), 'Singapore-China Special Economic Relations: In Search of Business Opportunities' in *Ritsumeikan International Affairs*, **3**.

Shepard, Wade (2016), 'China's One Belt, One Road Plan Covers more than Half of the Population, 75 per cent of Energy Resources and 40 per cent of World's GDP' in *South China Morning Post* (21 June 2016).

Song, Teng Siow (2009), 'FTAs, China, the ASEAN Charter and the ASEAN Economic Community' in Kok Kheng Yeoh (eds), *China-ASEAN Relations: Economic Engagement and Policy Reform*, Kuala Lumpur: University of Malaya Press.

State Council of China (2014), 'White Paper: The Practice of the "One Country, Two Systems" Policy in the Hong Kong Special Administrative Region'. Online. Available at: www.china.org.cn/government/whitepaper/node_7207387.htm.

Studwell, Joe (2013), *How Asia Works: Success and Failure in the World's Most Dynamic Region*, New York: Profile Books.

Subacchi, Paola; Huang, Helena; Molajoni, Alberta; and Varghese, Richard (2012), 'Shifting Capital: The Rise of Financial Centres in Greater China' Chatham House Report. Online. Available at: www.chathamhouse.org/publications/papers/view/183257.

Tang, Frank (2017), 'How does China's 'One Belt, One Road' Match up against the TPP?' in *South China Morning Post* (24 January 2017).

Teo, John (2017), 'Malaysia One of Greatest Beneficiaries of OBOR' in *New Straits Times* (16 May 2017).

Thangavelu, Shandre; Yong, Yik Wei; and Chongvilaivan, Aekapol (2009), 'FDI, Growth and Financial Crisis: The Experience of Selected Asian Countries' in *World Economy*, **32**.

Tille, Cedric (201), 'Sailing through the Storm? Capital Flows in Asia during the Crisis' in *Pacific Economic Review*, **17**.

Turner, Philip (2007), 'Are Banking Systems in East Asia Stronger?' in *Asian Economic Policy Review*, **2**.

UNCTAD (2007), 'Rising FDI into China: The Facts behind the Numbers' Investment Brief No. 2 2007. Online. Available at: http://unctad.org/en/Docs/iteiiamisc20075_en.pdf.

Van den Bossche, Peter and Zdouc, Werner (2013), *The Law and Policy of the World Trade Organisation*, Cambridge: CUP.

Villafuerte, James; Corong, Erwin; and Zhuang, Juzhong (2017), 'The One Belt, One Road Initiative-Impact on Trade and Growth' 19th Annual Conference on Global Economic Analysis Paper. Online. Available at: www.gtap.agecon.purdue.edu/resources/download/8280.pdf.

Wang, Jiangyu (2004), 'China's Regional Trade Agreements: The Law, Geopolitics, and Impact on the Multilateral Trading System' in *Singapore Year Book of International Law*, **8**.

Weinland, Don (2017), 'China Warned of Risk to Banks from One Belt, One Road Initiative' in *Financial Times* (26 January 2017).

Williams, Brock (2013), 'Trans-Pacific Partnership (TPP) Countries: Comparative Trade and Economic Analysis' Congressional Research Service Paper. Online. Available at: http://digitalcommons.ilr.cornell.edu/cgi/viewcontent.cgi?article=2020&context=key_workplace.

World Economic Forum (2015), 'What is the Future of the WTO?' Online. Available at: www.weforum.org/agenda/2015/09/how-can-the-wto-remain-relevant.

World Economic Forum (2016), 'The ASEAN Economic Community: What You Need to Know'. Online. Available at: www.weforum.org/agenda/2016/05/asean-economic-community-what-you-need-to-know.

World Trade Organisation (2008), 'Trade Policy Review: Report by the Secretariat Singapore' Document WT/TPR/S/202.

World Trade Organisation (2010), 'Trade Policy Review: Report by the Secretariat Hong Kong' Document WT/TPR/S/241.

World Trade Organisation (2015), *Understanding the WTO*, Geneva: WTO.

World Trade Organisation (2017), 'Regional Trade Agreements'. Online. Available at: www.wto.org/english/tratop_e/region_e/region_e.htm.

Yeoh, Kok-Kheng; Yoo, Im-Soo; and Liong, Lionel (2011), 'The Role of China in Asia-Pacific Trade Framework in the Context of APEC' in Lok Sang Ho and John Wong (eds), *APEC and the Rise of China*, Singapore: World Scientific.

Yu, Tony (2007), *Entrepreneurship and Economic Development in Hong Kong*, Abingdon: Routledge.

Zhang, Shu and Miller, Matthew (2017), 'Behind China's Silk Road Vision: Cheap Funds, Heavy Debt, Growing Risk' in *Reuters* (15 May 2017). Online. Available at: http://in.reuters.com/article/china-silk-road-finance/behind-chinas-silk-road-vision-cheap-funds-heavy-debt-growing-risk-idINKCN18B0XY.

Zhang, Yang and Tong, Sarah (2009), 'Hong Kong's Economy in the Financial Crisis' EAI Background Brief No. 448. Online. Available at: www.eai.nus.edu.sg/publications/files/BB448.pdf.

8 Conclusion

This book has provided a holistic and comprehensive account of the growth stories of four Asian economies, namely China, Hong Kong, Singapore and Malaysia, and their cities. They do not have a uniform degree of economic development. According to the categorisation by the World Bank, Hong Kong and Singapore are regarded as high-income economies, whereas China and Malaysia are upper-middle income economies.[1] If one considers an important economic indicator, GDP per capita, Singapore (US$52,960.7) perhaps is the most successful among the four, followed by Hong Kong (US$ 43,681.1), then Malaysia (US$9,502.6) and finally China (US$8,123.2).[2] Meanwhile, it is undeniable that China, as the second largest economy in the world, is now regarded as an economic and political superpower which can easily dwarf the other three economies. Historically, the Song Dynasty of China (*c.* AD 1200) created one of the most magnificent civilisations the world had ever seen, accounting for 25 per cent to 30 per cent of global output.[3] In contrast, Hong Kong, Singapore and Malaysia had had very humble beginnings until their fortune was reversed by the colonisation of the British Empire. From this point, their economies started to take off.

Following the decolonisation movement in Asia, Malaysia and Singapore became independent in 1957 and 1963 respectively. Meanwhile, Hong Kong remained under British rule for a few more decades until its sovereignty was handed back to China in 1997. Following their independence, both Singapore and Malaysia were committed to industrialisation by introducing various programmes of economic reform. Even without active coordination from the government, Hong Kong was going in a largely similar direction, trying hard to reinvent itself from an entrepot into a manufacturing base. On the other hand, in China at that time economic development was significantly hampered by unsuccessful reforms like the Great Leap Forward and political turmoil brought about by the Cultural Revolution. From around late 1970s and early 1980s, all the economies have continued to experience transformation. In China, national economic reform was initiated, which has laid down the foundation of an economic miracle. Hong Kong was adversely affected by this, owing to the migration of factories to the north to take advantage of the cheap production costs in China. This prompted Hong Kong to transform into a services-oriented economy.

Meanwhile, Singapore and Malaysia have continued to move up the value chain in their industrialisation process.

Nowadays, the economies have their own characteristics. China is seen as the world's factory.[4] In 1990 it produced less than 3 per cent of global manufacturing output by value; its share now is nearly a quarter. China produces about 80 per cent of the world's air-conditioners, 70 per cent of its mobile phones and 60 per cent of its shoes. Like Singapore, the industries have tried their best to move up the value chain and some world leading technology companies are now seen in China, such as Tencent, Alibaba and Huawei. Also, China has its own financial centre in Shanghai, which is competing with Hong Kong. Hong Kong has long and firmly established itself as an international financial centre, which serves as an important fund-raising ground for Chinese companies. The city has fully embraced finance and trade, with an almost negligible manufacturing sector.[5] In comparison, Singapore has a more diversified economy. The services industry has flourished to form one of the pillars of Singapore's economy, along with the field key industries, namely chemicals, electronics, engineering and biotechnology. In Malaysia, despite an attempt to focus more on manufacturing and services, the commodity sector remains one of the most important sectors for Malaysia's economy.

The economic development of the four economies can be briefly summarised as above. The core concern of this book is the institutional conditions which support their growth. Again using the analytical framework in Chapter 2, this conclusion will compare and contrast the key findings made in previous chapters for the four economies under four general headings: legal, political, cultural and infrastructure.

Legal institutions

Thanks to their colonial origin, Hong Kong, Singapore and Malaysia have inherited a ready-made legal framework from Britain to support their economic activities. For example, the first Companies Ordinance[6] in Hong Kong was a reproduction of the English Companies Act of 1862. Likewise, following their independence, the first Companies Acts in Singapore and Malaysia were largely based on the UK Companies Act 1948. Over the years, the jurisdictions have put a lot of effort into reforming their regimes so as to attract and retain businesses. Nowadays, their regimes are the most protective of investors, as recognised by the World Bank.[7] For example, Singapore was one of the first jurisdictions in the world to introduce a statutory derivative action into its company law in 1993, so as to increase shareholder's access to litigation. Hong Kong and Malaysia also followed suit in 2004 and 2007 respectively. In sharp contrast, China's first company law was introduced in 1993 to support the emerging business activities after their economic reform towards late 1970s. Although the current legal framework in China in terms of investor protection is not highly regarded by the World Bank, an academic study argues that China's system has greatly improved over the past decades and is now one of the best systems in the world.[8] All four jurisdictions, apart from company laws, also have their securities laws and corporate governance codes to make sure that a complete regulatory structure is in place to support local corporate and financial activities.

A complete regulatory structure also entails enforcement. All four jurisdictions have largely relied on public enforcement instead of private enforcement to keep the market players in check. One explanation is that all of them have a vibrant financial sector. As a result, the governments are willing to devote significant resources to strengthen the capacity of the regulators. Strong public enforcement is essential to fill the void of private enforcement when investors are not actively seeking to safeguard their own interests. In a nutshell, there is a degree of resemblance in their legal institutions that they all have strong laws, coupled with strong public enforcement. Private enforcement has not been their major landscape of governance.

Political institutions

Again all four economies share a common characteristic in this regard. They have a largely authoritarian state. This challenges traditional thinking about the relationship between democracy and economic development.[9] There is a de facto one-party system in China, Singapore and Malaysia. Although Hong Kong is an autonomous region of China, it is virtually impossible for the people to choose their own government. On the other hand, there are dissimilarities between the four economies. China, Singapore and Malaysia all have very well defined economic plans. The prosperity of China has largely come from the adjustment by Deng Xiaoping of a strictly socialist model to a 'socialist market economy with Chinese characteristics'. The state's domination in Singapore's economy can be exemplified by a quote from Paul Krugman, who once said 'Singapore grew through a mobilisation of resources that would have done Stalin proud.'[10] Similarly, economic development in Malaysia has been guided by their Malaysia Plans. In sharp contrast, Hong Kong has adopted a laissez-faire capitalist model. Milton Friedman referred to Hong Kong as an example of capitalism in action.[11] Their government has always tried to maintain a low profile in the economy and a positive non-interventionist philosophy in governance.

Meanwhile, all four economies have their own problems. Chinese President, Xi Jinping has recognised that corruption had long been a problem in China and could threaten Communist Party rule.[12] Unfortunately, Xi's anticorruption campaign has yielded limited success thus far. In Singapore and Hong Kong, political instability is a problem after the death of Lee Kuan Yew and the Umbrella Revolution, respectively. For Malaysia, inter-racial conflicts have long been a problem, which prompted the government to incorporate social goals into their economic plans.

Cultural institutions

The societies of Singapore and Malaysia are multiracial and multicultural. In China and Hong Kong, there is a predominantly Chinese society. Confucianism has not only been practised by local people, but also has affected the cultural values of many Asians. Confucianism has focused on the connections between people, which remain important in the Chinese business sector in the form of *guanxi*. Owing to the blurred line between *guanxi* and corruption, corruption is perceived as widespread in China and Malaysia, but has been successfully controlled in Singapore and Hong Kong. In Hong Kong, Singapore and Malaysia, the dynamic Chinese family businesses have formed a core part of their respective economies. Despite the fact that the Chinese community in Malaysia is an ethnic minority, the Malaysian economy has been controlled by a number of wealthy Chinese businessmen.

Infrastructure

All four economies, especially China, Singapore and Hong Kong, have some of the world largest ports to support their trade. Furthermore, they have invested hugely in infrastructure so as to ensure that, for example, there are adequate transportation links, such as airports, to support growth. Free trade zones, business parks and industrial estates, normally with preferential policies, have continually been built to attract businesses. Furthermore, talents are either attracted from overseas or trained locally, to ensure an adequate supply of human capital.

In a nutshell, it can be seen that China, Hong Kong, Singapore and Malaysia all have tried their best to ensure that they have the perfect mix of institutional advantages to support their sustained economic growth. Certain institutional changes are far easier than others. For example, it has been common for the economies to draw on the experience of their counterparts to formulate their legal reform. For example, as early as the 1970s, Canadian jurisdictions began implementing statute-based derivative actions into their company acts.[13] If the economies believe that it is an efficient arrangement, then all they have to do is to copy it (and they did). Likewise, if they believe public enforcement is important, then all they have to do is to increase the amount of resources available to the regulators. Moreover, if they believe they need more ports, bridges and airports, all they have to do is to invest. However, certain institutional changes may take time and experience more hindrance, for example, an authoritarian political regime, and the culture of local people.[14] As a result, continual evolution of their institutional conditions can slow down in line with their stages of economic development. Also, from the experience of the four economies, having an authoritarian regime is not necessarily a disadvantage which needs to be changed.

As a result, future economic growth apparently will be dependent on how they grow together as an economic or trading bloc. For a very long period of time, Hong Kong has been relying on China as a driver of its economic growth. As predicted by the IMF, Asia as a region will continue to be the leader of global growth.[15] There are many exciting opportunities ahead. Whilst ASEAN can continue to grow as a bloc of ten Southeast Asian countries, the ASEAN-China Free Trade Area can inject the much needed momentum for further growth. Building on the existing WTO framework, wider regional and transcontinental collaboration, in the form of TPP (though falling through for the time being) and OBOR can certainly present new opportunities to the economies. The institutional advantages, possessed by the four economies studied by this book, namely China, Hong Kong, Singapore and Malaysia, can mean that they are better placed than others to capitalise on these opportunities.

Notes

1 World Bank (2017), 'World Bank Country and Lending Groups'. Online. Available: https://datahelpdesk.worldbank.org/knowledgebase/articles/906519-world-bank-country-and-lending-groups.
2 GDP per capita as of 2016; data from the World Bank.
3 Chris Matthews (2014), 'Fortune 5: The Most Powerful Economic Empires of all Time' in *Fortune* (5 October 2014).
4 Economist (2015), 'Made in China? Global Manufacturing' in *Economist* (14 March 2015).
5 Manufacturing only contributed to 1.1 per cent of the city's GDP in 2015, compared to 92.7 per cent from services. See Census and Statistics Department of Hong Kong (2017), 'Gross Domestic Product (GDP) by Economic Activity'. Online. Available at: www.censtatd.gov.hk/hkstat/sub/sp250.jsp?tableID=036&ID=0&productType=8.
6 Companies Ordinance of 1865.
7 World Bank (2017), 'Doing Business'. Online. Available at: www.doingbusiness.org.
8 Ibid. See also Dionysia Katelouzou and Mathias Siems (2015), 'Disappearing Paradigms in Shareholder Protection: Leximetric Evidence for 30 Countries, 1990–2013' in *Journal of Corporate Law Studies*, **15**.
9 Adam Przeworski and Fernando Limongi (1993), 'Political Regimes and Economic Growth' in *Journal of Economic Perspectives*, **7**; and Robert Barro (1999), 'Determinants of Democracy' in *Journal of Political Economy*, **107**.
10 Paul Krugman (1994), 'The Myth of Asia's Miracle' in *Foreign Affairs*, **73**, p. 70.
11 Milton Friedman (1997), 'The Real Lesson of Hong Kong'. Online. Available at: http://miltonfriedman.hoover.org/friedman_images/Collections/2016c21/MFlecture_05_14_1997.pdf.
12 Hudson Lockett (2016), 'China Anti-corruption Campaign Backfires' in *Financial Times* (9 October 2016).
13 Arad Reisberg (2007), *Derivative Actions and Corporate Governance*, Oxford: OUP, p. 176.
14 William Easterly (2008), 'Institutions: Top Down or Bottom Up?' in *American Economic Review: Papers and Proceedings*, **98**.
15 International Monetary Fund (2017), 'Asia's Dynamic Economies Continue to Lead Global Growth'. Online. Available at: www.imf.org/en/News/Articles/2017/05/08/NA050917-Asia-Dynamic-Economies-Continue-to-Lead-Global-Growth.

References

Barro, Robert (1999), 'Determinants of Democracy' in *Journal of Political Economy*, **107**.

Census and Statistics Department of Hong Kong (2017), 'Gross Domestic Product (GDP) by Economic Activity'. Online. Available at: www.censtatd.gov.hk/hkstat/sub/sp250.jsp?tableID=036&ID=0&productType=8.

Easterly, William (2008), 'Institutions: Top Down or Bottom Up?' in *American Economic Review: Papers and Proceedings*, **98**.

Economist (2015), 'Made in China? Global Manufacturing' in *Economist* (14 March 2015).

Friedman, Milton (1997), 'The Real Lesson of Hong Kong'. Online. Available at: http://miltonfriedman.hoover.org/friedman_images/Collections/2016c21/MFlecture_05_14_1997.pdf.

International Monetary Fund (2017), 'Asia's Dynamic Economies Continue to Lead Global Growth'. Online. Available at: www.imf.org/en/News/Articles/2017/05/08/NA050917-Asia-Dynamic-Economies-Continue-to-Lead-Global-Growth.

Katelouzou, Dionysia and Siems, Mathias (2015), 'Disappearing Paradigms in Shareholder Protection: Leximetric Evidence for 30 Countries, 1990–2013' in *Journal of Corporate Law Studies*, **15**.

Krugman, Paul (1994), 'The Myth of Asia's Miracle' in *Foreign Affairs*, **73**.

Lockett, Hudson (2016), 'China Anti-corruption Campaign Backfires' in *Financial Times* (9 October 2016).

Matthews, Chris (2014), 'Fortune 5: The Most Powerful Economic Empires of all Time' in *Fortune* (5 October 2014).

Przeworski, Adam and Limongi, Fernando (1993), 'Political Regimes and Economic Growth' in *Journal of Economic Perspectives*, **7**.

Reisberg, Arad (2007), *Derivative Actions and Corporate Governance*, Oxford: OUP.

World Bank (2017), 'World Bank Country and Lending Groups'. Online. Available: https://datahelpdesk.worldbank.org/knowledgebase/articles/906519-world-bank-country-and-lending-groups.

World Bank (2017), 'Doing Business'. Online. Available at: www.doingbusiness.org.

Index

Page numbers in **bold** denote tables, those in *italics* denote figures.

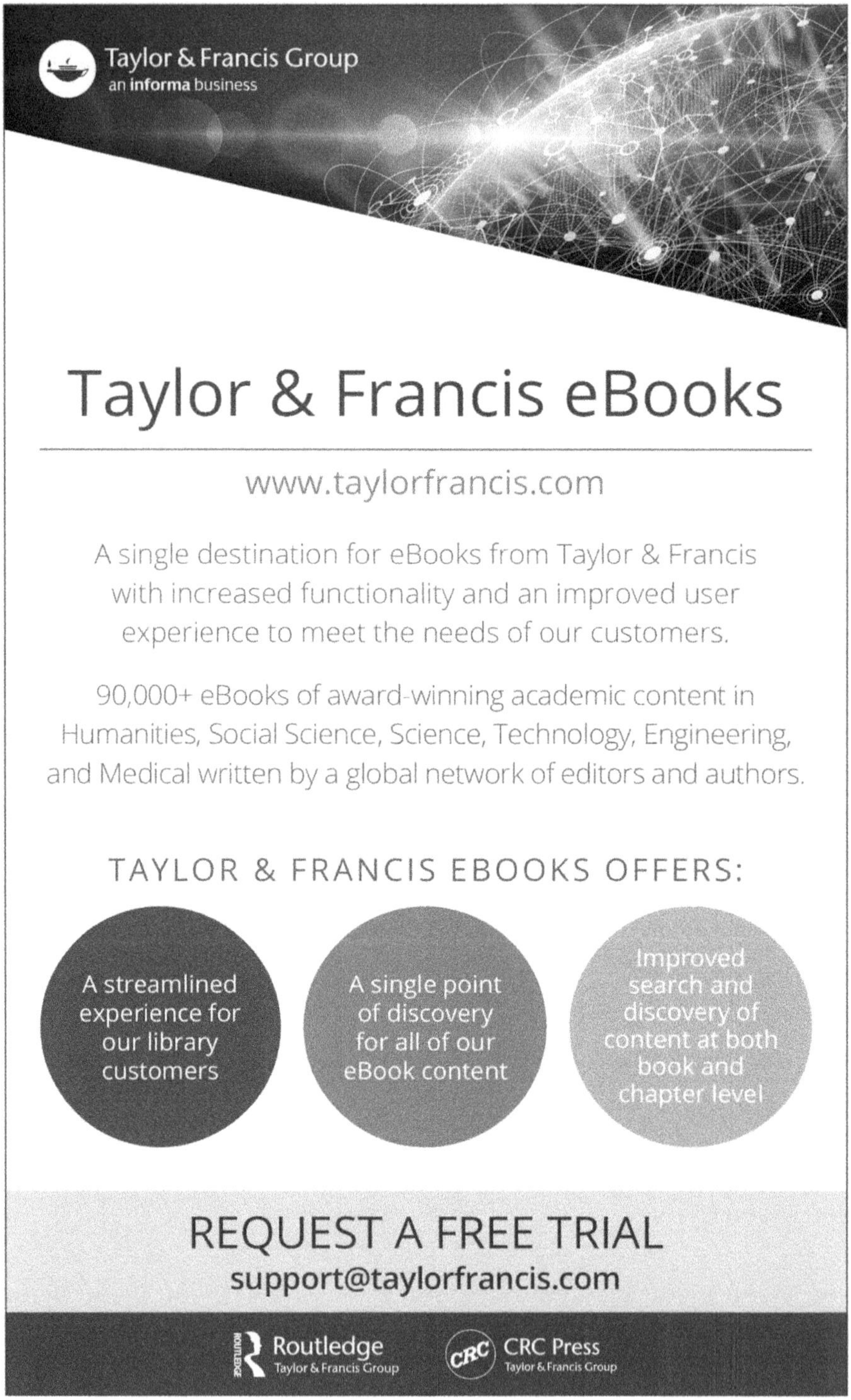
Taylor & Francis Group
an informa business
Taylor & Francis eBooks
www.taylorfrancis.com
A single destination for eBooks from Taylor & Francis with increased functionality and an improved user experience to meet the needs of our customers.
90,000+ eBooks of award-winning academic content in Humanities, Social Science, Science, Technology, Engineering, and Medical written by a global network of editors and authors.
TAYLOR & FRANCIS EBOOKS OFFERS:
A streamlined experience for our library customers
A single point of discovery for all of our eBook content
Improved search and discovery of content at both book and chapter level
REQUEST A FREE TRIAL
support@taylorfrancis.com
Routledge
Taylor & Francis Group
CRC Press
Taylor & Francis Group

For Product Safety Concerns and Information please contact our EU
representative GPSR@taylorandfrancis.com
Taylor & Francis Verlag GmbH, Kaufingerstraße 24, 80331 München, Germany

www.ingramcontent.com/pod-product-compliance
Ingram Content Group UK Ltd.
Pitfield, Milton Keynes, MK11 3LW, UK
UKHW022010180926
475701UK00003B/299

* 9 7 8 0 3 6 7 5 9 1 8 8 5 *